THEORIES OF DEMOCRACY

THEORIES OF DEMOCRACY

A READER

RONALD J. TERCHEK
AND THOMAS C. CONTE

ROWMAN & LITTLEFIELD PUBLISHERS, INC.
LANHAM • BOULDER • NEW YORK • OXFORD

ROWMAN & LITTLEFIELD PUBLISHERS, INC.

Published in the United States of America
by Rowman & Littlefield Publishers, Inc.
4720 Boston Way, Lanham, Maryland 20706
www.rowmanlittlefield.com

12 Hid's Copse Road
Cumnor Hill, Oxford OX2 9JJ, England

British Library Cataloguing-in-Publication Information Available

Library of Congress Cataloging-in-Publication Data

Theories of democracy : a reader / [edited by] Ronald J. Terchek and Thomas C. Conte.
    p. cm.
  Includes bibliographical references and index.
  ISBN 0-8476-9724-X (alk. paper) — ISBN 0-8476-9725-8 (pbk. : alk. paper)
    1. Democracy. 2. Democracy—History. I. Terchek, Ronald, 1936– II. Conte, Thomas
C., 1964–

JC423 .T398 2001
321.8—dc21

                                       2001019692

Printed in the United States of America.

♾™ The paper used in this publication meets the minimum requirements of American
National Standard for Information Sciences—Permanence of Paper for Printed Library
Materials, ANSI/NISO Z39.48-1992.

To my students, particularly Ana, Dave, and Thomas, for all they have taught me.

&

To Renee and Max for their patience and steady encouragement.

CONTENTS

Acknowledgments and Credits

Beacon Press: *Race Matters*, by Cornel West, Boston: Beacon Press, pp. 1–8. Copyright © 1993 Cornel West. Reprinted by permission of Beacon Press, Boston.

Beyond Law: "Conditionality, Human Rights, and Democracy: The Latin American Experience," by Adolfo Pérez Esquivel, from *Beyond Law*, vol. 5, nos. 15–16, pp. 75–81. Copyright © 1996 Adolfo Pérez Esquivel. Reprinted by permission of *Beyond Law* and Adolfo Pérez Esquivel.

Doubleday: *No Future without Forgiveness*, by Desmond Mpilo Tutu, New York: Doubleday. Copyright © 1999 Desmond Tutu. Reprinted by permission of Doubleday, a division of Random House, Inc.

HarperCollins Publishers: *Capitalism, Socialism and Democracy*, 1st ed., by Joseph Schumpeter, New York: Harper & Brothers, pp. 250–52, 258–64, 269–73, 282–83, and 290–93. Copyright © 1942 Joseph A. Schumpeter. Copyright renewed 1975. Reprinted by permission of HarperCollins Publishers, Inc.

Harvard University Press: *A Theory of Justice*, by John Rawls, Cambridge, Mass.: The Belknap Press of Harvard University Press. Copyright © 1971 the President and Fellows of Harvard College. Reprinted by permission of the Harvard University Press.

Navajivan Trust: *Hind Swaraj*, by M. K. Gandhi, chaps. 7, 14, and 17. Copyright © 1963 Navajivan Trust. Reprinted by permission of the Navajivan Trust.

Navajivan Trust: "Speech at Muir College Economic Society," by M. K. Gandhi, from *The Collected Works of Mahatma Gandhi*, vol. 13, pp. 311–17. Copyright © 1954 Navajivan Trust. Reprinted by permission of the Navajivan Trust.

Orbis Books: *Aristide: An Autobiography*, by Jean-Bertrand Aristide with Christophe Wargny, translated by Linda Maloney, Maryknoll, N.Y.: Orbis Books, pp. 189–202. Copyright © 1993 Orbis Books. Reprinted by permission of Orbis Books.

Pennsylvania State University Press: *Engendering Democracy*, by Anne Phillips, University Park: Pennsylvania State University Press, pp. 101–4 and 110–19. Copyright © 1991 the Pennsylvania State University Press. Reprinted by permission of the Pennsylvania State University Press.

Princeton University Press: *Justice and the Politics of Difference*, by Iris Marion Young, Princeton, N.J.: Princeton University Press, pp. 156–59, 163–66, 168, 171, 173–74, 183–87, and 189–90. Copyright © 1990 Princeton University Press. Reprinted by permission of the Princeton University Press.

Princeton University Press: "Three Normative Models of Democracy," by Jürgen Habermas, from *Democracy and Difference: Testing the Boundaries of the Political*, edited by Seyla Benhabib, Princeton, N.J.: Princeton University Press, pp. 21–30. Copyright © 1996 Princeton University Press. Reprinted by permission of the Princeton University Press.

Random House: *Power/Knowledge: Selected Interviews and Other Writings, 1972–1977*, by Michel Foucault, translated and edited by Colin Gordon, New York: Pantheon Books, pp. 88–99 and 102–8. Copyright © 1972, 1975, 1976, 1977 Michel Foucault. This collection copyright © 1980 Harvester Press. Reprinted by permission of Pantheon Books, a division of Random House, Inc.

Sage Publications: "The Liberal/Democratic Divide," by Sheldon Wolin, from *Political Theory*, vol. 24, no. 1 (1996), pp. 97–98, 101–7, and 117–119. Copyright © 1996 Sage Publications, Inc. Reprinted by permission of Sage Publications, Inc.

Southern Illinois University Press: "Democratic Ends Need Democratic Methods for Their Realization," by John Dewey, from *Dewey Later Works Volume 14*, Carbondale: Southern Illinois University Press, pp. 367–68. Copyright © 1991 the Board of Trustees, Southern Illinois University. Reprinted by permission of Southern Illinois University Press.

Southern Illinois University Press: "The Problem of Method," by John Dewey, from *Dewey Later Works Volume 2*, Carbondale: Southern Illinois University Press, pp. 362–67. Copyright © 1988 the Board of Trustees, Southern Illinois University. Reprinted by permission of Southern Illinois University Press.

University of California Press: *Economy and Society*, 2 vols., by Max Weber, translated and edited by Guenther Roth and Claus Wittichby, Berkeley: University of California Press, pp. 948, 973–75, 979–80, 983–85, 987–88, 990–92, 1393–94, 1403, 1407–8, and 1414. Copyright © 1978 the Regents of the University of California. Reprinted by permission of the University of California.

University of California Press: *Strong Democracy: Participatory Politics for a New Age*, by Benjamin Barber, Berkeley: University of California Press, pp. 145–55. Copyright © 1984 University of California Press. Reprinted by permission of the University of California.

University of Chicago Press: "An Economic Theory of Political Action in a Democracy," by Anthony Downs, from *Journal of Political Economy*, vol. 64 (1957), pp. 135–41 and 147–49. Copyright © 1957 the University of Chicago Press. Reprinted by permission of the University of Chicago Press.

University of Chicago Press: *Law, Legislation and Liberty*, vol. 3, by Friedrich Hayek, Chicago: University of Chicago Press, pp. 1–2, 6, 9–11, 13, and 128–34. Copyright © 1979 the University of Chicago Press. Reprinted by permission of the University of Chicago Press.

University of Chicago Press: "The Role of Government in a Free Society," from *Capitalism and Freedom,* by Milton Friedman, Chicago: University of Chicago Press, pp. 22–36. Copyright © 1962 the University of Chicago Press. Reprinted by permission of the University of Chicago Press.

University of Minnesota Press: *The Future of Democracy: A Defense of the Rules of the Game,* by Norberto Bobbio, translated by Robert Griffin, edited by Richard Bellamy, Minneapolis: University of Minnesota Press. Copyright ©1987 Polity Press. Reprinted by permission of the University of Minnesota Press.

University of Minnesota Press: "Radical Democracy: Modern or Postmodern?" by Chantal Mouffe, from *Universal Abandon? The Politics of Postmodernism,* edited by Andrew Ross, Minneapolis: University of Minnesota Press, pp. 31–45. Copyright © 1988 the University of Minnesota Press. Reprinted by permission of the University of Minnesota Press.

University of Wisconsin Press: "Democracy and Normalization," from *Politics and Ambiguity,* by William E. Connolly, Madison: University of Wisconsin Press, pp. 3–16. Copyright © 1987 the University of Wisconsin Press. Reprinted by permission of the University of Wisconsin Press.

Viking Penguin: "Quest of Democracy" from *Freedom from Fear and Other Writings,* rev. ed., by Aung San Suu Kyi, translated and edited by Michael Aris, New York: Penguin Books. Copyright © 1991, 1995 Aung San Suu Kyi and Michael Aris. Reprinted by permission of Viking Penguin, a division of Penguin Putnam, Inc.

Yale University Press: *Dilemmas of Pluralist Democracy,* by Robert Dahl, New Haven, Conn.: Yale University Press, pp. 4–11, 31–36, and 40–43. Copyright © 1982 Yale University Press. Reprinted by permission of Yale University Press.

INTRODUCTION

This collection builds on Robert Dahl's observation that there is no single theory of democracy—only theories.[1] Yet however different many of them are from one another, these theories belong to a family, and they share some family resemblances. Most obviously, they reject the idea that one person or a few have any warrant to rule the rest. The reason this is so for most democrats is that they hold that persons are equal in some important ways and all deserve a voice in their governance. Democratic theories also share the view that each member of the political community carries elementary rational capacities that are sufficient to judge the conduct of government. For such judgments to have meaning, democratic citizens are expected to be free in several important respects; they must be free regarding such matters as speech, assembly, and conscience. For some, these sorts of freedoms are liberal rights, but for many democrats, these and allied freedoms are valued independently of our liberal inheritance as essential components of an open regime that is accountable to citizens.

Over the centuries, democrats have been proud of the fact that this form of government assures a peaceful transition from one set of officials to another. Public office is not the property of incumbents but theoretically belongs to the citizens who can reclaim it in an orderly, peaceful way. Moreover, democrats hold as an ideal that public power flows from public approval and that the law reflects public preferences. The credibility of these arguments depends upon the existence of choice among candidates and policies. This becomes particularly important as new issues arise that cast previous political settlements in a new light. The logic of the democratic model, therefore, assumes that public officials are responsible for their conduct and accountable to citizens and that present politics can be challenged. These characteristics of democracy might be taken as some of its minimal features, and, as we shall see, some democrats will want to move beyond this conception.

For these democrats, part of the problem with minimalist conceptions is that they mask the tendencies of all governments, including democratic ones, to become secret and its officials to become manipulative. Moreover, some democrats fear that in practice, conventional forms of participation promote a politics that is likely to become remote from the everyday concerns of ordinary citizens who have an increasingly difficult time registering their views. Another set of complaints about minimalist conceptions of democracy focuses on the many forms of nonpolitical power that are seen invading public space and directing public policy, bypassing citizen input. When this happens, the common good, difficult to achieve under the best of circumstances, becomes even more illusive. Other critics of minimalist democracy want to make democracy more inclusive, not only by drawing more people into decision-making processes but also by expanding the sites of democratic control. These critiques are presented as strengthening democracy from within by extending the logic of democratic organization to new spheres of social experience.

Through its long and turbulent history, democracy has undergone a series of critical reinterpretations. Taken together, these differing interpretations have produced profound disagreements, some of which can be traced to the permanent tension between democracy as an ideal, on the one hand, and as a set of actual public institutions on the other. Yet even within the former sphere, competing conceptualizations of the key components of the democratic ideal and their proper relationship to each other continue to fuel contentious debates. Although all theories of democracy share a vision of government by free and equal citizens who participate in their own governance, it turns out that each of these terms has various meanings. Aristotle's view of democratic government does not mesh with most contemporary theories, such as Robert Dahl's pluralism, nor with the views of feminist writers like Anne Phillips or the postmodern orientation of William Connolly. For some, democracy is about protecting freedom from a government that favors rulers and their friends at the expense of the rest. For others, democracy should reflect the interests of citizens and remain responsive to the concerns of organized groups. Alternate democratic voices call for a more active government to address the problems of the most vulnerable citizens. Still others see obstacles to full democratic citizenship coming not only from the state but located throughout society in ways that diminish the egalitarian principle of democratic politics and, therefore, need to be resisted.

The variety of meanings attached to a term like democracy is also evidenced in allied terms such as citizenship, freedom, equality, and participation. Although many of these and other terms are used in similar ways in some theories, it is important to notice that these same words often take on distinctive meanings in other theories. Take the idea of citizenship. Aristotle ties it to the ownership of private property, but virtually all twentieth-century democratic theorists deny the connection. Friedrich Hayek thinks democratic citizens should most value their freedom and use their democratic resources to resist intervention by the state in what should be private. Yet this position is rejected by most other contemporary theorists who, for all of their different ideas about where to draw the line between the public and private, generally give the democratic state greater latitude than Hayek. Civic republicans and communitarians proceed with the argument that the free citizen can only flourish politically in a community where traditions are strong and civic duty is widely respected. Such an approach, however, troubles liberal democrats who worry that an emphasis on community and duty can displace fundamental rights as the central commitment of a democratic regime. Still other democrats want to extend the scope of citizenship beyond conventional participation, such as voting, to previously nonpolitical areas of life.

One of the primary, if not the primary, characteristics of politics is power. In this context, democratic politics aims at the widest distribution of power among the citizenry. Yet disputes among democratic theorists about what power means and how it can enable or disable full and equal citizenship are legion. Indeed, the very same features of political life that some identify as abuses of power in a democracy, others find to be essential to the emancipation of individuals and an indispensable component of full political equality. For some, the primary site of the abuse of power is located in the state, with its proclivity to interfere with the freedom of its citizens. For other democrats, however, power has myriad locations, and they look at civil society or the market to consider the ways in which nonpolitical advantages and resources are converted into political influence. For this group, democratic government is called upon to resist the demands of concentrated private power, particularly the power of status and wealth. But the question of power takes on still other dimensions in the writings of many modern feminists and postmodernists. As they understand matters, power is not confined to institutional sites, public or private, but circulates throughout society: in the family and race relations, in schools and the media, in the workplace, and even within the seemingly neutral spheres of knowledge, the sciences and technology. Working with this understanding, they move beyond earlier conceptions of the state as the center of contestation and extend their democratic impulses to other spheres of activity, many of which have traditionally been considered to operate below the threshold of democratic politics.

Democratic theories also depart from one another in what they expect from citizens. For civic republicans and communitarians, the character of its citizens determines the character of the republic. If citizens are civically virtuous, the republic can be expected to thrive, but if they are self-involved or lethargic, we should anticipate a politics of fragmentation and corruption leading toward decay. Others find that citizens must prize their liberty and be ever vigilant against efforts to involve the state in more areas of private and social life. Still others hold that a democratic form of government, if properly ordered, does not depend on virtuous or restrained citizens. What is needed is a diffusion of power and group competition. The first is needed to avoid any inordinate concentration of power by a single group and the latter to assure political opportunities to organize with like-minded citizens to influence public policy. Yet others want citizens who not only speak but also listen to divergent positions and who are open to finding common solutions to common problems.

But differences in democratic theory do not stop here. One of the most contentious issues has to do with the role of interests in a democracy. Why should interests be so important in politics? Socrates puts the negative case about interests in poignant and blunt terms. His *Republic* is built around a theory of justice where all of the parts cohere harmoniously. But the search for justice is undermined when those who rule put their interests ahead of the good of the whole. For this reason, Socrates wants his philosopher kings and queens to do without family (that is, spouses and children of their own) and without private property. As he understands matters, such attachments distract rulers from searching for justice and so, he reasons, interests need to be banished from politics. Even though civic republicans reject Socrates' strictures regarding the family and property, they retain his hostility to interests as a driving force in politics. And so do many other contemporary critics of liberal democratic practice. For these authors, politics cannot be primarily about serving individual interests but must attend to what is common. When viewed through this lens, real democrats will resist moves to use public power to serve the interests of some at the expense of the whole. These critics find that interests corrupt political language and make agreement about a common good difficult, if not impossible. For their part, supporters of interests in democratic politics find that interests are an inescapable and necessary part of political life, and efforts to silence or thwart them threaten to disarm the many against those who already enjoy a preponderance of power.

Such debates about power, equality, freedom, justice, and interests are the subject matter of this collection. They appear in the voices of those who have championed influential theories concerning the opportunities and dangers associated with democratic politics. Their writings are offered as contributions regarding the value of democracy and the diverse ways that it is understood and practiced. Our goal in drawing these authors together is not to promote a particular way of looking at democracy but rather to assemble key materials that will enable the reader to carry on an informed discourse concerning the meaning and purposes of democracy.

In this collection, we have assembled the works of classical, modern, and contemporary commentators on democracy. We have included some classical texts to show the deep but diverse roots of the democratic commitment as well as to provide materials for thinking about the way some contemporary theories build on different traditions of democratic theorizing. However, we do not organize the texts chronologically but rather collect them under several different and distinctive theories to highlight the many ways that principled democrats have thought about the subject. The texts in this collection include many of the major contributors in various theories of democracy and serve as representative voices of those approaches to democratic government. Despite their many differences, however, they share a common dedication to the idea that democratic politics, for all of its variability and problems, must be the politics of any good regime.

NOTE

1. *A Preface to Democratic Theory* (Chicago: University of Chicago Press, 1965), 1.

NOTE TO THE READER

In assembling this collection we have aimed at breadth and depth. In the interests of balancing these priorities we have deleted some materials from individual selections. Sometimes the deleted material was highly topical and would have served to distract the reader rather than inform. Sometimes we removed material because it referred to earlier passages by the author that were not included in this collection. Other times, we removed material because it was redundant. These deletions, however, are identified within the text.

We have also removed some footnotes but have not indicated their omissions. Footnotes were not included when they referred to literature in a foreign language, were tied to a particular time, or did not substantially add to the argument.

LIBERALISM AND REPUBLICANISM

THE EVOLVING LIBERAL TRADITION

Before the rise of democratic government as we know it today, with the extension of the franchise to all adult citizens, the idea of government based on the consent of the governed had already found a determined voice in the writings of the classic liberals.[1] Unlike some other schools of democratic thought, the liberal tradition makes the rights-carrying individual the central concern of politics. Invested with the principles of rights, reason, and equality, each individual is thought to deserve to be free from the unwanted interference of other citizens and the state. The arguments that liberals have with one another involve the meaning of rights and how equality is to be understood. Yet for their many disagreements, they remain committed to the idea of individual rights as the foundation of any desirable politics. As liberalism eventually came to embrace democracy as a means of better securing individual rights these two schools of thought were consolidated in modern constitutions. Still, this merger did not eliminate certain internal tensions that continue to drive debate concerning the proper role of the state and individual liberty.[2]

With early liberals, such as John Locke, we are introduced to the concept of the consent of the governed and the value of popular institutions. Locke seeks to empower an elected legislature to check the ambitions of the crown. For him, a popular presence is the best guardian of liberty because it requires government to be accountable to the governed. This commitment is connected to the premise that what people most want is their freedom, and they rightly resist efforts by the state to deprive them of it. Many later liberals want to move beyond this minimalist character of democracy and some, such as John Stuart Mill, look to greater participation to enliven debate as well as improve the character of democratic citizens. At the same time, Mill invests public discourse among diverse participants with the ability to uncover what is defective in public life as well as highlight what is worthwhile there.

The need for liberal democratic citizens to move beyond their own interests is stressed by Alexis de Tocqueville in his discussion of the importance of religion and an extended associational life to democracy. As society becomes more complex, industrialized, and urbanized, some latter liberals, such as T. H. Green and Leonard Hobhouse in Great Britain and Herbert Croly in the United States, shift the emphasis of liberal government and look to an expansion of the state to meet the educational and welfare needs of the most vulnerable members of society. More recently, John Rawls offers a theory of justice for liberal-democratic societies that speaks to the needs of its most vulnerable citizens. What we have with the evolution of liberal-democratic theory is not the replacement of early theories by later ones. Instead, later theories compete with variations of earlier ones for the allegiance of liberal citizens who continue to prize both their rights and democratic governance.

Locke is known to us as one of the leading theorists and founders of liberalism. In his *Second Treatise on Government,* he lays out a justification for equal rights for everyone, along with an argument that we all have elementary rational capacities that enable us to make choices for ourselves. What he does not do in this work or in his other writings is to call for a universal franchise or for a government that is popularly elected. Rather, he accepts the practices of his time that extend the vote to some, though not to all, to elect a legislature to check the monarchy. What enables us to think about Locke as an early but cautious liberal-democrat are his arguments that government must be based on the consent of the governed and that this is reflected in a popularly elected legislature, which has wide powers and is guided by the principle of majority rule. The democratic features of his theory are meant to protect rights by dispersing governmental power.

Locke prizes the consent of the governed because he sees it as the best protection for the natural rights of individuals. In his discussion of the state of nature, Locke works with the view that everyone is equal and invests each person with the rights to life, liberty, and property. To deprive someone of these rights without the person's voluntary consent is contrary to the laws of nature and reason and needs to be resisted. In his influential discussion of property, Locke holds that in the state of nature it is our labor that establishes our claim to ownership. Locke makes private property a central right in his liberalism, something that some later liberals as well as several nonliberal thinkers will discount.

For Locke, there are two principle dangers to our freedom. The obvious one comes from a tyrannical government which, he holds, should be resisted by a majority. The second threat comes from public opinion, a topic he takes up in his *Essay Concerning Human Understanding.* There, he argues that freedom often consists of standing still and thinking for oneself rather than allowing society do our thinking for us. The danger that Locke detects comes when people blindly follow public opinion. In such circumstances, he argues that individuals do not really govern themselves.

For his part, Thomas Paine sees democratic citizens valuing their freedom and wanting to be left alone to pursue their own private lives. As he understands matters, society is natural and brings out the best in human beings; government, on the other hand, is a reflection of our failures and is, at best, a necessary evil. The harm government can do is enormous, according to Paine, and its actions must therefore be strictly constrained. What it should do is provide the conditions for our freedom and security, but what it too often does is deny us each. For this reason, Paine joins Locke to insist that government must rest on the consent of the governed. With this in mind, Paine turns to a democratic government that, he believes, is able to protect both liberty and security because this is what people most want for themselves and will resist efforts by the state to deprive them of it. As Paine understands matters, good government is minimal government because it safeguards opportunities for ordinary men and women to go about their own affairs without the interference of the state.

James Madison wonders how someone committed to popular government can work both to protect liberty as well as avoid what he takes to be the most dangerous effects of democracy, that is, factions that can gain control of government and destroy the rights of the minority. Madison fears that when factions form a majority and grasp political power, they will serve their own interests at the expense of others, including the liberty of others. When the interests of the majority faction are fused with political power, then the winners need pay no mind to the losers and can trample on their rights. This is particularly troubling to Madison, who holds that parties should not be judges in their own cases. He argues that this is what happens when a faction becomes a majority and gains control of government. On Madison's account, one way we can purge politics of self-interests is to get rid of freedom, something he rejects. As a practical alternative he offers the new American constitution as the best way of keeping factions in check.

Madison holds that factions are unlikely to form when constitutional arrangements disperse power and when a continental republic houses so many diverse interests that they do not have much in common with one another. Through such arrangements, he reasons that no majority faction will be constructed to work its mischief on republican government or individual liberty. One striking feature of Madison's confidence in institutional solutions appears in his view that the character of citizens is not as important as the civic republican writers, who we encounter in the next section, had thought. For Madison, it is impossible to abolish self-interest and make citizens civically virtuous; therefore, the task of a constitutional, popular government is to assure that interests do not dominate government.

A very different view of liberal democracy is supplied by Alexis de Tocqueville. As he understands matters, the spirit of equality permeates the modern age, depriving the old aristocratic order of a moral grounding but also weakening religion, tradition, and the heroic virtues. Tocqueville finds democracy resting on the expanding conception of equality where people resist traditional claims of hierarchy. They want to decide what is important to them and be in charge of their own lives rather than be directed by the old authorities. Yet, he notes that the new opportunities of democracy are not cost-free, and he attempts to alert his readers to the dangerous possibilities of the new era, particularly the ones he believes flow from individualism and the conflict between equality and liberty.

He fears that democracy can be endangered by democracy itself. Its thirst for equality has undermined traditional ways of supplying persons with identity and purpose, leaving them to look elsewhere for standards of judgment. Traditional standards, Tocqueville tells us, are replaced by the will of the majority. But the majority is given to tyrannical behavior, which threatens to smother liberty beneath its unrestrained claim to broad social powers. Although he identifies this threat to freedom as lurking inside every democracy, he also insists that there exist powerful means to combat it, many of which he finds at work in American democracy. There, he recognizes how people often reach beyond their individual interests to engage in larger, shared projects. His Americans achieve this connectedness through their rich associational lives and their attachments to government at the local level. Moreover, Tocqueville believes that democracy requires religion as a way of dampening the self-interest that arises in the modern age. For him, religion teaches men and women that they are not the center of the universe and that democratic citizens should be concerned not only about the present, as many democrats are apt to do, but also about the future as well. As Tocqueville understands matters, religion can challenge the individualism and materialism that reside in any democratic, egalitarian society. He also admires what he terms self-interests rightly understood, which enable democratic citizens to reach beyond a narrow construction of the self, not in ancient, heroic ways, but in small and steady ways that rebound to their own good and the good of their community.

John Stuart Mill not only wants to universalize the franchise but also sees in liberal-democracy a forum for education and enlightenment. For Mill, human beings are "progressive beings," and their progress is most likely to flourish in a free society with active and self-governing members. In *On Liberty*, he identifies the critical contributions that free speech makes to individuality and social development. For him, every society carries not only positive aspects but also prejudices and other impediments to human development. He also sees the pressures to conform threatening to stifle liberty. The only reliable remedy, according to Mill, is to promote a citizenry that is not only tolerant in its legal codes but equally tolerant in its outlooks and orientations. Without such commitments, public opinion can prove just as powerful a source of censorship as the most repressive laws.

For Mill, no government can adequately speak for those who have been excluded, no matter how generous and well meaning officeholders might be. This is why he wants to extend the franchise to all adults, including previously disenfranchised workers and women. Another reason that Mill wants broad participation is because of what it does for the participants. He sees them growing and developing in their activities in the civic arena and believes they become not only better citizens but better people as well. However, a universal franchise does not guarantee that citizens will actually become actively involved in their government. Like Tocqueville, Mill is troubled by the dangers associated with a lethargic citizen body that relinquishes its responsibilities of political participation to the "good despot" in return for promises of comfort and conveniences. When material self-interest and pleasure become the most important things in the lives of citizens, he warns that they will lose their liberty as well as control of their own roles in popular government.

As we show in the next section, liberals have been roundly criticized for their emphasis on rights. For liberals, however, this criticism is misplaced for several reasons. For one, the problems that trouble us today have a multitude of causes reflecting a technologically changing society with greater bureaucracy, centralization, and impersonality. The issue for these liberals, whether on the left or right of the political spectrum, is the preservation or extension of rights, and efforts to discount basic rights need to be resisted. For many contemporary liberals, it is impossible to think that a regime is good if it is prepared to deny equal respect and regard to everyone.

For the most part, liberals recognize that all is not well today but hold the problem is not, as some of their critics claim, that we have too much in the way of rights. For some liberals, the disabilities of the past, particularly in regard to such issues as race and gender, weigh heavily upon the present and rights must remain at the center of public policy. To call up such other goods as stability or community of a certain sort runs the danger, on this liberal account, of neglecting the rights of some of the most vulnerable members of society.

This is the position of the last liberal we consider. John Rawls seeks to construct a democratic regime that speaks to justice and recognizes the integrity of each of its citizens; along the way, he also wants to defeat the role of interests in public life. He pursues these ends by making his principles of justice trump other considerations, such as making morality the subject matter of politics. He reaches his conclusions about justice by imagining a representative individual behind a veil of ignorance or what he calls the original position. There, the person is unaware of his or her personal attributes and does not know whether he or she will be in a favorable position or not upon entering society, rich or poor, healthy or disabled, bright or slow—characteristics that Rawls refers to as morally arbitrary. Rawls believes that behind the veil of ignorance, his representative person will decide that it makes sense to be concerned about the least well-off in society, since that is where he or she might wind up in the real world. With this strategy, Rawls develops his theory of justice, which speaks to the basic liberties of everyone, the necessity of equality of opportunity, and the need to justify inequalities in terms of how they affect the most disadvantaged. He reaches this conclusion by reasoning that people in the original position are risk adverse rather than driven by greed or ambition or by altruism. For Rawls, greed and ambition arise in real societies when some, taking advantage of their positions or attributes, are ready to help themselves at the expense of others; for this reason, he argues, we need institutions that embody his principles of justice.

READINGS

JOHN LOCKE, SELECTIONS FROM *THE SECOND TREATISE ON GOVERNMENT* (1688)

To understand Political Power right, and derive it from its Original, we must consider what State all Men are naturally in, and that is, a *State of perfect Freedom* to order their Actions, and dispose of their Possessions, and Persons as they think fit, within the bounds of the Law of Nature, without asking leave, or depending upon the Will of any other Man.

A *State* also *of Equality,* wherein all the Power and Jurisdiction is reciprocal, no one having more than another: there being nothing more evident, than that Creatures of the same species and rank promiscuously born to all the same advantages of Nature, and the use of the same faculties, should also be equal one amongst another without Subordination or Subjection, unless the Lord and Master of them all, should by any manifest Declaration of his Will set one above another, and confer on him by an evident and clear appointment an undoubted Right to Dominion and Sovereignty. [. . . .]

But though this be a *State of Liberty,* yet it is *not a State of Licence,* though Man in that State have in uncontroleable Liberty, to dispose of his Person or Possessions, yet he has not Liberty to destroy himself, or so much as any Creature in his Possession, but where some nobler use, than its bare Preservation calls for it. The *State of Nature* has a Law of Nature to govern it, which obliges every one: And Reason, which is that Law, teaches all Mankind, who will but consult it, that being all equal and independent, no one ought to harm another in his Life, Health, Liberty, or Possessions. For Men being all the Workmanship of one Omnipotent, and infinitely wise Maker; All the Servants of one Sovereign Master, sent into the World by his order and about his business, they are his Property, whose Workmanship they are, made to last during his, not one another's Pleasure. And being furnished with like Faculties, sharing all in one Community of Nature, there cannot be supposed any such *Subordination* among us, that may Authorize us to destroy one another, as if we were made for one another's uses, as the inferior ranks of Creatures are for ours. Every one as he is *bound to preserve himself,* and not to quit his Station wilfully; so by the like reason when his own Preservation comes not in competition, ought he, as much as he can, *to preserve the rest of Mankind,* and may not unless it be to do Justice on an Offender, take away, or impair the life, or what tends to the Preservation of the Life, the Liberty, Health, Limb or Goods of another.

And that all Men may be restrained from invading others' Rights, and from doing hurt to one another, and the Law of Nature be observed, which willeth the Peace and *Preservation of all Mankind,* the *Execution* of the Law of Nature is in that State, put into every Man's hands, whereby every one has a right to punish the transgressors of that Law to such a Degree, as may hinder its Violation. For the *Law of Nature* would, as all other Laws that concern Men in this World, be in vain, if there were no body that in the State of Nature, had a *Power to Execute* that Law, and thereby preserve the innocent and restrain offenders, and if any one in the State of Nature may punish another, for any evil he has done, every one may do so. For in that *State of perfect Equality,* where naturally there is no superiority or jurisdiction of one, over another, what any may do in Prosecution of that Law, every one must needs have a Right to do. [. . . .]

Of Property

Though the Earth, and all inferior Creatures be common to all Men, yet every Man has a *Property* in his own *Person.* This no Body has any Right to but himself. The *Labour* of his Body, and the *Work* of his Hands, we may say, are properly his. Whatsoever then he removes out of the State that Nature hath provided, and left it in, he hath mixed his *Labour* with, and joyned to it something that is his own, and thereby makes it his *Property.* It being by him removed from the common state Nature placed it in, it hath by his *labour* something annexed to it, that excludes the common right of other Men. For this *Labour* being the unquestionable Property of the Labourer, no Man but he can have a right to what that is once joyned to, at least where there is enough, and as good left in common for others.

He that is nourished by the Acorns he picked up under an Oak, or the Apples he gathered from the Trees in the Wood, has certainly appropriated them to himself. No Body can deny but the nourishment is his. I ask then, When did they begin to be his? When he digested? Or when he eat? Or when he boiled? Or when he brought them home? Or when he picked them up? And 'tis plain, if the first gathering made them not his, nothing else could. That *labour* put a distinction between them and common. That added something to them more than Nature, the common Mother of all, had done; and so they became his private right. And will any one say he had no right to those Acorns or Apples he thus appropriated, because he had not the consent of all Mankind to make them his? Was it a Robbery thus to assume to himself what belonged to all in Common? If such a consent as that was necessary, Man had starved, notwithstanding the Plenty God had given him. We see in *Commons,* which remain so by Compact, that 'tis the taking any part of what is common, and removing it out of the state Nature leaves it in, which *begins the Property;* without which the Common is of no use. And the taking of this or that part, does not depend on the express consent of all the Commoners. Thus the Grass my Horse has bit; the Turfs my Servant has cut; and the Ore I have digg'd in any place where I have a right to them in common with others, become my *Property,* without the assignation or consent of any body. The *labour* that was mine, removing them out of that common state they were in, hath *fixed* my *Property* in them. [. . . .]

It will perhaps be objected to this, That if gathering the Acorns, or other Fruits of the Earth, etc. makes a right to them, then any one may *ingross* as much as he will. To which I Answer, Not so. The same Law of Nature, that does by this means give us Property, does also *bound* that *Property* too. *God has given us all things richly,* I Tim. vi. 17. is the Voice of

Reason confirmed by, Inspiration. But how far has he given it us? *To enjoy.* As much as any one can make use of to any advantage of life before it spoils; so much he may by his labor fix a Property in. Whatever is beyond this, is more than his share, and belongs to others. Nothing was made by God for Man to spoil or destroy. And thus considering the plenty of natural Provisions there was a long time in the World, and the few spenders, and to how small a part of that provision the industry of one Man could extend it self, and ingross it to the prejudice of others; especially keeping within the *bounds,* set by reason of what might serve for his *use*; there could be then little room for Quarrels or Contentions about Property so establish'd.

But the *chief matter of Property* being now not the Fruits of the Earth, and the Beasts that subsist on it, but the *Earth it self*; as that which takes in and carries with it all the rest: I think it is plain, that *Property* in that too is Acquired as the former. *As much Land* as a Man Tills, Plants, Improves, Cultivates, and can use the product of, so much is his *Property.* He by his Labour does as it were, inclose it from the Common. Nor will it invalidate his right to say, Every body else has an equal Title to it; and therefore he cannot appropriate, he cannot inclose, without the Consent of all his Fellow-Commoners, all Mankind. God, when he gave the World in common to all Mankind, commanded Man also to labour, and the penury of his Condition required it of him. God and his Reason commanded him to subdue the Earth, *i.e.,* improve it for the benefit of Life, and therein lay out something upon it that was his own, his labour. He that in Obedience to this Command of God, subdued, tilled and sowed any part of it, thereby annexed to it something that was his *Property,* which Another had no Title to, nor could without injury take from him.

Nor was this *appropriation* of any parcel of *Land,* by improving it, any prejudice to any other Man, since there was still and as good left; and more than the yet unprovided could use. So that in effect, there was never the less left for others because of his inclosure for himself. For he that leaves as much as another can make use of, does as good as take nothing at all. No Body could think himself injur'd by the drinking of another Man, though he took a good Draught, who had a whole River of the same Water left him to quench his thirst. And the Case of Land and Water, where there is enough of both, is perfectly the same.

God gave the World to Men in Common; but since he gave it them for their benefit, and the greatest Conveniencies of life they were capable to draw from it, it cannot be supposed he meant it should always remain common and uncultivated. He gave it to the use of the Industrious and Rational, (and *Labour* was to be *his Title* to it) not to the Fancy or Covetousness of the Quarrelsom and Contentious. He that had as good left for his Improvement, as was already taken up, needed not complain, ought not to meddle with what was already improved by another's Labour: If he did, 'tis plain he desired the benefit of another's Pains, which he had no right to, and not the Ground which God had given him in common with others to labour on, and whereof there was as good left, as that already possessed, and more than he knew what to do with, or his Industry could reach to.

'Tis true, in *Land* that is *common* in *England,* or any other Country, where there is Plenty of People under Government, who have Money and Commerce, no one can inclose or appropriate any part, without the consent of all his Fellow-Commoners: Because this is left common by Compact, *i.e.,* by the Law of the Land, which is not to be violated. And though it be Common, in respect of some Men, it is not so to all Mankind; but is the joint property of this Country, or this Parish. Besides, the remainder, after such inclosure, would not be as good to the rest of the Commoners as the whole was, when they could all make use of the whole: whereas in the beginning and first peopling of the great Common of the World, it was quite otherwise. The Law Man was under, was rather for *appropriating*. God Commanded, and his Wants forced him to *labour*. That was his *Property* which could not be taken from him where-ever he had fixed it. And hence subduing or cultivating the Earth, and having Dominion, we see are joyned together. The one gave Title to the other. So that God, by commanding to subdue, gave Authority so far to *appropriate*. And the Condition of Humane Life, which requires Labour and Materials to work on, necessarily introduces *private Possessions*.

The measure of Property, Nature has well set, by the Extent of Men's *Labour, and the Conveniency of Life*: No Man's Labour could subdue, or appropriate all: nor could his Enjoyment consume more than a small part; so that it was impossible for any Man, this way, to intrench upon the right of another, or acquire, to himself, a Property, to the Prejudice of his Neighbour, who would still have room, for as good, and as large a Possession (after the other had taken out his) as before it was appropriated. This *measure* did confine every Man's *Possession,* to a very moderate Proportion, and such as he might appropriate to himself, without Injury to any Body in the first Ages of the World, when Men were more in danger to be lost, by wandering from their Company, in the then vast Wilderness of the Earth, than to be straitned for want of room to plant in. And the same *measure* may be allowed still, without prejudice to any Body, as full as the World seems. For supposing a Man, or Family, in the state they were, at first peopling of the World by the Children of *Adam,* or *Noah;* let him plant in some in-land, vacant places of *America,* we shall find that the *Possessions* he could make himself upon the *measures* we have given, would not be very large, nor, even to this day, prejudice the rest of Mankind, or give them reason to complain, or think themselves injured by this Man's Incroachment, though the Race of Men have now spread themselves to all the corners of the World, and do infinitely exceed the small number [that] was at the beginning. Nay, the extent of *Ground* is of so little value, *without labour,* that I have heard it affirmed, that in *Spain* it self, a Man may be permitted to plough, sow, and reap, without being disturbed, upon Land he has no other Title to, but only his making use of it. But, on the contrary, the Inhabitants think themselves beholden to him, who, by his Industry on neglected, and consequently waste Land, has increased the stock of Corn, which they wanted. But be this as it will, which I lay no stress on; This I dare boldly affirm, That the same *Rule of Property, (viz.)* that every Man should have as much as he could make use of, would hold still in the World, without straitning any body, since there is Land enough in the World to suffice double the Inhabitants had not the *Invention of Money,* and the tacit Agreement of Men to put a value on it, introduced (by Consent) larger Possessions, and a Right to them; which, how it has done, I shall, by and by, shew more at large.

This is certain, That in the beginning, before the desire of having more than Men needed, had altered the intrinsick value of things, which depends only on their usefulness to the Life of Man; or had *agreed, that a little piece of yellow Metal,* which would keep without wasting or decay, should be worth a great piece of Flesh, or a whole heap of Corn; though Men had a Right to appropriate, by their Labour, each one to himself, as much of the things of Nature, as he could use: Yet this could not be much, nor to the Prejudice of others, where the same plenty was still left, to those who would use the same Industry. To which let me add, that he who appropriates land to himself by his labour, does not lessen but increase the common stock of mankind. For the provisions serving to the support of humane life, produced by one acre of inclosed and cultivated land, are (to speak much within compasse) ten times more, than those, which are yielded by an acre of Land, of an equal richnesse, lyeing wast in common. And therefore he, that incloses Land and has a greater plenty of the conveniencys of life from ten acres, than he could have from an hundred left to Nature, may truly be said, to give ninety acres to Mankind. For his labour now supplys him with provisions out of ten acres, which were but the product of an hundred lying in common. I have here rated the improved land very low in making its product but as ten to one, when it is much nearer an hundred to one. For I aske whether in the wild woods and uncultivated wast of America left to Nature, without any improvement, tillage or husbandry, a thousand acres will yield the needy and wretched inhabitants as many conveniencies of life as ten acres of equally fertile land doe in Devonshire where they are well cultivated?

Before the Appropriation of Land, he who gathered as much of the wild Fruit, killed, caught, or tamed, as many of the Beasts as he could; he that so employed his Pains about any of the spontaneous Products of Nature, as any way to alter them, from the state which Nature put them in, *by* placing any of his *Labour* on them, did thereby *acquire a Property in them*: But if they perished, in his Possession, without their due use; if the Fruits rotted, or the Venison putrified, before he could spend it, he offended against the common Law of Nature, and was liable to be punished; he invaded his Neighbour's share, for he had *no Right, farther than his Use* called for any of them, and they might serve to afford him Conveniencies of Life. [. . . .]

Of the Beginning of Political Society

Men being, as has been said, by Nature, all free, equal and independent, no one can be put out of this Estate, and subjected to the Political Power of another, without his own *Consent*. The only way whereby any one devests himself of his Natural Liberty, and *puts on the bonds of Civil Society* is by agreeing with other Men to joyn and unite into a Community, for their comfortable, safe, and peaceable living one amongst another, in a secure Enjoyment of their Properties, and a greater Security against any that are not of it. This any number of Men may do, because it injures not the Freedom of the rest; they are left as they were in the Liberty of the State of Nature. When any number of Men have so *consented to make one Community* or Government, they are thereby presently incorporated, and make *one Body Politick,* wherein the *Majority* have a Right to act and conclude the rest.

For when any number of Men have, by the consent of every individual, made a *Community,* they have thereby made that *Community* one Body, with a Power to Act as one Body, which is only by the will and determination of the *majority*. For that which acts any Community, being only the consent of the individuals of it, and it being necessary to that which is one body to move one way; it is necessary the Body should move that way whither the greater force carries it, which is the *consent of the majority*: or else it is impossible it should act or continue one Body, *one Community,* which the consent of every individual that united into it, agreed that it should; and so every one is bound by that consent to be concluded by the *majority*. And therefore we see that in Assemblies impowered to act by positive Laws where no number is set by that positive Law which impowers them, the *act of the Majority* passes for the act of the whole, and of course determines, as having by the Law of Nature and Reason, the power of the whole.

And thus every Man, by consenting with others to make one Body Politick under one Government, puts himself under an Obligation to every one of that Society, to submit to the determination of the *majority,* and to be concluded by it; or else this *original Compact,* whereby he with others incorporates into *one Society,* would signifie nothing, and be no Company, if he be left free, and under no other ties, than he was in before in the State of Nature.

For what appearance would there be of any Compact? What new Engagement if he were no farther tied by any Decrees of the Society, than he himself thought fit, and did actually consent to? This would be still as great a liberty, as he himself had before his Company, or any one else in the State of Nature hath, who may submit himself and consent to any acts of it if he thinks fit.

For if *the consent of the majority* shall not in reason, be received, as *the act of the whole,* and conclude every individual; nothing but the consent of every individual can make any thing to be the act of the whole: But such a consent is next impossible ever to be had, if we, consider the Infirmities of Health, and Avocations of Business, which in a number, though much less than that of a Common-wealth, will necessarily keep many away from the publick Assembly. To which if we add the variety of Opinions, and contrariety of Interests, which unavoidably happen in all Collections of Men, the coming into Society upon such terms, would be only like *Cato's* coming into the Theatre, only to go out again. Such a Constitution as this would make the mighty *Leviathan* of a shorter duration, than the feeblest Creatures; and not let it outlast the day it was born in: which cannot be suppos'd, till we can think, that Rational Creatures should desire and constitute Societies only to be dissolved. For where the *majority* cannot conclude the rest, there they cannot act as one Body, and consequently will be immediately dissolved again.

Whosoever therefore out of a state of Nature unite into a *Community,* must be understood to give up all the power, necessary to the ends for which they unite into Society, to the *majority* of the Community, unless they expressly agreed in any number greater than the majority. And this is done by barely agreeing to *unite into one Political Society,* which is *all the Compact* that is, or needs be, between the Individuals, that enter into, or make up a *Common-wealth.* And thus that, which begins and actually *constitutes any Political Society,* is nothing but the consent of any number of Freemen capable of a majority to unite and incorporate into such a Society. And this is that, and that only, which did, or could give *beginning* to any *lawful Government* in the World. [. . . .]

Of the Extent of the Legislative Power

The great end of Men's entring into Society, being the enjoyment of their Properties in Peace and Safety, and the great instrument and means of that being the Laws establish'd in that Society; the *first and fundamental positive Law* of all Common-wealths, *is the establishing of the Legislative* Power; as the *first and fundamental natural Law,* which is to govern even the Legislative it self, is *the preservation of the Society,* and (as far as will consist with the publick good) of every person in it. This *Legislative* is not only *the supream power* of the Common-wealth, but sacred and unalterable in the hands where the Community have once placed it; nor can any Edict of any Bodyelse, in what Form soever conceived, or by what Power soever backed, have the force and obligation of a *Law,* which has not its *Sanction from* that *Legislative,* which the publick has chosen and appointed. For without this the Law could not have that, which is absolutely necessary to its being a *Law, the consent of the Society,* over whom no Body can have a power to make Laws, but by their own consent, and by Authority received from them; and therefore all the *Obedience,* which by the most solemn Ties any one can be obliged to pay, ultimately terminates in this *Supream Power,* and is directed by those Laws which it enacts: nor can any Oaths to any Foreign Power whatsoever, or any Domestick Subordinate Power, discharge any Member of the Society from his *Obedience to the Legislative,* acting pursuant to their trust, nor oblige him to any Obedience contrary to the Laws so enacted, or farther than they do allow; it being ridiculous to imagine one can be tied ultimately to *obey* any *Power* in the Society, which is not *the Supream*. [. . . .]

But *Government* into whatsoever hands it is put, being as I have before shew'd, intrusted with this condition, and *for this end,* that Men might have and secure *their Properties,* the Prince or Senate, however it may have power to make Laws for the regulating of *Property* between the Subjects one amongst another, yet can never have a Power to take to themselves the whole or any part of the Subjects' *Property*, without their own consent. For this would be in effect to leave them no *Property* at all. And to let us see, that even *absolate Power,* where it is necessary, is *not Arbitrary* by being absolute, but is still limited by that reason, and confined to those ends, which required it in some Cases to be absolute, we need look no farther than the common practice of Martial Discipline. For the Preservation of the Army, and in it of the whole Commonwealth, requires an *absolute Obedience* to the Command of every Superiour Officer, and it is justly Death to disobey or dispute the most dangerous or unreasonable of them: but yet we see, that neither the Serjeant, that could command a Soldier to march up to the mouth of a Cannon, or stand in a Breach, where he is almost sure to perish, can command that Soldier to give him one penny of his Money; nor the *General,* that can condemn him to Death for deserting his Post, or for not obeying the most desperate Orders, can yet with all his absolute Power of Life and Death, dispose of one Farthing of that Soldiers Estate, or seize one jot of his Goods; whom yet he can command any thing, and hang for the least Disobedience. Because such a blind Obedience is necessary to that end for which the Commander has his Power, *viz.* the preservation of the rest; but the disposing of his Goods has nothing to do with it.

'Tis true, Governments cannot be supported without great Charge, and 'tis fit every one who enjoys his share of the Protection, should pay out of his Estate his proportion for the maintenance of it. But still it must be with his own Consent, *i.e.,* the Consent of the Majority, giving it either by themselves, or their Representatives chosen by them. For if any one shall claim a *Power to lay and levy Taxes* on the People, by his own Authority, and without such consent of the People, he thereby invades the *Fundamental Law of Property,* and subverts the end of Government. For what property have I in that which another may by right take, when he pleases to himself?

JOHN LOCKE, SELECTION FROM *AN ESSAY CONCERNING HUMAN UNDERSTANDING* (1689)

There being in us a great many *uneasinesses* always soliciting, and ready to determine the *will,* it is natural that the greatest, and the most pressing should determine the *will* to the next action; and so it does for the most part, but not always. For the mind having in most cases, as is evident in Experience, a power to *suspend* the execution and satisfaction of any of its desires, and so all one after another, is at liberty to consider the objects of them; examine them on all sides, and weigh them with others. In this lies the liberty Man has; and from the not using of it right comes all that variety of mistakes, errors, and faults which we run into, in the conduct of our lives, and our endeavors after happiness; whilst we precipitate the determination of our *wills,* and engage too soon before due *Examination.* To prevent this we have a power to *suspend* the prosecution of this or that desire, as every one daily may *Experiment* in himself. This seems to me the source of all liberty. . . . For during this *suspension* of any desire, before the *will* be determined to action and the action (which follows that determination) done, we have opportunity to examine, view, and judge, of the good or evil of what we are going to do; and when, upon due *Examination*, we have judg'd we have done our duty, all that we can, or ought to do, in pursuit of our happiness; and 'tis not a fault, but a perfection of our nature to desire, will, and act according to the last result of a fair *Examination*.

This is so far from being a restraint or diminution or *Freedom*, that it is the very improvement and benefit of it: 'tis not an Abridgment, 'tis the end use of our *Liberty*; and the farther we are removed from such a determination, the nearer we are to Misery and Slavery. A perfect Indifference in the Mind, not determinable by its last judgment of the Good or Evil, that is thought to attend its Choice, would be so far from being an advantage and excellency of any intellectual Nature, that it would be as great an imperfection, as the want of Indifference to act, or not to act, till determined by the *Will*, would be an imperfection on the other side. A Man is at liberty to lift up his Hand to his Head, or let it rest quiet: He is perfectly indifferent in either; and it would be an imperfection in him, if he wanted that Power, if he were deprived of that Indifference. But it would be as great an imperfection, if he had the same indifference, whether he would prefer the lifting up his Hand, or its remaining in rest, when it would save his Head or Eyes from a blow he sees coming: *'tis* as much *a perfection, that desire or the power of Preferring should be determined by Good*, as that the power of Acting should be determined by the *Will*, and the certainer such determination is, the greater is the perfection. Nay were we determined by anything but the last result of our own Minds, judging of the good or evil of any action, we were not free, the very end of our Freedom being, that we might attain the good we choose. And therefore every Man is put under a necessity by his constitution, as an intelligent Being, to be determined in *willing* by his own Thought and Judgment, what is best for him to do: else he would be under the determination of some other than himself, which is want of Liberty. And to deny, that a Man's *will*, in every determination, follows his own Judgment, is to say, that a Man *wills* and acts for an end that he would not have the time that he *wills* and acts for it. For if he prefers it in his present Thoughts before any other, 'tis plain he then thinks better of it, and would have it before any other, unless he can have, and not have it; *will* and not *will* it at the same time; a Contradiction too manifest to be admitted.

If we look upon those *superior Beings* among us, who enjoy perfect Happiness, we shall have reason to judge that they are more steadily *determined in their choice of Good* than we; and yet we have no reason to think they are less happy, or less free, than we are. And if it were fit for such poor finite Creatures as we are, to pronounce what infinite Wisdom and Goodness could do, I think, we might say, That God himself cannot choose what is not good; the Freedom of the Almighty hinders not his being determined by what is best.

But to give a right view of this mistaken part of Liberty, let me ask, Would any one be a Changeling, because he is less determined, by wise Considerations, than a wise Man? Is it worth the Name of *Freedom* to be at liberty to play the Fool, and draw Shame and Misery upon a Man's self? If to break loose from the conduct of Reason, and to want that restraint of Examination and Judgment, which keeps us from choosing or doing the worse, be *Liberty*, true Liberty, mad Men and Fools are the only Freemen: but yet, I think, nobody would choose to be mad for the sake of such *Liberty*, but he that is mad already. The constant desire of Happiness, and the constraint it puts upon us to act for it, no Body, I think, accounts an abridgment of *Liberty*, or at least an abridgment of Liberty to be complain'd of. God

Almighty himself is under the necessity of being happy; and the more any intelligent Being is so, the nearer is its approach to infinite perfection and happiness. That in this state of Ignorance we short-sighted Creatures might not mistake true felicity, we are endowed with a power to suspend any particular desire, and keep it from determining the *will*, and engaging us in action. This is *standing still*, where we are not sufficiently assured of the way: Examination is *consulting a guide.* The determination of the *will* upon inquiry is *following the direction of that Guide:* And he that has a power to act, or not to act according as such determination directs, is a *free Agent*; such determination abridges not that Power wherein Liberty consists. He that has his Chains knocked off, and the Prison-doors set open to him, is perfectly at *liberty*, because he may either go or stay, as he best likes; though his preference be determined to stay, by the darkness of the Night, or illness of the Weather, or want of other Lodging. He ceases not to be free; though the desire of some convenience to be had there, absolutely determines his preference, and makes him stay in his Prison.

As therefore the highest perfection of intellectual nature, lies in a careful and constant pursuit of true and solid happiness; so the care of ourselves, that we, mistake not imaginary for real happiness, is the necessary foundation of our *liberty*. The stronger ties, we have, to an unalterable pursuit of happiness in general, which is our greatest good, and which as such our desires always follow, the more are we free from any necessary determination of our *will* to any particular action, and from a necessary compliance with our desire, set upon any particular, and then appearing preferable good, till we have duly examin'd, whether it has a tendency to, or be inconsistent with our real happiness; and therefore till we are as much informed upon this enquiry, as the weight of the matter, and the nature of the case demands, we are by the necessity of preferring and pursuing true happiness as our greatest good, obliged to suspend the satisfaction of our desire in particular cases. [. . . .]

From what has been said, it is easy to give an account, how it comes to pass, that though all Men desire Happiness, yet their *wills carry them so contrarily*, and consequently some of them to what is Evil. And to this I say, that the various and contrary choices, that Men make in the World, do not argue, that they do not all pursue Good; but that the same thing is not good to every Man alike. This variety of pursuits shows, that every one does not place his happiness in the same thing, or choose the same way to it. Were all the Concerns of Man terminated in this Life, why one followed Study and Knowledge, and another Hawking and Hunting; why one chose Luxury and Debauchery, and another Sobriety and Riches, would not be, because every one of these did not aim at his own happiness; but because their *Happiness* was placed in different things. And therefore 'twas a right Answer of the Physician to his Patient, that had sore Eyes. If you have more Pleasure in the Taste of Wine, than in the use or your Sight, Wine is good for you; but if the Pleasure of Seeing be greater to you, than that of Drinking, Wine is naught.

The Mind has a different relish, as well as the Palate; and you will as fruitlessly endeavor to delight all Men with Riches or Glory, (which yet some Men place their Happiness in) as you would to satisfy all Men's Hunger with Cheese or Lobsters; which, though very agreeable and delicious fare to some, are to others is extremely nauseous and offensive: and many People would with Reason preferr the griping of an hungry Belly, to those Dishes, which are a Feast to others. Hence it was, I think, that the Philosophers of old did in vain enquire, whether *Summum bonum* consisted in Riches, or bodily Delights, or Virtue, or Contemplation: And they might have as reasonably disputed, whether the best Relish were to be found in Apples, Plumbs, or Nuts; and have divided themselves into Sects upon it. For as pleasant Tastes depend not on the things themselves, but their agreeableness to this or that particular Palate, wherein there is great variety: so the greatest Happiness consists, in the having those things, which produce the greatest Pleasure; and in the absence of those, which Cause any disturbance, any pain. Now these, to different Men, are very different things. If therefore Men in this Life only have hope; if in this Life they can only enjoy, 'tis not strange, nor unreasonable, that they should seek their Happiness by avoiding all things, that disease them here, and by pursuing that delight them; wherein it will be no wonder to find variety and difference. For if there be no Prospect beyond the Grave, the inference is certainly right, *Let us eat and drink,* let us enjoy what we delight in, *for to morrow we shall die.* This, I think, may serve to shew us the Reason, why, though all Men's desires tend to Happiness, yet they are not moved by the same Object. Men may choose different things, and yet all choose right, supposing them only like a Company of poor Insects, whereof some are Bees, delighted with Flowers, and their sweetness; others, Beetles, delighted with other kind of Viands; which having enjoyed for a season, they should cease to be, and exist no more for ever.

These things duly weigh'd, will give us, as I think, a clear view into the state of humane Liberty. Liberty 'tis plain consists in a Power to do, or not to do; to do, or forbear doing as we *will.* This cannot be deny'd But this seeming to comprehend only the actions of a Man consecutive to volition, it is farther enquired, whether he be at Liberty to *will,* or no? and to this it has been answered, that in most cases a Man is not at Liberty to forbear the act of volition; he must exert an act of his *will,* whereby the action proposed, is made to exist, or not to exist. But yet there is a case wherein a Man is at Liberty in respect of *willing,* and that is the choosing of a remote Good as an end to be pursued. Here a Man may suspend the act of his choice from being determined for or against the thing proposed, till he has examined, whether it be really of a nature in it self and consequences to make him happy, or no. For when he has once chosen it, and thereby it is become a part of his Happiness, it raises desire, and that proportionably gives him *uneasiness,* which determines his *will,* and sets him at work in pursuit of his choice on all occasions that offer. And here we may see how it comes to pass, that a Man may justly incur punishment, though it be certain that in all the particular actions that he *wills,* he does, and necessarily does will that, which he then judges to be good. For though his *will* be always determined by that, which is judg'd good by his Understanding, yet it excuses him not: Because, by a too hasty choice of his own making, he has imposed on himself wrong measures of good and evil; which however false and fallacious, have the same influence on all his future conduct, as if they were true and right. He has vitiated his own Palate, and must be answerable to himself for the sickness and death that follows from it. The eternal Law and Nature of things must not be alter'd to comply with his ill-order'd choice. If the neglect or abuse of the Liberty he had, to examine what would really and truly make for his Happiness, misleads him, the miscarriages that follow on it, must be imputed to his own election. He had a Power to suspend his determination: It was given him, that he might examine, and take care of his own Happiness, and look that he were not deceived. And he could never judge, that it was better to be deceived, than not, in a matter of so great and near concernment.

THOMAS PAINE, SELECTIONS FROM *COMMON SENSE* (1776)

Some writers have so confounded society with government, as to leave little or no distinction between them; whereas they are not only different, but have different origins. Society is produced by our wants and government by our wickedness; the former promotes our happiness *positively* by uniting our affections, the latter *negatively* by restraining our vices. The one encourages intercourse, the other creates distinctions. The first is a patron, the last a punisher.

Society in every state is a blessing, but government, even in its best state, is but a necessary evil; in its worst state an intolerable one: for when we suffer, or are exposed to the same miseries *by a government*, which we might expect in a country *without government*, our calamity is heightened by reflecting that we furnish the means by which we suffer. Government, like dress, is the badge of lost innocence; the palaces of kings are built upon the ruins of the bowers of paradise. For were the impulses of conscience clear, uniform and irresistibly obeyed, man would need no other lawgiver; but that not being the case, he finds it necessary to surrender up a part of his property to furnish means for the protection of the rest; and this he is induced to do by the same prudence which in every other case advises him, out of two evils to choose the least. Wherefore, security being the true design and end of government, it unanswerably follows that whatever form thereof appears most likely to ensure it to us, with the least expense and greatest benefit, is preferable to all others.

In order to gain a clear and just idea of the design and end of government, let us suppose a small number of persons settled in some sequestered part of the earth, unconnected with the rest; they will then represent the first peopling of any country, or of the world. In this state of natural liberty, society will be their first thought. A thousand motives will excite them thereto; the strength of one man is so unequal to his wants, and his mind so unfitted for perpetual solitude, that he is soon obliged to seek assistance and relief of another, who in his turn requires the same. Four or five united would be able to raise a tolerable dwelling in the midst of a wilderness, but one man might labor out the common period of life without accomplishing any thing; when he had felled his timber he could not remove it, nor erect it after it was removed; hunger in the mean time would urge him to quit his work, and every different want would call him a different way. [. . . .]

Thus necessity, like a gravitating power, would soon form our newly arrived emigrants into society, the reciprocal blessings of which would supercede, and render the obligations of law and government unnecessary while they remained perfectly just to each other; but as nothing but Heaven is impregnable to vice, it will unavoidably happen that in proportion as they surmount the first difficulties of emigration, which bound them together in a common cause, they will begin to relax in their duty and attachment to each other: and this remissness will point out the necessity of establishing some form of government to supply the defect of moral virtue.

Some convenient tree will afford them a State House, under the branches of which the whole colony may assemble to deliberate on public matters. It is more than probable that their first laws will have the title only of regulations and be enforced by no other penalty than public disesteem. In this first parliament every man by natural right will have a seat.

But as the colony increases, the public concerns will increase likewise, and the distance at which the members may be separated, will render it too inconvenient for all of them to meet on every occasion as at first, when their number was small, their habitations near, and the public concerns few and trifling. This will point out the convenience of their consenting to leave the legislative part to be managed by a select number chosen from the whole body, who are supposed to have the same concerns at stake which those have who appointed them, and who will act in the same manner as the whole body would act were they present. If the colony continue increasing, it will become necessary to augment the number of representatives, and that the interest of every part of the colony may be attended to, it will be found best to divide the whole into convenient parts, each part sending its proper number: and that the *elected* might never form to themselves an interest separate from the *electors*, prudence will point out the propriety of having elections often because as the *elected* might by that means return and mix again with the general body of the *electors* in a few months, their fidelity to the public will be secured by the prudent reflection of not making a rod for themselves. And as this frequent interchange will establish a common interest with every part of the community, they will mutually and naturally support each other, and on this (not on the unmeaning name of king) depends the *strength of government, and the happiness of the governed.*

Here then is the origin and rise of government; namely, a mode rendered necessary by the inability of moral virtue to govern the world; here too is the design and end of government, viz. freedom and security. And however our eyes may be dazzled with show, or our ears deceived by sound; however prejudice may warp our wills, or interest darken our understanding, the simple voice of nature and reason will say, 'tis right.

I draw my idea of the form of government from a principle in nature which no art can overturn, viz. that the more simple any thing is, the less liable it is to be disordered, and the easier repaired when disordered; and with this maxim in view I offer a few remarks on the so much boasted Constitution of England. That it was noble for the dark and slavish times in which it was erected, is granted. When the world was overrun with tyranny the least remove there from was a glorious rescue. But that it is imperfect, subject to convulsions, and incapable of producing what it seems to promise, is easily demonstrated.

Absolute governments (though the disgrace of human nature) have this advantage with them, they are simple; if the people suffer, they know the head from which their suffering springs; know likewise the remedy and are not bewildered by a variety of causes and cures. But the Constitution of England is so exceedingly complex, that the nation may suffer for years together without being able to discover in which part the fault lies; some will say in one and some in another, and every political physician will advise a different medicine.

I know it is difficult to get over local or long standing prejudices, yet if we will suffer ourselves to examine the component parts of the English Constitution, we shall find them to be the base remains of two ancient tyrannies, compounded with some new Republican materials.

First—The remains of monarchical tyranny in the person of the king.

Secondly—The remains of aristocratical tyranny in the persons of the peers.

Thirdly—The new Republican materials, in the persons of the Commons, on whose virtue depends the freedom of England.

The two first, by being hereditary, are independent of the people; wherefore in a *constitutional sense* they contribute nothing towards the freedom of the State.

To say that the Constitution of England is an *union* of three powers, reciprocally *checking* each other, is farcical; either the words have no meaning, or they are flat contradictions.

To say that the Commons is a check upon the king presupposes two things.

First—That the king is not to be trusted without being looked after; or in other words, that a thirst for absolute power is the natural disease of monarchy.

Secondly—That the Commons, by being appointed for that purpose, are either wiser or more worthy of confidence than the crown.

But as the same constitution which gives the Commons a power to check the king by withholding the supplies, gives afterwards the king a power to check the Commons by empowering him to reject their other bills; it again supposes that the king is wiser than those whom it has already supposed to be wiser than him. A mere absurdity!

There is something exceedingly ridiculous in the composition of monarchy; it first excludes a man from the means of information, yet empowers him to act in cases where the highest judgment is required. The state of a king shuts him from the world, yet the business of a king requires him to know it thoroughly; wherefore the different parts, by unnaturally opposing and destroying each other, prove the whole character to be absurd and useless.

Some writers have explained the English Constitution thus: the king, say they, is one, the people another; the peers are a house in behalf of the king, the Commons in behalf of the people; but this hath all the distinctions of a house divided against itself; and though the expressions be pleasantly arranged, yet when examined they appear idle and ambiguous; and it will always happen, that the nicest construction that words are capable of, when applied to the description of something which either cannot exist, or is too incomprehensible to be within the compass of description, will be words of sound only, and though they may amuse the ear, they cannot inform the mind: for this explanation includes a previous question, viz. *how came the king by a power which the people are afraid to trust, and always obliged to check?* Such a power could not be the gift of a wise people, neither can any power, *which needs checking*, be from God; yet the provision which the Constitution makes supposes such a power to exist.

But the provision is unequal to the task; the means either cannot or will not accomplish the end, and the whole affair is a *Felo de se:* for as the greater weight will always carry up the less, and as all the wheels of a machine are put in motion by one, it only remains to know which power in the constitution has the most weight, for that will govern: and though the others, or a part of them, may clog, or, as the phrase is, check the rapidity of its motion, yet so long as they cannot stop it, their endeavors will be ineffectual: The first moving power will at last have its way, and what it wants in speed is supplied by time.

That the crown is this overbearing part in the English Constitution needs not be mentioned, and that it derives its whole consequence merely from being the giver of places and pensions is self-evident; wherefore, though we have been wise enough to shut and lock a door against absolute Monarchy, we at the same time have been foolish enough to put the crown in possession of the key.

The prejudice of Englishmen, in favor of their own government, by king, lords and Commons, arises as much or more from national pride than reason. Individuals are undoubtedly safer in England than in some other countries: but the will of the king is as much the law of the land in Britain as in France, with this difference, that instead of proceeding directly from his mouth, it is handed to the people under the formidable shape of an act of Parliament. For the fate of Charles the First hath only made kings more subtle—not more just.

Wherefore, laying aside all national pride and prejudice in favor of modes and forms, the plain truth is that *it is wholly owing to the constitution of the people, and not to the constitution of the government* that the crown is not as oppressive in England as in Turkey.

An inquiry into the *constitutional errors* in the English form of government, is at this time highly necessary; for as we are never in a proper condition of doing justice to others, while we continue under the influence of some leading partiality, so neither are we capable of doing it to ourselves while we remain fettered by any obstinate prejudice. And as a man who is attached to a prostitute is unfitted to choose or judge of a wife, so any prepossession in favor of a rotten constitution of government will disable us from discerning a good one. [. . . .]

In the following pages I offer nothing more than simple facts, plain arguments, and common sense: and have no other preliminaries to settle with the reader, than that he will divest himself of prejudice and prepossession, and suffer his reason and his feelings to determine for themselves: that he will put on or rather that he will not put off, the true character of a man, and generously enlarge his views beyond the present day. [. . . .]

I have heard it asserted by some, that as America has flourished under her former connection with Great Britain, the same connection is necessary towards her future happiness, and will always have the same effect. Nothing can be more fallacious than this kind of argument. We may as well assert that because a child has thrived upon milk, that it is never to have meat, or that the first twenty years of our lives is to become a precedent for the next twenty. But even this is admitting more than is true; for I answer roundly, that America would have flourished as much, and probably much more, had no European power taken any notice of her. The commerce by which she hath enriched herself are the necessaries of life, and will always have a market while eating is the custom of Europe.

But she has protected us, say some. That she hath engrossed us is true, and defended the continent at our expense as well as her own, is admitted; and she would have defended Turkey from the same motive, viz. for the sake of trade and dominion.

Alas! we have been long led away by ancient prejudices and made large sacrifices to superstition. We have boasted the protection of Great Britain, without considering, that her motive was *interest* not *attachment*; and that she did not protect us from *our enemies* on *our account*; but from *her enemies* on *her own account*, from those who had no quarrel with us on any *other account*, and who will always be our enemies on the *same account*. Let Britain waive her pretensions to the continent, or the continent throw off the dependence, and we should be at peace with France and Spain, were they at war with Britain. The miseries of Hanover's last war ought to warn us against connections.

It hath lately been asserted in Parliament, that the colonies have no relation to each other but through the parent country, *i.e.*, that Pennsylvania and the Jerseys, and so on for the rest, are sister colonies by the way of England; this is certainly a very roundabout way of proving relationship, but it is the nearest and only true way of proving enmity (or enemyship, if I may so call it). France and Spain never were, nor perhaps ever will be, our enemies as *Americans*, but as our being the *subjects of Great Britain*.

But Britain is the parent country, say some. Then the more shame upon her conduct. Even brutes do not devour their young, nor savages make war upon their families, wherefore, the assertion, if true, turns to her reproach; but it happens not to be true, or only partly so, and the phrase *parent* or *mother county* hath been jesuitically adopted by the king and his parasites, with a low papistical design of gaining an unfair bias on the credulous weakness of our minds. Europe, and not England, is the parent country of America. This new world hath been the asylum for the persecuted lovers of civil and religious liberty from *every part* of Europe. Hither have they fled, not from the tender embraces of the mother, but from the cruelty of the monster; and it is so far true of England, that the same tyranny which drove the first emigrants from home, pursues their descendants still.

In this extensive quarter of the globe, we forget the narrow limits of three hundred and sixty miles (the extent of England) and carry our friendship on a larger scale; we claim brotherhood with every European Christian, and triumph in the generosity of the sentiment. [. . . .]

But, admitting that we were all of English descent, what does it amount to? Nothing. Britain, being now an open enemy, extinguishes every other name and title: and to say that reconciliation is our duty, is truly farcical. The first king of England, of the present line

(William the Conqueror) was a Frenchman, and half the peers of England are descendants from the same country; wherefore, by the same method of reasoning, England ought to be governed by France.

Much hath been said of the united strength of Britain and the colonies, that in conjunction they might bid defiance to the world. But this is mere presumption; the fate of war is uncertain, neither do the expressions mean any thing; for this continent would never suffer itself to be drained of inhabitants, to support the British arms in either Asia, Africa or Europe.

Besides, what have we to do with setting the world at defiance? Our plan is commerce, and that, well attended to, will secure us the peace and friendship of all Europe; because it is the interest of all Europe to have America a free port. Her trade will always be a protection, and her barrenness of gold and silver secure her from invaders.

I challenge the warmest advocate for reconciliation to show a single advantage that this continent can reap by being connected with Great Britain. I repeat the challenge; not a single advantage is derived. Our corn will fetch its price in any market in Europe, and our imported goods must be paid for by them where we will.

But the injuries and disadvantages which we sustain by that connection, are without number; and our duty to mankind at large, as well as to ourselves, instruct us to renounce the alliance: because, any submission to, or dependence on, Great Britain, tends directly to involve this continent in European wars and quarrels, and set us at variance with nations who would otherwise seek our friendship, and against whom we have neither anger nor complaint. As Europe is our market for trade, we ought to form no partial connection with any part of it. It is the true interest of America to steer clear of European contentions, which she never can do, while, by her dependence on Britain, she is made the makeweight in the scale of British politics. [. . . .]

Another reason why the present time is preferable to all others, is, that the fewer our numbers are, the more land there is yet unoccupied, which, instead of being lavished by the king on his worthless dependents, may be hereafter applied, not only to the discharge of the present debt, but to the constant support of government. No nation under heaven hath such an advantage as this.

The infant state of the colonies, as it is called, so far from being against, is an argument in favor of independence. We are sufficiently numerous, and were we more so we might be less united. 'Tis a matter worthy of observation, that the more a country is peopled, the smaller their armies are. In military numbers, the ancients far exceeded the moderns: and the reason is evident, for trade being the consequence of population, men became too much absorbed thereby to attend to any thing else. Commerce diminishes the spirit both of patriotism and military defense. And history sufficiently informs us, that the bravest achievements were always accomplished in the non-age of a nation. With the increase of commerce England hath lost its spirit. The city of London, notwithstanding its numbers, submits to continued insults with the patience of a coward. The more men have to lose, the less willing are they to venture. The rich are in general slaves to fear, and submit to courtly power with the trembling duplicity of a spaniel.

Youth is the seed-time of good habits as well in nations as in individuals. It might be difficult, if not impossible, to form the continent into one government half a century hence.

The present time, likewise, is that peculiar time which never happens to a nation but once, viz. the time of forming itself into a government. Most nations have let slip the opportunity, and by that means have been compelled to receive laws from their conquerors, instead of making laws for themselves. First, they had a king, and then a form of government; whereas the articles or charter of government should be formed first, and men delegated to execute them afterwards: but from the errors of other nations let us learn wisdom, and lay hold of the present opportunity—*to begin government at the right end.*

JAMES MADISON, "FEDERALIST NO. 10" (1787)

Among the numerous advantages promised by a well-constructed Union, none deserves to be more accurately developed than its tendency to break and control the violence of faction. The friend of popular governments never finds himself so much alarmed for their character and fate as when he contemplates their propensity to this dangerous vice. He will not fail, therefore, to set a due value on any plan, which, without violating the principles to which he is attached, provides a proper cure for it. The instability, injustice, and confusion introduced into the public councils have, in truth, been the mortal diseases under which popular governments have everywhere perished, as they continue to be the favorite and fruitful topics from which the adversaries to liberty derive their most specious declamations. The valuable improvements made by the American constitutions on the popular models, both ancient and modern, cannot certainly be too much admired; but it would be an unwarrantable partiality to contend that they have as effectually obviated the danger on this side, as was wished and expected. Complaints are everywhere heard from our most considerate and virtuous citizens, equally the friends of public and private faith and of public and personal liberty, that our governments are too unstable, that the public good is disregarded in the conflicts of rival parties, and that measures are too often decided, not according to the rules of justice and the rights of the minor party, but by the superior force of an interested and overbearing majority. However anxiously we may wish that these complaints had no foundation, the evidence of known facts will not permit us to deny that they are in some degree true. It will be found, indeed, on a candid review of our situation, that some of the distresses under which we labor have been erroneously charged on the operation of our governments; but it will be found, at the same time, that other causes will not alone account for many of our heaviest misfortunes; and, particularly, for that prevailing and increasing distrust of public engagements and alarm for private rights which are echoed from one end of the continent to the other. These must be chiefly, if not wholly, effects of the unsteadiness and injustice with which a factious spirit has tainted our public administration.

By a faction I understand a number of citizens, whether amounting to a majority or minority of the whole, who are united and actuated by some common impulse of passion, or of interest, adverse to the rights of other citizens, or to the permanent and aggregate interests of the community.

There are two methods of curing the mischiefs of faction: the one, by removing its causes; the other, by controlling its effects.

There are again two methods of removing the causes of faction: the one, by destroying the liberty which is essential to its existence; the other, by giving to every citizen the same opinions, the same passions, and the same interests.

It could never be more truly said than of the first remedy that it was worse than the disease. Liberty is to faction what air is to fire, an aliment without which it instantly expires. But it could not be a less folly to abolish liberty, which is essential to political life, because it nourishes faction than it would be to wish the annihilation of air, which is essential to animal life, because it imparts to fire its destructive agency.

The second expedient is as impracticable as the first would be unwise. As long as the reason of man continues fallible, and he is at liberty to exercise it, different opinions will be formed. As long as the connection subsists between his reason and his self-love, his opinions and his passions will have a reciprocal influence on each other; and the former will be objects to which the latter will attach themselves. The diversity in the faculties of men, from which the rights of property originate, is not less an insuperable obstacle to a uniformity of interests. The protection of these faculties is the first object of government. From the protection of different and unequal faculties of acquiring property, the possession of different degrees and kinds of property immediately results; and from the influence of these on the sentiments and views of the respective proprietors ensues a division of the society into different interests and parties.

The latent causes of faction are thus sown in the nature of man; and we see them everywhere brought into different degrees of activity, according to the different circumstances of civil society. A zeal for different opinions concerning religion, concerning government, and many other points, as well of speculation as of practice; an attachment to different leaders ambitiously contending for pre-eminence and power: or to persons of other descriptions whose fortunes have been interesting to the human passions, have, in turn, divided mankind into parties, inflamed them with mutual animosity, and rendered them much more disposed to vex and oppress each other than to co-operate for their common good. So strong is this propensity of mankind to fall into mutual animosities that where no substantial occasion presents itself the most frivolous and fanciful distinctions have been sufficient to kindle their unfriendly passions and excite their most violent conflicts. But the most common and durable source of factions has been the various and unequal distribution of property. Those who hold and those who are without property have ever formed distinct interests in society. Those who are creditors, and those who are debtors, fall under a like discrimination. A landed interest, a manufacturing interest, a mercantile interest, a moneyed interest, with many lesser interests, grow up of necessity in civilized nations, and divide them into different classes, actuated by different sentiments and views. The regulation of these various and interfering interests forms the principal task of modern legislation and involves the spirit of party and faction in the necessary and ordinary operations of government.

No man is allowed to be a judge in his own cause because his interest would certainly bias his judgment, and, not improbably, corrupt his integrity. With equal, nay with greater reason, a body of men are unfit to be both judges and parties at the same time; yet what are many of the most important acts of legislation but so many judicial determinations, not indeed concerning the rights of single persons, but concerning the rights of large bodies of citizens? And what are the different classes of legislators but advocates and parties to the causes which they determine? Is a law proposed concerning private debts? It is a question to which the creditors are parties on one side and the debtors on the other. Justice ought to hold the balance between them. Yet the parties are, and must be, themselves the judges; and the most numerous party, or in other words, the most powerful faction I must be expected to prevail. Shall domestic manufacturers be encouraged, and in what degree, by restrictions on foreign manufacturers? are questions which would be differently decided by the landed and the manufacturing classes, and probably by neither with a sole regard to justice and the public good. The apportionment of taxes on the various descriptions of property is an act which seems to require the most exact impartiality; yet there is, perhaps, no legislative act in which greater opportunity and temptation are given to a predominant party to trample on the rules of justice. Every shilling with which they overburden the inferior number is a shilling saved to their own pockets.

It is in vain to say that enlightened statesmen will be able to adjust these clashing interests and render them all subservient to the public good. Enlightened statesmen will not always be at the helm. Nor, in many cases, can such an adjustment be made at all without taking into view indirect and remote considerations, which will rarely prevail over the immediate interest which one party may find in disregarding the rights of another or the good of the whole.

The inference to which we are brought is that the *causes* of faction cannot be removed and that relief is only to be sought in the means of controlling its *effects*.

If a faction consists of less than a majority, relief is supplied by the republican principle, which enables the majority to defeat its sinister views by regular vote. It may clog the administration, it may convulse the society; but it will be unable to execute and mask its violence under the forms of the Constitution. When a majority is included in a faction, the form of popular government, on the other hand, enables it to sacrifice to its ruling passion or interest both the public good and the rights of other citizens. To secure the public good and private rights against the danger of such a faction, and at the same time to preserve the spirit and the form of popular government, is then the great object to which our inquiries are directed. Let me add that it is the great desideratum by which alone this form of government can be rescued from the opprobrium under which it has so long labored and be recommended to the esteem and adoption of mankind.

By what means is this object attainable? Evidently by one of two only. Either the existence of the same passion or interest in a majority at the same time must be prevented, or the majority, having such coexistent passion of interest, must be rendered, by their number and local situation, unable to concert and carry into effect schemes of oppression. If the impulse and the opportunity be suffered to coincide, we well know that neither moral nor religious motives can be relied on as an adequate control. They are not found to be such on the injustice and violence of individuals, and lose their efficacy in proportion to the number combined together, that is, in proportion as their efficacy becomes needful.

From this view of the subject it may be concluded that a pure democracy, by which I mean a society consisting of a small number of citizens, who assemble and administer the government in person, can admit of no cure for the mischiefs of faction. A common passion or interest will, in almost every case, be felt by a majority of the whole; a communication and concert results from the form of government itself; and there is nothing to check the inducements to sacrifice the weaker party or an obnoxious individual. Hence it is that such democracies have ever been spectacles of turbulence and contention; have ever been found incompatible with personal security or the rights of property; and have in general been as short in their lives as they have been violent in their deaths. Theoretic politicians, who have patronized this species of government, have erroneously supposed that by reducing mankind to a perfect equality in their political rights, they would at the same time be perfectly equalized and assimilated in their possessions, their opinions, and their passions.

A republic, by which I mean a government in which the scheme of representation takes place, opens a different prospect and promises the cure for which we are seeking. Let us examine the points in which it varies from pure democracy, and we shall comprehend both the nature of the cure and the efficacy which it must derive from the Union.

The two great points of difference between a democracy and a republic are: first, the delegation of the government, in the latter, to a small number of citizens elected by the rest: secondly, the greater number of citizens and greater sphere of country over which the latter may be extended.

The effect of the first difference is, on the one hand, to refine and enlarge the public views by passing them through the medium of a chosen body of citizens, whose wisdom may best discern the true interest of their country and whose patriotism and love of justice will be least likely to sacrifice it to temporary or partial considerations. Under such a regulation it may well happen that the public voice, pronounced by the representatives of the people, will be more consonant to the public good than if pronounced by the people themselves, convened for the purpose. On the other hand, the effect may be inverted. Men of factious tempers, of local prejudices, or of sinister designs, may, by intrigue, by corruption, or by other means, first obtain the suffrages, and then betray the interests of the people. The question resulting is, whether small or extensive republics are most favorable to the election of proper guardians of the public weal; and it is clearly decided in favor of the latter by two obvious considerations.

In the first place it is to be remarked that however small the republic may be the representatives must be raised to a certain number in order to guard against the cabals of a few; and that however large it may be they must be limited to a certain number in order to guard against the confusion of a multitude. Hence, the number of representatives in the two cases not being in proportion to that of the constituents, and being proportionally greatest in the small republic, it follows that if the proportion of fit characters be not less in the large than in the small republic, the former will present a greater option, and consequently a greater probability of a fit choice.

In the next place, as each representative will be chosen by a greater number of citizens in the large than in the small republic, it will be more difficult for unworthy candidates to practice with success the vicious arts by which elections are too often carried; and the suffrages of the people being more free, will be more likely to center on men who possess the most attractive merit and the most diffusive and established characters.

It must be confessed that in this, as in most other cases, there is a mean, on both sides of which inconveniences will be found to lie. By enlarging too much the number of electors, you render the representative too little acquainted with all their local circumstances and lesser interests; as by reducing it too much, you render him unduly attached to these, and too little fit to comprehend and pursue great and national objects. The federal Constitution forms a happy combination in this respect; the great and aggregate interests being referred to the national, the local and particular to the State legislatures.

The other point of difference is the greater number of citizens and extent of territory which may be brought within the compass of republican than of democratic government; and it is this circumstance principally which renders factious combinations less to be dreaded in the former than in the latter. The smaller the society, the fewer probably will be the distinct parties and interests composing it; the fewer the distinct parties and interests, the more frequently will a majority be found of the same party; and the smaller the number of individuals composing a majority, and the smaller the compass within which they are placed, the more easily will they concert and execute their plans of oppression. Extend the sphere and you take in a greater variety of parties and interests; you make it less probable that a majority of the whole will have a common motive to invade the rights of other citizens; or if such a common motive exists, will be more difficult for all who feel it to discover their own strength and to act in unison with each other. Besides other impediments, it may be remarked that, where there is a consciousness of unjust or dishonorable purposes, communication is always checked by distrust in proportion to the number whose concurrence is necessary.

Hence, it clearly appears that the same advantage which a republic has over a democracy in controlling the effects of faction is enjoyed by a large over a small republic is enjoyed by the Union over the States composing it. Does this advantage consist in the substitution of representatives whose enlightened views and virtuous sentiments render them superior to local prejudices and to schemes of injustice? It will not be denied that the representation of the Union will be most likely to possess these requisite endowments. Does it consist in the greater security afforded by a greater variety of parties, against the event of any one party being able to outnumber and oppress the rest? In an equal degree does the increased variety of parties comprised within the Union increase this security. Does it, in fine, consist in the greater obstacles opposed to the concert accomplishment of the secret wishes of an unjust and interested majority? Here again the extent of the Union gives it the most palpable advantage.

The influence of factious leaders may kindle a flame within their particular States but will be unable to spread a general conflagration through the other States. A religious sect may degenerate into a political faction in a part of the Confederacy; but the variety of sects dispersed over the entire face of it must secure the national councils against any danger from that source. A rage for paper money, for an abolition of debts, for an equal division of property, or for any other improper or wicked project, will he less apt to pervade the whole body of the Union than a particular member of it, in the same proportion as such a malady is more likely to taint a particular county or district than an entire State.

In the extent and proper structure of the Union, therefore, we behold a republican remedy for the diseases most incident to republican government. And according to the degree of pleasure and pride we feel in being republicans ought to be our zeal in cherishing the spirit and supportive the character of federalists.

ALEXIS DE TOCQUEVILLE, SELECTIONS FROM *DEMOCRACY IN AMERICA* (1835 AND 1840)

Introduction

Amongst the novel objects that attracted my attention during my stay in the United States, nothing struck me more forcibly than the general equality of conditions. I readily discovered the prodigious influence which this primary fact exercises on the whole course of society, by giving a certain direction to public opinion, and a certain tenor to the laws; by imparting new maxims to the governing powers, and peculiar habits to the governed.

I speedily perceived that the influence of this fact extends far beyond the political character and the laws of the country, and that it has no less empire over civil society than over the Government; it creates opinions, engenders sentiments, suggests the ordinary practices of life, and modifies whatever it does not produce. [. . . .]

The various occurrences of national existence have everywhere turned to the advantage of democracy; all men have aided it by their exertions: those who have intentionally labored in its cause, and those who have served it unwittingly; those who have fought for it, and those who have declared themselves its opponents—have all been driven along in the same track, have all labored to one end, some ignorantly and some unwillingly; all have been blind instruments in the hands of God.

The gradual development of the equality of conditions is therefore a providential fact, and it possesses all the characteristics of a Divine decree: it is universal, it is durable, it constantly eludes all human interference, and all events as well as all men contribute to its progress. [. . . .]

If the men of our time were led by attentive observation and by sincere reflection, to acknowledge that the gradual and progressive development of social equality is at once the past and future of their history, this solitary truth would confer the sacred character of a divine decree upon the change. To attempt to check democracy would be in that case to resist the will of God; and the nations would then be constrained to make the best of the social lot awarded to them by Providence.

The Christian nations of our age seem to me to present a most alarming spectacle; the impulse which is bearing them along is so strong that it cannot stopped, but it is not yet so rapid that it cannot be guided: their fate is in their hands; yet a little while and it may be so no longer.

The first duty which is at this time imposed upon those who direct our affairs is to educate the democracy; to warm its faith, if that be possible; to purify its morals; to direct its energies; to substitute a knowledge of business for its inexperience, and an acquaintance with its true interests for its blind propensities; to adapt its government to time and place, and to modify it in compliance with the occurrences and the actors of the age.

A new science of politics is indispensable to a new world. [. . . .]

Political Associations in the United States

In no country in the world has the principle of association been more successfully used, or more unsparingly applied to a multitude of different objects, than in America. Besides the permanent associations which are established by law under the names of townships, cities, and counties, a vast number of others are formed and maintained by the agency of private individuals.

The citizen of the United States is taught from his earliest infancy to rely upon his own exertions, in order to resist the evils and the difficulties of life; he looks upon the social authority with an eye of mistrust and anxiety, and he only claims its assistance when he is quite unable to shift without it. This habit may even be traced in the schools of the rising generation, where the children in their games are wont to submit to rules which they have themselves established, and to punish misdemeanors which they have themselves defined. The same spirit pervades every act of social life. If a stoppage occurs in a thoroughfare, and the circulation of the public is hindered, the neighbors immediately constitute a deliberative body; and this extemporaneous assembly gives rise to an executive power, which remedies the inconvenience, before anybody has thought of recurring to an authority superior to that of the persons immediately concerned. If the public pleasures are concerned, an association is formed to provide for the splendor and the regularity of the entertainment. Societies are formed to resist enemies which are exclusively of a moral nature, and to diminish the vice of intemperance: in the United States associations are established to promote public order, commerce, industry, morality, and religion; for there is no end which the human will, seconded by the collective exertions of individuals, despairs of attaining.

I shall hereafter have occasion to show the effects of association upon the course of society, and I must confine myself for the present to the political world. When once the right of association is recognized, the citizens may employ it in several different ways.

An association consists simply in the public assent which a number of individuals give to certain doctrines; and in the engagement which they contract to promote the spread of those doctrines by their exertions. The right of associating with these views is very analogous to the liberty of unlicensed writing; but societies thus formed possess more authority than the press. When an opinion is represented by a society it necessarily assumes a more exact and explicit form. It numbers its partisans, and compromises their welfare in its cause; they, on the other hand, become acquainted with each other, and their zeal is increased by their number. An association unites the efforts of minds which have a tendency to diverge, in one single channel, and urges them vigorously towards one single end which it points out.

The second degree in the right of association is the power of meeting. When an association is allowed to establish centres of action at certain important points in the country, its activity is increased, and its influence extended. Men have the opportunity of seeing each other; means of execution are more readily combined; and opinions are maintained with a degree of warmth and energy which written language cannot approach.

Lastly, in the exercise of the right of political association, there is a third degree: the partisans of an opinion may unite in electoral bodies, and choose delegates to represent them in a central assembly. This is, properly speaking, the application of the representative system to a party. [. . . .]

The more we consider the independence of the press in its principal consequences, the more are we convinced that it is the chief, and, so to speak, the constitutive element of freedom in the modern world. A nation which is determined to remain free, is therefore right in demanding the unrestrained exercise of this independence. But the *unrestrained* liberty of political association cannot be entirely assimilated to the liberty of the press. The one is at the same time less necessary and more dangerous than the other. A nation may confine it within certain limits without forfeiting any part of its self-control; and it may sometimes be obliged to do so in order to maintain its own authority. [. . . .]

The omnipotence of the majority appears to me to present such extreme perils to the American Republics, that the dangerous measure which is used to repress it seems to be more advantageous than prejudicial. And here I am about to advance a proposition which may remind the reader of what I said before in speaking of municipal freedom: There are no countries in which associations are more needed, to prevent the despotism of faction or the arbitrary power of a prince, than those which are democratically constituted. In aristocratic nations, the body of the nobles and the more opulent part of the community are in themselves natural associations, which act as checks upon the abuses of power. In countries in which those associations do not exist, if private individuals are unable to create an artificial and a temporary substitute for them, I can imagine no permanent protection against the most galling tyranny; and a great people may be oppressed by a small faction, or by a single individual with impunity. [. . . .]

Power Exercised by the Majority in America upon Opinion

It is in the examination of the display of public opinion in the United States, that we clearly perceive how far the power of the majority surpasses all the powers with which we are acquainted in Europe. Intellectual principles exercise an influence which is so invisible and often so inappreciable, that they baffle the toils of oppression. At the present time the most absolute monarchs in Europe are unable to prevent certain notions, which are opposed to their authority, from circulating in secret through out their dominions, and even in their courts. Such is not the case in America; as long as the majority is still undecided, discussion is carried on; but as soon as its decision is irrevocably pronounced, a submissive silence is observed; and the friends, as well as the opponents of the measure, unite in assenting to its propriety. The reason for this is perfectly clear: no monarch is so absolute as to combine all the powers of society in his own hands, and to conquer all opposition, with the energy of a majority, which, invested with the right of making and of executing the laws.

The authority of a king is purely physical, and it controls the actions of the subject without subduing his private will; but the majority possesses a power which is physical and moral at the same time; it acts upon the will as well as upon the actions of men, and it represses not only all contest, but all controversy

I know of no country in which there is so little true independence of mind and freedom of discussion as in America. In any constitutional state in Europe every sort of religious and political theory may be advocated and propagated abroad; for there is no country in Europe so subdued by any single authority, as not to contain citizens who are ready to protect the man who raises his voice in the cause of truth, from the consequences of his hardihood. If he is unfortunate enough to live under an absolute government, the people is upon his side; if he inhabits a free country, he may find a shelter behind the authority of the throne, if he require one. The aristocratic part of society supports him in some countries, and the democracy in others. But in a nation where democratic institutions exist, organized like those of the United States, there is but one sole authority, one single element of strength and of success, with nothing beyond it.

In America, the majority raises very formidable barriers to the liberty of opinion: within these barriers an author may write whatever he pleases, but he will repent it if he ever step beyond them. Not that he is exposed to the terrors of an auto-da-fé, but he is tormented by the slights and persecutions of daily obloquy. His political career is closed for ever, since he has offended the only authority which is able to promote his success. Every sort of compensation, even that of celebrity, is refused to him. Before he published his opinions, he imagined that he held them in common with many others; but no sooner has he declared them openly, than he is loudly censured by his overbearing opponents, whilst those who think, without having the courage to speak, like him, abandon him in silence. He yields at length, oppressed by the daily efforts he has been making, and he subsides into silence, as if he was tormented by remorse for having spoken the truth.

Fetters and headsmen were the coarse instruments which tyranny formerly employed; but the civilization of our age has refined the arts of despotism, which seemed however to have been sufficiently perfected before. The excesses of monarchical power had devised a variety of physical means of oppression; the democratic republics of the present day have rendered it as entirely an affair of the mind, as that will which it is intended to coerce. Under the, absolute sway of an individual despot, the body was attacked, in order to subdue the soul; and the soul escaped the blows which were directed against it, and rose superior to the attempt; but such is not the course adopted by tyranny in democratic republics; there the body is left free and the soul is enslaved. The sovereign can no longer say, 'You shall think as I do on pain of death;' but he says, 'You are free to think differently from me, and to retain your life, your property, and all that you possess; but if such be your determination, you are henceforth an alien among your people. You may retain your civil rights, but they will be useless to you, for you will never be chosen by your fellow-citizens, if you solicit their suffrages; and they will affect to scorn you, if you solicit their esteem. You will remain among men, but you will be deprived of the rights of mankind. Your fellow-creatures will shun you like an impure being; and those who are most persuaded of your innocence will abandon you too, lest they should be shunned in their turn. Go in peace! I have given you your life, but it is an existence incomparably worse than death.'

Absolute monarchies have thrown an odium upon despotism; let us beware lest democratic republics should restore oppression, and should render it less odious and less degrading in the eyes of the many, by making it still more onerous to the few.

Works have been published in the proudest nations of the Old World, expressly intended to censure the vices and deride the follies of the time: Labruyère inhabited the palace of Louis XIV when he composed his chapter upon the Great, and Molière criticized the courtiers in the very pieces which were acted before the Court. But the ruling power in the United States is not to be made game of; the smallest reproach irritates its sensibility, and the slightest joke which has any foundation in truth renders it indignant; from the style of its language to the more solid virtues of its character, everything must be made the subject of encomium. No writer, whatever be his eminence, can escape from this tribute of adulation to his fellow-citizens. The majority lives in the perpetual practice of self-applause; and there are certain truths which the Americans can only learn from strangers or from experience.

If great writers have not at present existed in America, the reason is very simply given in these facts; there can be no literary genius without freedom of opinion, and freedom of opinion does not exist in America. The Inquisition has never been able to prevent a vast number of anti-religious books from circulating in Spain. The empire of the majority succeeds much better in the United States, since it actually removes the wish of publishing them. Unbelievers are to be met with in America, but, to say the truth, there is no public organ of infidelity. Attempts have been made by some governments to protect the morality of nations by prohibiting licentious books. In the United States no one is punished for this sort of works, but no one is induced to write them; not because all the citizens are immaculate in their manners, but because the majority of the community is decent and orderly.

In these cases the advantages derived from the exercise of this power are unquestionable; and I am simply discussing the nature of the power itself. This irresistible authority is a constant fact, and its judicial exercise is an accidental occurrence. [. . . .]

Indirect Influence of Religious Opinions upon Political Society in the United States

The sects which exist in the United States are innumerable. They all differ in respect to the worship which is due from man to his Creator; but they all agree in respect to the duties which are due from man to man. Each sect adores the Deity in its own peculiar manner; but all the sects preach the same moral law in the name of God. If it be of the slightest importance to man, as an individual, that his religion should be true, the case of society is not the same. Society has no future life to hope for or to fear; and provided the citizens profess a religion, the peculiar tenets of that religion are of very little importance to its interests. Moreover, almost all the sects of the United States are comprised within the great unity of Christianity and Christian morality is everywhere the same.

It may be believed without unfairness, that a certain number of Americans pursue a particular form of worship, from habit more than from conviction. In United States the sovereign authority is religious, and consequently hypocrisy must be common; but there is no country in the whole world in which the Christian religion retains greater influence over the souls of men than in America; and there can be no greater proof of its utility, and of its conformity to human nature, than that its influence is most powerfully felt over the most enlightened and free nation of the earth.

I have remarked that the members of the American clergy in general, without even excepting those who do not admit religious liberty, are all in favor of civil freedom; but they do not support any particular political system. They keep aloof from parties, and from public affairs. In the United States religion exercises but little influence upon the laws, and upon the details of public opinion; but it directs the manners of the community, and by regulating domestic life, it regulates the State. [. . . .]

The imagination of the Americans, even in its greatest flights, is circumspect and undecided; its impulses are checked, and its works unfinished. These habits of restraint recur in political society, and are singularly favorable both to the tranquillity of the people and to the durability of the institutions it has established. Nature and circumstances concurred to make the inhabitants of the United States bold men, as is sufficiently attested by the enterprising spirit with which they seek for fortune. If the minds of the Americans were free from all trammels, they would very shortly become the most daring innovators and the most implacable disputants in the world. But the revolutionists of America are obliged to profess an ostensible respect for Christian morality and equity, which does not easily permit them to violate the laws that oppose their designs; nor would they find it easy to surmount the scruples of their partisans, even if they were able to get over their own. Hitherto no one, in the United States, has dared to advance the maxim, that everything is permissible with a view to the interests of society; an impious adage, which seems to have been invented in an age of freedom to shelter all the tyrants of future ages. Thus whilst the law permits the Americans to do what they please, religion prevents them from conceiving, and forbids them to commit what is rash or unjust.

Religion in America takes no direct part in the government of society, but it must nevertheless be regarded as the foremost of the political institutions of that country; for if it does not impart a taste for freedom, it facilitates the use of free institutions. Indeed, it is in this same point of view that the inhabitants of the United States themselves look upon religious belief. I do not know whether all the Americans have a sincere faith in their religion; for who can search the human heart? but I am certain that they hold it to be indispensable to the maintenance of republican institutions. This opinion is not peculiar to a class of citizens or to a party, but it belongs to the whole nation, and to every rank of society. [. . . .]

Of Individualism in Democratic Countries

I have shown how it is that in ages of equality every man seeks for his opinions within himself; I am now to show how it is that in the same ages all his feelings are turned towards himself alone. *Individualism* is a novel expression, to which a novel idea has given birth. Our fathers were only acquainted with *égoïsme* (selfishness). Selfishness is a passionate and exaggerated love of self, which leads a man to connect everything with himself and to prefer himself to everything in the world. Individualism is a mature and calm feeling, which disposes each member of the community to sever himself from the mass of his fellows and to draw apart with his family and his friends, so that after he has thus formed a little circle of his own, he willingly leaves society at large to itself. Selfishness originates in blind instinct; individualism proceeds from erroneous judgment more than from depraved feelings; it originates as much in deficiencies of mind as in perversity of heart.

Selfishness blights the germ of all virtue; individualism, at first, only saps the virtues of public life; but in the long run it attacks and destroys all others and is at length absorbed in downright selfishness. Selfishness is a vice as old as the world, which does not belong to one form of society more than to another; individualism is of democratic origin, and it threatens to spread in the same ratio as the equality of condition.

Among aristocratic nations, as families remain for centuries in the same condition, often on the same spot, all generations become, as it were, contemporaneous. A man almost always knows his forefathers and respects them; he thinks he already sees his remote descendants and he loves them. He willingly imposes duties on himself towards the former and the latter, and he will frequently sacrifice his personal gratifications to those who went before and to those who will come after him. Aristocratic institutions: moreover, have the effect of closely binding every man to several of his fellow citizens. As the classes of an aristocratic people are strongly marked and permanent, each of them is regarded by its own members as a sort of lesser country, more tangible and more cherished than the country at large. As in aristocratic communities all the citizens occupy fixed positions, one above another, the result is that each of them always sees a man above himself whose patronage is necessary to him, and below himself another man whose co-operation he may claim. Men living in aristocratic ages are therefore almost always closely attached to something placed out of their own sphere, and they are often disposed to forget themselves. It is true that in these ages the notion of human fellowship is faint and that men seldom think of sacrificing themselves for mankind; but they often sacrifice themselves for other men. In democratic times, on the contrary, when the duties of each individual to the race are much more clear, devoted service to any one man becomes more rare; the bond of human affections extended, but it is relaxed.

Among democratic nations new families are constantly springing up, others are constantly falling away, and all that remain change their condition; the woof of time is every instant broken and the track of generations effaced. Those who went before are soon forgotten; of those who will come after, no one has any idea: the interest of man is confined to those in close propinquity to himself. As each class gradually approaches others and mingles with them, its members become undifferentiated and lose their class identity for each other. Aristocracy had made a chain of the members of the community, from the peasant to the king; democracy breaks that chain and severs every link of it.

As social conditions become more equal, the number of persons increases who, although they are neither rich nor powerful enough to exercise any great influence over their fellows, have nevertheless acquired or retained sufficient education and fortune to satisfy their own wants. They owe nothing to any man, they expect nothing from any man; they acquire the habit of always considering themselves as standing alone, and they are apt to imagine that their whole destiny is in their own hands.

Thus not only does democracy make every man forget his ancestors, but it hides his descendants and separates his contemporaries from him; it throws him back forever upon himself alone and threatens in the end to confine him entirely within the solitude of his own heart.

How the Americans Combat Individualism by the Principle of Self-Interest Rightly Understood

When the world was managed by a few rich and powerful individuals, these persons loved to entertain a lofty idea of the duties of man. They were fond of professing that it is praiseworthy to forget oneself and that good should be done without hope of reward, as it is by the Deity himself. Such were the standard opinions of that time in morals.

I doubt whether men were more virtuous in aristocratic ages than in others, but they were incessantly talking of the beauties of virtue, and its utility was only studied in secret. But since the imagination takes less lofty flights, and every man's thoughts are centered in himself, moralists are alarmed by this idea of self-sacrifice and they no longer venture to present it to the human mind. They therefore content themselves with inquiring whether the personal advantage of each member of the community does not consist in working for the good of all; and when they have hit upon some point on which private interest and public interest meet and amalgamate, they are eager to bring it into notice. Observations of this kind are gradually multiplied; what was only a single remark becomes a general principle, and it is held as a truth that man serves himself in serving his fellow creatures and that his private interest is to do good.

I have already shown, in several parts of this work, by what means the inhabitants of the United States almost always manage to combine their own advantage with that of their fellow citizens; my present purpose is to point out the general rule that enables them to do so. In the United States hardly anybody talks of the beauty of virtue, but they maintain that virtue is useful and prove it every day. The American moralists do not profess that men ought to sacrifice themselves for their fellow creatures *because* it is noble to make such sacrifices, but they boldly aver that such sacrifices are as necessary to him who imposes them upon himself as to him for whose sake they are made.

They have found out that in their country and their age, man is brought home to himself by an irresistible force; and, losing all hope of stopping that force, they turn all their thoughts to the direction of it. They therefore do not deny that every man may follow his own interest, but they endeavor to prove that it is the interest of every man to be virtuous. I shall not here enter into the reasons they allege, which would divert me from my subject; suffice it to say that they have convinced their fellow countrymen.

Montaigne said long ago: "Were I not to follow the straight road for its straightness, I should follow it for having found by experience that in the end it is commonly the happiest and most useful track." The doctrine of interest rightly understood is not then new, but among the Americans of our time it finds universal acceptance; it has become popular there; you may trace it at the bottom of all their actions, you will remark it in all they say. It is as often asserted by the poor man as by the rich. In Europe the principle of interest is much grosser than it is in America, but it is also less common and especially it is less avowed; among us, men still constantly feign great abnegation which they no longer feel.

The Americans, on the other hand, are fond of explaining almost all the actions of their lives by the principle of self-interest rightly understood; they show with complacency how enlightened regard for themselves constantly prompts them to assist one another and inclines them willingly to sacrifice a portion of their time and property to the welfare of the state. In this respect I think they frequently fail to do themselves justice; for in the United States as well as elsewhere people are sometimes seen to give way to those disinterested and spontaneous impulses that are natural to man; but the Americans seldom admit that they yield to emotions of this kind; they are more anxious to do honor to their philosophy than to themselves.

I might here pause without attempting to pass a judgment on what I have described. The extreme difficulty of the subject would be my excuse, but I shall not avail myself of it; and I had rather that my readers, clearly perceiving my object, would refuse to follow me than that I should leave them in suspense.

The principle of self-interest rightly understood is not a lofty one, but it is clear and sure. It does not aim at mighty objects, but it attains without excessive exertion all those at which it aims. As it lies within the reach of all capacities, everyone can without difficulty learn and retain it. By its admirable conformity to human weaknesses it easily obtains great dominion; nor is that dominion precarious, since the principle checks one personal interest by another, and uses, to direct the passions, the very same instrument that excites them.

The principle of self-interest rightly understood produces no great acts of self-sacrifice, but it suggests daily small acts of self-denial. By itself it cannot suffice to make a man virtuous; but it disciplines a number of persons in habits of regularity, temperance, moderation, foresight, self-command; and if it does not lead men straight to virtue by the will, it gradually draws them in that direction by their habits. If the principle of interest rightly understood were to sway the whole moral world, extraordinary virtues would doubtless be more rare; but I think that gross depravity would then also be less common. The principle of interest rightly understood perhaps prevents men from rising far above the level of mankind, but a great number of other men, who were falling far below it, are caught and restrained by it. Observe some few individuals, they are lowered by it; survey mankind, they are raised.

I am not afraid to say that the principle of self-interest rightly understood appears to me the best suited of all philosophical theories to the wants of the men of our time, and that I regard it as their chief remaining security against themselves. Towards it, therefore, the minds of the moralists of our age should turn; even should they judge it to be incomplete, it must nevertheless be adopted as necessary.

JOHN STUART MILL, SELECTIONS FROM *ON LIBERTY* (1859)

Introductory

The subject of this Essay is not the so-called Liberty of the Will, so unfortunately opposed to the misnamed doctrine of Philosophical Necessity; but Civil, or Social Liberty: the nature and limits of the power which can be legitimately exercised by society over the individual. A question seldom stated, and hardly ever discussed, in general terms, but which profoundly influences the practical controversies of the age by its latent presence, and is likely soon to make itself recognized as the vital question of the future. It is so far from being new, that, in a certain sense, it has divided mankind, almost from the remotest ages; but in the stage of progress into which the more civilized portions of the species have now entered, it presents itself under new conditions, and requires a different and more fundamental treatment.

The struggle between Liberty and Authority is the most conspicuous feature in the portions of history with which we are earliest familiar, particularly in that of Greece, Rome, and England. But in old times this contest was between subjects, or some classes of subjects, and the Government. By liberty, was meant protection against the tyranny of the political rulers. The rulers were conceived (except in some of the popular governments of Greece) as in a necessarily antagonistic position to the people whom they ruled. They consisted of a governing One, or a governing tribe or caste, who derived their authority from inheritance or conquest, who, at all events, did not hold it at the pleasure of the governed, and whose supremacy men did not venture, perhaps did not desire, to contest, whatever precautions might be taken against its oppressive exercise. Their power was regarded as necessary, but also as highly dangerous; as a weapon which they would attempt to use against their subjects, no less than against external enemies. To prevent the weaker members of the community from being preyed upon by innumerable vultures, it was needful that there should be an animal of prey stronger than the rest, commissioned to keep them down. But as the king of the vultures would be no less bent upon preying on the flock than any of the minor harpies, it was indispensable to be in a perpetual attitude of defence against his beak and claws. The aim, therefore, of patriots was to set limits to the power which the ruler should be suffered to exercise over the community; and this limitation was what they meant by liberty. It was attempted in two ways. First, by obtaining a recognition of certain immunities, called political liberties or rights, which it was to be regarded as a breach of duty in the ruler to infringe, and which, if he did infringe, specific resistance, or general rebellion, was held to be justifiable. A second, and generally a later expedient, was the establishment of constitutional checks, by which the consent of the community, or of a body of some sort, supposed to represent its interests, was made a necessary condition to some of the more important acts of the governing power. To the first of these modes of limitation, the ruling power, in most European countries, was compelled, more or less, to submit. It was not so with the second; and, to attain this, or when already in some degree possessed, to attain it more completely, became everywhere the principal object of the lovers of liberty. And so long as mankind were content to combat one enemy by another, and to be ruled by a master, on condition of being guaranteed more or less efficaciously against his tyranny, they did not carry their aspirations beyond this point.

A time, however, came, in the progress of human affairs, when men ceased to think it a necessity of nature that their governors should be an independent power, opposed in interest to themselves. It appeared to them much better that the various magistrates of the State should be their tenants or delegates, revocable at their pleasure. In that way alone, it seemed, could they have complete security that the powers of government would never be abused to their disadvantage. By degrees this new demand for elective and temporary rulers became the prominent object of the exertions of the popular party, wherever any such party existed; and superseded, to a considerable extent, the previous efforts to limit the power of rulers. As the struggle proceeded for making the ruling power emanate from the periodical choice of the ruled, some persons began to think that too much importance had been attached to the limitation of the power itself. *That* (it might seem) was a resource against rulers whose interests were habitually opposed to those of the people. What was now wanted was, that the rulers should be identified with the people; that their interest and will should be the interest and will of the nation. The nation did not need to be protected against its own Will. There was no fear of its tyrannising over itself. Let the rulers be effectually responsible to it, promptly removable by it, and it could afford to trust them with power of which it could itself dictate the use to be made. Their power was but the nation's own power, concentrated, and in a form convenient for exercise. This mode of thought, or rather perhaps of feeling, was common among the last generation of European liberalism, in the Continental section of which it still apparently predominates. Those who admit any limit to what a government may do, except in the case of such governments as they think ought not to exist, stand out as brilliant exceptions among the political thinkers of the Continent. A similar tone of sentiment might by this time have been prevalent in our own country, if the circumstances which for a time encouraged it, had continued unaltered.

But, in political and philosophical theories, as well as in persons, success discloses faults and infirmities which failure might have concealed from observation. The notion, that the people have no need to limit their power over themselves, might seem axiomatic, when popular government was a thing only dreamed about, or read of as having existed at some distant period of the past. Neither was that notion necessarily disturbed by such temporary aberrations as those of the French Revolution, the worst of which were the work of an usurping few, and which, in any case, belonged, not to the permanent working of popular institutions, but to a sudden and convulsive outbreak against monarchical and aristocratic despotism. In time, however, a democratic republic came to occupy a large portion of the earth's surface, and made itself felt as one of the most powerful members of the community of nations; and elective and responsible government became subject to the observations and criticisms which wait upon a great existing fact. It was now perceived that such phrases as 'self-government,' and 'the power of the people over themselves,' do not express the true state of the case. The 'people' who exercise the power are not always the same people with those over whom it is exercised; and the 'self-government' spoken of is not the government of each by himself, but of each by all the rest. The will of the people, moreover, practically means the will of the most numerous or the most active *part* of the people; the majority, or those who succeed in making themselves accepted as the majority; the people, consequently, *may* desire to oppress a part of their number; and precautions are as much needed against this as against any other abuse of power. The limitation, therefore, of the power of government over individuals loses none of its importance when the holders of power are regularly accountable to the community, that is, to the strongest party therein. This view of things, recommending itself equally to the intelligence of thinkers and to the inclination of those important classes in European society to whose real or supposed interests democracy is adverse, has had no difficulty in establishing itself; and in political speculations 'the tyranny of the majority' is now generally included among the evils against which society requires to be on its guard.

Like other tyrannies, the tyranny of the majority was at first, and is still vulgarly, held in dread, chiefly as operating through the acts of the public authorities. But reflecting persons perceived that when society is itself the tyrant—society collectively, over the separate individuals who compose it—its means of tyrannising are not restricted to the acts which it may do by the hands of its political functionaries. Society can and does execute its own mandates: and if it issues wrong mandates instead of right, or any mandates at all in things with which it ought not to meddle, it practices a social tyranny more formidable than many kinds of political oppression, since, though not usually upheld by such extreme penalties, it leaves fewer means of escape, penetrating much more deeply into the details of life, and enslaving the soul itself. Protection, therefore, against the tyranny of the magistrate is not enough: there needs protection also against the tyranny of the prevailing opinion and feeling; against the tendency of society to impose, by other means than civil penalties, its own ideas and practices as rules of conduct on those who dissent from them; to fetter the development, and, if possible, prevent the formation, of any individuality not in harmony with its ways, and compel all characters to fashion themselves upon the model of its own. There is a limit to the legitimate interference of collective opinion with individual independence: and to find that limit, and maintain it against encroachment, is as indispensable to a good condition of human affairs, as protection against political despotism.

But though this proposition is not likely to be contested in general terms, the practical question, where to place the limit—how to make the fitting adjustment between individual independence and social control—is a subject on which nearly everything remains to be done. All that makes existence valuable to any one, depends on the enforcement of restraints upon the actions of other people. Some rules of conduct, therefore, must be imposed, by law in the first place, and by opinion on many things which are not fit subjects for the operation of law. What these rules should be is the principal question of human affairs; but if we except a few of the most obvious cases, it is one of those which least progress has been made in resolving. No two ages, and scarcely any two countries, have decided it alike; and the decision of one age or country is a wonder to another. Yet the people of any given age and country no more suspect any difficulty in it, than if it were a subject on which mankind had always been agreed. The rules which obtain among themselves appear to them self-evident and self-justifying. This all but universal illusion is one of the examples of the magical influence of custom, which is not only, as the proverb says, a second nature, but is continually mistaken for the first. The effect of custom, in preventing any misgiving respecting the rules of conduct which mankind impose on one another, is all the more complete because the subject is one on which it is not generally considered necessary that reasons should be given, either by one person to others, or by each to himself. People are accustomed to believe, and have been encouraged in the belief by some who aspire to the character of philosophers, that their feelings, on subjects of this nature, are better than reasons, and render reasons unnecessary. The practical principle which guides them to their opinions on the regulation of human conduct, is the feeling in each person's mind that everybody should be required to act as he, and those with whom he sympathises, would like them to act. No one, indeed, acknowledges to himself that his standard of judgment is his own liking; but an opinion on a point of conduct, not supported by reasons, can only count as one person's preference; and if the reasons, when given, are a mere appeal to a similar preference felt by other people, it is still only many people's liking instead of one. To an ordinary man, however, his own preference, thus supported, is not only a perfectly satisfactory reason, but the only one he generally has for any of his notions of morality, taste, or propriety, which are not expressly written in his religious creed; and his chief guide in the interpretation even of that. Men's opinions, accordingly, on what is laudable or blameable, are affected by all the multifarious causes which influence their wishes in regard to the conduct of others, and which are as numerous as those which determine their wishes on any other subject. Sometimes their reason—at other times their prejudices or superstitions: often their social affections, not seldom their antisocial ones, their envy or jealousy, their arrogance or contemptuousness: but most commonly, their desires or fears for themselves—their legitimate or illegitimate self-interest. Where there is an ascendant class, a large portion of the morality of the country emanates from its class interests, and its feelings of class superiority. The morality between Spartans and Helots, between planters and negroes, between princes and subjects, between nobles and returners, between men and women, has been for the most part the creation of these class interests and feelings: and the sentiments thus generated, react in turn upon the moral feelings of the members of the ascendant class, in the relations among themselves. Where, on the other hand, a class, formerly ascendant, has lost its ascendancy, or where its ascendancy is unpopular, the prevailing moral sentiments frequently bear the impress of an impatient dislike of superiority. Another grand determining principle of the rules of conduct, both in act and forbearance, which have been enforced by law or opinion, has been the servility of mankind towards the supposed preferences or aversions of their temporal masters, or of their gods. This servility, though essentially selfish, is not hypocrisy; it gives rise to perfectly genuine sentiments of abhorrence; it made men burn magicians and heretics. Among so many baser influences, the general and obvious interests of society have of course had a share, and a large one, in the direction of the moral sentiments: less, however, as matter of reason, and on their own account, than as a consequence of the sympathies and antipathies which grew out of them: and sympathies and antipathies which had little or nothing to do with the interests of society, have made themselves felt in the establishment of moralities with quite as great a force.

The likings and dislikings of society, or of some powerful portion of it, are thus the main thing which has practically determined the rules laid down for general observance, under the penalties of law or opinion. And in general, those who have been in advance of society in thought and feeling, have left this condition of things unassailed in principle, however they may have come into conflict with it in some of its details. They have occupied themselves rather in inquiring what things society ought to like or dislike, than in questioning whether its likings or dislikings should be a law to individuals. They preferred endeavouring to alter the feelings of mankind on the particular points on which they were themselves heretical, rather than make common cause in defense of freedom, with heretics generally. [. . . .]

The object of this Essay is to assert one very simple principle, as entitled to govern absolutely the dealings of society with the individual in the way of compulsion and control, whether the means used be physical force in the form of legal penalties, or the moral coercion of public opinion. That principle is, that the sole end for which mankind are warranted, individually or collectively, in interfering with the liberty of action of any of their number, is self-protection. That the only purpose for which power can be rightfully exercised over any member of a civilized community, against his will, is to prevent harm to others. His own good, either physical or moral, is not a sufficient warrant. He cannot rightfully be compelled to do or forbear because it will be better for him to do so, because it will make him happier, because, in the opinions of others, to do so would be wise, or even right. These are good reasons for remonstrating with him, or reasoning with him, or persuading him, or entreating him, but not for compelling him, or visiting him with any evil in case he do otherwise. To justify that, the conduct from which it is desired to deter him, must be calculated to produce evil to some one else. The only part of the conduct of any one, for which he is amenable to society, is that which concerns others. In the part which merely concerns himself, his independence is, of right, absolute. Over himself, over his own body and mind, the individual is sovereign. [. . . .]

It is proper to state that I forego any advantage which could be derived to my argument from the idea of abstract right, as a thing independent of utility. I regard utility as the ultimate appeal on all ethical questions; but it must be utility in the largest sense, grounded on the permanent interests of man as a progressive being. Those interests, I contend, authorise the subjection of individual spontaneity to external control, only in respect to those actions of each, which concern the interest of other people. If any one does an act hurtful to others, there is a *primâ facie* case for punishing him, by law, or, where legal penalties are not safely applicable, by general disapprobation. There are also many positive acts for the benefit of others, which he may rightfully be compelled to perform; such as, to give evidence in a court of justice; to bear his fair share in the common defence, or in any other joint work necessary to the interest of the society of which he enjoys the protection; and to perform certain acts of individual beneficence, such as saving a fellow-creature's life, or interposing to protect the defenceless against ill-usage, things which whenever it is obviously a man's duty to do, he may rightfully be made responsible to society for not doing. A person may cause evil to others not only by his actions but by his inaction, and in either case he is justly accountable to them for the injury. The latter case, it is true, requires a much more cautious exercise of compulsion than the former. To make any one answerable for doing evil to others, is the rule; to make him answerable for not preventing evil, is, comparatively speaking, the exception. Yet there are many cases clear enough and grave enough to justify that exception. In all things which regard the external relations of the individual, he is *de jure* amenable to those whose interests are concerned, and if need be, to society as their protector. There are often good reasons for not holding him to the responsibility; but these reasons must arise from the special expediencies of the case: either because it is a kind of case in which he is on the whole likely to act better, when left to his own discretion, than when controlled in any way in which society have it in their power to control him; or because the attempt to exercise control would produce other evils, greater than those which it would prevent. When such reasons as these preclude the enforcement of responsibility, the conscience of the agent himself should step into the vacant judgment seat, and protect those interests of others which have no external protection; judging himself all the more rigidly, because the case does not admit of his being made accountable to the judgment of his fellow-creatures.

But there is a sphere of action in which society, as distinguished from the individual, has, if any, only an indirect interest; comprehending all that portion of a person's life and conduct which affects only himself, or if it also affects others, only with their free, voluntary, and undeceived consent and participation. When I say only himself, I mean directly, and in the first instance: for whatever affects himself, may affect others through himself; and the objection which may be grounded on this contingency, will receive consideration in the sequel. This, then, is the appropriate region of human liberty. It comprises, first, the inward domain of consciousness; demanding liberty of conscience, in the most comprehensive sense; liberty of thought and feeling; absolute freedom of opinion and sentiment on all subjects, practical or speculative, scientific, moral, or theological. The liberty of expressing and publishing opinions may seem to fall under a different principle, since it belongs to that part of the conduct of an individual which concerns other people; but, being almost of as much importance as the liberty of thought itself, and resting in great part on the same reasons, is practically inseparable from it. Secondly, the principle requires liberty of tastes and pursuits; of framing the plan of our life to suit our own character; of doing as we like, subject to such consequences as may follow: without impediment from our fellow-creatures, so long as what we do does not harm them, even though they should think our conduct foolish, perverse, or wrong. Thirdly, from this liberty of each individual, follows the liberty, within the same limits, of combination among individuals; freedom to unite, for any purpose not involving harm to others: the persons combining being supposed to be of full age, and not forced or deceived.

No society in which these liberties are not, on the whole, respected, is free, whatever may be its form of government; and none is completely free in which they do not exist absolute and unqualified. The only freedom which deserves the name, is that of pursuing our own good in our own way, so long as we do not attempt to deprive others of theirs, or impede their efforts to obtain it. Each is the proper guardian of his own health, whether bodily, or mental and spiritual. Mankind are greater gainers by suffering each other to live as seems good to themselves, than by compelling each to live as seems good to the rest. [. . . .]

Of Individuality, As One of the Elements of Well-Being

No one pretends that actions should be as free as opinions. On the contrary, even opinions lose their immunity, when the circumstances in which they are expressed are such as to constitute their expression a positive instigation to some mischievous act. An opinion that corn-dealers are starvers of the poor, or that private property is robbery, ought to be unmolested when simply circulated through the press, but may justly incur punishment when delivered orally to an excited mob assembled before the house of a corn-dealer, or when handed about among the same mob in the form of a placard. Acts, of whatever kind, which, without justifiable cause, do harm to others, may be, and in the more important cases absolutely require to be, controlled by the unfavourable sentiments, and, when needful, by the active interference of mankind. The liberty of the individual must be thus far limited; he must not make himself a nuisance to other people. But if he refrains from molesting others in what concerns them, and merely acts according to his own inclination and judgment in things which concern himself, the same reasons which show that opinion should be free, prove also that he should be allowed, without molestation, to carry his opinions into practice at his own cost. That mankind are not infallible; that their truths, for the most part, are only half-truths; that unity of opinion, unless resulting from the fullest and freest comparison of opposite opinions, is not desirable, and diversity not an evil, but a good, until mankind are much more capable than at present of recognising all sides of the truth, are principles applicable to men's modes of action, not less than to their opinions. As it is useful that while mankind are imperfect there should be different opinions, so is it that there should be different experiments of living; that free scope should be given to varieties of character, short of injury to others; and that the worth of different modes of life should be proved practically, when any one thinks fit to try them. It is desirable, in short, that in things which do not primarily concern others, individuality should assert itself. Where, not the person's own character, but the traditions or customs of other people are the rule of conduct, there is wanting one of the principal ingredients of human happiness, and quite the chief ingredient of individual and social progress.

In maintaining this principle, the greatest difficulty to be encountered does not lie in the appreciation of means towards an acknowledged end, but in the indifference of persons in general to the end itself. If it were felt that the free development of individuality is one of the leading essentials of well-being; that it is not only a coordinate element with all that is designated by the terms civilization, instruction, education, culture, but is itself a necessary part and condition of all those things; there would be no danger that liberty should be undervalued, and the adjustment of the boundaries between it and social control would present no extraordinary difficulty. But the evil is, that individual spontaneity is hardly recognised by the common modes of thinking, as having any intrinsic worth, or deserving any regard on its own account. The majority, being satisfied with the ways of mankind as they now are (for it is they who make them what they are), cannot comprehend why those ways should not be good enough for everybody; and what is more, spontaneity forms no part of the ideal of the majority of moral and social reformers, but is rather looked on with jealousy, as a troublesome and perhaps rebellious obstruction to the general acceptance of what these reformers, in their own judgment, think would be best for mankind. Few persons, out of Germany, even comprehend the meaning of the doctrine which Wilhelm Von Humboldt, so eminent both as a *savant* and as a politician, made the text of a treatise—that 'the end of man, or that which is prescribed by eternal or immutable dictates of reason, and not suggested by vague and transient desires, is the highest and most harmonious development of his powers to a complete and consistent whole'; that therefore, the object 'towards which every human being must ceaselessly direct his efforts, and on which especially those who design to influence their fellow-men must ever keep their eyes, is the individuality of power and development'; that for this there are two requisites, 'freedom, and variety of situations';

and that from the union of these arise 'individual vigour and manifold diversity,' which combine themselves in 'originality.'[3]

Little, however, as people are accustomed to a doctrine like that of Von Humboldt, and surprising as it may be to them to find so high a value attached to individuality, the question, one must nevertheless think, can only be one of degree. No one's idea of excellence in conduct is that people should do absolutely nothing but copy one another. No one would assert that people ought not to put into their mode of life, and into the conduct of their concerns, any impress whatever of their own judgment, or of their own individual character. On the other hand, it would be absurd to pretend that people ought to live as if nothing whatever had been known in the world before they came into it; as if experience had as yet done nothing towards showing that one mode of existence, or of conduct, is preferable to another. Nobody denies that people should be so taught and trained in youth, as to know and benefit by the ascertained results of human experience. But it is the privilege and proper condition of a human being, arrived at the maturity of his faculties, to use and interpret experience in his own way. It is for him to find out what part of recorded experience is properly applicable to his own circumstances and character. The traditions and customs of other people are, to a certain extent, evidence of what their experience has taught *them;* presumptive evidence, and as such, have a claim to his deference: but, in the first place, their experience may be too narrow; or they may not have interpreted it rightly. Secondly, their interpretation of experience may be correct, but unsuitable to him. Customs are made for customary circumstances, and customary characters; and his circumstances or his character may be uncustomary. Thirdly, though the customs be both good as customs, and suitable to him, yet to conform to custom, merely *as* custom, does not educate or develope in him any of the qualities which are the distinctive endowment of a human being. The human faculties of perception, judgment, discriminative feeling, mental activity, and even moral preference, are exercised only in making a choice. He who does anything because it is the custom, makes no choice. He gains no practice either in discerning or in desiring what is best. The mental and moral, like the muscular powers, are improved only by being used. The faculties are called into no exercise by doing a thing merely because others do it, no more than by believing a thing only because others believe it. If the grounds of an opinion are not conclusive to the person's own reason, his reason cannot be strengthened, but is likely to be weakened, by his adopting it; and if the inducements to an act are not such as are consentaneous to his own feelings and character (where affection, or the rights of others, are concerned) it is so much done towards rendering his feelings and character inert and torpid, instead of active and energetic.

He who lets the world, or his own portion of it, choose his plan of life for him, has no need of any other faculty than the ape-like one of imitation. He who chooses his plan for himself, employs all his faculties. He must use observation to see, reasoning and judgment to foresee, activity to gather materials for decision, discrimination to decide, and when he has decided, firmness and self-control to hold to his deliberate decision. And these qualities he requires and exercises exactly in proportion as the part of his conduct which he determines according to his own judgment and feelings is a large one. It is possible that he might be guided in some good path, and kept out of harm's way, without any of these things. But what will be his comparative worth as a human being? It really is of importance, not only what men do, but also what manner of men they are that do it. Among the works of man, which human life is rightly employed in perfecting and beautifying, the first in importance surely is man himself. Supposing it were possible to get houses built, corn grown, battles fought, causes tried, and even churches erected and prayers said, by machinery—by automatons in human form—it would be a considerable loss to exchange for these automatons even the men and women who at present inhabit the more civilized parts of the world, and who assuredly are but starved specimens of what nature can and will produce. Human nature is not a machine to be built after a model, and set to do exactly the work prescribed for it, but a tree, which requires to grow and develope itself on all sides, according to the tendency of the inward forces which make it a living thing. [. . . .]

A person whose desires and impulses are his own—are the expression of his own nature, as it has been developed and modified by his own culture—is said to have a character. One whose desires and impulses are not his own, has no character, no more than a steam-engine has a character. If, in addition to being his own, his impulses are strong, and are under the government of a strong will, he has an energetic character. Whoever thinks that individuality of desires and impulses should not be encouraged to unfold itself, must maintain that society has no need of strong natures—is not the better for containing many persons who have much character—and that a high general average of energy is not desirable.

JOHN STUART MILL, SELECTIONS FROM *CONSIDERATIONS ON REPRESENTATIVE GOVERNMENT* (1861)

That the Ideally Best Form of Government Is Representative Government

It has long (perhaps throughout the entire duration of British freedom) been a common saying, that if a good despot could be ensured, despotic monarchy would be the best form of government. I look upon this as a radical and most pernicious misconception of what good government is; which, until it can be got rid of, will fatally vitiate all our speculations on government.

The supposition is, that absolute power, in the hands of an eminent individual, would ensure a virtuous and intelligent performance of all the duties of government. Good laws would be established and enforced, bad laws would be reformed; the best men would be placed in all situations of trust; justice would be as well administered, the public burdens would be as light and as judiciously imposed, every branch of administration would be as purely and as intelligently conducted, as the circumstances of the country and its degree of intellectual and moral cultivation would admit. I am willing, for the sake of the argument, to concede all this; but I must point out how great the concession is; how much more is needed to produce even an approximation to these results, than is conveyed in the simple expression, a good despot. Their realization would in fact imply, not merely a good monarch, but an all-seeing one. He must be at all times informed correctly, in considerable detail, of the conduct and working of every branch of administration, in every district of the country, and must be able, in the twenty-four hours per day which are all that is granted to a king as to the humblest labourer, to give an effective share of attention and superintendence to all parts of this vast field; or he must at least be capable of discerning and choosing out, from among the mass of his subjects, not only a large abundance of honest and able men, fit to conduct every branch of public administration under supervision and control, but also the small number of men of eminent virtues and talents who can be trusted not only to do without that supervision, but to exercise it themselves over others. So extraordinary are the faculties and energies required for performing this task in any supportable manner, that the good despot whom we are supposing can hardly be imagined as consenting to undertake it, unless as a refuge from intolerable evils, and a transitional preparation for something beyond. But the argument can do without even this immense item in the account. Suppose the difficulty vanquished. What should we then have? One man of superhuman mental activity managing the entire affairs of a mentally passive people. Their passivity is implied in the very idea of absolute power. The nation as a whole, and every individual composing it, are without any potential voice in their own destiny. They exercise no will in respect to their collective interests. All is decided for them by a will not their own, which it is legally a crime for them to disobey. What sort of human beings can be formed under such a regimen? What development can either their thinking or their active faculties attain under it? On matters of pure theory they might perhaps be allowed to speculate, so long as their speculations either did not approach politics, or had not the remotest connection with its practice. On practical affairs they could at most be only suffered to suggest; and even under the most moderate of despots, none but persons of already admitted or reputed superiority could hope that their suggestions would be known to, much less regarded by, those who had the management of affairs. A person must have a very unusual taste for intellectual exercise in and for itself, who will put himself to the trouble of thought when it is to have no outward effect, or qualify himself for functions which he has no chance of being allowed to exercise. The only sufficient incitement to mental exertion, in any but a few minds in a generation, is the prospect of some practical use to be made of its results. It does not follow that the nation will be wholly destitute of intellectual power. The common business of life, which must necessarily be performed by each individual or family for themselves, will call forth some amount of intelligence and practical ability, within a certain narrow range of ideas. There may be a select class of *savants*, who cultivate science with a view to its physical uses, or for the pleasure of the pursuit. There will be a bureaucracy, and persons in training for the bureaucracy, who will be taught at least some empirical maxims of government and public administration. There may be, and often has been, a systematic organization of the best mental power in the country in some special direction (commonly military) to promote the grandeur of the despot. But the public at large remain without information and without interest on all the greater matters of practice; or, if they have any knowledge of them, it is but a *dilettante* knowledge, like that which people have of the mechanical arts who have never handled a tool. Nor is it only in their intelligence that they suffer. Their moral capacities are equally stunted. Wherever the sphere of action of human beings is artificially circumscribed, their sentiments are narrowed and dwarfed in the same proportion. The food of feeling is action: even domestic affection lives upon voluntary good offices. Let a person have nothing to do for his country, and he will not care for it. [. . . .]

A good despotism means a government in which, so far as depends on the despot, there is no positive oppression by officers of state, but in which all the collective interests of the people are managed for them, all the thinking that has relation to collective interests done for them, and in which their minds are formed by, and consenting to, this abdication of their own energies. Leaving things to the Government, like leaving them to Providence, is synonymous with caring nothing about them, and accepting their results, when disagreeable, as visitations of Nature. With the exception, therefore, of a few studious men who take an intellectual interest in speculation for its own sake, the intelligence and sentiments of the whole people are given up to the material interests, and when these are provided for, to the amusement and ornamentation, of private life. But to say this is to say, if the whole testimony of history is worth anything, that the era of national decline has arrived. [. . . .]

It is not much to be wondered at, if impatient or disappointed reformers, groaning under the impediments opposed to the most salutary public improvements by the ignorance, the indifference, the intractableness, the perverse obstinacy of a people, and the corrupt combinations of selfish private interests armed with the powerful weapons afforded by free institutions, should at times sigh for a strong hand to bear down all these obstacles, and compel a recalcitrant people to be better governed. But (setting aside the fact, that for one despot who now and then reforms an abuse, there are ninety-nine who do nothing but create them) those who look in any such direction for the realization of their hopes leave out of the idea of good government its principal element, the improvement of the people themselves. One of the benefits of freedom is that under it the ruler cannot pass by the people's minds, and amend their affairs for them without amending them. If it were possible for the people to be well governed in spite of themselves, their good government would last no longer than the freedom of a people usually lasts who have been liberated by foreign arms without their own co-operation. It is true, a despot may educate the people; and to do so really would be the best apology for his despotism. But any education which aims at making human beings other than machines, in the long run makes them claim to have the control of their own actions. [. . . .]

There is no difficulty in showing that the ideally best form of government is that in which the sovereignty, or supreme controlling power in the last resort, is vested in the entire aggregate of the community; every citizen not only having a voice in the exercise of that ultimate sovereignty, but being, at least occasionally, called on to take an actual part in the government, by the personal discharge of some public function, local or general. [. . . .]

Its superiority in reference to present well-being rests upon two principles, of as universal truth and applicability as any general propositions which can be laid down respecting human affairs. The first is, that the rights and interests of every or any person are only secure from being disregarded, when the person interested is himself able, and habitually disposed, to stand up for them. The second is, that the general prosperity attains a greater height, and is more widely diffused, in proportion to the amount and variety of the personal energies enlisted in promoting it. [. . . .]

We need not suppose that when power resides in an exclusive class, that class will knowingly and deliberately sacrifice the other classes to themselves: it suffices that, in the absence of its natural defenders, the interest of the excluded is always in danger of being overlooked; and, when looked at, is seen with very different eyes from those of the persons whom it directly concerns. In this country, for example, what are called the working classes may be considered as excluded from all direct participation in the government. I do not believe that the classes who do participate in it, have in general any intention of sacrificing the working classes to themselves. They once had that intention; witness the persevering attempts so long made to keep down wages by law. But in the present day, their ordinary disposition is the very opposite: they willingly make considerable sacrifices, especially of their pecuniary interest, for the benefit of the working classes, and err rather by too lavish and in discriminating beneficence; nor do I believe that any rulers in history have been actuated by a more sincere desire to do their duty towards the poorer portion of their countrymen. Yet does Parliament, or almost any of the members composing it, ever for an instant look at any question with the eyes of a working man? When a subject arises in which the laborers as such have an interest, is it regarded from any point of view but that of the employers of labor? I do not say that the working men's view of these questions is in general nearer to truth than the other: but it is sometimes quite as near; and in any case it ought to be respectfully listened to, instead of being, as it is, not merely turned away from, but ignored. [. . . .]

It is not sufficiently considered how little there is in most men's ordinary life to give any largeness either to their conceptions or to their sentiments. Their work is a routine; not a labour of love, but of self-interest in the most elementary form, the satisfaction of daily wants; neither the thing done, nor the process of doing it, introduces the mind to thoughts or feelings extending beyond individuals; if instructive books are within their reach, there is no stimulus to read them; and in most cases the individual has no access to any person of cultivation much superior to his own. Giving him something to do for the public, supplies, in a measure, all these deficiencies. If circumstances allow the amount of public duty assigned him to be considerable, it makes him an educated man. Notwithstanding the defects of the social system and moral ideas of antiquity, the practice of the dicastery and the ecclesia raised the intellectual standard of an average Athenian citizen far beyond anything of which there is yet an example in any other mass of men, ancient or modern. . . . [W]e need scarcely look further than to the high quality of the addresses which [the] great orators [of ancient Greece] deemed best calculated to act with effect on their understanding and will. A benefit of the same kind, though far less in degree, is produced on Englishmen of the lower middle class by their liability to be placed on juries and to serve parish offices; which, though it does not occur to so many, nor is so continuous, nor introduces them to so great a variety of elevated considerations, as to admit of comparison with the public education which every citizen of Athens obtained from her democratic institutions, must make them nevertheless very different beings, in range of ideas and development of faculties, from those who have done nothing in their lives but drive a quill, or sell goods over a counter. Still more salutary is the moral part of the instruction afforded by the participation of the private citizen, if even rarely, in public functions. He is called upon, while so engaged, to weigh interests not his own; to be guided, in case of conflicting claims, by another rule than his private partialities; to apply, at every turn, principles and maxims which have for their reason of existence the common good: and he usually finds associated with him in the same work minds more familiarized than his own with these ideas and operations, whose study it will be to supply reasons to his understanding, and stimulation to his feeling for the general interest. He is made to feel himself one of the public, and whatever is for their benefit to be for his benefit. Where this school of public spirit does not exist, scarcely any sense is entertained that private persons, in no eminent social situation, owe any duties to society, except to obey the laws and submit to the government. There is no unselfish sentiment of identification with the public. Every thought or feeling, either of interest or of duty, is absorbed in the individual and in the family. The man never thinks of any collective interest, of any objects to be pursued jointly with others, but only in competition with them, and in some measure at their expense. A neighbour, not being an ally or an associate, since he is never engaged in any common undertaking for joint benefit, is therefore only a rival. Thus even private morality suffers, while public is actually extinct. Were this the universal and only possible state of things, the utmost aspirations of the lawgiver or the moralist could only stretch to making the bulk of the community a flock of sheep innocently nibbling the grass side by side.

From these accumulated considerations it is evident, that the only government which can fully satisfy all the exigencies of the social state, is one in which the whole people participate; that any participation, even in the smallest public function, is useful; that the participation should everywhere be as great as the general degree of improvement of the community will allow; and that nothing less can be ultimately desirable, than the admission of all to a share in the sovereign power of the state. But since all cannot, in a community exceeding a single small town, participate personally in any but some very minor portions of the public business, it follows that the ideal type of a perfect government must be representative.

JOHN RAWLS, SELECTION FROM *A THEORY OF JUSTICE* (1971)

The Main Idea of the Theory of Justice

My aim is to present a conception of justice which generalizes and carries to a higher level of abstraction the familiar theory of the social contract as found, say, in Locke, Rousseau, and Kant. In order to do this we are not to think of the original contract as one to enter a particular society or to set up a particular form of government. Rather, the guiding idea is that the principles of justice for the basic structure of society are the object of the original agreement. They are the principles that free and rational persons concerned to further their own interests would accept in an initial position of equality as defining the fundamental terms of their association. These principles are to regulate all further agreements; they specify the kinds of social cooperation that can be entered into and the forms of government that can be established. This way of regarding the principles of justice I shall call justice as fairness.

Thus we are to imagine that those who engage in social cooperation choose together, in one joint act, the principles which are to assign basic rights and duties and to determine the division of social benefits. Men are to decide in advance how they are to regulate their claims against one another and what is to be the foundation charter of their society. Just as each person must decide by rational reflection what constitutes his good, that is, the system of ends which it is rational for him to pursue, so a group of persons must decide once and for all what is to count among them as just and unjust. The choice which rational men would make in this hypothetical situation of equal liberty, assuming for the present that this choice problem has a solution, determines the principles of justice.

In justice as fairness the original position of equality corresponds to the state of nature in the traditional theory of the social contract. This original position is not, of course, thought of as an actual historical state of affairs, much less as a primitive condition of culture. It is understood as a purely hypothetical situation characterized so as to lead to a certain conception of justice. Among the essential features of this situation is that no one knows his place in society, his class position or social status, nor does any one know his fortune in the distribution of natural assets and abilities, his intelligence, strength, and the like. I shall even assume that the parties do not know their conceptions of the good or their special psychological propensities. The principles of justice are chosen behind a veil of ignorance. This ensures that no one is advantaged or disadvantaged in the choice of principles by the outcome of natural chance or the contingency of social circumstances. Since all are similarly situated and no one is able to design principles to favor his particular condition, the principles of justice are the result of a fair agreement or bargain. For given the circumstances of the original position, the symmetry of everyone's relations to each other, this initial situation is fair between individuals as moral persons, that is, as rational beings with their own ends and capable, I shall assume, of a sense of justice. The original position is, one might say, the appropriate initial status quo, and thus the fundamental agreements reached in it are fair. This explains the propriety of the name "justice as fairness": it conveys the idea that the principles of justice are agreed to in an initial situation that is fair. The name does not mean that the concepts of justice and fairness are the same, any more than the phrase "poetry as metaphor" means that the concepts of poetry and metaphor are the same.

Justice as fairness begins, as I have said, with one of the most general of all choices which persons might make together, namely, with the choice of the first principles of a conception of justice which is to regulate all subsequent criticism and reform of institutions. Then, having chosen a conception of justice, we can suppose that they are to choose a constitution and a legislature to enact laws, and so on, all in accordance with the principles of justice initially agreed upon. Our social situation is just if it is such that by this sequence of hypothetical agreements we would have contracted into the general system of rules which defines it. Moreover, assuming that the original position does determine a set of principles (that is, that a particular conception of justice would be chosen), it will then be true that whenever social institutions satisfy these principles those engaged in them can say to one another that they are cooperating on terms to which they would agree if they were free and equal persons whose relations with respect to one another were fair. They could all view their arrangements as meeting the stipulations which they would acknowledge in an initial situation that embodies widely accepted and reasonable constraints on the choice of principles. The general recognition of this fact would provide the basis for a public acceptance of the corresponding principles of justice. No society can, of course, be a scheme of cooperation which men enter voluntarily in a literal sense; each person finds himself placed at birth in some particular position in some particular society, and the nature of this position materially affects his life prospects. Yet a society satisfying the principles of justice as fairness comes as close as a society can to being a voluntary scheme, for it meets the principles which free and equal persons would assent to under circumstances that are fair. In this sense its members are autonomous and the obligations they recognize self-imposed.

One feature of justice as fairness is to think of the parties in the initial situation as rational and mutually disinterested. This does not mean that the parties are egoists, that is, individuals with only certain kinds of interests, say in wealth, prestige, and domination. But they are conceived as not taking an interest in one another's interests. They are to presume that even their spiritual aims may be opposed, in the way that the aims of those of different religions may be opposed. Moreover, the concept of rationality must be interpreted as far as possible in the narrow sense, standard in economic theory, of taking the most effective means to given ends. I shall modify this concept to some extent. . . , but one must try to avoid introducing into it any controversial ethical elements. The initial situation must be characterized by stipulations that are widely accepted.

In working out the conception of justice as fairness one main task clearly is to determine which principles of justice would be chosen in the original position. To do this we must describe this situation in some detail and formulate with care the problem of choice which it presents. . . . [O]nce the principles of justice are thought of as arising from an original agreement in a situation of equality, it is an open question whether the principle of utility would be acknowledged. Offhand it hardly seems likely that persons who view themselves as equals, entitled to press their claims upon one another, would agree to a principle which may require lesser life prospects for some simply for the sake of a greater sum of advantages enjoyed by others. Since each desires to protect his interests, his capacity to advance his conception of the good, no one has a reason to acquiesce in an enduring loss for himself in order to bring about a greater net balance of satisfaction. In the absence of strong and lasting benevolent impulses, a rational man would not accept a basic structure merely because it maximized the algebraic sum of advantages irrespective of its permanent effects on his own basic rights and interests. Thus it seems that the principle of utility is incompatible with the conception of social cooperation among equals for mutual advantage. It appears to be inconsistent with the idea of reciprocity implicit in the notion of a well-ordered society. Or, at any rate, so I shall argue.

I shall maintain instead that the persons in the initial situation would choose two rather different principles: the first requires equality in the assignment of basic rights and duties, while the second holds that social and economic inequalities, for example inequalities of wealth and authority, are just only if they result in compensating benefits for everyone, and in particular for the least advantaged members of society. These principles rule out justifying institutions on the grounds that the hardships of some are offset by a greater good in the aggregate. It may be expedient but it is not just that some should have less in order that others may prosper. But there is no injustice in the greater benefits earned by a few provided that the situation of persons not so fortunate is thereby improved. The intuitive idea is that since everyone's well-being depends upon a scheme of cooperation without which no one could have a satisfactory life, the division of advantages should be such as to draw forth the willing cooperation of everyone taking part in it, including those less well situated. Yet this can be expected only if reasonable terms are proposed. The two principles mentioned seem to be a fair agreement on the basis of which those better endowed, or more fortunate in their social position, neither of which we can be said to deserve, could expect the willing cooperation of others when some workable scheme is a necessary condition of the welfare of all. Once we decide to look for a conception of justice that nullifies the accidents of natural endowment and the contingencies of social circumstance as counters in quest for political and economic advantage, we are led to these principles. They express the result of leaving aside those aspects of the social world that seem arbitrary from a moral point of view.

The problem of the choice of principles, however, is extremely difficult. I do not expect the answer I shall suggest to be convincing to everyone. It is, therefore, worth noting from the outset that justice as fairness, like other contract views, consists of two parts: (1) an interpretation of the initial situation and of the problem of choice posed there, and (2) a set of principles which, it is argued, would be agreed to. One may accept the first part of the theory (or some variant thereof), but not the other, and conversely. The concept of the initial contractual situation may seem reasonable although the particular principles proposed are rejected. To be sure, I want to maintain that the most appropriate conception of this situation does lead to principles of justice contrary to utilitarianism and perfectionism, and therefore that the contract doctrine provides an alternative to these views. Still, one may dispute this contention even though one grants that the contractarian method is a useful way of studying ethical theories and of setting forth their underlying assumptions.

Justice as fairness is an example of what I have called a contract theory. Now there may be an objection to the term "contract" and related expressions, but I think it will serve reasonably well. Many words have misleading connotations which at first are likely to confuse. The terms "utility" and "utilitarianism" are surely no exception. They too have unfortunate suggestions which hostile critics have been willing to exploit; yet they are clear enough for those prepared to study utilitarian doctrine. The same should be true of the term "contract" applied to moral theories. As I have mentioned, to understand it one has to keep in mind that it implies a certain level of abstraction. In particular, the content of the relevant agreement is not to enter a given society or to adopt a given form of government, but to accept certain moral principles. Moreover, the undertakings referred to are purely hypothetical: a contract view holds that certain principles would be accepted in a well-defined initial situation.

The merit of the contract terminology is that it conveys the idea that principles of justice may be conceived as principles that would be chosen by rational persons, and that in this way conceptions of justice may be explained and justified. The theory of justice is a part, perhaps the most significant part, of the theory of rational choice. Furthermore, principles of justice deal with conflicting claims upon the advantages won by social cooperation; they apply to the relations among several persons or groups. The word "contract" suggests this plurality as well as the condition that the appropriate division of advantages must be in accordance with principles acceptable to all parties. The condition of publicity for principles of justice is also connoted by the contract phraseology. Thus, if these principles are the outcome of an agreement, citizens have a knowledge of the principles that others follow. It is characteristic of contract theories to stress the public nature of political principles. Finally there is the long tradition of the contract doctrine. Expressing the tie with this line of thought helps to define ideas and accords with natural piety. There are then several advantages in the use of the term "contract." With due precautions taken, it should not be misleading.

A final remark. Justice as fairness is not a complete contract theory. For it is clear that the contractarian idea can be extended to the choice of more or less an entire ethical system, that is, to a system including principles for all the virtues and not only for justice. Now for the most part I shall consider only principles of justice and others closely related to them; I make no attempt to discuss the virtues in a systematic way. Obviously if justice as fairness succeeds reasonably well, a next step would be to study the more general view suggested by the name "rightness as fairness." But even this wider theory fails to embrace all moral relationships, since it would seem to include only our relations with other persons and to leave out of account how we are to conduct ourselves toward animals and the rest of nature. I do not contend that the contract notion offers a way to approach these questions which are certainly of the first importance; and I shall have to put them aside. We must recognize the limited scope of justice as fairness and of the general type of view that it exemplifies. How far its conclusions must be revised once these other matters are understood cannot be decided in advance.

NOTES

1. The term liberal as used in this collection reflects the common usage of political theorists in talking about rights-based theories of politics. This meaning of "liberal" should be distinguished from contemporary, conventional applications of the term that generally refer to positions on the left of the political spectrum and are sometimes labeled revisionary or welfare state liberalism.

2. For a discussion of the continuities and discontinuities between liberalism and democracy see Norberto Bobbio, *Liberalism and Democracy* (New York: Verso, 1990). For an influential discussion of liberalism, see Isaiah Berlin, *Four Essays on Liberty* (Oxford: Oxford University Press, 1969). For a discussion of rights in early liberal theory and their standing in contemporary liberal thought, see Ian Shapiro, *The Evolution of Rights in Liberal Theory* (Cambridge: Cambridge University Press, 1986).

3. *The Sphere and Duties of Government*, from the German of Baron Wilhelm von Humboldt, 11, 13.

2

THE CIVIC REPUBLICAN TRADITION
AND COMMUNITARIANS

In this section we take up the civic republicanism of Aristotle, Machiavelli, Rousseau, and two versions of American republicanism.[1] We then turn to the contemporary communitarian Robert Bellah. For each of these authors, the good republic is more than a set of institutional arrangements. Instead, it is inexorably related to the character of its citizens. Civic republicans work with a set of assumptions that is absent from most of the dominant democratic theories we have today. Aristotle, Machiavelli, and Rousseau celebrate the need for a vibrant civic life, a continuing commitment to the common good, and an enhanced appreciation of the role of civic virtue. Along the way, they fear that when self-interests invade the public sphere, politics becomes corrupt and the common good becomes illusive or is eclipsed altogether. What makes Aristotle, Machiavelli, and Rousseau civic republicans is that although they make the republican tradition and civic education a vital part of what defines and sustains the good polity, they do not presume that this is all that is necessary. For them, it is also important to consider the economic well-being and autonomy of each citizen. For these thinkers, if citizens share a common education and tradition but do not all share in what should make the republic valuable to everyone, we should not expect republican principles, such as the promotion of the common good, to serve as a compass in pubic life.

At the very beginning of *Politics*, Aristotle tells us that the state is the highest good, higher than the family or any isolated individual. This is so because it is only in the state that we have what is necessary to lead the good life. Although the good state cannot ensure that its citizens will invariably find happiness, without it we would not have what is necessary for the good life, according to Aristotle. But not all states are the same, and Aristotle offers us two ways of thinking about any regime. Quantitatively, we ask whether power is placed in one person, the few, or the many; qualitatively, we ask whether the regime aims at the good the whole or the good of the rulers (at the expense of the rest).

With Aristotle we also find an early and often repeated argument about the role of public speech among equals in a democracy. For him, decisions are better apt to be made by a collection of citizens who listen to each other and fashion a solution acceptable to all rather than suffer the decisions that are made by the limited insight of one or a few persons who hold power over the rest. Unlike Socrates, Aristotle argues that the concerns of ordinary people about their households are natural to political life. By this Aristotle means that people do not give up caring about themselves in a republic. Instead they recognize that their personal well-being depends on the success of their republic. But he also recognizes that self-interests can run wild and destroy democracy. This happens when citizens mistake their freedom for a license to do whatever they want. To confront this danger, Aristotle calls for an education for democrats to teach people an appreciation of the responsibilities of citizenship through the skills of ruling and obedience alike. These points are interrelated for Aristotle since, if citizens misunderstand liberty and believe that they are free to do whatever pleases them, then the regime will only be a collection of self-regarding individuals who use politics to further their own self-interests, something he believes is contrary to any good regime. At such times, citizens lose the virtue of moderation and forget their duty to the well-being of the republic.

Ultimately, Aristotle fears that all pure forms of government, including democracies, tend to push their defining principle to extremes and in so doing serve to undermine their own integrity. When this happens in democracies, society becomes disorganized and shared understandings of the common good collapse. Yet he insists that the self-destructive trajectory of democracy can be held in check. This occurs when political life is structured in a polity in which class antagonisms are mitigated by a large and politically active middle class that practices a politics of moderation and forbearance.

For Machiavelli, the republic represents the ideal government; it disperses power in order to protect liberty and it requires virtuous citizens to cooperate in their shared projects as they seek a common good. One good that all of Machiavelli's citizens share is their liberty, which in turn rests upon their republican institutions. The maintenance of a healthy republic, according to Machiavelli, requires a strong sense of civic virtue as well as a readiness to resist the temptations to become corrupt.[2] The divisive force of corruption weakens the unity of the state and leaves it vulnerable to the ambitions of aggressive neighboring states as well as the domineering initiatives of citizens at home. Machiavelli's freedom depends not only on laws, but equally on those civic virtues, customs, and habits that succeed in persuading citizens of the value of working for the good of the whole. Such virtues, customs, and habits are inspired by a love of liberty and the recognition that these civic practices are required to protect liberty. In this model, the strength and longevity of the republic depend on its capacity to distribute the responsibilities of political life broadly among citizens.

Like Tocqueville in another context, Machiavelli also looks to religion to aid politics. He sees it teaching discipline, unity, and goodness and showing citizens that they must move beyond their own immediate self-interests. Religion, along with the principles of the founding, is essential for Machiavelli's republic, enabling it to move beyond a concern about materialism or status and address the common good. This good is exemplified by Machiavelli's ideal citizen, Cincinnatus, someone without personal ambition but driven by his civic virtue. For him, the honor of his fellow citizens, not power or wealth, is the real prize to be won in the good republic.

Machiavelli opens *The Discourses* with a discussion of the founding of states and claims that one of its central aims is to promote justice as security and liberty. Yet he observes from history that pure forms of the state quickly degenerate and are overthrown in a political cycle that leads to a succession of unstable governments, some of which degenerate into despotic forms. Machiavelli announces that he seeks a republic that can break the conflicts of pure forms of government, and he turns to a mixed regime where the many have a prominent and decisive place. Yet the threats facing a free republic are not eliminated with this choice, and one of the most prominent dangers in this regard is the corrosive force of avarice. Along with many other civic republicans, Machiavelli holds that a society preoccupied with material goods is in the grip of civil decay. At such a time, he thinks that economics, rather than politics, captures the attention of citizens who turn away from the public good to pursue their own private concerns. This shift leaves the affairs of the republic to those who grasp public power in order to use it for their own private advantages. In such times, he reasons, the common good is shattered as the incentive to public service is reduced. With a diminishing commitment to the common good, the integrity of the republic is jeopardized and with it the liberty of its citizens.

Turning to Rousseau, we find many of these same republican themes at work, but new ones appear as well. For him, all politics is a historical construction that has subverted the natural equality and liberty that everyone enjoyed in an imagined state of nature. The task Rousseau sets for himself is to offer a way of thinking about how the liberty and equality that have been lost can be recovered without having to return to the original state of nature. This he does with his ingenious solution to self-governance in his *Social Contract* where he expects the general will to rule and particular wills, such as self-interests or factions, are banished. Rousseau's general will reflects the will of the citizens to protect their own liberty and equality, and when the general will is the basis of law, he reasons, we are not obeying some alien will but our own will. However, when particular wills carry the day and become public law, we no longer obey our own will, according to Rousseau, but the will of those who wield power at the time.

With these claims, he calls attention to one of the great dangers he sees facing the republic; namely, the ease with which public power can be usurped by private interests. To counter this threat to equality and liberty, he urges citizens to be politically active. If they think that politics need not concern them and that they have better things to do than protect their liberty, then they will find that those who remain politically active will use their power for their own purposes.

To achieve his good republic, Rousseau relies heavily on the conditions of its founding, which teach that there is something more important than one's immediate interests and that citizens must appreciate how their own welfare is inexorably tied to the good of the whole. Along with many other civic republicans, Rousseau holds that the founding represents the highest ideals of the republic; it is not about economics or individual advantage, but about the moral and civic aspirations of a community. It is the primary responsibility of the founder or legislator to inculcate the principles of civic duty as the guiding motivations of citizens. When these principles are ignored or become merely ritualistic, he fears the republic is on its way to corruption and decay. For him, this deterioration can effectively be challenged by the active participation of free and equal citizens. But the effectiveness of civic involvement is judged by the extent to which it helps citizens to recognize that their own good cannot be separated from the good of the republic. If they believe they can ignore politics or use it to enhance their own personal advantage, then the very institutions that secure the liberty of each citizen will be destroyed.

The republican tradition also found voice in North America, and one of the earliest and arguably most articulate expressions comes from John Winthrop. In "A Modell of Christian Charity," he emphasizes the good of each can only be achieved within the good of the whole. This means that each person must regard all of the others in his or her community as equals and be ready to help one another in time of need. As he puts it, the "care of the publique must oversway all private respects." Those with much are expected to assist those with less and refuse to make material self-interest their touchstone. Winthrop sees the Puritans ready to build a "City upon a hill," a place where men and women will be free from the corruption of Europe and live in the light of God in a community that is held together by "brotherly Affection." For him, their experiment is not guaranteed to be successful; everything depends on the character of the members of the community and their determination not to be seduced by "pleasures and profits."

Character is on the mind of a later American author, Horace Mann, when he worries about the dual nature of liberty. He sees it releasing the many talents and aspirations that had been denied by arbitrary government, but he also believes that it can easily unleash a selfish and destructive side of human beings as well. For Mann, freedom is essential to the good life, but not sufficient to assure it. With this in mind, he observes that "without intelligence and virtue. . . , we shall perish at the first storm." What is necessary then is to develop the kind of moral character that can both discipline the weaker side of the self and simultaneously bring out the best in human beings. For Mann, the issue is not whether people pursue wealth, but whether they do so by honest means. The economic issues that were important to many earlier civic republicans are left behind by Mann, who emphasizes the importance of education in developing both a moral and civic character, which remains central to many communitarians today.

The modern heirs to the civic republican tradition are contemporary communitarians who lament what they take to be the shattered, materialistic, morally empty character of society today.[3] They find its politics bereft of any conception of a common good and any sense of social coherence and civic-mindedness in deplorable decline. For communitarians, contemporary society is fractured, its citizens atomistic, the bonds of community weak, and a pervasive consumerism rules the land.[4] When many communitarians survey liberal-democratic society today they find a fragmented, unsituated liberal self without attachments, commitments, or duties.[5] These authors trace the source of our discontents to our liberal inheritance and what they take to be its exaggerated preoccupation with personal rights.[6] On this account, liberalism gives individuals permission to make themselves the center and to ignore their interconnectedness with others. In such a milieu, we share little and are left to seek our own advantage, even at the expense of others. To correct this, many communitarians point to the need to reconstruct democratic life around a robust, coherent community where citizens realize that they have duties as well as rights and where people recognize that they are not alone but part of a common project.

Robert Bellah captures many communitarian themes in his discussions of community. Against those critics who associate strong community standards with norms that can be oppressive to the individual, he argues that such standards do not require unanimity nor close off avenues for modifying the terms of agreement. Rather, such agreements are presented as the substance of social life and an invaluable addition to the stark contractual model of liberalism. Bellah wants us to visualize a common good. For him, the overreliance on either the market or the state as the primary sites of social action neglects the critical role of civil society in providing both organizational coherence and the motive for collective initiatives. For Bellah, we need to acknowledge the necessity of morality in political life if we are to salvage a desirable and responsive politics.

READINGS

ARISTOTLE, SELECTIONS FROM *POLITICS* (335–323 B.C.)

Every state is a community of some kind, and every community is established with a view to some good; for mankind always act in order to obtain that which they think good. But, if all communities aim at some good, the state or political community, which is the highest of all, and which embraces all the rest, aims at good in a greater degree than any other, and at the highest good.

Some people think that the qualifications of a statesman, king, householder, and master are the same, and that they differ, not in kind, but only in the number of their subjects. For example, the ruler over a few is called a master; over more, the manager of a household; over a still larger number, a statesman or king, as if there were no difference between a great household and a small state. The distinction which is made between the king and the statesman is as follows: when the government is personal, the ruler is a king; when, according to the rules of the political science, the citizens rule and are ruled in turn, then he is called a statesman.

But all this is a mistake; for governments differ in kind, as will be evident to any one who considers the matter according to the method which has hitherto guided us. As in other departments of science, so in politics, the compound should always be resolved into the simple elements or least parts of the whole. We must therefore look at the elements of which the state is composed, in order that we may see in what the different kinds of rule differ from one another, and whether any scientific result can be attained about each one of them. [   ]

The family is the association established by nature for the supply of men's everyday wants, and the members of it are called by Charondas 'companions of the cupboard,' and by Epimenides the Cretan, 'companions of the manger.' But when several families are united, and the association aims at something more than the supply of daily needs, the first society to be formed is the village. And the most natural form of the village appears to be that of a colony from the family, composed of the children and grandchildren, who are said to be 'suckled with the same milk.' And this is the reason why Hellenic states were originally governed by kings; because the Hellenes were under royal rule before they came together, as the barbarians still are. Every family is ruled by the eldest, and therefore in the colonies of the family the kingly form of government prevailed because they were of the same blood. [. . . .]

For they lived dispersedly, as was the manner in ancient times. Wherefore men say that the Gods have a king, because they themselves either are or were in ancient times under the rule of a king. For they imagine, not only the forms of the Gods, but their ways of life to be like their own.

When several villages are united in a single complete community, large enough to be nearly or quite self-sufficing, the state comes into existence, originating in the bare needs of life, and continuing in existence for the sake of a good life. And therefore, if the earlier forms of society are natural, so is the state, for it is the end of them, and the nature of a thing is its end. For what each thing is when fully developed, we call its nature, whether we are speaking of a man, a horse, or a family. Besides, the final cause and end of a thing is the best, and to be self-sufficing is the end and the best.

Hence it is evident that the state is a creation of nature, and that man is by nature a political animal. And he who by nature and not by mere accident is without a state, is either a bad man or above humanity; he is like the

'Tribeless, lawless, heartless one,'

whom Homer denounces—the natural outcast is forthwith a lover of war; he may be compared to an isolated piece at draughts.

Now, that man is more of a political animal than bees or any other gregarious animals is evident. Nature, as we often say, makes nothing in vain, and man is the only animal whom she has endowed with the gift of speech. And whereas mere voice is but an indication of pleasure or pain and is therefore found in other animals (for their nature attains to the perception of pleasure and pain and the intimation of them to one another, and no further), the power of speech is intended to set forth the expedient and inexpedient, and therefore likewise the just and the unjust. And it is a characteristic of man that he alone has any sense of good and evil, of just and unjust, and the like, and the association of living beings who have this sense makes a family and a state.

Further, the state is by nature clearly prior to the family and to the individual, since the whole is of necessity prior to the part; for example, if the whole body be destroyed, there will be no foot or hand, except in an equivocal sense, as we might speak of a stone hand; for when destroyed the hand will be no better than that. But things are defined by their working and power; and we ought not to say that they are the same when they no longer have their proper quality, but only that they have the same name. The proof that the state is a creation of nature and prior to the individual is that the individual, when isolated, is not self-sufficing; and therefore he is like a part in relation to the whole. But he who is unable to live in society or who has no need because he is sufficient for himself, must be either a beast or a god: he is no part of a state. A social instinct is implanted in all men by nature, and yet he who first founded the state was the greatest of benefactors. For man, when perfected, is the best of animals, but, when separated from law and justice, he is the worst of all; since armed injustice is the more dangerous, and he is equipped at birth with arms, meant to be used by intelligence and virtue, which he may use for the worst ends. Wherefore, if he have not virtue, he is the most unholy and the most savage of animals, and the most full of lust and gluttony. But justice is the bond of men in states, for the administration of justice, which is the determination of what is just, is the principle of order in political society. [. . . .]

Property is a part of the household, and the art of acquiring property is a part of the art of managing the household; for no man can live well, or indeed live at all, unless he be provided with necessaries. And as in the arts which have a definite sphere the workers must have their own proper instruments for the accomplishment of their work, so it is in the management of a household. [. . . .]

[W]e have next to consider whether there is only one form of government or many, and if many, what they are, and how many, and what are the differences between them.

A constitution is the arrangement of magistracies in a state, especially of the highest of all. The government is everywhere sovereign in the state, and the constitution is in fact the government. For example, in democracies the people are supreme, but in oligarchies, the few; and, therefore, we say that these two forms of government also are different: and so in other cases.

First, let us consider what is the purpose of a state, and how many forms of government there are by which human society is regulated. We have already said, in the first part of this treatise, when discussing household management and the rule of a master, that man is by nature a political animal. And therefore, men, even when they do not require one another's help, desire to live together; not but that they are also brought together by their common interests in proportion as they severally attain to any measure of well-being. This is certainly the chief end, both of individuals and of states. And also for the sake of mere life (in which there is possibly some noble element so long as the evils of existence do not greatly overbalance the good) mankind meet together and maintain the political community. And we all see that men cling to life even at the cost of enduring great misfortune, seeming to find in life a natural sweetness and happiness. [. . . .]

[W]e have next to consider how many forms of government there are, and what they are; and in the first place what are the true forms, for when they are determined the perversions of them will at once be apparent. The words constitution and government have the same meaning, and the government, which is the supreme authority in states, must be in the hands of one, or of a few, or of the many. The true forms of government, therefore, are those in which the one, or the few, or the many, govern with a view to the common interest; but governments which rule with a view to the private interest, whether of the one, or of the few, or of the many, are perversions. For the members of a state, if they are truly citizens, ought to participate in its advantages. Of forms of government in which one rules, we call that which regards the common interests, kingship or royalty; that in which more than one, but not many, rule, aristocracy; and it is so called, either because the rulers are the best men, or because they have at heart the best interests of the state and of the citizens. But when the citizens at large administer the state for the common interest, the government is called by the generic name— a constitution. And there is a reason for this use of language. One man or a few may excel in virtue; but as the number increases it becomes more difficult for them to attain perfection in every kind of virtue, though they may in military virtue, for this is found in the masses. Hence in a constitutional government the fighting-men have the supreme power, and those who possess arms are the citizens.

Of the above-mentioned forms, the perversions are as follows—of royalty, tyranny; of aristocracy, oligarchy; of constitutional government, democracy. For tyranny is a kind of monarchy which has in view the interest of the monarch only; oligarchy has in view the interest of the wealthy; democracy, of the needy: none of them, the common good of all. [. . . .]

Let us begin by considering the common definitions of oligarchy and democracy, and what is justice oligarchical and democratical. For all men cling to justice of some kind, but their conceptions are imperfect and they do not express the whole idea. For example, justice is thought by them to be, and is, equality, not, however, for all, but only for equals. And inequality is thought to be, and is, justice; neither is this for all, but only for unequals. When the persons are omitted, then men judge erroneously. The reason is that they are passing judgement on themselves, and most people are bad judges in their own I case. And whereas justice implies a relation to persons as well as to things, and a just distribution, as I have already said in the *Ethics*, implies the same ratio between the persons and between the things, they agree about the equality of the things, but dispute about the equality of the persons, chiefly for the reason which I have just given—because they are bad judges in their own affairs; and secondly, because both the parties to the argument are speaking of a limited and partial justice, but imagine themselves to be speaking of absolute justice. For the one party, if they are unequal in one respect, for example wealth, consider themselves to be unequal in all; and the other party, if they are equal in one respect, for example free birth, consider themselves to be equal in all. But they leave out the capital point. For if men met and associated out of regard to wealth only, their share in the state would be proportioned to their property, and the oligarchical doctrine would then seem to carry the day. It would not be just, that he who paid one mina should have the same share of a hundred minae, whether of the principal or of the profits, as he who paid the remaining ninety-nine. But a state exists for the sake of a good life, and not for the sake of life only: if life only were the object, slaves and brute animals might form a state, but they cannot, for they have no share in happiness or in a life of free choice. Nor does a state exist for the sake of alliance and security from injustice, nor yet for the sake of exchange and mutual intercourse; for then the Tyrrhenians and the Carthaginians, and all who have commercial treaties with one another, would be the citizens of one state. True, they have agreements about imports, and engagements that they will do no wrong to one another, and written articles of alliance. But there are no magistracies common to the contracting parties who will enforce their engagements; different states have each their own magistracies. Nor does one state take care that the citizens of the other are such as they ought to be, nor see that those who come under the terms of the treaty do no wrong or wickedness at all, but only that they do no injustice to one another. Whereas, those who care for good government take into consideration virtue and vice in states. Whence it may be further inferred that virtue must be the care of a state which is truly so called, and not merely enjoys the name: for without this end the community becomes a mere alliance which differs only in place from alliances of which the members live apart; and law is only a convention, 'a surety to one another of justice,' as the sophist Lycophron says, and has no real power to make the citizens good and just. [. . . .]

Our conclusion, then, is that political society exists for the sake of noble actions, and not of mere companionship. Hence they who contribute most to such a society have a greater share in it than those who have the same or a greater freedom or nobility of birth but are inferior to them in political virtue; or than those who exceed them in wealth but are surpassed by them in virtue.

From what has been said it will be clearly seen that all the partisans of different forms of government speak of a part of justice only. [. . . .]

The principle that the multitude ought to be supreme rather than the few best is one that is maintained, and, though not free from difficulty, yet seems to contain an element of truth. For the many, of whom each individual is but an ordinary person, when they meet together may very likely be better than the few good, if regarded not individually but collectively, just as a feast to which many contribute is better than a dinner provided out of a single purse. For each individual among the many has a share of virtue and prudence, and when they meet together, they become in a manner one man, who has many feet, and hands, and senses; that is a figure of their mind and disposition. Hence the many are better judges than a single man of music and poetry; for some understand one part, and some another, and among them they understand the whole. There is a similar combination of qualities in good men, who differ from any individual of the many, as the beautiful are said to differ from those who are not beautiful, and works of art from realities, because in them the scattered elements are combined, although, if taken separately, the eye of one person or some other feature in another person would be fairer than in the picture. Whether this principle can apply to every democracy, and to all bodies of men, is not clear. Or rather, by heaven, in some cases it is impossible of application; for the argument would equally hold about brutes; and wherein, it will be asked, do some men differ from brutes? But there may be bodies of men about whom our statement is nevertheless true. And if so, the difficulty which has been already raised, and also another which is akin to it—viz. what power should be assigned to the mass of freemen and citizens, who are not rich and have no personal merit—are both solved. There is still a danger in allowing them to share the great offices of state, for their folly will lead them into error, and their dishonesty into crime. But there is a danger also in not letting them share, for a state in which many poor men are excluded from office will necessarily be full of enemies. [. . . .]

In our original discussion about governments we divided them into three true forms: kingly rule, aristocracy, and constitutional government, and three corresponding perversions—tyranny, oligarchy and democracy. Of kingly rule and of aristocracy we have already spoken, for the inquiry into the perfect state is the same thing with the discussion of the two forms thus named, since both imply a principle of virtue provided with external means. We have already determined in what aristocracy and kingly rule differ from one another, and when the latter should be established. In what follows we have to describe the so-called constitutional government, which bears the common name of all constitutions, and the other forms, tyranny, oligarchy, and democracy.

It is obvious which of the three perversions is the worst, and which is the next in badness. That which is the perversion of the first and most divine is necessarily the worst. And just as a royal rule, if not a mere name, must exist by virtue of some great personal superiority in the king, so tyranny, which is the worst of governments, is necessarily the farthest removed from a well-constituted form; oligarchy is little better, for it is a long way from aristocracy, and democracy is the most tolerable of the three. [. . . .]

The reason why there are many forms of government is that every state contains many elements. In the first place we see that all states are made up of families, and in the multitude of citizens there must be some rich and some poor, and some in a middle condition; the rich are heavy-armed, and the poor not. Of the common people, some are husbandmen, and some traders, and some artisans. There are also among the notables differences of wealth and property—for example, in the number of horses which they keep, for they cannot afford to keep them unless they are rich. And therefore in old times the cities whose strength lay in their cavalry were oligarchies, and they used cavalry in wars against their neighbours; as was the practice of the Eretrians and Chalcidians, and also of the Magnesians on the river Maeander, and of other peoples in Asia. Besides differences of wealth there are differences of rank and merit, and there are some other elements which were mentioned by us when in treating of aristocracy we enumerated the essentials of a state. Of these elements, sometimes all, sometimes the lesser and sometimes the greater number, have a share in the government. It is evident then that there must be many forms of government, differing in kind, since the parts of which they are composed differ from each other in kind. For a constitution is an organization of offices, which all the citizens distribute among themselves, according to the power which different classes possess, for example the rich or the poor, or according to some principle of equality which includes both. There must therefore be as many forms of government as there are modes of arranging the offices, according to the superiorities and the differences of the parts of the state. [. . . .]

We have now to inquire what is the best constitution for most states, and the best life for most men, neither assuming a standards of virtue which is above ordinary persons, nor an education which is exceptional favoured by nature and circumstances, nor yet an ideal state which is an aspiration only, but having regard to the life in which the majority are able to share, and to the form of government which states in general can attain. . . . For if what was said in the *Ethics* is true, that the happy life is the life according to virtue lived without impediment, and that virtue is a mean,[7] then the life which is in a mean, and in a mean attainable by every one, must be the best. And the same principles of virtues and vice are characteristic of cities and of constitutions; for the constitution is in a figure the life of the city.

Now in all states there are three elements: one class is very rich, another very poor and a third in a mean. It is admitted that moderation and the mean are best, and therefore it will clearly be best to possess the gifts of fortune in moderation; for in that condition of life men are most ready to follow rational principle. But he who greatly excels in beauty, strength, birth, or wealth, or on the other hand who is very poor, or very weak, or very much disgraced, finds it difficult to follow rational principle. Of these two, the one sort grow into violent and great criminals, the others into rogues and petty rascals. And two sorts of offences correspond to them, the one committed from violence, the other from roguery. Again, the middle class is least likely to shrink from rule, or to be over-ambitious for it; both of which are injuries to the state. Again, those who have too much of the goods of fortune, strength, wealth, friends, and the like are neither willing nor able to submit to authority. The evil begins at home; for when they are boys, by reason of the luxury in which they are brought up, they never learn, even at school, the habit of obedience. On the other hand, the very poor, who are in the opposite extreme, are too degraded. So that the one class cannot obey and can only rule despotically; the other knows not how to command and must be ruled like slaves. Thus arises a city, not of freemen, but of masters and slaves, the one despising, the other envying; and nothing can be more fatal to friendship and good fellowship in states than this: for good fellowship springs from friendship; when men are at enmity with one another, they would rather not even share the same path. But a city ought to be composed, as far as possible, of equals and similars; and these are generally the middle classes. Wherefore, the city which is composed of middle-class citizens is necessarily best constituted in respect of the elements of which we say the fabric of the state naturally consists. And this is the class of citizens which is most secure in a state, for they do not, like the poor, covet their neighbour's goods; nor do others covet theirs, as the poor covet the goods of the rich; and as they neither plot against others, nor are themselves plotted against others, they pass though life safely. Wisely then did Phocylides pray—'Many things are best in the mean; I desire to be of a middle condition in my city.'

Thus it is manifest that the best political community is formed by citizens of the middle class, and that those states are likely to be well-administered, in which the middle class is large, and stronger if possible than both the other classes, or at any rate than either singly; for the addition of the middle class turns the scale, and prevents either of the extremes from being dominant. Great then is the good fortune of a state in which the citizens have a moderate and sufficient property; for where some possess much, and the others nothing, there may arise an extreme democracy, or a pure oligarchy; or a tyranny may grow out of either extreme—either out of the most rampant democracy, or out of an oligarchy; but it is not so likely to arise out of the middle constitutions and those akin to them. [. . . .] The mean condition of states is clearly best, for no other is free from faction; and where the middle class is large, there are least likely to be factions and dissensions. [. . . .]

The basis of a democratic state is liberty; which, according to the common opinion of men, can only be enjoyed in such a state—this they affirm to be the great end of every democracy. One principle of liberty is for all to rule and be ruled in turn, and indeed democratic justice is the application of numerical not proportionate equality; whence it follows that the majority must be supreme, and that whatever the majority approve must be the end and the just. Every citizen, it is said, must have equality, and therefore in a democracy the poor have more power than the rich, because there are more of them, and the will of the majority is supreme. This, then, is one note of liberty which all democrats affirm to be the principle of their state. Another is that a man should live as he likes. This, they say, is the privilege of a freeman, since, on the other hand, not to live as a man likes is the mark of a slave. This is the second characteristic of democracy, whence has arisen the claim of men to be ruled by none, if possible, or, if this is impossible, to rule and be ruled in turns; and so it contributes to the freedom based upon equality.

Such being our foundation and such the principle from which we start, the characteristics of democracy are as follows—the election of officers by all out of all; and that all should rule over each, and each in his turn over all; that the appointment to all offices, or to all but those which require experience and skill, should be made by lot; that no property qualification should be required for offices, or only a very low one; that a man should not hold the same office twice, or not often, or in the case of few except military offices: that the tenure of all offices, or of as many as possible, should be brief; that all men should sit in judgement, or that judges selected out of all should judge, in all matters, or in most and in the greatest and most important—such as the scrutiny of accounts, the constitution, and private contracts; that the assembly should be supreme over all causes, or at any rate over the most important, and the magistrates over none or only over a very few. Of all magistracies, a council is the most democratic when there is not the means of paying all the citizens, but when they are paid even this is robbed of its power, for the people then draw all cases to themselves, as I said in the previous discussion. The next characteristic of democracy is payment for services; assembly, law-courts, magistrates, everybody receives pay, when it is to be had; or when it is not to be had for all, then it is given to the law-courts and to the stated assemblies, to the council and to the magistrates, or at least to any of them who are compelled to have their meals together. And whereas oligarchy is characterized by birth, wealth, and education, the notes of democracy appear to be the opposite of these—low birth, poverty, mean employment. Another note is that no magistracy is perpetual, but if any such have survived some ancient change in the constitution it should be stripped of its power, and the holders should be elected by lot and no longer by vote. These are the points common to all democracies; but democracy and demos in their truest form are based upon the recognized principle of democratic justice, that all should count equally; for equality implies that the poor should have no more share in the government than the rich, and should not be the only rulers, but that all should rule equally according to their numbers. And in this way men think that they will secure equality and freedom in their state.

NICCOLÒ MACHIAVELLI, SELECTIONS FROM *THE DISCOURSES* (1531)

Desiring . . . to discuss the nature of the government of Rome, and to ascertain the accidental circumstances which brought it to its perfection, I say, as has been said before by many who have written of Governments, that of these there are three forms, known by the names Monarchy, Aristocracy, and Democracy, and that those who give its institutions to a State have recourse to one or other of these three, according as it suits their purpose. Other, and, as many have thought, wiser teachers, will have it, that there are altogether six forms of Government, three of them utterly bad, the other three good in themselves, but so readily corrupted that they too are apt to become hurtful. The good are the three above named; the bad, three others dependent upon these, and each so like that to which it is related, that it is easy to pass imperceptibly from the one to the other. For a Monarchy readily becomes a Tyranny, an Aristocracy an Oligarchy, while a Democracy tends to degenerate into Anarchy. So that if the founder of a State should establish, any one of these three forms of Government, he establishes it for a short time only, since no precaution he may take can prevent it from sliding into its contrary, by reason of the close resemblance which, in this case, the virtue bears to the vice.

These diversities in the form of Government spring up among men by chance. For in the beginning of the world, its inhabitants, being few in number, for a time lived scattered after the fashion of beasts; but afterwards, as they increased and multiplied, gathered themselves into societies, and, the better to protect themselves, began to seek who among them was the strongest and of the highest courage, to whom, making him their head, they rendered obedience. Next arose the knowledge of such things as are honourable and good, as opposed to those which are bad and shameful. For observing that when a man wronged his benefactor, hatred was universally felt for the one and sympathy for the other, and that the ungrateful were blamed, while those who showed gratitude were honoured, and reflecting that the wrongs they saw done to others might be done to themselves, to escape these they resorted to making laws and fixing punishments against any who should transgress them; and in this way grew the recognition of justice. Whence it came that afterwards, in choosing their rulers, men no longer looked about for the strongest, but for him who was the most prudent and the most just.

But, presently, when sovereignty grew to be hereditary, and no longer elective, hereditary sovereigns began to degenerate from their ancestors, and, quitting worthy courses, took up the notion that princes had nothing to do but to surpass the rest of the world in sumptuous display, and wantonness, and whatever else ministers to pleasure; so that the prince coming to be hated, and therefore to feel fear, and passing from fear to infliction of injuries, a tyranny soon sprang up. Forthwith there began movements to overthrow the prince, and plots and conspiracies against him, undertaken not by those who were weak, or afraid for themselves, but by such as being conspicuous for their birth, courage, wealth, and station, could not tolerate the shameful life of the tyrant. The multitude, following the lead of these powerful men, took up arms against the prince, and, he being got rid of, obeyed these others as their liberators who, on their part, holding in hatred the name of sole ruler, formed themselves into a government; and at first, while the recollection of past tyranny was still fresh, observed the laws they themselves made, and postponing personal advantage to the common welfare, administered affairs both publicly and privately with the utmost diligence and zeal. But this government passing, afterwards, to their descendants who, never having been taught in the school of Adversity, knew nothing of the vicissitudes of Fortune, these not choosing to rest content with mere civil equality, but abandoning themselves to avarice, ambition, and lust, converted, without respect to civil rights, what had been a government of the best into a government of the few; and so very soon met with the same fate as the tyrant.

For the multitude loathing its rulers, lent itself to any who ventured, in whatever way, to attack them; when some one man speedily arose who with the aid of the people overthrew them. But the recollection of the tyrant and of the wrongs suffered at his hands being still fresh in the minds of the people, who therefore felt no desire to restore the monarchy, they had recourse to a popular government, which they established on such a footing that neither king nor nobles had any place in it. And because all governments inspire respect at the first, this government also lasted for a while, but not for long, and seldom after the generation which brought it into existence had died out. For, suddenly, liberty passed into license, wherein neither private worth nor public authority was respected, but every one living as he liked, a thousand wrongs were done daily. Whereupon, whether driven by necessity, or on the suggestion of some wiser man among them and to escape anarchy, the people reverted to a monarchy, from which, step by step, in the manner and for the causes already assigned, they came round once more to license. For this is the circle revolving within which all States are and have been governed; although in the same State the same forms of Government rarely repeat themselves, because hardly any State can have such vitality as to pass through such a cycle more than once, and still hold together. For it may be expected that in some season of disaster, when a State must always be wanting in prudent counsels and in strength, it will become subject to some neighbouring and better-governed State; though assuming this not to happen, it might well pass for an indefinite period from one of these forms of government to another.

I say, then, that all these six forms of government are pernicious—the three good kinds, from their brief duration; the three bad, from their inherent badness. Wise legislators, therefore, knowing these defects, and avoiding each of these forms in its simplicity, have made choice of a form which shares in the qualities of all the first three, and which they judge to be more stable and lasting than any of them separately. For where we have a monarchy, an aristocracy, and a democracy existing together in the same city, each of the three serves as a check upon the other.

Among those who have earned special praise by devising a constitution of this nature, was Lycurgus, who, so framed the laws of Sparta as to assign their proper functions to kings, nobles, and commons; and in this way established a government, which, to his great glory and to the peace and tranquillity of his country, lasted for more than eight hundred years. The contrary, however, happened in the case, of Solon; who by the turn he gave to the institutions of Athens, created there a purely democratic government; of such brief duration, that he himself lived to witness the beginning of the despotism of Pisistratus. And although, forty years later, the heirs of Pisistratus were driven out, and Athens recovered her freedom, nevertheless because she reverted to the same form of government as had been established by Solon, she could maintain it for only a hundred years more; for though to preserve it, many ordinances were passed for repressing the ambition of the great and the turbulence of the people, against which Solon had not provided, still, since neither the monarchic nor the aristocratic element was given a place in her constitution, Athens, as compared with Sparta, had but a short life.

But let us now turn to Rome, which city, although she had no Lycurgus to give her from the first such a constitution as would preserve her long in freedom, through a series of accidents, caused by the contests between the commons and the senate, obtained by chance what the foresight of her founders failed to provide. So that Fortune, if she bestowed not her first favours on Rome, bestowed her second; because, although the original institutions of this city were defective, still they lay not outside the true path which could bring them to perfection. For Romulus and the other kin made many and good laws, and such as were not incompatible with freedom; but because they sought to found a kingdom and not a commonwealth, when the city became free many things were found wanting which in the interest of liberty it was necessary to supply, since these kings had not supplied them. And although the kings of Rome lost their sovereignty, . . . nevertheless those who drove them out, by at once creating two consuls to take their place, preserved in Rome the regal authority while banishing from it the regal name; so that as both senate and consuls were included in that republic, it in fact possessed two of the three elements above enumerated, to wit, the monarchic and the aristocratic.

It then only remained to assign its place to the popular element, and the Roman nobles growing insolent . . . the commons rose against them, when, not to lose the whole of their power, they were forced to concede a share to the people; while with the share which remained, the senate and consuls retained so much authority that they still held their own place in the republic. In this way the tribunes of the people came to be created, after whose creation the stability of the State was much augmented, since each of the three forms of government had now its due influence allowed it. And such was the good fortune of Rome that although her government passed from the kings to the nobles, and from these to the people, by the steps and for the reasons noticed above, still the entire authority of the kingly element was not sacrificed to strengthen the authority of the nobles, nor were the nobles divested of their authority to bestow it on the commons; but all three, blending together, made up a perfect State; which perfection . . . was reached through the dissensions of the commons and the senate. [. . . .]

Of the provisions made by wise founders of republics, one of the most necessary is for the creation of a guardianship of liberty; for according as this is placed in good or bad hands, the freedom of the State will be more or less lasting. And because in every republic we find the two parties of nobles and commons, the question arises, to which of these two this guardianship can most safely be entrusted. Among the Lacedaemonians of old, as now with the Venetians, it was placed in the hands of the nobles, but with the Romans it was vested in the commons. We have, therefore, to determine which of these States made the wiser choice. If we look to reasons, something is to be said on both sides of the question; though were we to look to results, we should have to pronounce in favour of the nobles, inasmuch as the liberty of Sparta and Venice has had a longer life than that of Rome.

As touching reasons, it may be pleaded for the Roman method, that they are most fit to have charge of a thing, who least desire to pervert it to their own ends. And, doubtless, if we examine the aims which the nobles and the commons respectively set before them, we shall find in the former a great desire to dominate, in the latter merely a desire not to be dominated over, and hence a greater attachment to freedom, since they have less to gain than the others by destroying it. Wherefore, when the commons are put forward as the defenders of liberty, they may be expected to take better care of it, and, as they have no desire to tamper with it themselves, to be less apt to suffer others to do so. [. . . .]

Though Rome had Romulus for her first founder, and as a daughter owed him her being and nurture, nevertheless, when the institutions of Romulus were seen by Heaven to be insufficient for so great a State, the Roman senate were moved to choose Numa Pompilius as his successor, that he might look to all matters which Romulus had neglected. He finding the people fierce and turbulent, and desiring with the help of the peaceful arts to bring them to order and obedience, called in the aid of religion as essential to the maintenance of civil society, and gave it such a form, that for many ages God was nowhere so much feared as in that republic. The effect of this was to render easy any enterprise in which the senate or great men of Rome thought fit to engage. And whosoever pays heed to an infinity of actions performed, sometimes by the Roman people collectively, often by single citizens, will see that esteeming the power of God beyond that of man, they dreaded far more to violate their oath than, to transgress the laws; as is clearly shown by the examples of Scipio and of Manlius Torquatus. For after the defeat of the Romans by Hannibal at Cannae, many citizens meeting together, resolved, in their terror and dismay, to abandon Italy and seek refuge in Sicily. But Scipio, getting word of this, went among them, and menacing them with his naked sword, made them swear never to abandon their country. Again, when Lucius Manlius was accused by the tribune Marcus Pomponius, before the day fixed for the trial, Titus Manlius, afterwards named Torquatus, son to Lucius, went to seek this Marcus, and threatening him with death if he did not withdraw the charge against his father, compelled him to swear compliance; and he, through fear, having sworn, kept his oath. In the first of these two instances, therefore, citizens whom love of their country and its laws could not have retained in Italy, were kept there by the oath forced upon them; and in the second, the tribune Marcus, to keep his oath, laid aside the hatred he bore the father, and overlooked the injury done him by the son, and his own dishonour. And this from no other cause than the religion which Numa had impressed upon this city.

And it will be plain to any one who carefully studies Roman History, how much religion helped in disciplining the army, in uniting the people, in keeping good men good, and putting bad men to shame; so that had it to be decided to which prince, Romulus or Numa, Rome owed the greater debt, I think the balance must turn in favour of Numa; for when religion is once established you may readily bring in arms; but where you have arms without religion it is not easy afterwards to bring in religion. [. . . .]

And as the observance of the ordinances of religion is the cause of the greatness of a State, so their neglect is the occasion of its decline; since a kingdom without the fear of God must either fall to pieces, or must be maintained by the fear of some prince who supplies that influence not supplied by religion. But since the lives of princes are short, the life of this prince, also, and with it his influence, must soon come to an end; whence it happens that a kingdom which rests wholly on the qualities of its prince, lasts for a brief time only; because these qualities, terminating with his life, are rarely renewed in his successor. [. . . .]

It follows, therefore, that the safety of a commonwealth or kingdom lies, not in its having a ruler who governs it prudently while he lives, but in having one who so orders things, that when he dies, the State may still maintain itself. [. . . .]

Doubtless, all the things of this world have a limit set to their duration; yet those of them the bodies whereof have not been suffered to grow disordered, but have been so cared for that either no change at all has been wrought in them, or, if any, a change for the better and not for the worse, will run that course which Heaven has in a general way appointed them. And since I am now speaking of mixed bodies, for States and Sects are so to be regarded, I say that for them these are wholesome changes which bring them back to their first beginnings.

Those States consequently stand surest and endure longest which, either by the operation of their institutions can renew themselves, or come to be renewed by accident apart from any design. Nothing, however, can be clearer than that unless thus renewed these bodies do not last. Now the way to renew them is, as I have said, to bring them back to their beginnings, since all beginnings of sects, commonwealths, or kingdoms must needs have in them a certain excellence, by virtue of which they gain their first reputation and make their first growth. But because in progress of time this excellence becomes corrupted, unless something be done to restore it to what it was at first, these bodies necessarily decay; for as the physicians tell us in speaking of the human body, *"Something or other is daily added which sooner or later will require treatment."*

As regards commonwealths, this return to the point of departure is brought about either by extrinsic accident or by intrinsic foresight. As to the first, we have seen how it was necessary that Rome should be taken by the Gauls, that being thus in a manner reborn, she might recover life and vigour, and resume the observances of religion and justice which she had suffered to grow rusted by neglect. This is well seen from those passages of Livius wherein he tells us that when the Roman army was sent forth against the Gauls, and again when tribunes were created with consular authority, no religious rites whatever were celebrated and wherein he further relates how the Romans not only failed to punish the three Fabii, who contrary to the law of nations had fought against the Gauls, but even clothed them with honour. For, from these instances, we may well infer that the rest of the wise ordinances instituted by Romulus, and the other prudent kings, had begun to be held of less account than they deserved, and less than was essential for the maintenance of good government.

And therefore it was that Rome was visited by this calamity from without, to the end that all her ordinances might be reformed, and the people taught that it behoved them not only to maintain religion and justice, but also to esteem their worthy citizens, and to prize their virtues beyond any advantages of which they themselves might seem to have been deprived at their instance. And this, we find, was just the effect produced. For no sooner was the city retaken, than all thé ordinances of the old religion were at once restored; the Fabii, who had fought in violation of the law of nations, were punished; and the worth and excellence of Camillus so fully recognized, that the senate and the whole people, laying all jealousies aside, once more committed to him the entire charge of public affairs.

It is necessary then, as I have said already, that where men dwell together in a regulated society, they be often reminded of those ordinances in conformity with which they ought to live, either by something inherent in these, or else by some external accident. A reminder is given in the former of these two ways, either by the passing of some law whereby the members of the society are brought to an account; or else by some man of rare worth arising among them, whose virtuous life and example have the same effect as a law. In a Commonwealth, accordingly, this end is served either by the virtues of some one of its citizens, or by the operation of its institutions. [. . . .]

Elsewhere I have shown that no ordinance is of such advantage to a commonwealth, as one which enforces poverty on its citizens. And although it does not appear what particular law it was that had this operation in Rome (especially since we know the agrarian law to have been stubbornly resisted), we find, as a fact, that four hundred years after the city was founded, great poverty still prevailed there; and may assume that nothing helped so much to produce this result as the knowledge that the path to honours and preferment was closed to none, and that merit was sought after wheresoever it was to be found; for this manner of conferring honours made riches the less courted. In proof whereof I shall cite one instance only.

When the consul Minutius was beset in his camp by the Equians, the Roman people were filled with such alarm lest their army should be destroyed, that they appointed a dictator, always their last stay in seasons of peril. Their choice fell on Lucius Quintius Cincinnatus, who at the time was living on his small farm of little more than four acres, which he tilled with his own hand. The story is nobly told by Titus Livius where he says: "*This is worth listening to by those who contemn all things human as compared with riches, and think that glory and excellence can have no place unless accompanied by lavish wealth.*" Cincinnatus, then, was ploughing in his little field, when there arrived from Rome the messengers sent by the senate to tell him he had been made dictator, and inform him of the dangers which threatened the Republic. Putting on his gown, he hastened to Rome, and getting together an army, marched to deliver Minutius. But when he had defeated and spoiled the enemy, and released Minutius, he would not suffer the army he had rescued to participate in the spoils, saying, "*I will not have you share in the plunder of those to whom you had so nearly fallen a prey.*" Minutius he deprived of his consulship, and reduced to be a subaltern, in which rank he bade him remain till he had learned how to command. And before this he had made Lucius Tarquininus, although forced by his poverty to serve on foot, his master of the knights.

JEAN-JACQUES ROUSSEAU, SELECTIONS FROM *THE SOCIAL CONTRACT* (1762)

The Social Compact

I suppose men to have reached the point at which the obstacles in the way of their preservation in the state of nature show their power of resistance to be greater than the resources at the disposal of each individual for his maintenance in that state. That primitive condition can then subsist no longer; and the human race would perish unless it changed its manner of existence.

But as men cannot engender new forces, but only unite and direct existing ones, they have no other means of preserving themselves than the formation, by aggregation, of a sum of forces great enough to overcome the resistance. These they have to bring into play by means of a single motive power, and cause to act in concert.

This sum of forces can arise only where several persons come together: but, as the force and liberty of each man are the chief instruments of his self-preservation, how can he pledge them without harming his own interests, and neglecting the care he owes to himself? This difficulty, in its bearing on my present subject, may be stated in the following terms:

'The problem is to find a form of association which will defend and protect with the whole common force the person and goods of each associate, and in which each, while uniting himself with all, may still obey himself alone, and remain as free as before.' This is the fundamental problem of which the social contract provides the solution.

The clauses of this contract are so determined by the nature of the act that the slightest modification would make them vain and ineffective; so that, although they have perhaps never been formally set forth, they are everywhere the same and everywhere tacitly admitted and recognized, until, on the violation of the social compact, each regains his original rights and resumes his natural liberty, while losing the conventional liberty in favour of which he renounced it.

These clauses, properly understood, may be reduced to one—the total alienation of each associate, together with all his rights, to the whole community; for, in the first place, as each gives himself absolutely, the conditions are the same for all; and, this being so, no one has any interest in making them burdensome to others.

Moreover, the alienation being without reserve, the union is as perfect as it can be, and no associate has anything more to demand: for, if the individuals retained certain rights, as there would be no common superior to decide between them and the public, each, being on one point his own judge, would ask to be so on all; the state of nature would thus continue, and the association would necessarily become inoperative or tyrannical.

Finally, each man, in giving himself to all, gives himself to nobody; and as there is no associate over which he does not acquire the same right as he yields others over himself, he gains an equivalent for everything he loses, and an increase of force for the preservation of what he has.

If then we discard from the social compact what is not of its essence, we shall find that it reduces itself to the following terms:

'*Each of us puts his person and all his power in common under the supreme direction of the general will, and, in our corporate capacity, we receive each member as an indivisible part of the whole.*'

At once, in place of the individual personality of each contracting party, this act of association creates a corporate and collective body, composed of as many members as the assembly contains voters, and receiving from this act its unity, its common identity, its life, and its will. This public person, so formed by the union of all other persons, formerly took the name of *city*[8] and now takes that of *Republic* or *body politic;* it is called by its members *State* when passive, *Sovereign* when active, and *Power* when compared with others like itself. Those who are associated in it take collectively the name of *people,* and severally are called *citizens,* as sharing in the sovereign authority, and *subjects,* as being under the laws of the State. But these terms are often confused and taken one for another: it is enough to know how to distinguish them when they are being used with precision. [. . . .]

Whether the General Will Is Infallible

[T]he general will is always upright and always tends to the public advantage, but it does not follow that the deliberations of the people always have the same rectitude. Our will is always for our own good, but we do not always see what that is; the people is never corrupted, but it is often deceived, and on such occasions only does it seem to will what is bad.

There is often a great deal of difference between the will of all and the general will; the latter considers only the common interest, while the former takes private interest into account, and is no more than a sum of particular wills: but take away from these same wills the pluses and minuses that cancel one another[9] and the general will remains as the sum of the differences.

If, when the people, being furnished with adequate information, held its deliberations, the citizens had no communication one with another, the grand total of the small differences would always give the general will, and the decision would always be good. But when intrigues arise, and partial associations are formed at the expense of the great association, the will of each of these associations becomes general in relation to its members, while it remains particular in relation to the State: it may then be said that there are no longer as many votes as there are men, but only as many as there are associations. The differences become less numerous and give a less general result. Lastly, when one of these associations is so great as to prevail over all the rest, the result is no longer a sum of small differences, but a single difference; in this case there is no longer a general will, and the opinion which prevails is purely particular.

It is therefore essential, if the general will is to be able to make itself known, that there should be no partial society in the state and that each citizen should express only his own opinion:[10] which was indeed the sublime and unique system established by the great Lycurgus. But if there are partial societies, it is best to have as many as possible and to prevent them from being unequal, as was done by Solon, Numa, and Servius. These precautions are the only ones that can guarantee that the general will shall be always enlightened, and that the people shall in no way deceive itself. [. . . .]

The Legislator

In order to discover the rules of society best suited to nations, a superior intelligence beholding all the passions of men without experiencing any of them would be needed. This intelligence would have to be wholly unrelated to our nature, while knowing it through and through; its happiness would have to be independent of us, and yet ready to occupy itself with ours; and lastly, it would have, in the march of time, to look forward to a distant glory, and, working in one century, to be able to enjoy in the next.[11] It would take gods to give men laws.

What Caligula argued from the facts, Plato, in the dialogue called the *Politicus*, argued in defining the civil or kingly man, on the basis of right. But if great princes are rare, how much more so are great legislators! The former have only to follow the pattern which the latter have to lay down. The legislator is the engineer who invents the machine, the prince merely the mechanic who sets it up and makes it go. 'At the birth of societies,' says Montesquieu, 'the rulers of Republics establish institutions, and afterwards the institutions mould the rulers.'

He who dares to undertake the making of a people's institutions ought to feel himself capable, so to speak, of changing human nature, of transforming each individual, who is by himself a complete and solitary whole, into part of a greater whole from which he in a manner receives his life and being; of altering man's constitution for the purpose of strengthening it; and of substituting a partial and moral existence for the physical and independent existence nature has conferred on us all. He must, in a word, take away from man his own resources and give him instead new ones alien to him, and incapable of being made use of without the help of other men. The more completely these natural resources are annihilated, the greater and the more lasting are those which he acquires, and the more stable and perfect the new institutions; so that if each citizen is nothing and can do nothing without the rest, and the resources acquired by the whole are equal or superior to the aggregate of the resources of all the individuals, it may be said that legislation is at the highest possible point of perfection. [. . . .]

He, therefore, who draws up the laws has, or should have, no right of legislation, and the people cannot, even if it wishes, deprive itself of this incommunicable right, because, according to the fundamental compact, only the general will can bind the individuals, and there can be no assurance that a particular will is in conformity with the general will, until it has been put to the free vote of the people. This I have said already; but it is worth while to repeat it.

Thus in the task of legislation we find together two things which appear to be incompatible: an enterprise too difficult for human powers, and, for its execution, an authority that is no authority.

There is a further difficulty that deserves attention. Wise men, if they try to speak their language to the common herd instead of its own, cannot possibly make themselves understood. There are a thousand kinds of ideas which it is impossible to translate into popular language. Conceptions that are too general and objects that are too remote are equally out of its range: each individual, having no taste for any other plan of government than that which suits his particular interest, finds it difficult to realize the advantages he might hope to draw from the continual privations good laws impose. For a young people to be able to relish sound principles of political theory and follow the fundamental rules of statecraft, the effect would have to become the cause; the social spirit, which should be created by these institutions, would have to preside over their very foundation; and men would have to be before law what they should become by means of law. The legislator therefore, being unable to appeal to either force or reason, must have recourse to an authority of a different order, capable of constraining without violence and persuading without convincing.

This is what has, in all ages, compelled the fathers of nations to have recourse to divine intervention and credit the gods with their own wisdom, in order that the peoples, submitting to the laws of the State as to those of nature, and recognizing the same power in the formation of the city as in that of man, might obey freely, and bear with docility the yoke of the public happiness.

This sublime reason, far above the range of the common herd, is that whose decisions the legislator puts into the mouth of the immortals, in order to constrain by divine authority those whom human prudence could not move.[12] But it is not anybody who can make the gods speak, or get himself believed when he proclaims himself their interpreter. The great soul of the legislator is the only miracle that can prove his mission. Any man may grave tablets of stone, or buy an oracle, or feign secret intercourse with some divinity, or train a bird to whisper in his ear, or find other vulgar ways of imposing on the people. He whose knowledge goes no further may perhaps gather round him a band of fools; but he will never found an empire, and his extravagances will quickly perish with him. Idle tricks form a passing tie; only wisdom can make it lasting. The Judaic law, which still subsists, and that of the child of Ishmael, which, for ten centuries, has ruled half the world, still proclaim the great men who laid them down; and, while the pride of philosophy or the blind spirit of faction sees in them no more than lucky impostures, the true political theorist admires, in the institutions they set up, the great and powerful genius which presides over things made to endure.

We should not. . .conclude from this that politics and religion have among us a common object, but that, in the first periods of nations, the one is used as an instrument for the other.

The People

As, before putting up a large building, the architect surveys and sounds the site to see if it will bear the weight, the wise legislator does not begin by laying down laws good in themselves, but by investigating the fitness of the people, for which they are destined, to receive them. Plato refused to legislate for the Arcadians and the Cyrenaeans, because he knew that both peoples were rich and could not put up with equality; and good laws and bad men were found together in Crete, because Minos had inflicted discipline on a people already burdened with vice.

A thousand nations have achieved earthly greatness, that could never have endured good laws; even such as could have endured them could have done so only for a very brief period of their long history. Most peoples, like most men, are docile only in youth; as they grow old they become incorrigible. When once customs have become established and prejudices inveterate, it is dangerous and useless to attempt their reformation; the people, like the foolish and cowardly patients who rave at sight of the doctor, can no longer bear that any one should lay hands on its faults to remedy them.

There are indeed times in the history of States when, just as some kinds of illness turn men's heads and make them forget the past, periods of violence and revolutions do to peoples what these crises do to individuals: horror of the past takes the place of forgetfulness, and the State, set on fire by civil wars, is born again, so to speak, from its ashes, and takes on anew, fresh from the jaws of death, the vigour of youth. Such were Sparta at the time of Lycurgus, Rome after the Tarquins, and, in modern times, Holland and Switzerland after the expulsion of the tyrants.

But such events are rare; they are exceptions, the cause of which is always to be found in the particular constitution of the State concerned. They cannot even happen twice to the same people, for it can make itself free as long as it remains barbarous, but not when the civic impulse has lost its vigour. Then disturbances may destroy it, but revolutions cannot mend it: it needs a master, and not a liberator. Free peoples, be mindful of this maxim: 'Liberty may be gained, but can never be recovered.' [. . . .]

Deputies or Representatives

As soon as public service ceases to be the chief business of the citizens, and they would rather serve with their money than with their persons, the State is not far from its fall. When it is necessary to march out to war, they pay troops and stay at home: when it is necessary to meet in council, they name deputies and stay at home. By reason of idleness and money, they end by having soldiers to enslave their country and representatives to sell it.

It is through the hustle of commerce and the arts, through the greedy self-interest of profit, and through softness and love of amenities that personal services are replaced by money payments. Men surrender a part of their profits in order to have time to increase them at leisure. Make gifts of money, and you will not be long without chains. The word 'finance' is a slavish word, unknown in the city-state. In a country that is truly free, the citizens do everything with their own arms and nothing by means of money; so far from paying to be exempted from their duties, they would even pay for the privilege of fulfilling them themselves. I am far from taking the common view: I hold enforced labour to be less opposed to liberty than taxes.

The better the constitution of a State is, the more do public affairs encroach on private in the minds of the citizens. Private affairs are even of much less importance, because the aggregate of the common happiness furnishes a greater proportion of that of each individual, so that he has less need to seek it in private interests. In a well-ordered city every man files to the assemblies: under a bad government no one cares to stir a step to get to them, because no one is interested in what happens there, because it is foreseen that the general will will not prevail, and lastly because domestic cares are all-absorbing. Good laws lead to the making of better ones; bad ones bring about worse. As soon as any man says of the affairs of State *What does it matter to me?* the State may be given up for lost.

The lukewarmness of patriotism, the activity of private interest, the vastness of States, conquest, and the abuse of government suggested the method of having deputies or representatives of the people in the national assemblies. These are what, in some countries, man have presumed to call the Third Estate. Thus the individual interest of two orders is put first, and second; the public interest occupies only the third place.

Sovereignty, for the same reason as it makes it inalienable, cannot be represented; it lies essentially in the general will, and will does not admit of representation: it is either the same, or other, there is no intermediate possibility. The deputies of the people, therefore, are not and cannot be its representatives: they are merely its stewards, and can carry through no definitive acts. Every law the people has not ratified in person is null and void—is in fact, not a law. The people of England regards itself as free; but it is greatly mistaken; it is free only during the election of members of parliament. As soon as they are elected, slavery overtakes it, and it is nothing. The use it makes of the short moments of liberty it enjoys shows indeed that it deserves to lose them.

The idea of representation is modern; it comes to us from feudal government, from that iniquitous and absurd system which degrades humanity and dishonours the name of man. In ancient republics and even in monarchies, the people never had representatives; the word itself was unknown. It is very singular that in Rome, where the tribunes were so sacrosanct, it was never imagined that they could usurp the functons of the people, and that in the midst of so great a multitiude they never attempted to pass on their own authority a single *plebiscitum.* We can however, form an idea of the difficulties caused sometimes by the people being so numerous, from what happened in the time of the Gracchi, when some of the citizens had to cast their votes from the roofs of buildings.

Where right and liberty are everything, disadvantages count for nothing. Among this wise people everything was given its just value, its lictors were allowed to do what its tribunes would never have dared to attempt; for it had no fear that its lictors would try to represent it.

To explain, however, in what way the tribunes did sometimes represent it, it is enough to conceive how the government represents the Sovereign. Law being purely the declaration of the general will, it is clear that, in the exercise of the legislative power, the people cannot be represented; but in that of the executive power, which is only the force that is applied to give the law effect, it both can and should be represented. We thus see that if we looked closely into the matter we should find that very few nations have any laws. However that may be, it is certain that the tribunes, possessing no executive power, could never represent the Roman people by right of the powers entrusted to them, but only by usurping those of the senate.

In Greece, all that the people had to do, it did for itself; it was constantly assembled in the public square. The Greeks lived in a mild climate; they had no natural greed; slaves did their work for them; their great concern was with liberty. Lacking the same advantages, how can you preserve the same rights? Your severer climates add to your needs; for half the year your public squares are uninhabitable; the flatness of your languages unfits them for being heard in the open air; you sacrifice more for profit than for liberty, and fear slavery less than poverty.

What then? Is liberty maintained only by the help of slavery? It may be so. Extremes meet. Everything that is not in the course of nature has its disadvantages, civil society most of all. There are some unhappy circumstances in which we can only keep our liberty at others' expense, and where the citizen can be perfectly free only when the slave is most a slave. Such was the case with Sparta. As for you, modern peoples, you have no slaves, but you are slaves yourselves; you pay for their liberty with your own. It is in vain that you boast of this preference; I find in it more cowardice than humanity.

I do not mean by all this that it is necessary to have slaves, or that the right of slavery is legitimate: I am merely giving the reasons why modern peoples, believing themselves to be free, have representatives, while ancient peoples had none. In any case, the moment a people allows itself to be represented, it is no longer free: it no longer exists.

All things considered, I do not see that it is possible henceforth for the Sovereign to preserve among us the exercise of its rights, unless the city is very small. [. . . .]

How to Check the Usurpations of Government

[T]he institution of government is not a contract, but a law; that the depositories of the executive power are not the people's masters, but its officers; that it can set them up and pull them down when it likes; that for them there is no question of contract, but of obedience; and that in taking charge of the functions the State imposes on them they are doing no more than fulfilling their duty as citizens, without having the remotest right to argue about the conditions.

When therefore the people sets up an hereditary government, whether it be monarchical and confined to one family, or aristocratic and confined to a class, what it enters into is not an undertaking; the administration is given a provisional form, until the people chooses to order it otherwise.

It is true that such changes are always dangerous, and that the established government should never be touched except when it comes to be incompatible with the public good; but the circumspection this involves is a maxim of policy and not a rule of right, and the State is no more bound to leave civil authority in the hands of its rulers than military authority in the hands of its generals.

It is also true that it is impossible to be too careful to observe, in such cases, all the formalities necessary to distinguish a regular and legitimate act from a seditious tumult, and the will of a whole people from the clamour of a faction. Here above all no more weight should be given to invidious cases than that which is demanded by the strictest interpretation of the law. From this obligation the prince derives a great advantage in preserving his power despite the people, without its being possible to say he has usurped it; for, seeming to avail himself only of his rights, he finds it very easy to extend them, and to prevent, under the pretext of keeping the peace, assemblies that are destined to the reestablishment of order; with the result that he takes advantage of a silence he does not allow to be broken, or of irregularities he causes to be committed, to assume that he has the support of those whom fear prevents from speaking, and to punish those who dare to speak. Thus it was that the decemvirs, first elected for one year and then kept on in office for a second, tried to perpetuate their power by forbidding the comitia to assemble, and by this easy method every government in the world, once clothed with the public power, sooner or later usurps the sovereign authority.

The periodical assemblies of which I have already spoken are designed to prevent or postpone this calamity, above all when they need no formal summoning; for in that case, the prince cannot stop them without openly declaring himself a law-breaker and an enemy of the State.

The opening of these assemblies, whose sole object is the maintenance of the social treaty, should always take the form of putting two propositions that may not be suppressed, which should be voted on separately.

The first is: 'Does it please the Sovereign to preserve the present form of government?' The second is: 'Does it please the people to leave its administration in the hands of those who are actually in charge of it?'

I am here assuming what I think I have shown; that there is in the State no fundamental law that cannot be revoked, not excluding the social compact itself; for if all the citizens assembled of one accord to break the compact, it is impossible to doubt that it would be very legitimately broken. Grotious even thinks that each man can renounce his membership of his own State, and recover his natural liberty and his goods on leaving the country.[13] It would be indeed absurd if all the citizens in assembly could not do what each can do by himself.

JOHN WINTHROP, SELECTION FROM "A MODELL OF CHRISTIAN CHARITY" (1630)

A Modell Hereof

God Almightie in his most holy and wise providence hath soe disposed of the Condicion of mankinde, as in all times some must be rich some poore, some highe and eminent in power and dignitie; others meane and in subjeccion.

The Reason Hereof

1. REAS: First, to hold conformity with the rest of his workes, being delighted to shewe forthe the glory of his wisdome in the variety and differance of the Creatures and the glory of his power, in ordering all these differences for the preservacion and good of the whole, and the glory of his greatnes that as it is the glory of princes to have many officers, soe this great King will have many Stewards counting himselfe more honoured in dispenceing his guifts to man by man, then if hee did it by his owne immediate hand.

2. REAS: Secondly, That he might have the more occasion to manifest the worke of his Spirit: first, upon the wicked in moderateing and restraineing them: soe that the riche and mighty should not eate upp the poore, nor the poore, and dispised rise upp against theire superiours, and shake off theire yoake: 2ly in the regenerate in exerciseing his graces in them, as in the greate ones, theire love mercy, gentlenes, temperance etc., in the poore and inferiour sorte, theire faithe patience, obedience etc:

3. REAS: Thirdly, That every man might have need of other, and from hence they might be all knitt more nearly together in the Bond of brotherly affeccion; from hence it appears plainely that noe man is made more honourable than another or more wealthy etc., out of any perticuler and singuler respect to himselfe but for the glory of his Creator and the Common good of the Creature. Man; Therefore God still reserves the propperty of these guifts to himselfe as Zech. 16:17. he there calls wealthe his gold and his silver etc. Prov. 3:9, he claimes theire service as his due[.] honour the Lord with thy riches etc. . . . There is likewise a double Lawe by which wee are regulated in our conversacion one towardes another: in both the former respects, the lawe of nature and the lawe of grace, or the morrall lawe or the lawe of the gospell, to omitt the rule of Justice as not propperly belonging to this purpose otherwise then it may fall into consideracion in some perticuler Cases; By the first of these lawes man as he was enabled soe withall [is] commaunded to love his neighbour as himselfe[.] upon this ground stands all the precepts of the morrall lawe, which concernes our dealings with men. To apply this to the works of mercy this lawe requires two things[,] first that every man afford his help to another in every want or distresse. Secondly, That hee performe this out of the same affeccion, which makes him carefull of his owne good according to that of our Saviour Math. [7:12] Whatsoever ye would that men should doe to you. This was practised by Abraham and Lott in entertaineing the Angells and the old man of Gibea.

The Lawe of Grace or the Gospell hath some differance from the former as in these respectes first the lawe of nature was given to man in the estate of innocency; this of the gospell in the estate of regeneracy: 2ly, the former propounds one man to another, as the same fleshe and Image of God, this as a brother in Christ allsoe, and in the Communion of the same spirit and soe teacheth us to put a difference betweene Christians and others. Doe good to all especially to the household of faith [Gal. 6:10]; upon this ground the Israelites were to putt a difference betweene the brethren of such as were strangers though not of the Canaanites. 3ly. The Lawe of nature could give noe rules for dealeing with enemies for all to be considered as freinds in the estate of innocency, but the Gospell commaunds love to an enemy. proofe. If thine Enemic hunger feede him; Love your Enemies doe good to them that hate you Math. 5:44.

This Laawe of the Gospell propoundes likewise a difference of seasons and occasions: there is a time when a christian must sell all and give to the poore as they did in the Apostles times. There is a tyme allsoe when a christian (though they give not all yet) must give beyond theire abillity as they of Macedonia Cor. 2:6. likewise community of perills calls for extraordinary liberallity and soe doth Community in some speciall service for the Churche. Lastly, when there is noe other meanes whereby our Christian brother may be releived in this distresse wee must help him beyond our ability, rather than tempt God, in putting him upon help by miraculous or extraordinary meanes.

This duty of mercy is exercised in the kindes, Giveing, lending, and forgiveing. . . .

Question: What rule must wee observe in lending?

Answer: Thou must observe whether thy brother hath present or probable, or possible meanes of repayeing thee, if ther be none of these, thou must give him according to his necessity, rather than lend him as hee requires: if he hath present meanes of repayeing thee, thou art to looke at him, not as an Act of mercy, but by way of Commerce; wherein thou arte to walke by the rule of Justice, but, if his meanes of repayeing thee be onely probable or possible then is hee an object of thy mercy thou must lend him, though there be danger of looseing it Deut. 15:7. If any of thy brethren be poore etc. thou shalt lend him sufficient that men might not shift off this duty by the apparent hazzard, he tells them that though the Yeare of Jubile were at hand (when he must remitt it., if hee were not able to repay it before) yet he must lend him and that chearefully; it may not greive thee to give him (saith hee) and because some might object, why soe I should soone impoverishe my selfe and my family, he adds with all thy Worke etc. for our Saviour Math. 5:42. From him that would borrow of thee turne not away. [. . . .]

The diffinition which the Scripture gives us of love is this Love is the bond of perfection [Col. 3:14]. First, it is a bond, or ligament. 2ly, it makes the worke perfect. There is noe body but consistes of partes and that which knitts these partes together gives the body its perfeccion, because it makes each parte soe contiguous to other as thereby they doe mutually participate with cache other, both in strengthe and infirmity in pleasure and paine, to instance in the most perfect of all bodies, Christ and his church make one body: the severall parties of this body considered aparte before they were united were as disproportionate and as much disordering as soe many contrary quallities or elements but when christ comes and by his spirit and love knitts all these partes to himselfe and each to other, it become the most perfect and best proportioned body in the world Eph. 4:16. Christ by whome all the body being knitt together by every ioynt for the furniture thereof according to the effectuall power which is in the measure of every perfeccion of partes a glorious body without spott or wrinckle the ligaments hereof being Christ or his love for Christ is love 1 John 4:8. Soe this definition is right. Love is the bond of perfeccion.

From hence wee may frame these Conclusions.

1. First all true Christians are of one body in Christ 1. Cor. 12:12–13. 17. [27.] Ye are the body of Christ. [. . . .]
2ly. The ligamentes of this body which knitt together are love.
3ly. Noe body can be perfect which wants its propper ligamentes.
4ly. All the partes of this body being thus united are made soe contiguous in a speciall relacion as they must needes partake of each others strength and infirmity, ioy, and sorrowe, weale and woe. 1. Cor. 12:26. If one member suffers all suffer with it, if one be in honour, all reioyce with it.
5ly. This sensiblenes and Sympathy of each others Condicions will necessarily infuse into each parte a native desire and endeavour, to strengthen defend preserve and comfort the other.

To insist a little on this Conclusion being the product of all the former the truthe hereof will appeare both by precept and patterne i. John 3:10. yee ought to lay downe your lives for the brethren Gal. 6:2. beare ye one anothers burthens and soe fulfill the lawe of Christ. . . .

The next consideracion is how this love comes to be wrought; Adam in his first estate was a perfect modell of mankinde in all theire generacions, and in him this love was perfected in regard of the habit, but Adam Rent in himselfe from his Creator, rent all his posterity allsoe one from another, whence it comes that every man is home with this principle in him, to love and seeke himselfe onely and thus a man continueth till Christ comes and takes possession of the soule, and infuseth another principle of love to God and our brother, and this latter haveing continuall supply from Christ, as the head and roote by which hee is united get the predominency in the soule, soe by little and little expells the former 1 John 4:7. love cometh of god and every one that loveth is borne of god, soe that this love is the fruite of the new birthe, and none can have it but the new Creature, now when this quality is thus formed in the soules of men it workes like the Spirit upon the drie bones [Zech 37] bone came to bone, it gathers together the scattered bones or perfect old man Adam and knitts them into one body againe in Christ whereby a man is become againe a liveing soule. [. . . .]

It rests now to make some application of this discourse by the present designe which gave the occasion of writeing of it. Herein are 4 things to be propounded: first the persons, 2ly, the worke, 3ly, the end, 4ly the meanes.

1. For the persons, wee are a Company professing our selves fellow members of Christ, In which respect onely though wee were absent from eache other many miles, and had our ilmploymentes as farre distant, yet wee ought to account our selves knitt together by this bond of love, and live in the exercise of it, if wee would have comforte of our being in Christ, this was notorious in the practise of the Christians in former times. . . .
2ly. For the Worke wee have in hand, it is by a mutuall consent through a speciall over-ruleing providence, and a more then an ordinary approbation of the Churches of Christ to seeke out a place of Cohabitation and Consorteshipp under a due forme of Government both civill and ecclesiasticall. In such cases as this the care of the publique must oversway all private respects, by which not onely conscience, but meare Civill pollicy doth binde us; for it is a true rule that perticuler Estates cannott subsist in the ruine of the publique.

3ly. The end is to improve our lives to doe more service to the Lord the comforte and encrease of the body of christe whereof wee are members that our selves and posterity may be the better preserved from the Common corrupcions of this evill world to serve the Lord and worke out our Salvacion under the power and purity of his holy Ordinances.

4ly. For the meanes whereby this must bee effected, they are 2fold, a Conformity with the worke and end wee aime at, these wee see are extraordinary, therefore wee must not content our selves with usuall ordinary meanes whatsoever wee did or ought to have done when wee lived in England, the same must wee doe and more allsoe where wee goe; That which the most in theire Churches maineteine as a truthe in profession onely, wee must bring into familiar and constant practise, as in this duty of love wee must love brotherly without dissimulation, wee must love one another with a pure hearte fervently wee must beare one anothers burtheens, wee must not looke onely on our owne things, but allsoe on the things of our brethren, neither must wee think that the lord will beare with such faileings at our hands as hee dothe from those among whome wee have lived. [. . . .]

When God gives a speciall Commission he lookes to have it strictly observed in every Article. . . . [W]ee are entered into Covenant with him for this worke, wee have taken out a Commission. the Lord hath given us leave to drawe our owne Articles wee have professed to enterprise these Accions upon these and these ends, we have hereupon besought him of favour and blessing; Now if the Lord shall please to heare us, and bring us in peace to the place wee desire, then hath hee ratified this Covenant and sealed our Commission, [and] will expect a strickt performance of the Articles contained in it, but if wee shall neglect the observacion of these Articles which are the ends wee have propounded, and dissembling with our God, shall fall to embrace this present world and prosecute our carnall intencions, seekeing great things for our selves and our posterity, the Lord will surely breake out in wrathe against us be revenged of such a periured people and make us knowe the price of the breache of such a Covenant.

Now the onely way to avoyde this shipwracke and to provide for our posterity is to followe the Counsell of Micah, to doe Justly, to love mercy, to walke humbly with our God, for this end wee must be knitt together in this worke as one man, wee must entertainee each other in brotherly Affeccion, wee must be willing to abridge our selves of our superfluities, for the supply of others necessities, wee must uphold a familiar Commerce together in all meekenes, gentlenes, patience and liberallity, wee must delight in eache other, make others Condicions our owne reioyce together, mourne together, labour, and suffer together, allwayes haveing before our eyes our Commission and Community in the worke, our Community as members of the same body, soe shall wee keepe the unitie of the spirit in the bond of peace, the Lord will be our God and delight to dwell among us, as his owne people and will commaund a blessing upon us in all our wayes, soe that wee shall see much more of his wisdome power goodnes and truthe then formerly wee have beene acquainted with, wee shall finde that the God of Israel is among us. When tenn of us shall be able to resist a thousand of our enemies, when hee shall make us a prause and glory, that men shall say of succeeding plantacions: the lord make it like that of New England; for wee must Consider that wee shall be as a Citty upon a Hill, the Eies of all people are upoon us; soe that if wee shall deale falsely with our god in this worke wee have undertaken and soe cause him to withdrawe his present help from us, wee shall be made a story and a by-word through the world, wee shall open the mouthes of enemies to speake evill of the wayes of god and all professours for Gods sake; wee shall shame the faces of many of gods worthy servants, and cause theire prayers to be turned into Cursses upon us till wee be consumed out of the good land whether wee are goeing; And to shutt upp this Discourse with that ex- hortacion of Moses that faithfull servant of the Lord in his last farewell to Israeli Deut. 30: [15–19]. Beloved there is now sett before us life, and good, deathe and evill in that wee are Commaunded this day to love the Lord our God, and to love one another to walke in his wayes and to keepe his Commaundements and his Ordinance, and his lawes, and the Arti- cles of our Covenant with him that wee may live and be multiplyed, and that the Lord our God may blesse us in the land whether wee goe to possesse it: But if our heartes shall turne away soe that wee will not obey, but shall be seduced and worshipp other Gods our pleas- ures, and proffitts, and serve them; it is propounded unto us this day, wee shall surely per- ishe out of the good Land whether wee passe over this vast Sea to possesse it;

> Therefore lett us choose life,
> that wee, and our Seede,
> may live; by obeying his
> voyce, and cleaveing to him,
> for hee is our life, and
> our prosperity.

HORACE MANN, SELECTION FROM "THE NECESSITY OF EDUCATION IN A REPUBLICAN GOVERNMENT" (1839)

It is a truism, that free institutions multiply human energies. A chained body cannot do much harm; a chained mind can do as little. In a despotic government, the human faculties are be- numbed and paralyzed; in a Republic, they glow with an intense life, and burst forth with un- controllable impetuosity. In the former, they are circumscribed and straitened in their range of action; in the latter, they have "ample room and verge enough," and may rise to glory or plunge into ruin. Amidst universal ignorance, there cannot be such wrong notions about right, as there may be in a community partially enlightened; and false conclusions which have been reasoned out, are infinitely worse than blind impulses.

To demonstrate the necessity of education in our government, I shall not attempt to de- rive my proofs from the history of other Republics. Such arguments are becoming stale. Be- sides, there are so many points of difference between our own political institutions, and those of any other government calling itself free, which has ever existed, that the objector perpetu- ally eludes or denies the force of our reasoning, by showing some want of analogy between the cases presented.

I propose, therefore, on this occasion, not to adduce, as proofs, what has been true only in past times; but what is true, at the present time, and must always continue to be true. I shall rely, not on precedents, but on the nature of things; and draw my arguments less from history than from humanity.

Now it is undeniable that, with the possession of certain higher faculties—common to all mankind—whose proper cultivation will bear us upward to hitherto undiscovered re- gions of prosperity and glory, we possess, also, certain lower faculties or propensities— equally common—whose improper indulgence leads, inevitably, to tribulation, and anguish, and ruin. The propensities to which I refer, seem indispensable to our temporal existence, and if restricted within proper limits, they are promotive of our enjoyment; but, beyond those limits, they work dishonor and infatuation, madness and despair. As servants, they are indispensable; as masters, they torture as well as tyrannize. Now despotic and arbitrary governments have dwarfed and crippled the powers of doing evil as much as the powers of doing good; but a republican government, from the very fact of its freedom, un-reins their speed, and lets loose their strength. It is justly alleged against despotisms, that they fetter, mutilate, almost extinguish the noblest powers of the human soul; but there is a *per contra* to this, for which we have not given them credit—they circumscribe the ability to do the greatest evil, as well as to do the greatest good.

My proposition, therefore, is simply this—If republican institutions do wake up unexampled energies in the whole mass of a people, and give them implements of unexampled power wherewith to work out their will; then these same institutions ought also to confer upon that people unexampled wisdom and rectitude. If these institutions give greater scope and impulse to the lower order of faculties belonging to the human mind, then, they must also give more authoritative control, and more skillful guidance to the higher ones. If they multiply temptations, they must fortify against them. If they quicken the activity and enlarge the sphere of the appetites and passions, they must, at least in an equal ration, establish the authority and extend the jurisdiction of reason and conscience. In a word, we must not add to the impulsive, without also adding to the regulating forces.

If we maintain institutions, which bring us within the action of new and unheard-of powers, without taking any corresponding measures for the government of those powers, we shall perish by the very instruments prepared for our happiness.

The truth has been so often asserted, that there is no security for a republic but in morality and intelligence, that a repetition of it seems hardly in good taste. But all permanent blessings being founded on permanent truths, a continued observance of the truth is the condition of a continued enjoyment of the blessing. I know we are often admonished that, without intelligence and virtue, as a chart and a compass, to direct us in our untried political voyage, we shall perish in the first storm; but I venture to add that, without these qualities, we shall not wait for a storm—we cannot weather a calm. If the sea is as smooth as glass we shall founder, for we are in a stoneboat. Unless these qualities pervade the general head and the general heart, not only will republican institutions vanish from amongst us, but the words *prosperity* and *happiness* will become obsolete. And all this may be affirmed, not from historical examples merely, but from the very constitution of our nature. We are created and brought into life with a set of innate, organic dispositions or propensities, which a free government rouses and invigorates, and which, if not bridled and tamed, by our actually seeing the eternal laws of justice, as plainly as we can see the sun in the heavens—and by our actually feeling the sovereign sentiment of duty, as plainly as we feel the earth beneath our feet—will hurry us forward into regions populous with every form of evil. [. . . .]

From the accursed thirst for gold have come the felon frauds of the marketplace, and the more wicked pious frauds of the church, the robber's blow, the burglar's stealthy step around the midnight couch, the pirate's murders, the rapine of cities, the plundering and captivity of nations. Even now, in self-styled Christian communities, are there not men who, under the sharp goadings of this impulse, equip vessels to cross the ocean—not to carry the glad tidings of the gospel to heathen lands, but to descend upon defenceless villages in a whirlwind of fire and ruin, to kidnap men, women and children, and to transport them through all the horrors of the middle passage, where their cries of agony and despair outvoice the storm, that the wretched victims may at last be sold into remorseless bondage, to wear chains, and to bequeath chains—and all this is perpetrated and suffered because a little gold can be transmuted, by such fiery alchemy, from human tears and blood! Such is the inexorable power of cupidity, in self-styled Christian lands, in sight of the spires of God's temples pointing upward to heaven, which, if Truth had its appropriate emblems, would be reversed and point downward to hell. [. . . .]

Let the lover of wealth seek wealth by all honest means, and with earnestness, if he will—let him surround himself with the comforts and the embellishments of life, and add the pleasures of beauty to the pleasures of utility. Let every honorable man indulge a quick and sustaining confidence in his own worthiness, whenever disparaged or maligned; and let him count upon the affections of his friends, and the benedictions of his race, as a part of the solid rewards of virtue. These, and kindred feelings, are not to be crushed, extinguished. Let them rouse themselves in presence of their objects, and rush out to seize them, and neigh, like a war-horse for the battle—only let them know that they have a rider, to whose eye no mist can dim the severe line they are never to pass, and whose arm can bend every neck of them, like the twig of an osier.

But I must pass to the next topic for consideration—the stimulus which, in this country, is applied to the propensities; and the free, unbarred, unbounded career, which is here opened for their activity. In every other nation that has ever existed—not even excepting Greece and Rome—the mind of the masses has been obstructed in its development. Amongst millions of men, only some half dozen of individuals—often only a single individual—have been able to pour out the lava of their passions, with full, volcanic force. These few men have made the Pharaohs, the Neros, the Napoleons of the race. The rest have usually been subjected to a systematic course of blinding, deafening, crippling. As an inevitable consequence of this, the minds of men have never yet put forth one thousandth part of their tremendous energies. Bad men have swarmed upon the earth, it is true, but they have been weak men. Another consequence is, that we, by deriving our impressions from history, have formed too low an estimate of the marvellous powers and capacities of the human being for evil as well as for good. The general estimate is altogether inadequate to what the common mind will be able to effect, when apt instruments are put into its hands, and the wide world is opened for its sphere of operations. [. . . .]

Nor let it be forgotten, in contemplating our condition, that the human passions, as unfolded and invigorated by our institutions, are not only possessed of all the prerogatives, and equipped with all the implements of sovereignty; but that they are forever roused and spurred to the most vehement efforts. It is a law of the passions, that they exert strength in proportion to the causes which excite them—a law which holds true in cases of sanity, as well as in the terrible strength of insanity. And with what endless excitements are the passions of men here plied! . . .

All objects which stimulate the passions of men, are made to pass before the eyes of all, as in a circling panorama. In very truth we are hung upon the same electrical wire, and if the ignorant and vicious get possession of the apparatus, the intelligent and the virtuous must take such shocks as the stupid or profligate experimenters may choose to administer.

So the inordinate love of office will present the spectacle of gladiatorial contests—of men struggling for station as for life, and using against each other the poisonous weapons of calumny and vituperation—while the abiding welfare, the true greatness and prosperity of the people will be like the soil of some neutral Flanders, over which the hostile bands of parti-sans will march and countermarch, and convert it into battlefields—so that, whichever side may triumph, the people will be ruined. And even after one cause or one party has prevailed, the conquered land will not be wide enough to settle a tithe of the conquerors upon. [. . . .]

With exceptions comparatively few, we have but two classes of ignorant persons amongst us, and they are harmless. Infants and idiots are ignorant; few others are so. Those whom we are accustomed to call ignorant, are full of false notions, as much worse than ignorance as wisdom is better. A merely ignorant man has no skill in adapting means to ends, whereby to jeopard the welfare of great interests or great numbers. Ignorance is blankness; or, at most, a lifeless, inert mass, which can, indeed, be moved and placed where you please, but will stay where it is placed. In Europe, there are multitudes of ignorant men—men into whose minds no idea ever entered respecting the duties of society or of government, or the conditions of human prosperity. They, like their work-fellows, the cattle, are obedient to their masters; and the range of their ideas on political or social questions, is hardly more extensive than that of the brutes. But with our institutions, this state of things, to any great extent, is impossible. The very atmosphere we breathe is freighted with the ideas of property, of acquisition and trans-mission; of wages, labor and capital; of political and social rights; of the appointment to, and tenure of offices; of the reciprocal relations between the great departments of government—executive, legislative, and judicial. Every native-born child amongst us imbibes notions, either false or true, on these subjects. Let these notions be false; let an individual grow up, with false ideas of his own nature and destiny as an immortal being, with false views respecting what government, laws, customs, should be; with no knowledge of the works, or the opinions of those great men who framed our government, and adjusted its various parts to each other—and when such an individual is invested with the political rights of citizenship, with power to give an authoritative voice and vote upon the affairs of his country, he will look upon all ex-isting things as rubbish which it is his duty to sweep away, that he may have room for the erection of other structures, planned after the model of his own false ideas. [. . . .]

And now, my friends, I ask, with the deepest anxiety, what institutions exist amongst us, which at once possess the power and are administered with the efficiency, requisite to save us from the dangers that spring up in our own bosoms? That the propensities, which each generation brings into the world, possess terrific power, and are capable of inflicting the completest ruin, none can deny. Nor will it be questioned that amongst *us*, they have an open career, and a command of means, such as never before coëxisted. What antago-nist power have we provided against them? By what exorcism can we lay the spirits we have raised? Once, brute force, directed by a few men, trampled upon the many. Here, the many are the possessors of that very force, and have almost abolished its use as a means of government. The French *gendarmerie*, the British horse-guards, the dreadful punish-ment of the Siberian mines, will never be copied here. Should the government resort to a standing army, that army would consist of the very forces they dread, organized, equipped and officered. Can laws save us? With us, the very idea of legislation is reversed. Once, the law prescribed the actions and shaped the wills of the multitude; here, the wills of the mul-titude prescribe and shape the law. With us, legislators study the will of the multitude, just as natural philosophers study a volcanoc—not with any expectation of doing aught to the volcano, but to see what the volcano is about to do to them. While the law was clothed with majesty and power, and the mind of the multitude was weak, then, as in all cases of a conflict between unequal forces, the law prevailed. But now, when the law is weak, and the passions of the multitude have gathered irresistible strength, it is fallacious and insane to look for security in the moral force of the law. [. . . .]

But perhaps others may look for security to the public Press, which has now taken its place amongst the organized forces of modern civilization. Probably its political department supplies more than half the reading of the mass of our people. But, bating the point, whether, in times of public excitement, when the sobriety and thoughtfulness of wisdom, when severe and exact truth are, more than ever else, necessary—whether, at such times, the press is not itself liable to be inflamed by the heats it should allay, and to be perverted by the obliquities it should rectify—bating this point, it is still obvious that its principal efforts are expended upon one department only of all our social duties. The very existence of the newspaper press, for any useful purpose, presupposes that the people are already supplied with the elements of knowledge and inspired with the love of right; and are therefore prepared to decide, with intelligence and honesty, those complicated and conflicting claims, which the tide of events is constantly presenting, and which, by the myriad messengers of the press, are carried to every man's fireside for his adjudication. For, of what value is it, that we have the most wisely-framed government on earth; to what end is it, that the wisest schemes which a phil-anthropic statesmanship can devise, are propounded to the people, if this people has not the intelligence to understand, or the integrity to espouse them? Each of two things is equally nec-essary to our political prosperity; namely, just principles of government and administration, on one side, and a people able to understand and resolute to uphold them, on the other. Of what use is the most exquisite music ever composed by the greatest masters of the art, until you have orchestra or choir that can perform the pieces? Pupils must thoroughly master the vocal elements, musical language must be learned, voices must be long and severely trained, or the divinest compositions of Haydn or Mozart would only set the teeth of an auditory on edge. And so must it be with our government and laws—the best will be useless, unless we have a people who will appreciate and uphold them. [. . . .]

The same Almighty power which implants in our nature the germs of these terrible propensities, has endowed us also, with reason and conscience and a sense of responsibility to Him; and, in his providence, he has opened a way by which these nobler faculties can be elevated into dominion and supremacy over the appetites and passions. But if this is ever done, it must be mainly done, during the docile and teachable years of childhood. I repeat it, my friends, *if this is ever done, it must be mainly done, during the docile and teachable years of childhood.* Wretched, incorrigible, demoniac, as any human being may ever have become, there was a time when he took the first step in error and in crime; when, for the first time, he just nodded to his fall, on the brink of ruin. Then, ere he was irrecoverably lost, ere he plunged into the abyss of infamy and guilt, he might have been recalled, as it were by the waving of the hand. Fathers, mothers, patriots, Christians! it is this very hour of peril through which our children are now passing. They know it not, but we know it; and where the knowl-edge is, there rests the responsibility. Society is responsible—not society considered as an ab-straction, but society as it consists of living members, which members we are. Clergymen are responsible—all men who have enjoyed the opportunities of a higher education in colleges and universities are responsible, for they can convert their means, whether of time or of tal-ent, into instruments for elevating the masses of the people. The conductors of the public press are responsible, for they have daily access to the public ear, and can infuse just notions of this high duty into the public mind. Legislators and rulers are responsible. In our country, and in our times, no man is worthy the honored name of a statesman, who does not include the highest practicable education of the people in all his plans of administration. He may have eloquence, he may have a knowledge of all history, diplomacy, jurisprudence, and by these he might claim, in other countries, the elevated rank of a statesman; but, unless he speaks, plans, labors, at all times and in all places, for the culture and edification of the whole people, he is not, he cannot be, an American statesman.

Robert Bellah, "Community Properly Understood: A Defense of 'Democratic Communitarianism'" (1988)

The word "community" leads a double life. It makes most people feel good, associated as it is with warmth, friendship, and acceptance. But among academics the word arouses suspicion. Doesn't community imply the abandonment of ethical universalism and the withdrawal into closed particularistic loyalties? Doesn't it perhaps lead even to ethnic cleansing?

The word community is a good word and worthy of continued use if it is carefully defined. My fellow authors and I attempted such a definition in *Habits of the Heart,* but it was often ignored. The primary problem is that the word is frequently used to mean small-scale, face-to-face groups like the family, the congregation, and the small town—what the Germans call *Gemeinschaft.* There is a long tradition of extolling this kind of community in America. But when that is all that community means, it is basically sentimental and, in the strict sense of the word, nostalgic. And nostalgia, as Christopher Lasch wrote, is merely a psychological placebo that allows one to accept regretfully but uncritically whatever is currently being served up in the name of progress. It inhibits, rather than serves, serious social criticism.

Thus if the term community is to be useful, it must mean something more. Those philosophical liberals who tend to reject the term community altogether see society as based on a social contract establishing procedures of fairness, but otherwise leaving individuals free to serve their own interests. They argue that under modern conditions, if we think of community as based on shared values and shared goals, community can exist only in small groups and is not possible or desirable in large-scale societies or institutions.

A deeper analysis, however, reveals that it is possible to see this supposed contrast of contract versus community as a continuum, or even as a necessary complementarity, rather than as an either/or proposition. Surely procedural norms of fairness are necessary in large-scale social institutions; but any group of any size, if it has a significant breadth of involvement and lasts a significant length of time, must have some shared values and goals. Consequently societies and institutions can never be based solely on contract, striving to maximize the opportunities of individuals. They must also, to some extent, be communities with shared values and goals.

But this reformulation leads to a further problem. Those who think of community as a form of *Gemeinschaft,* as well as their liberal critics, tend to think consensus about values and goals must be complete or nearly complete. Is such complete consensus realistic, or even desirable, in modern societies?

The answer, of course, is no. Yet this lack of unanimity need not create problems for supporters of community. While community-shared values and goals do imply something more than procedural agreement—they do imply some agreements about substance—they do not require anything like total or unarguable agreement. A good community is one in which there is argument, even conflict, about the meaning of the shared values and goals, and certainly about how they will be actualized in everyday life. Community is not about silent consensus; it is a form of intelligent, reflective life, in which there is indeed consensus, but where the consensus can be challenged and changed—often gradually, sometimes radically—over time.

Thus we are led to the question of what makes any kind of group a community and not just a contractual association. The answer lies in a shared concern with the following question: "What will make this group a *good* group?" Any institution, such as a university, a city, or a society, insofar as it is or seeks to be a community, needs to ask what is a good university, city, society, and so forth. So far as it reaches agreement about the good it is supposed to realize (and that will always be contested and open to further debate), it becomes a community with some common values and some common goals. ("Goals" are particularly important, as the effort to define a good community also entails the goal of trying to create a good one—or, more modestly and realistically, a better one than the current one.)

The Individual Reconsidered

Even given the claim that community does not require complete consensus, some people view with skepticism any effort to reach some common agreement about the good. Such a view is rooted in our culture's adherence to "ontological individualism"—the belief that the truth of our condition is not in our society or in our relation to others, but in our isolated and inviolable selves. It is this belief that tempts us to imagine that it is opportunity that will solve all our problems—if we could just provide individuals the opportunity to realize themselves, then everything else would take care of itself. If we focus on individual opportunity then we don't need to worry about substantive agreement or the common good, much less force any such notion on others. Each individual can concentrate on whatever good he or she chooses to pursue.

In seeking to solve our problems through individual opportunity we have come up with two master strategies. We will provide opportunity through the market or through the state. The great ideological wars of our current politics focus on whether the most effective provider of opportunity is the market or the state. On this issue we imagine a radical polarity between conservative and liberal, Republican and Democrat. What we often do not see is that this is a very tame polarity, because the opponents agree so deeply on most of the terms of the problem. Both solutions are individualistic. Whatever their opponents say, those who support a strong government seldom believe in government as such. They simply see it as the most effective provider of those opportunities that will allow individuals to have a fair chance at making something of themselves. Those who believe in the market think free competition is the best context for individual self-realization. Both positions are essentially technocratic. They do not imply much about substantive values, other than freedom and opportunity. They would solve our problems through economic or political mechanisms, not moral solidarity.

And yet the world of these ideological opponents, composed as it is of autonomous individuals, markets, and states, is not the world that anyone lives in—not even the free enterprise or welfare liberal ideologists. This ideological world is a world without families. It is also a world without neighborhoods, ethnic communities, churches, cities and towns, even nations (as opposed to states). It is, to use the terminology of the German sociologist-philosopher Jürgen Habermas, a world of individuals and systems (economic and administrative), but not a lifeworld. The lifeworld missing in these conservative and liberal ideologies is the place where we communicate with others, deliberate, come to agreements about standards and norms, pursue in common an effort to create a valuable form of life—in short, the lifeworld is the world of community.

Democratic Communitarianism

I want to sketch a framework that escapes the ideological blinders of current American politics and highlights what is missing in much of our debate. As opposed to free market conservatism and welfare state liberalism, I want to describe another approach to our common problems which I will call—borrowing from Jonathan Boswell in *Community and the Economy: The Theory of Public Co-operation*—democratic communitarianism. Democratic communitarianism does not pit itself against the two reigning ideologies as a third way. It accepts the value and inevitability of both the market and the state, but it insists that the function of the market and the state is to serve us, not to dominate us. Democratic communitarianism seeks to provide a humane context within which to think about the market and the state. Its first principle is the one already enunciated in what I have said about community: it seeks to define and further the good which is the community's purpose. I want to offer four values to which democratic communitarianism is committed and which give its notion of the good somewhat more specificity:

1. Democratic communitarianism is based on the value of the sacredness of the individual, which is common to most of the great religions and philosophies of the world. (It is expressed in biblical religion through the idea that we are created in the image and likeness of God.) Anything that would oppress individuals, or operate to stunt individual development, would be contrary to the principles of democratic communitarianism. However, unlike its ideological rivals, democratic communitarianism does not think of individuals as existing in a vacuum or as existing in a world composed only of markets and states. Rather, it believes that individuals are realized only in and through communities, and that strong, healthy, morally vigorous communities are the prerequisite for strong, healthy, morally vigorous individuals.

2. Democratic communitarianism, therefore, affirms the central value of solidarity. Solidarity points to the fact that we become who we are through our relationships—that reciprocity, loyalty, and shared commitment to the good are defining features of a fully human life.

3. Democratic communitarianism believes in what Boswell has called "complementary association." By this he means a commitment to "varied social groupings: the family, the local community, the cultural or religious group, the economic enterprise, the trade union or profession, the nation-state." Through this principle it is clear that community does not mean small-scale, all-inclusive, total groups. In our kind of society an individual will belong to many communities and ultimately the world itself can be seen as a community. Democratic communitarianism views such a multiplicity of belonging as a positive good, as potentially and in principle complementary.

4. Finally, democratic communitarianism is committed to the idea of participation as both a right and a duty. Communities become positive goods only when they provide the opportunity and support to participate in them. A corollary of this principle is the principle of subsidiarity, derived from Catholic social teaching. This idea asserts that the

groups closest to a problem should attend to it, receiving support from higher level groups only if necessary. To be clear, democratic communitarianism does not adhere to Patrick Buchanan's interpretation of subsidiarity, which projects a society virtually without a state. A more legitimate understanding of subsidiarity realizes the inevitability and necessity of the state. It has the responsibility of nurturing lower-level associations wherever they are weak, as they normally are among the poor and the marginalized. Applying this perspective to current events, at a moment when powerful political forces in the United States are attempting to dismantle a weak welfare state, democratic communitarians will defend vigorous and responsible state action.

Nothing in this argument is meant to imply that face-to-face community is not a good thing. It is, and in our society it needs to be strengthened. But the argument for democratic community—rooted in the search for the common good—applies to groups of any size, and ultimately to the world as a community. It is a political argument grounded on the belief that a politics based on the summing of individual preferences is inadequate and misleading. Democratic communitarianism presumes that morality and politics cannot be separated and that moral argument, painful and difficult though it sometimes is, is fundamental to a defensible stance in today's world.

NOTES

1. It is important not to confuse the Republican Party in the United States with civic republicans. The former is an organized political party with commitments to individual rights. As we shall see, civic republicans value liberty but always place it in the context of robust communities. For a discussion of civic republicanism, see J. G. A. Pocock, *The Machiavellian Moment* (Princeton, N.J.: Princeton University Press, 1975) and Quentin Skinner, *The Foundations of Modern Political Thought,* vol. 1. (Cambridge: Cambridge University Press, 1978); also see Ronald Terchek, *Republican Paradoxes and Liberal Anxieties* (Lanham, Md.: Rowman & Littlefield, 1997), chaps. 2–3.

2. When republicans talk about corruption, they have in mind a society that has become preoccupied with luxury and where civic virtue and a commitment to the common good are weak.

3. For a discussion of various modes of communitarian thinking, see Robert Booth Fowler, *The Dance with Community* (Lawrence: University of Kansas Press, 1991). Also see Aimed Asian, *New Communitarian Thinking* (Charlottesville: University Press of Virginia, 1995).

4. For a liberal critique of communitarianism, see Will Kymlicka *Liberalism, Community, and Culture* (Oxford: Oxford University Press, 1989).

5. See, for example, Michael Sandel, *Liberalism and the Limits of Justice* (New York: Cambridge University Press, 1982).

6. For a criticism of the role of rights in liberal society, see Mary Glendon, *Rights Talk: The Impoverishment of Political Discourse* (New York: Free Press, 1991).

7. For Aristotle, virtue is a mean located between what is excessive and deficient (*Ethics,* 1107a). Thus, courage falls between the deficiency of the coward and the excess of the rash person. *Eds.*

8. The real meaning of this word has been almost wholly lost in modern times; people mistake a town for a city, and a townsman for a citizen. They do not know that houses make a town, but citizens a city. The same mistake long ago cost the Carthaginians dear. I have never read of the title of citizens being given to the subjects of any prince, not even the ancient Macedonians or the English of today, though they are nearer liberty than any one else. The French alone everywhere familiarly adopt the name of citizens, because, as can be seen from their dictionaries, they have no idea of its meaning; otherwise they would be guilty in usurping it, of the crime of *lèse-majesté*; among them, the name expresses a virtue,

and not a right. When Bodin spoke of our citizens and townsmen, he fell into a bad blunder in taking the one class for the other. M. d'Alembert has avoided the error, and, in his article on Geneva, has clearly distinguished the four orders of men (or even five, counting mere foreigners) who dwell in our town, of which two only compose the Republic. No other French writer, to my knowledge, has understood the real meaning of the word citizen.

9. 'Every interest,' says the Marquis d'Argenson, 'has different principles. The agreement of two particular interests is formed by opposition to a third.' He might have added that the agreement of all interests is formed by opposition to that of each. If there were no different interests, the common interest would be barely felt, as it would encounter no obstacle; all would go on of its own accord, and politics would cease to be an art.

10. 'In fact,' says Machiavelli, 'there are some divisions that are harmful to a Republic and some that are advantageous. Those which stir up sections and followers are harmful; those attended by neither are advantageous. Since, then, the founder of a Republic cannot help enmities arising he ought at least to prevent them from growing into sections' (*History of Florence*, Book VII).

11. A people becomes famous only when its legislation begins to decline. We do not know for how many centuries the system of Lycurgus made the Spartans happy before the rest of Greece took any notice of it.

12. 'In truth,' says Machiavelli, 'there has never been, in any country, an extraordinary legislator who has not had recourse to God; for otherwise his laws would not have been accepted: there are, in fact, many useful truths of which a wise man may have knowledge without their having in themselves such clear reasons for their being so as to be able to convince others' (*Discourses on Livy*, Bk. v, ch. xi).

13. Provided, of course, he does not leave to escape his obligations and avoid having to serve his country in the hour of need. Flight in such a case would be criminal and punishable, and would be, not withdrawal, but desertion.

CONTEMPORARY THEORIES OF DEMOCRACY

Four of the most important contemporary theories of democracy are examined in this section. All four work within the broad constitutional frameworks that describe liberal democracies today, though each with a different emphasis and purpose. The first three make conventional democratic procedures central to their objectives while participatory theories look for new ways to extend existing ones. Each calls attention to specific aspects of the democratic enterprise, which it holds as central to popular governance. For protective democrats, popular rule should primarily mean one thing: checking an active government that attempts to use power for its own benefit as well as the benefit of its friends and patrons. What protective democracy defends, then, are the rights of citizens from an intrusive state. For pluralists, the basic unit of democratic politics is the group and pluralist politics is group competition. Advocates of this outlook find that citizens, through their membership in groups, have a continuing presence in public affairs between elections. Performance theories of democracy see government resting on the consent of the democratic citizen. In this model, the only relevant question citizens ask themselves when they vote is whether they are better or worse off with the present incumbents. Here, voters are driven by their immediate, individual, short-term interests and it is difficult to talk about a common good. For their part, participatory democrats find that voting and conventional interest-group memberships are inadequate to express the views of citizens and want democratic participation extended to realms beyond conventional mechanisms of political involvement. To do this, they frequently seek to democratize other areas of social life, such as the workplace or neighborhood, and to open existing arenas of formal decisionmaking to more direct modes of popular involvement.

PROTECTIVE DEMOCRACY

Fear of the real and potential abuse of the powers of government has long inspired democrats. In this respect, protective democracy is an extension of the early liberal theories of Locke, Paine, and Madison. For contemporary protective democrats, government is driven by its dual and sometimes competing commitments to liberty, on one hand, and its attentiveness to mass political interest groups on the other. Friedrich Hayek holds that an active government is a threat to freedom and that popular rule can serve the cause of liberty best when it commits itself to restraining government to the narrow confines of a predefined public sphere. By the same logic, Milton Friedman finds that it is by preserving the most minimal political arrangements that the government fulfills its obligations to provide the maximum freedom to its citizens at the lowest possible cost.

Although democrats have always worried about the dangers associated with empowering the few at the expense of the many, protectionist democrats have also sought to call attention to the dangers associated with empowering citizens in ways that extend beyond the formal guarantees of legal and political equality and freedom. For protective democrats such as Friedman, limited government promises the best possibility of social cohesion by reducing the scope of issues that are subject to political conflict. By immunizing the political sphere from those issues where people are prone to disagree, he holds that the minimal state is better able to provide for the stability of the regime and all the benefits that Friedman believes will follow from such conditions. At the same time, by relegating the activities of public power to the narrowest space of action that is compatible with the maintenance of social order, this model claims to ensure the broadest possible range of freedoms in the private sphere.

The containment of the state fosters a free market that provides an arena for uncoerced human activity. Although this sphere of freedom is described as essentially self-regulating, Friedman concedes that it does depend on a state capable of judging, enforcing, and when necessary modifying common rules. And while the logic of expediency might justify the state's incursion into a small set of social activities, such paternalistic initiatives, however well-meaning, are always viewed with deep suspicion by Friedman who insists that such activities inevitably compromise individual freedom and ought to considered only as a last resort.

With Hayek, we encounter one of the strongest contemporary statements of protective democracy, particularly in his assault on the modern welfare state.[1] Whatever the reasons, modern liberal democracy has become associated with the modern welfare state, despite recent efforts to scale back the latter's scope of activity. In an era of greater complexity and interdependence, as well as a persistent inequality of resources between citizens, the modern welfare state is called to provide a variety of services that once were the domain of individuals, families, and private associations or were left unattended. Today, the welfare state extends its involvement beyond the poorest and most vulnerable members of society to direct a wide variety of other areas as well. Education, transportation, health and safety legislation, environmental protection, social security, and a variety of other activities characterize a state that needs to tax as well as regulate conduct that was once considered nonpolitical.

Hayek takes many of these moves as posing a danger to liberty. For him, the modern democratic state is an intrusive state that has overstepped the boundaries originally assigned to the democratic polity and that increasingly undermines the spontaneously generated activities that, be believes, are the hallmark of liberty. For him, early democracy was guided by a "higher nomos," which held that freedom was the greatest good of everyone. Today this has been replaced by a government intent on pleasing interest groups—indeed, by a government directed by interest groups. On Hayek's reading, ruling elites attempt to maintain their power by promising more and more to groups that return the favor with their political support. What results, in Hayek's account, is the modern regulatory state that is committed not to safeguarding liberty but rather to keeping power for incumbents. This is not merely something that characterizes the politics of the left with its promises of more benefits to the working class and the poor. It is also a part of the politics of the right with its promises to trade associations and professional groups, which demand that the government protect and promote their interests. In responding to those pressures, he argues, the intrusive state replaces the voluntary associations and spontaneous order of a free society and sacrifices the liberty of its citizens in the process. Hayek wants a democratic government that gets its priorities straight, and for him this means that it secures liberty and private property from government intrusion. Hayek also fears that democracy undermines itself because citizens have lost control. What he takes to be the reckless promising of benefits by elected officials to interest groups means that, in each election cycle, candidates promise more and more in a spiral of decreasing respect for the primary obligations of a free government. When this happens, democracy is no longer the friend of freedom that it once was.

READINGS

FRIEDRICH A. HAYEK, SELECTIONS FROM *THE POLITICAL ORDER OF A FREE PEOPLE* (1979)

"Majority Opinion and Contemporary Democracy"

> But the great number [of the Athenian Assembly] cried out that it was monstrous if the people were to be prevented from doing whatever they wished. . . . Then the

Prytanes, stricken with fear, agreed to put the question to all of them except Socrates, the son of Sophroniscus; and he said that in no case would he act except in accordance with the law.

—Xenophon

The Progressive Disillusionment about Democracy

When the activities of modern government produce aggregate results that few people have either wanted or foreseen this is commonly regarded as an inevitable feature of democracy. It can hardly be claimed, however, that such developments usually correspond to the desires of any identifiable group of men. It appears that the particular process which we have chosen to ascertain what we call the will of the people brings about results which have little to do with anything deserving the name of the 'common will' of any substantial part of the population.

We have in fact become so used to regard as democratic only the particular set of institutions which today prevails in all Western democracies, and in which a majority of a representative body lays down the law *and* directs government, that we regard this as the only possible form of democracy. As a consequence we do not care to dwell on the fact that this system not only has produced many results which nobody likes, even in those countries in which on the whole it has worked well, but also has proved unworkable in most countries where these democratic institutions were not restrained by strong traditions about the appropriate tasks of the representative assemblies. Because we rightly believe in the basic ideal of democracy we feel usually bound to defend the particular institutions which have long been accepted as its embodiment, and hesitate to criticize them because this might weaken the respect for an ideal we wish to preserve.

It is no longer possible, however, to overlook the fact that in recent times in spite of continued lip-service and even demands for its further extension, there has arisen among thoughtful persons an increasing disquiet and serious alarm about the results it often produces. This does not everywhere take the form of that cynical realism which is characteristic of some contemporary political scientists who regard democracy merely as just another form of an inevitable struggle in which it is decided 'who gets what, when, and how.'[2] Yet that there prevails deep disillusionment and doubt about the future of democracy, caused by a belief that those developments of it which hardly anybody approves are inevitable, can scarcely be denied. It found its expression many years ago in Joseph Schumpeter's well-known contention that, although a system based on the free market would be better for most, it is doomed beyond hope, while socialism, though it cannot fulfill its promises, is bound to come.[3]

It seems to be the regular course of the development of democracy that after a glorious first period in which it is understood as and actually operates as a safeguard of personal freedom because it accepts the limitations of a higher nomos, sooner or later it comes to claim the right to settle any particular question in whatever manner a majority agrees upon. This is what happened to the Athenian democracy at the end of the fifth century, as shown by the famous occurrence to which the quotation at the head of this chapter refers; and in the next century Demosthenes (and others) were to complain that 'our laws are no better than so many decrees; nay, you will find that the laws which have to be observed in drafting the decrees are later than the decrees themselves.'[4]

In modern times a similar development started when the British Parliament claimed sovereign, that is unlimited, powers and in 1766 explicitly rejected the idea that in its particular decisions it was bound to observe any general rules not of its own making. Though for a time a strong tradition of the rule of law prevented serious abuse of the power that Parliament had arrogated to itself, it proved in the long run the great calamity of modern development that soon after representative government was achieved all those restraints upon the supreme power that had been painfully built up during the evolution of constitutional monarchy were successively dismantled as no longer necessary. That this in effect meant the abandonment of constitutionalism which consists in a limitation of all power by permanent principles of government was already seen by Aristotle when he maintained that 'where the laws are not sovereign . . . since the many are sovereign not as individuals but collectively . . . such a democracy is not a constitution at all';[5] and it was recently pointed out again by a modern author who speaks of 'constitutions which are so democratic that they are properly speaking no longer constitutions.'[6] Indeed, we are now told that the 'modern conception of democracy is a form of government in which no restriction is placed on the governing body'[7] and . . . some have already drawn the conclusion that constitutions are an antiquated survival which have no place in the modern conception of government.

Unlimited Power the Fatal Defect of the Prevailing Form of Democracy

The tragic illusion was that the adoption of democratic procedures made it possible to dispense with all other limitations on governmental power. It also promoted the belief that the 'control of government' by the democratically elected legislation would adequately replace the traditional limitations, while in fact the necessity of forming organized majorities for supporting a program of particular actions in favor of special groups introduced a new source of arbitrariness and partiality and produced results inconsistent with the moral principles of the majority. As we shall see, the paradoxical result of the possession of unlimited power makes it impossible for a representative body to make the general principles prevail on which it agrees, because under such a system the majority of the representative assembly, in order to remain a majority, *must* do what it can to buy the support of the several interests by granting them special benefits.

So it came about that the precious institutions of representative government Britain gave to the world also the pernicious principle of parliamentary sovereignty according to which the representative assembly is not only the highest but also an unlimited authority. The latter is sometimes thought to be a necessary consequence of the former, but this is not so. Its power may be limited, not by another superior 'will' but by the consent of the people on which all power and the coherence of the state rest. If that consent approves only of the laying down and enforcement of general rules of just conduct, and nobody is given power to coerce except for the enforcement of these rules (or temporarily during a violent disruption of order by some cataclysm), even the highest constituted power may be limited. Indeed, the claim of Parliament to sovereignty at first meant only that it recognized no other will above it; it only gradually came to mean that it could do whatever it liked—which does not necessarily follow from the first, because the consent on which the unity of the state and therefore the power of any of its organs are founded may only restrain power but not confer positive power to act. It is allegiance which creates power and the power thus created extends only so far as it has been extended by the consent of the people. It was because this was forgotten that the sovereignty of law became the same thing as the sovereignty of Parliament. And while the conception of the rule (reign, sovereignty or supremacy) of law presupposes a concept of law defined by the attributes of the rules, not by their source, *today legislatures are no longer so called because they make the laws, but laws are so called because they emanate from legislatures*, whatever the form or content of their resolutions.[8]

If it could be justly contended that the existing institutions produce results which have been willed or approved by a majority, the believer in the basic principle of democracy would of course have to accept them. But there are strong reasons to think that what those institutions in fact produce is in a great measure an unintended outcome of the particular kind of machinery we have set up to ascertain what we believe to be the will of the majority, rather than a deliberate decision of the majority or anybody else. It would seem that wherever democratic institutions ceased to be restrained by the tradition of the Rule of Law, they led not only to 'totalitarian democracy' but in due time even to a 'plebiscitary dictatorship.' This should certainly make us understand that what is a precious possession is not a particular set of institutions that are easily enough copied, but some less tangible traditions; and that the degeneration of these institutions may even be a necessary result wherever the inherent logic of the machinery is not checked by the predominance of the prevailing general conceptions of justice. May it not be true, as has been well said, that 'the belief in democracy presupposes belief in things higher than democracy'? And there is really no other way for people to maintain a democratic government than by handing over unlimited power to a group of elected representatives whose decisions must be guided by the exigencies of a bargaining process in which they bribe a sufficient number of voters to support an organized group of themselves numerous enough to outvote the rest?

The True Content of the Democratic Ideal

Though a great deal of nonsense has been and still is being talked about democracy and the benefits its further extension will secure, I am profoundly disturbed by the rapid decline of faith in it. This sharp decrease of the esteem in which democracy is held by critical minds ought to alarm even those who never shared the unmeasured and uncritical enthusiasm it used to inspire until recently, and which made the term describe almost anything that was good in politics. As seems to be the fate of most terms expressing a political ideal, 'democracy' has been used to describe various kinds of things which have little to do with the original meaning of the term, and now is even often used where what is really meant is 'equality.' Strictly speaking it refers to a method or procedure for determining governmental decisions and neither refers to some substantial good or aim of government (such as a sort of material equality), nor is it a method that can be meaningfully applied to non-governmental organizations (such as educational, medical, military or commercial establishments). Both of these abuses deprive the word 'democracy' of any clear meaning.[9]

But even a wholly sober and unsentimental consideration which regards democracy as a mere convention making possible a peaceful change of the holders of power should make us understand that it is an ideal worth fighting for to the utmost, because it is our only protection (even if in its present form, not a certain one) against tyranny. Though democracy itself is not freedom (except for that indefinite collective, the majority of 'the people') it is one of the most important safeguards of freedom. As the only method of peaceful change of government yet discovered, it is one of those paramount though negative values, comparable to sanitary precautions against the plague, of which we are hardly aware while they are effective, but the absence of which may be deadly.

The principle that coercion should be allowed only for the purpose of ensuring obedience to rules of just conduct approved by most, or at least by a majority, seems to be the essential condition for the absence of arbitrary power and therefore of freedom. It is this principle which has made possible the peaceful co-existence of men in a Great Society and the peaceful change of the directors of organized power. But that whenever common action is necessary it should be guided by the opinion of the majority, and that no power of coercion is legitimate unless the principle guiding it is approved by at least a majority, does not imply that the power of the majority must be unlimited—or even that there must be a possible way of ascertaining what it called the will of the majority on every conceivable subject. It appears that we have unwittingly created a machinery which makes possible a claim that the sanction of an alleged majority for measures which are in fact not desired by a majority, and which may even be disapproved by a majority of the people; and that this machinery produces an aggregate of measures that not only is not wanted by anybody, but that it could not as a whole be approved by any rational mind because it is inherently contradictory.

If all coercive power is to rest on the opinion of the majority, then it should also not extend further than the majority can genuinely agree. This does not mean that there must exist specific approval by the majority of any particular action of the government. Such a demand would clearly be impossible to fulfill in a complex modern society so far as the current direction of the detail of the government machinery is concerned, that is for all the day-to-day decisions about how the resources placed at the disposal of government are to be used. But it does mean that the individual should be bound to obey only such commands as necessarily follow from the general principles approved by the majority, and that the power of the representatives of the majority should be unrestricted only in the administration of the particular means placed at their disposal.

The ultimate justification of the conferment of a power to coerce is that such a power is required if a viable order is to be maintained, and that all have therefore an interest in the existence of such a power. But this justification does not extend further than the need. There is clearly no need that anybody, not even the majority, should have power over all the particular actions or things occurring in society. The step from the belief that only what is approved by the majority should be binding for all, to the belief that all that the majority approves shall have that force, may seem small. Yet it is the transition from one conception of government to an altogether different one: from the conception by which government has definite limited tasks required to bring about the formation of a spontaneous order to the conception that its powers are unlimited; or a transition from a system in which through recognized procedures we decide how certain common affairs are to be arranged, to a system in which one group of people may declare anything they like as a matter of common concern and on this ground subject it to those procedures. While the first conception refers to necessary common decisions requisite for the maintenance of peace and order, the second allows some organized sections of the people to control everything, and easily becomes the pretext of oppression.

There is, however, no more reason to believe in the case of the majority that because they want a particular thing this desire is an expression of their sense of justice, than there is ground for such a belief in the case of individuals. In the latter we know only too well that their sense of justice will often be swayed by their desire for particular objects. But as individuals we have generally been taught to curb illegitimate desires, though we sometimes have to be restrained by authority. Civilization largely rests on the fact that the individuals have learnt to restrain their desires for particular objects and to submit to generally recognized rules of just conduct. Majorities, however, have not yet been civilized in this manner because they do not have to obey rules. What would we not all do if we were genuinely convinced that our desire for a particular action proves that it is just? The result is not different if people are persuaded that the agreement of the majority on the advantage of a particular measure proves that it is just. When people are taught to believe that what they agree is necessarily just, they will indeed soon cease to ask whether it is so. Yet the belief that all on which a majority can agree is by definition just has for several generations been impressed upon popular opinion. Need we be surprised that in the conviction that what they resolve is necessarily just, the existing representative assemblies have ceased even to consider in the concrete instances whether this is really so?[10]

While the agreement among many people on the justice of a particular *rule* may indeed be a good though not an infallible test of its justice, it makes nonsense of the conception of justice if we define as just whatever particular measure the majority approves justifiable only by the positivist doctrine that there are no objective tests of justice. . . . There exists a great difference between what a majority may decide on any particular question and the general principle relevant to the issue which it might be willing to approve if it were put to it, as there will exist among individuals. There is, therefore, also great need that a majority be required to prove its conviction that what it decides is just by *committing* itself to the universal application of the rules on which it acts in the particular case; and its power to coerce should be confined to the enforcement of rules to which it is prepared to commit itself.

The belief that the will of the majority on particular matters determines what is just leads to the view, now widely regarded as self-evident, that the majority cannot be arbitrary. This appears to be a necessary conclusion only if, according to the prevalent interpretation of democracy (and the positivistic jurisprudence as its foundation), the source from which a decision emanates rather than its conformity with a rule on which the people agree, is regarded as the criterion of justice, and 'arbitrary' is arbitrarily defined as not determined by democratic procedure. 'Arbitrary' means, however, action determined by a particular will unrestrained by a general rule—irrespective of whether this will is the will of one or a majority. It is, therefore, not the agreement of a majority on a particular action, nor even its conformity with a constitution, but only the willingness of a representative body to commit itself to the universal application of a rule which requires the particular action, that can be regarded as evidence that its members regard as just what they decide. Today, however, the majority is not even asked whether it regards a particular decision as just; nor could its individual members assure themselves that the principle that is applied in the particular decision will also be applied in all similar instances. Since no resolution of a representative body binds it in its future decisions, it is in its several measures not bound by any general rules.

The Weakness of an Elective Assembly with Unlimited Powers

The crucial point is that votes on rules applicable to all, and votes on measures which directly affect only some, have a wholly different character. Votes on matters that concern all, such as general rules of just conduct, are based on a lasting strong opinion and thus something quite different from votes on particular measures for the benefit (and often also at the expense) of unknown people generally in the knowledge that such benefits will be distributed from the common purse in any case, and that all the individual can do is to guide this expenditure in the direction he prefers. Such a system is bound to produce the most paradoxical results in a

Great Society, however expedient it may be for arranging local affairs where all are fairly familiar with the problems, because the number and complexity of the tasks of the administration of a Great Society far exceed the range where the ignorance of the individual could be remedied by better information at the disposal of the voters or representatives.[11]

The classical theory of representative government assumed that the deputies

> when they make no laws but what they themselves and their posterity must be subject to; when they can give no money, but what they must pay their share of; when they can do no mischief, but what must fall upon their own heads in common with their countrymen; their principals may expect then good laws, little mischief, and much frugality.[12]

But the electors of a 'legislature' whose members are mainly concerned to secure and retain the votes of particular groups by procuring special benefits for them will care little about what others will get and be concerned only with what they gain in the haggling. They will normally merely agree to something being given to others about whom they know little, and usually at the expense of third groups, as the price for having their own wishes met, without any thought whether these various demands are just. Each group will be prepared to consent even to iniquitous benefits for other groups out of the common purse if this is the condition for the consent of the others to what this group has learnt to regard as its right. The result of this process will correspond to nobody's opinion of what is right, and to no principles; it will not be based on a judgment of merit but on political expediency. Its main object is bound to become the sharing out of funds extorted from a minority. That this is the inevitable outcome of the actions of an unrestrained 'interventionist' legislature was clearly foreseen by the early theorists of representative democracy.[13] Who indeed would pretend that in modern times the democratic legislatures have granted all the special subsidies, privileges and other benefits which so many special interests enjoy because they regard these demands as just. That A be protected against the competition of cheap imports and B against being undercut by a less highly trained operator, C against a reduction in his wages, and D against the loss of his job is not in the general interest, however much the advocates of such a measure pretend that this is so. And it is not chiefly because the voters are convinced that it is in the general interest but because they want the support of those who make these demands that they are in turn prepared to support *their* demands. The creation of the myth of 'social justice' . . . is indeed largely the product of this particular democratic machinery, which makes it necessary for the representatives to invent a moral justification for the benefits they grant to particular interests.

Indeed people often come genuinely to believe that it must in some sense be just if the majority regularly concedes special benefits to particular groups—as if it had anything to do with justice (or any moral consideration) if every party that wants majority support must promise special benefits to some particular groups (such as the farmers or peasants, or legal privileges to the trade unions) whose votes may shift the balance of power. Under the existing system thus every small interest group can enforce its demands, not by persuading a majority that the demands are just or equitable, but by threatening to withhold that support which the nucleus of agreed individuals will need to become a majority. The pretence that the democratic legislatures have granted all the special subsidies, privileges and other benefits which so many particular interests today enjoy because they thought these to be just would of course be simply ridiculous. Though skillful propaganda may occasionally have moved a few soft-hearted individuals on behalf of special groups, and though it is of course useful to the legislators to claim that they have been moved by considerations of justice, the artifacts of the voting machinery which we call the will of the majority do certainly not correspond to any opinion of the majority about what is right or wrong.

An assembly with power to vote on benefits to particular groups must become one in which bargains or deals among the majority rather than substantive agreement on the merits of the different claims will decide. The fictitious 'will of the majority' emerging from this bargaining process is no more than an agreement to assist its supporters at the expense of the rest. It is to the awareness of this fact that policy is largely determined by a series of deals with special interests that 'politics' owes its bad reputation among ordinary men.

Indeed, to the high-minded who feel that the politician should concern himself exclusively with the common good the reality of constant assuaging of particular groups by throwing them tidbits or more substantial gifts must appear as outright corruption. And the fact that majority government does not produce what the majority wants but what each of the groups making up the majority must concede to the others to get their support for what it wants itself amounts to that. That this is so is today accepted as one of the commonplaces of everyday life and that the experienced politician will merely pity the idealist who is naive enough to condemn this and to believe it could be avoided if only people were more honest, is therefore perfectly true so far as the existing institutions are concerned, and wrong only in taking it as an inevitable attribute of all representative or democratic government, an inherent corruption which the most virtuous and decent man cannot escape. It is however not a necessary attribute of all representative or democratic government, but a necessary product only of all unlimited or omnipotent government dependent on the support of numerous groups. Only limited government can be decent government, because there does not exist (and cannot exist) general moral rules for the assignments of particular benefits (as Kant put it), because 'welfare has no principle but depends on the material content of the will and therefore is incapable of a general principle.' It is not democracy or representative government as such, but the particular institution, chosen by us, of a single omnipotent legislature that make it necessarily corrupt.

Corrupt at the same time weak: unable to resist pressure from the component groups the governing majority *must do what it can do* to gratify the wishes of the groups from which it needs support, however harmful to the rest such measures may be—at least so long as this is not too easily seen or the groups who have to suffer are not too popular. While immensely and oppressively powerful and able to overwhelm all resistance from a minority, it is wholly incapable of pursuing a consistent course of action, lurching like a steam roller driven by one who is drunk. If no superior judiciary authority can prevent the legislature from granting privileges to particular groups there is no limit to the blackmail to which government will be subject. If government has the power to grant their demands it becomes their slave—as in Britain where they make impossible any policy that might pull the country out of its economic decline. If government is going to be strong enough to maintain order and justice we must deprive the politicians of that cornucopia the possession of which makes them believe that they can and ought 'to remove all sources of discontent.'[14] Unfortunately, every necessary adaptation to changed circumstances is bound to cause widespread discontent, and what will be mainly demanded from politicians is to make these unwelcome changes unnecessary for the individuals.

One curious effect of this condition in which the granting of special benefits is guided not by a general belief of what is just but by 'political necessity' is that it is apt to create erroneous beliefs of the following kind: if a certain group is regularly favored because it may swing the balance of the votes the myth will arise that it is generally agreed that it deserves this. But it would of course be absurd to conclude if the farmers, the small business men, or the municipal workers got their demands regularly satisfied that they must have a just claim, if in reality this merely happens because without the support of a substantial part of these groups no government would have a majority. Yet there seems to be a paradoxical reversal of what democratic theory assumes to happen: that the majority is not guided by what is generally believed to be right, but what it thinks it is necessary to do in order to maintain its coherence is being regarded as just. It is still believed that consent of the majority is proof of the justice of a measure, although most members of the majority will often consent only as payment of the price for the fulfillment of their own sectional demands. Things come to be regarded as 'socially just' merely because they are regularly done, not because anyone except the beneficiaries regards them as just on their own merits. But the necessity of constantly wooing splinter groups produces in the end purely fortuitous moral standards and often leads people to believe that the favored social groups are really specially deserving because they are regularly singled out for special benefits. Sometimes we do encounter the argument that all modern democracies have found it necessary to do this or that, used as if it were proof of the desirability of a measure rather than merely the blind result of a particular mechanism.

Thus the existing machinery of unlimited democratic government produces a new set of democratic pseudo-morals, an artifact of the machinery which makes people regard as socially just what is regularly done by democracies, or can by clever use of this machinery be extorted from democratic governments. The spreading awareness that more and more incomes are determined by government action will lead to ever new demands by groups whose position is still left to be determined by market forces for similar assurance of what they believe they deserve. Every time the income of some group is increased by government action a legitimate claim for similar treatment is provided for other groups. It is merely the expectations of many which legislatures have created by the boons they have already conferred on certain groups that they will be treated in the same manner that underlies most of the demands for 'social justice.'

Coalitions of Organized Interests and the Apparatus of Para-Government

So far we have considered the tendency of the prevailing democratic institutions only in so far as it is determined by the necessity to bribe the individual voter with promises of special benefits for his group, without taking into account a factor which greatly accentuates the influence of some particular interests, their ability to organize and to operate as organized pressure groups.[15] This leads to the particular political parties being united not by any principles but merely as coalitions or organized interests in which the concerns of those pressure groups that are capable of effective organization greatly preponderate over those that for one reason or another cannot form effective organizations.[16] This greatly enhanced influence of the organizable groups further distorts the distribution of benefits and makes it increasingly unrelated to the requirements of efficiency or any conceivable principle of equity. The result is a distribution of incomes chiefly determined by political power. The 'incomes policy' nowadays advocated as a supposed means to combat inflation is in fact largely inspired by the monstrous idea that all material benefits should be determined by the holders of such power.

It is part of this tendency that in the course of this century an enormous and exceedingly wasteful apparatus of para-government has grown up, consisting of trade associations, trades unions and professional organizations, designed primarily to divert as much as possible of the stream of governmental favor to their members. It has come to be regarded as obviously necessary and unavoidable, yet has arisen only in response to (or partly as defense against being disadvantaged in) the increasing necessity of an all-mighty majority government maintaining its majority by buying the support of particular small groups.

Political parties in these conditions become in fact little more than of organized interests whose actions are determined by the inherent logic of their mechanics rather than by any general principles or ideals on which they are agreed. Except for some ideological parties in the West who disapprove of the system now prevailing in their countries and aim at wholly replacing these by some imaginary utopia, it would indeed be difficult to discern in the programs, and even more in the actions, of any major party a consistent conception of the sort of social order on which its followers agree. They are all driven, even if that is not their agreed aim, to use their power to impose some particular structure upon society i.e. some form of socialism, rather than create the conditions in which society can gradually evolve improved formations.

The inevitability of such developments in a system where the legislature is omnipotent is clearly seen if we ask how a majority united on common action and capable of directing current policy can be formed. The original democratic ideal was based on the conception of a common opinion on what is right being held by most of the people. But community of opinion on basic values is not sufficient to determine a program for current governmental action. The specific program that is required to unite a body of supporters of a government, or to hold together such a party, must be based on some aggregation of different interests which can only be achieved by a process of bargaining. It will not be an expression of common desire for the particular results to be achieved; and, as it will be concerned with the use of the concrete resources at the disposal of government for particular purposes, it will generally rest on the consent of the several groups to particular services rendered to some of them in return for other services offered to each of the consenting groups.

It would be mere pretense to describe a program of action thus decided upon in a bargaining democracy as in any sense an expression of the common opinion of the majority. Indeed, there may exist nobody who desires or even approves of all the things contained in such a program; for it will often contain elements of such contradictory character that no thinking person could ever desire them all for their own sake. Considering the process by which such programs for common action are agreed upon, it would indeed be a miracle if the outcome were anything but a conglomerate of the separate and incoherent wishes of many different individuals and groups. On many of the items included in the program most members of the electorate (or many of the representative assembly) will have no opinion at all because they know nothing of the circumstances involved. Towards many more they will be indifferent or even adversely disposed, but prepared to consent as payment for the realization of their own wishes. For most individuals the choice between party programs will therefore be mainly a choice between evils, namely between different benefits to be provided for others at their expense.

The purely additive character of such a program for governmental action stands out most clearly if we consider the problem that will face the leader of the party. He may or he may not have some chief objective for which he deeply cares. But whatever his ultimate objective, what he needs to achieve it is power. For this he needs the support of a majority which he can get only by enlisting people who are little interested in the objectives which guide him. To build up support for his program he will therefore have to offer effective enticements to a sufficient number of special interests to bring together a majority for the support of his program as a whole.

The agreement on which such a program for governmental action is based is something very different from that common opinion of a majority which it was hoped would be the determining force in a democracy. Nor can this kind of bargaining be regarded as the kind of compromise that is inevitable whenever people differ and must be brought to agree on some middle line which does not wholly satisfy anybody. A series of deals by which the wishes of one group are satisfied in return for the satisfaction of the wishes of another (and frequently at the expense of a third who is not consulted) may determine aims for common action of a coalition, but does not signify popular approval of the overall results. The outcome may indeed be wholly contrary to any principles which the several members of the majority would approve if they ever had an opportunity to vote on them.

This domination of government by coalitions of organized interests (when they were first observed they were generally described as 'sinister interests') is usually regarded by the outsider as an abuse, or even a kind of corruption. It is, however, the inescapable result of a system in which government has unlimited powers to take whatever measures are required to satisfy wishes on whose support it relies. A government with such powers cannot refuse to exercise them and still retain the support of a majority. We have no right to blame the politicians for doing what they must do in the position in which we have placed them. We have created conditions in which it is known that the majority has power to give any particular section of the population whatever it demands. But a government that possesses such unlimited powers can stay in office only by satisfying a sufficiently large number of pressure groups to assure itself of the support of a majority.

Government, in the narrow sense of the administration of the special resources set aside for the satisfaction of common needs, will to some extent always have that character. Its task is to hand out particular benefits to different groups, which is altogether distinct from that of legislation proper. But while this weakness is comparatively innocuous as long as government is confined to determining the use of an amount of resources placed at its disposal according to rules it cannot alter (and particularly when, as in local government, people can escape exploitation by voting with their feet), it assumes alarming proportions when government and rulemaking come to be confused and the persons who administer the resources of government also determine how much of the total resources it ought to control. To place those who ought to define what is right in a position in which they can maintain themselves only by giving their supporters what they want, is to place at their disposal all the resources of society for whatever purpose they think necessary to keep them in power.

If the elected administrators of a certain share of the resources of a society were under a law which they could not alter, though they would have to use them so as to satisfy their supporters, they could not be driven beyond what can be done without interfering with the freedom of the individual. But if they are at the same time also the makers of those rules of conduct, they will be driven to use their power to organize not only the resources belonging to government, but all the resources of society, including the individual's, to serve the particular wishes of their constituents.

We can prevent government from serving special interests only by depriving it of the power to use coercion in doing so, which means that we can limit the powers of organized interests only by limiting the powers of government. A system in which the politicians believe that it is their duty, and in their power, to remove all dissatisfaction, must lead to a complete manipulation of the people's affairs by the politicians. If that power is unlimited, it will and must be used in the service of particular interests, and it will induce all the organizable interests to combine in order to bring pressure upon government. The only defense that a politician has against such pressure is to point to an established principle which prevents him from complying and which he cannot alter. No system in which those who direct the use of the resources of government are not bound by unalterable rules can escape becoming an instrument of the organized interests.

Agreement on General Rules and on Particular Measures

We have repeatedly stressed that in a Great Society nobody can possess knowledge of or have any views about all the particular facts which might become the object of decisions by government. Any member of such a society can know no more than some small part of the comprehensive structure of relationships which makes up the society, but his wishes concerning the shaping of the sector of the overall pattern to which he belongs will inevitably conflict with the wishes of the others.

Thus, while nobody knows all, the separate desires will often clash in their effects and must be reconciled if agreement is to be reached. Democratic *government* (as distinguished from democratic legislation) requires that the consent of the individuals extend much beyond the particular facts of which they can be aware; and they will submit to a disregard of their own wishes only if they have come to accept some general rules which guide all particular measures and by which even the majority will abide. That in such situations conflict can be avoided only by agreement on general rules while, if agreement on the several particulars were required, conflicts would be irreconcilable, seems to be largely forgotten today.

True general agreement, or even true agreement among a majority will, in a Great Society, rarely extend beyond some general principles, and can be maintained only on such particular measures as can be known to most of its members.[17] Even more important, such a society will achieve a coherent and self-consistent overall order only if it submits to general rules in its particular decisions, and does not permit even the majority to break these rules unless this majority is prepared to commit itself to a new rule which it undertakes henceforth to apply without exception.

We have seen . . . that commitment to rules is in some degree necessary even to a single individual who endeavors to bring order into a complex of actions he cannot know in detail in advance. It is even more necessary where the successive decisions will be made by different groups of people with reference to different parts of the whole. Successive votes on particular issues would in such conditions not be likely to produce an aggregate result of which anyone would approve, unless they were all guided by the same general rules.

It has in a great measure been an awareness of the unsatisfactory results of the established procedures of democratic decision-making that has led to the demand for an overall plan whereby all government action will be decided upon for a long period ahead. Yet such a plan would not really provide a solution for the crucial difficulty. At least, as it is usually conceived, it would still be the result of a series of particular decisions on concrete issues and its determination would therefore raise the same problems. The effect of the adoption of such a plan is usually that it becomes a substitute for real criteria of whether the measures for which it provides are desirable.

The decisive facts are that not only will a true majority view in a Great Society exist only on general principles, but also that a majority can exercise some control over the out-

come of the market process only if it confines itself to the laying down of general principles and refrains from interfering with the particulars even if the concrete results are in
conflict with its wishes. It is inevitable that, when for the achievement of some of our purposes we avail ourselves of a mechanism that responds in part to circumstances unknown
to us, its effects on some particular results should be contrary to our wishes, and that there
will therefore often arise a conflict between the general rules we wish to see obeyed and
the particular results that we desire.

In collective action this conflict will manifest itself most conspicuously because, while as
individuals we have in general learned to abide by rules and are able to do so consistently, as
members of a body that decides by majority votes we have no assurance that future majorities will abide by those rules which might forbid us to vote for particulars which we like but
which are obtainable only by infringing an established rule. Though as individuals we have
learnt to accept that in pursuing our aims we are limited by established rules of just conduct,
when we vote as members of a body that has power to alter these rules, we often do not feel
similarly restrained. In the latter situation most people will indeed regard it as reasonable to
claim for themselves benefits of a kind which they know are being granted to others, but
which they also know cannot be granted universally and which they would therefore perhaps
prefer not to see granted to anybody at all. In the course of the particular decisions on specific issues the voters or their representatives will therefore often be led to support measures
in conflict with principles which they would prefer to see generally observed. So long as there
exist no rules that are binding on those who decide on the particular measures, it is thus inevitable that majorities will approve measures of a kind which, if they were asked to vote on
the principle, they would probably prohibit once and for all.

The contention that in any society there will usually exist more agreement on general
principles than on particular issues will at first perhaps appear contrary to ordinary experience. Daily practice seems to show that it is usually easier to obtain agreement on a particular issue than on a general principle. This, however, is a consequence merely of the fact that
we usually do not explicitly know, and have never put into words, those common principles
on which we know well how to act and which normally lead different persons to agree in
their judgments. The articulation or verbal formulation of these principles will often be very
difficult. This lack of conscious awareness of the principles on which we act does not disprove, however, that in fact we usually agree on particular moral issues only because we
agree on the rules applicable to them. But we will often learn to express these common rules
only by the examination of the various particular instances in which we have agreed, and by
a systematic analysis of the points on which we agree.

If people who learn for the first time about the circumstances of a dispute will generally
arrive at similar judgements on its merits, this means precisely that, whether they know it or
not, they are in fact guided by the same principles, while, when they are unable to agree, this
would seem to show that they lack such common principles. This is confirmed when we examine the nature of the arguments likely to produce agreement among parties who first disagreed on the merits of a particular case. Such arguments will always consist of appeals to
general principles, or at least to facts which are relevant only in the light of some general principle. It will never be the concrete instance as such, but always its character as one of a class
of instances, or as one that falls under a particular rule, that will be regarded as relevant. The
discovery of such a rule on which we can agree will be the basis for arriving at an agreement
on the particular issue.

"The Containment of Power and the Dethronement of Politics"

> We are living at a time when justice has vanished. Our parliaments light-heartedly produce statutes which are contrary to justice. States deal with their subjects arbitrarily without attempting to preserve a sense of justice. Men who fall under the power of another nation find themselves to all intents and purposes outlawed. There is no longer any respect for their natural right to their homeland or their dwelling place or property, their right to earn a living or to sustenance, or to anything whatever. Our trust in justice has been wholly destroyed.
>
> —Albert Schweitzer

Limited and Unlimited Power

The effective limitation of power is the most important problem of social order. Government is indispensable for the formation of such an order only to protect all against coercion and violence from others. But as soon as, to achieve this, government successfully claims the monopoly of coercion and violence, it becomes also the chief threat to individual freedom. To limit this power was the great aim of the founders of constitutional government in the seventeenth and eighteenth centuries. But the endeavor to contain the powers of government was almost inadvertently abandoned when it came to be mistakenly believed that democratic control of the exercise of power provided a sufficient safeguard against its excessive growth.[18]

We have since learnt that the very omnipotence conferred on democratic representative assemblies exposes them to irresistible pressure to use their power for the benefit of special interests, a pressure a majority with unlimited powers cannot resist if it is to remain a majority. This development can be prevented only by depriving the governing majority of the power to grant discriminatory benefits to groups or individuals. This has generally been believed to be impossible in a democracy because it appears to require that another will be placed above that of the elected representatives of a majority. In fact democracy needs even more severe restraints on the discretionary powers government can exercise than other forms of government because it is much more subject to effective pressure from special interests, perhaps of small numbers, on which its majority depends.

The problem seemed insoluble, however, only because an older ideal had been forgotten, namely that the power of all authorities exercising governmental functions ought to be limited by long run rules which nobody has the power to alter or abrogate in the service of particular ends: principles which are the terms of association of the community that recognizes an authority because this authority is committed to such long-term rules. It was the constructivistic–positivist superstition which led to the belief that there must be some single unlimited supreme power from which all other power is derived, while in fact the supreme authority owes its respect to restraint by limiting general rules.

What today we call democratic government serves, as a result of its construction, not the opinion of the majority but the varied interests of a conglomerate of pressure groups whose support the government must buy by the grant of special benefits, simply because it cannot retain its supporters when it refuses to give them something it has the power to give. The resulting progressive increase of discriminating coercion now threatens to strangle the growth of a civilization which rests on individual freedom. An erroneous constructivistic interpretation of the order of society, combined with mistaken understanding of the meaning of justice, has indeed become the chief danger to the future not only of wealth, but of morals and peace.

Nobody with open eyes can any longer doubt that the danger to personal freedom comes chiefly from the left, not because of any particular ideals it pursues, but because the various socialist movements are the only large organized bodies which, for aims which appeal to many, want to impose upon society a preconceived design. This must lead to the extinction of all moral responsibility of the individual and has already progressively removed, one after the other, most of those safeguards of individual freedom which had been built up through centuries of the evolution of law.

To regain certain fundamental truths which generations of demagoguery have obliterated, it is necessary to learn again to understand why the basic values of a great or open society must be negative, assuring the individual of the right within a known domain to pursue his own aims on the basis of his own knowledge. Only such negative rules make possible the formation of a self-generating order, utilizing the knowledge, and serving the desires, of the individuals. We shall have to reconcile ourselves to the still strange fact that in a society of free men the highest authority must in normal times have no power of positive commands whatever. Its sole power should be that of prohibition according to rule, so that it would owe its supreme position to its commitment with every act to a general principle.

Peace, Freedom, and Justice: The Three Great Negatives

The fundamental reason why the best that a government can give a great society of free men is negative is the unalterable ignorance of any single mind, or any organization that can direct human action, of the immeasurable multitude of particular acts which must determine the order of its activities. Only fools believe that they know all, but there are many. This ignorance is the cause why government can only assist (or perhaps make possible) the formation of an abstract pattern or structure in which the several expectations of the members approximately match each other, through making these members observe certain negative rules or prohibitions which are independent of particular purposes. It can only assure the abstract character and not the positive content of the order that will arise from the individuals' use of their knowledge for their purpose by delimiting their domains against each other by abstract and negative rules. Yet this very fact that in order to make most effective the use by the individuals of the information they possess for their own purposes, the chief benefit government can offer them must be 'merely' negative, most people find difficult to accept. In consequence all constructivists try to chisel on the original conception of these ideals.

Perhaps the only one of the great ideals with regard to which people are generally prepared to accept its negative character and would at once reject any attempt at chiseling is peace. I hope, at least, that if, say, a Krushchev had used the popular socialist gambit to agree to peace provided it was 'positive peace,' everybody would have understood that this simply meant peace only if he could do what he liked. But few seem to recognize that if the intellectual chiselers demand that liberty, or justice, or law be made 'positive,' this is a similar attempt to pervert and abuse the basic ideals. As in the case of many other good things, such as quiet, health, leisure, peace of mind, or a good conscience, it is the absence of certain evils rather than the presence of positive goods which is the pre-condition of the success of individual endeavors.

Current usage, which has come to employ 'positive' and 'negative' almost as equivalent to 'good' and 'bad,' and makes people feel that a 'negative value' is the opposite of a value, a disvalue or a harm, blinds many people to the crucial character of the greatest benefits our society can offer to us.

The three great negatives of Peace, Freedom, and Justice are in fact the sole indispensable foundations of civilization which government must provide. They are necessarily absent in the 'natural' condition of primitive man, and man's innate instincts do not provide them for his fellows. They are . . . the most important yet still only imperfectly assured products of the rules of civilization.

Coercion can assist freemen in the pursuit of their ends only by the enforcement of a framework of universal rules which do not direct them to particular ends, but, by enabling them to create for themselves a domain protected against unpredictable disturbance caused by other men—including agents of government—to pursue their own ends. And if the greatest need is security against infringement of such a protected sphere by others, including government, the highest authority needed is one who can merely say 'no' to others but has itself no 'positive' powers.

The conception of a highest authority which cannot issue any commands sounds strange and even contradictory to us because it has come to be believed that a highest authority must be all comprehensive, omnipotent authority which comprises all the powers of the subordinate authorities. But there is no justification for all this 'positivist' belief. Except when as a result of external human or natural forces the self-generating order is disturbed and emergency measures are required to restore the conditions for its operation, there is no need for such 'positive' powers of the supreme authority. Indeed, there is every reason to desire as the highest authority such a one that all its powers rest on its committing itself to the kind of abstract rules which, independently of the particular consequences, require it to prevent interference with the acquired rights of the individuals by government or private agencies. Such an authority which normally is committed to certain recognized principles and then can order enforcement of such general rules, but so long as society is not threatened by outside forces has no other coercive powers whatever, may still be above all governmental powers—even be the only common power over a whole territory, while all the properly governmental powers might be separate for the different regions.

Centralization and Decentralization

The amount of centralization which we take for granted and in which the supreme legislature and the supreme governmental power are part of the same unitary organization of what we call a nation or a state (and which is little reduced even in federal states), is essentially the effect of the need of making this organization strong for war. But now, when at least in Western Europe and North America we believe we have excluded the possibility of war between the associated nations and are relying for defense (we hope effectively) on a supranational organization, we ought gradually to discover that we can reduce the centralization and cease to entrust so many tasks to the national government, merely to make that government strong against external enemies.

It was necessary, in the interest of clarity, in the context of this book to discuss the changes in the constitutional structure, required if individual freedom is to be preserved, with reference to the most familiar type of a unitary state. But they are in fact even more suitable for a decentralized hierarchic structure on federal lines. We can here mention only a few major aspects of this.

The bicameral system, usually regarded as essential for a federal constitution, has under the scheme proposed here been preempted for another purpose; but its function in a federation could be achieved by other means, such as a system of double counting of votes, at least in the governmental assembly: once according to heads and once according to the number of states represented in the central assembly. It would probably be desirable to restrict federal arrangements to government proper and to have a single legislative assembly for the whole federation. But it is not really necessary always to have both legislative assemblies and governmental assemblies on the same level of the hierarchy provided that the governmental power, whether extending to a smaller or a larger territory than the legislative power, is always limited by the latter. This would seem to make it desirable that the legislative power should extend over a larger territory than the governmental one; but there exist of course several instances (Great Britain with a different system of private law in England and Scotland, the USA with the common law in most states and the Code Napoleon in one) with a central governmental executive ruling over territories with different law, and a few (the British Commonwealth of Nations to some extent and for a period) where the highest power determining the law (the court of last instance) was common to a number of otherwise wholly independent governments.

More important for our purposes are, however, the desirable devolutions which would become possible once the power of a supranational authority to say 'no' to actions harmful to associated states had reduced the necessity of a strong central national government for defense purposes. Most service activities of government might then indeed with advantage be delegated to regional or local authorities, wholly limited in their coercive powers by the rules laid down by a higher legislative authority.

There exists, of course, neither on the national nor on the international level, a moral ground why poorer regions should be entitled to tap for their purposes the wealth of richer regions. Yet centralization advances, not because the majority of the people in the large region are anxious to supply the means for assistance to the poorer regions, but because the majority, to be a majority, needs the additional votes from the regions which benefit from sharing in the wealth of the larger unit. And what is happening in the existing nations is beginning to happen on an international scale, where, by a silly competition with Russia, the capitalist nations, instead of lending capital to enterprise in countries which pursue economic policies which they regard as promising, are actually subsidizing on a large scale the socialist experiments of underdeveloped countries where they know that the funds that they supply will be largely wasted.

The Rule of the Majority Versus the Rule of Laws Approved by the Majority

Not only peace, justice, and liberty, but also democracy is basically a negative value, a procedural rule which serves as protection against despotism and tyranny, and certainly no more but not much less important than the first Three Great Negatives—or, to put it differently, a convention which mainly serves to prevent harm. But, like liberty and justice, it is now being destroyed by endeavours to give it a 'positive' content. I am fairly certain that the days of unlimited democracy are numbered. We will, if we are to preserve the basic values of democracy, have to adopt a different form of it, or sooner or later lose altogether the power of getting rid of an oppressive government. [. . . .]

[U]nder the prevailing system it is not the common opinion of a majority that decides on common issues, but a majority that owes its existence and power to the gratifying of the special interests of numerous small groups, which the representatives cannot refuse to grant if they are to remain a majority. But while agreement of the majority of a great society on general rules is possible, the so-called approval by the majority of a conglomerate of measures serving particular interests is a farce. Buying majority support by deals with special interests, though this is what contemporary democracy has come to mean, has nothing to do with the original ideal of democracy, and is certainly contrary to the more fundamental moral conception that all use of force ought to be guided and limited by the opinion of the majority. The vote-buying process which we have come to accept as a necessary part of the democracy we know, and which indeed is inevitable in a representative assembly which has the power both to pass general laws and to issue commands, is morally indefensible and produces all that which to the outsider appears as contemptible in politics. It is certainly not a necessary consequence of the ideal that the opinion of the majority should rule, but is in conflict with it.

This error is closely connected with the misconception that the majority must be free to do what it likes. A majority of the representatives of the people based on bargaining over group demands can never represent the opinion of the majority of the people. Such 'freedom of Parliament' means the oppression of the people. It is wholly in conflict with the conception of a constitutional limitation of governmental power, and irreconcilable with the ideal of a society of free men. The exercise of the power of a representative democracy beyond the range where voters can comprehend the significance of its decisions can correspond to (or be controlled by) the opinion of the majority of the people only if in all its coercive measures government is confined to rules which apply equally to all members of the community.

So long as the present form of democracy persists, decent government cannot exist, even if the politicians are angels or profoundly convinced of the supreme value of personal freedom. We have no right to blame them for what they do, because it is we who, by maintaining the present institutions, place them in a position in which they can obtain power to do any good only if they commit themselves to secure special benefits for various groups. This has led to the attempt to justify these measures by the construction of a pseudo-ethics, called 'social justice,' which fails every test which a system of moral rules must satisfy in order to secure a peace and voluntary co-operation of free men.

It is the crucial contention of this book that what in a society of free men can alone justify coercion is a predominant opinion on the principles which ought to govern and restrain individual conduct. It is obvious that a peaceful and prosperous society can exist only if some such rules are generally obeyed and, when necessary, enforced. This has nothing to do with any 'will' aiming at a particular objective.

What to most people still seems strange and even incomprehensible is that in such a society the supreme power must be a limited power, not all-comprehensive but confined to restraining both organized government and private persons and organizations by the enforcement of general rules of conduct. Yet it can be the condition of submission which creates the state that the only authorization for coercion by the supreme authority refers to the enforcement of general rules of conduct equally applicable to all. Such a supreme power ought to owe the allegiance and respect which it claims to its commitment to the general principles, to secure obedience to which is the sole task for which it may use coercion. It is to make these principles conform to general opinion that the supreme legislature is made representative of the views of the majority of the people.

Moral Confusion and the Decay of Language

Under the influence of socialist agitation in the course of the last hundred years the very sense in which many of the key words describing political ideals are used has so changed meaning that one must today hesitate to use even words like 'liberty,' 'justice,' 'democracy' or 'law,' because they no longer convey the meaning they once did. But, as Confucius is reported to have said, 'when words lose their meaning, people will lose their liberty.' It was, unfortunately, not only ignorant propagandists but often grave social philosophers who contributed to this decay of language by twisting well established words to seduce people to serve what they imagined to be good purposes. When a John Dewey defines liberty as 'the effective power to do specific things'[19] this might seem a devious trick to delude innocents. But if another social philosopher argues in discussing democracy that 'the most promising line of approach is to say that democracy . . . is considered good because on the whole it is the best device for securing certain elements of social justice,'[20] it is evidently just incredible naivety.

The younger generation of social philosophers apparently do not even know what the basic concepts once meant. Only thus can it be explained when we find a young scholar seriously asserting that the usage of speaking of a 'just state of affairs . . . must be regarded as the primary one, for when we describe a man as just we mean that he usually attempts to act in such a way that a just state of affairs results'[21] and even adding a few pages later that 'there appears [!] to be a category of "private justice" which concerns the dealing of a man with his fellows where he is not acting as a participant in one of the major or social institutions.'[22] This may perhaps be accounted for by the fact that today a young man will first encounter the term 'justice' in some such connection, but it is of course a travesty of the evolution of the concept. As we have seen, a state of affairs which has not been deliberately brought about by men can possess neither intelligence nor virtue, nor justice, nor any other attribute of human values—not even if it is the unpredictable result of a game which people have consented to play by entering in their own interest into exchange relations with others. Justice is, of course, not a question of the aims of an action but of its obedience to rules which it obeys.

These instances, culled almost at random, of the current abuse of political terms in which those who have skill with words, by shifting the meaning of concepts they have perhaps never quite understood, have gradually emptied them of all clear content, could be increased indefinitely. It is difficult to know what to do when the enemies of liberty describe themselves as liberals, as is today common practice in the USA—except calling them persistently, as we ought to do, pseudo-liberals—or when they appeal to democracy when they mean egalitarianism. It is all part of that 'Treason of the Intellectuals' which Julien Benda castigated forty years ago, but which has since succeeded in creating a reign of untruthfulness which has become habitual in discussion issues of 'social' policy, and in the current language of politicians who habitually employ this makebelieve without themselves knowing it as such.

But it is not merely the confessed socialists who drive us along that road. Socialist ideas have so deeply penetrated general thought that it is not even only those pseudo-liberals who merely disguise their socialism by the name they have assumed, but also many conservatives who have assumed socialist ideas and language and constantly employ them in the belief that they are an established part of current thought. Nor is it only people who have strong views on, or take an active part in public affairs. Indeed the most active spreading of socialist conceptions still takes place through what David Hume called the fiction of poets,[23] the ignorant literati who are sure that the appealing words they employ have definite meaning. Only because we are so habituated to this can it be explained that, for instance, hundreds of thousands of business men all over the world still allow over their doorsteps journals which in their literary part will resort even to obscene language (such as 'the excremental abundance of capitalist production' in *Time* magazine of 27 June 1977) to ridicule capitalism. Though the principle of freedom requires that we tolerate such scandalous scurrilities, one might have hoped that the good sense of the readers would soon learn what publications they can trust.

Democratic Procedure and Egalitarian Objectives

Perhaps the worst sufferer in this process of the emptying of the meaning of words has in recent times been the word 'democracy' itself. Its chief abuse is to apply it not to a procedure of arriving at agreement on common action, but to give it a substantive content prescribing what the aim of those activities ought to be. However absurd this clearly is, many of the current invocations of democracy amount to telling democratic legislatures what they ought to do. Except so far as organization of government is concerned, the term 'democratic' says nothing about the particular aims people ought to vote for.

The true value of democracy is to serve as a sanitary precaution protecting us against an abuse of power. It enables us to get rid of a government and try to replace it by a better one. Or, to put it differently, it is the only convention we have yet discovered to make peaceful change possible. As such it is a high value well worth fighting for, since any government the people cannot get rid of by such an agreed procedure is bound to fall sooner or later into bad hands. But it is far from being the highest political value, and an unlimited democracy may well be worse than limited governments of a different kind.

In its present unlimited form democracy has today largely lost the capacity of serving as a protection against arbitrary power. It has ceased to be a safeguard of personal liberty, a restraint on the abuse of governmental power which it was hoped it would prove to be when it was naively believed that, when all power was made subject to democratic control, all the other restraints on governmental power could be dispensed with. It has, on the contrary, become the main cause of a progressive and accelerating increase of the power and weight of the administrative machine.

The omnipotent and omnicompetent single democratic assembly, in which a majority capable of governing can maintain itself only by trying to remove all sources of discontent of any supporter of that majority, is thereby driven to take control of all spheres of life. It is forced to develop and impose, in justification of the measures it must take to retain majority support, a non-existing and in the strict sense of the word inconceivable code of distributive justice. In such a society, to have political pull becomes much more rewarding than adding to the means of satisfying the needs of one's fellows. As everything tends to become a political issue for which the interference of the coercive powers of government can be invoked, an ever larger part of human activity is diverted from productive into political efforts—not only of the political machinery itself but, worse, of that rapidly expanding apparatus of para-government designed to bring pressure on government to favor particular interests.

What is still not understood is that the majority of a representative assembly with unlimited powers is neither able, nor constrained, to confine its activities to aims which all the members of the majority desire, or even approve of. If such an assembly has the power to grant special benefits, a majority can regularly be kept together only by paying off each of the special groups by which it is composed. In other words, we have under the false name democracy created a machinery in which not the majority decides, but each member of the majority has to consent to many bribes to get majority support for his own special demands. However admirable the principle of majority decisions may be with respect to matters which necessarily concern all, so vicious must be the result of an application of this procedure to distributing the booty which can be extracted from a dissident minority.

It seems to be inevitable that if we retain democracy in its present form, the concept itself is bound to become discredited to such an extent that even the legitimate case for majority decisions on questions of principle will go by default. Democracy is in danger because the particular institutions by which we have tried to realize it have produced effects which we mistake for those of the genuine article. As I have myself suggested before, I am even no longer certain that the name democracy can still be freed from the distaste with which increasing numbers of people for good reasons have come to regard it, even though few yet dare publicly to express their disillusionment.

The root of the trouble is, of course, to sum up, that in an unlimited democracy the holders of discretionary powers are forced to use them, whether they wish it or not, to favor particular groups on whose swing-vote their powers depend. This applies as much to government as to such democratically organized institutions as trades unions. Even if, in the case of government, some of these powers may serve to enable it to do much that might be desirable in itself, we must renounce conferring them since such discretionary powers inevitably and necessarily place the authority into a position in which it will be forced to do even more that is harmful.

MILTON FRIEDMAN, "THE ROLE OF GOVERNMENT IN A FREE SOCIETY" (1962)

A common objection to totalitarian societies is that they regard the end as justifying the means. Taken literally, this objection is clearly illogical. If the end does not justify the means, what does? But this easy answer does not dispose of the objection; it simply shows that the objection is not well put. To deny that the end justifies the means is indirectly to assert that the end in question is not the ultimate end, that the ultimate end is itself the use of the proper means. Desirable or not, any end that can be attained only by the use of bad means must give way to the more basic end of the use of acceptable means.

To the liberal, the appropriate means are free discussion and voluntary co-operation, which implies that any form of coercion is inappropriate. The ideal is unanimity among responsible individuals achieved on the basis of free and full discussion. This is another way of expressing the goal of freedom. . . .

From this standpoint, the role of the market is that it permits unanimity without conformity; that it is a system of effectively proportional representation. On the other hand, the characteristic feature of action through explicitly political channels is that it tends to require or to enforce substantial conformity. The typical issue must be decided "yes" or "no"; at most, provision can be made for a fairly limited number of alternatives. Even the use of proportional representation in its explicitly political form does not alter this conclusion. The number of separate groups that can in fact be represented is narrowly limited, enormously so by comparison with the proportional representation of the market. More important, the fact that the final outcome generally must be a law applicable to all groups, rather than separate legislative enactments for each "party" represented, means that proportional representation in its political version, far from permitting unanimity without conformity, tends toward ineffectiveness and fragmentation. It thereby operates to destroy any consensus on which unanimity with conformity can rest.

There are clearly some matters with respect to which effective proportional represen-tation is impossible. I cannot get the amount of national defense I want and you, a dif-ferent amount. With respect to such indivisible matters we can discuss, and argue, and vote. But having decided, we must conform. It is precisely the existence of such indivisi-ble matters—protection of the individual and the nation from coercion are clearly the most basic—that prevents exclusive reliance on individual action through the market. If we are to use some of our resources for such indivisible items, we must employ political channels to reconcile differences.

The use of political channels, while inevitable, tends to strain the social cohesion es-sential for a stable society. The strain is least if agreement for joint action need be reached only on a limited range of issues on which people in any event have common views. Every extension of the range of issues for which explicit agreement is sought strains further the delicate threads that hold society together. If it goes so far as to touch an issue on which men feel deeply yet differently, it may well disrupt the society. Fundamental differences in basic values can seldom if ever be resolved at the ballot box; ultimately they can only be decided, though not resolved, by conflict. The religious and civil wars of history are a bloody testament to this judgment.

The widespread use of the market reduces the strain on the social fabric by rendering conformity unnecessary with respect to any activities it encompasses. The wider the range of activities covered by the market, the fewer are the issues on which explicitly political deci-sions are required and hence on which it is necessary to achieve agreement. In turn, the fewer the issues on which agreement is necessary, the greater is the likelihood of getting agreement while maintaining a free society.

Unanimity is, of course, an ideal. In practice, we can afford neither the time nor the ef-fort that would be required to achieve complete unanimity on every issue. We must per-force accept something less. We are thus led to accept majority rule in one form or another as an expedient. That majority rule is an expedient rather than itself a basic principle is clearly shown by the fact that our willingness to resort to majority rule, and the size of the majority we require, themselves depend on the seriousness of the issue involved. If the matter is of little moment and the minority has no strong feelings about being overruled, a bare plurality will suffice. On the other hand, if the minority feels strongly about the issue involved, even a bare majority will not do. Few of us would be willing to have issues of free speech, for example, decided by a bare majority. Our legal structure is full of such dis-tinctions among kinds of issues that required different kinds of majorities. At the extreme are those issues embodied in the Constitution. These are the principles that are so impor-tant that we are willing to make minimal concessions to expediency. Something like es-sential consensus was achieved initially in accepting them, and we require something like essential consensus for a change in them.

The self-denying ordinance to refrain from majority rule on certain kinds of issues that is embodied in our Constitution and in similar written or unwritten constitutions elsewhere, and the specific provisions in these constitutions or their equivalents prohibiting coercion of indi-viduals, are themselves to be regarded as reached by free discussion and as reflecting essen-tial unanimity about means.

I turn now to consider more specifically, though still in very broad terms, what the areas are that cannot be handled through the market at all, or can be handled only at so great a cost that the use of political channels may be preferable.

Government as Rule-Maker and Umpire

It is important to distinguish the day-to-day activities of people from the general customary and legal framework within which these take place. The day-to-day activities are like the actions of participants in a game when they are playing it; the framework, like the rules of the game they play. And just as a good game requires acceptance by the players both of the rules and of the umpire to interpret and enforce them, so a good society requires that its members agree on the general conditions that will govern relations among them, on some means of arbitrating different interpretations of these conditions, and on some device for enforcing compliance with the generally accepted rules. As in games, so also in society, most of the general conditions are the unintended outcome of custom, accepted unthinkingly. At most, we consider explicitly only minor modifications in them, though the cumulative effect of a series of minor modifications may be a drastic alteration in the character of the game or of the society. In both games and society also, no set of rules can prevail unless most participants most of the time conform to them without external sanctions; unless that is, there is a broad underlying social consensus. But we cannot rely on custom or on this consensus alone to interpret and to enforce the rules; we need an umpire. These then are the basic roles of government in a free society: to provide a means whereby we can modify the rules, to mediate differences among us on the meaning of the rules, and to enforce compliance with the rules on the part of those few who would otherwise not play the game.

The need for government in these respects arises because absolute freedom is impossible. However attractive anarchy may be as a philosophy, it is not feasible in a world of imperfect men. Men's freedoms can conflict, and when they do, one man's freedom must be limited to preserve another's—as a Supreme Court justice once put it, "My freedom to move my fist must be limited by the proximity of your chin."

The major problem in deciding the appropriate activities of government is how to resolve such conflicts among the freedoms of different individuals. In some cases, the answer is easy. There is little difficulty in attaining near unanimity to the proposition that one man's freedom to murder his neighbor must be sacrificed to preserve the freedom of the other man to live. In other cases, the answer is difficult. In the economic area, a major problem arises in respect of the conflict between freedom to combine and freedom to compete. What meaning is to be attributed to "free" as modifying "enterprise"? In the United States, "free" has been understood to mean that anyone is free to set up an enterprise, which means that existing enterprises are not free to keep out competitors except by selling a better product at the same price or the same product at a lower price. In the continental tradition, on the other hand, the meaning has generally been that enterprises are free to do what they want, including the fixing of prices, division of markets, and the adoption of other techniques to keep out potential competitors. Perhaps the most difficult specific problem in this area arises with respect to combinations among laborers, where the problem of freedom to combine and freedom to compete is particularly acute.

A still more basic economic area in which the answer is both difficult and important is the definition of property rights. The notion of property, as it has developed over centuries and as it is embodied in our legal codes, has become so much a part of us that we tend to take it for granted, and fail to recognize the extent to which just what constitutes property and what rights the ownership of property confers are complex social creations rather than self-evident propositions. Does my having title to land, for example, and my freedom to use my property as I wish, permit me to deny to someone else the right to fly over my land in his airplane?

Or does his right to use his airplane take precedence? Or does this depend on how high he flies? Or how much noise he makes? Does voluntary exchange require that he pay me for the privilege of flying over my land? Or that I must pay him to refrain from flying over it? The mere mention of royalties, copyrights, patents; shares of stock in corporations; riparian rights, and the like, may perhaps emphasize the role of generally accepted social rules in the very definition of property. It may suggest also that, in many cases, the existence of a well-specified and generally accepted definition of property is far more important than just what the definition is.

Another economic area that raises particularly difficult problems is the monetary system. Government responsibility for the monetary system has long been recognized. It is explicitly provided for in the constitutional provision which gives Congress the power "to coin money, regulate the value thereof, and of foreign coin." There is probably no other area of economic activity with respect to which government action has been so uniformly accepted. This habitual and by now almost unthinking acceptance of governmental responsibility makes thorough understanding of the grounds for such responsibility all the more necessary, since it enhances the danger that the scope of government will spread from activities that are, to those that are not, appropriate in a free society, from providing a monetary framework to determining the allocation of resources among individuals. [. . . .]

In summary, the organization of economic activity through voluntary exchange presumes that we have provided, through government, for the maintenance of law and order to prevent coercion of one individual by another, the enforcement of contracts voluntarily entered into, the definition of the meaning of property rights, the interpretation and enforcement of such rights, and the provision of a monetary framework.

Action through Government on Grounds of Technical Monopoly and Neighborhood Effects

The role of government just considered is to do something that the market cannot do for itself, namely, to determine, arbitrate, and enforce the rules of the game. We may also want to do through government some things that might conceivably be done through the market but that technical or similar conditions render it difficult to do in that way. These all reduce to cases in which strictly voluntary exchange is either exceedingly costly or practically impossible. There are two general classes of such cases: monopoly and similar market imperfections, and neighborhood effects.

Exchange is truly voluntary only when nearly equivalent alternatives exist. Monopoly implies the absence of alternatives and thereby inhibits effective freedom of exchange. In practice, monopoly frequently, if not generally, arises from government support or from collusive agreements among individuals. With respect to these, the problem is either to avoid governmental fostering of monopoly or to stimulate the effective enforcement of rules such as those embodied in our anti-trust laws. However, monopoly may also arise because it is technically efficient to have a single producer or enterprise. I venture to suggest that such cases are more limited than is supposed but they unquestionably do arise. A simple example is perhaps the provision of telephone services within a community. I shall refer to such cases as "technical" monopoly.

When technical conditions make a monopoly the natural out come of competitive market forces, there are only three alternatives that seem available: private monopoly, public monopoly, or public regulation. All three are bad so we must choose among evils. Henry Simons, observing public regulation of monopoly in the United States, found the results so distasteful that he concluded public monopoly would be a lesser evil. Walter Eucken, a noted German liberal, observing public monopoly in German railroads, found the results so distasteful that he concluded public regulation would be a lesser evil. Having learned from both, I reluctantly conclude that, if tolerable, private monopoly may be the least of the evils.

If society were static so that the conditions which give rise to a technical monopoly were sure to remain, I would have little confidence in this solution. In a rapidly changing society, however, the conditions making for technical monopoly frequently change and I suspect that both public regulation and public monopoly, are likely to be less responsive to such changes in conditions, to be less readily capable of elimination, than private monopoly.

Railroads in the United States are an excellent example. A large degree of monopoly in railroads was perhaps inevitable on technical grounds in the nineteenth century. This was the justification for the Interstate Commerce Commission. But conditions have changed. The emergence of road and air transport has reduced the monopoly element in railroads to negligible proportions. Yet we have not eliminated the ICC. On the contrary, the ICC, which started out as an agency to protect the public from exploitation by the railroads, has become an agency to protect railroads from competition by trucks and other means of transport, and more recently even to protect existing truck companies from competition by new entrants. Similarly, in England, when the railroads were nationalized, trucking was at first brought into the state monopoly. If railroads had never been subjected to regulation in the United States, it is nearly certain that by now transportation, including railroads, would be a highly competitive industry with little or no remaining monopoly elements.

The choice between the evils of private monopoly, public monopoly, and public regulation cannot, however, be made once and for all, independently of the factual circumstances. If the technical monopoly is of a service or commodity that is regarded as essential and if its monopoly power is sizable, even the short-run effects of private unregulated monopoly may not be tolerable, and either public regulation or ownership may be a lesser evil.

Technical monopoly may on occasion justify a *de facto* public monopoly. It cannot by itself justify a public monopoly achieved by making it illegal for anyone else to compete. For example, there is no way to justify our present public monopoly of the post office. It may be argued that the carrying of mail is a technical monopoly and that a government monopoly is the least of evils. Along these lines, one could perhaps justify a government post office but not the present law, which makes it illegal for anybody else to carry mail. If the delivery of mail is a technical monopoly, no one will be able to succeed in competition with the government. If it is not, there is no reason why the government should be engaged in it. The only way to find out is to leave other people free to enter.

The historical reason why we have a post office monopoly is because the Pony Express did such a good job of carrying the mail across the continent that, when the government introduced transcontinental service, it couldn't compete effectively and lost money. The result was a law making it illegal for anybody else to carry the mail. That is why the Adams Express Company is an investment trust today instead of an operating company. I conjecture that if entry into the mail-carrying business were open to all, there would be a large number of firms entering it and this archaic industry would become revolutionized in short order.

A second general class of cases in which strictly voluntary exchange is impossible arises when actions of individuals have effects on other individuals for which it is not feasible to charge or recompense them. This is the problem of "neighborhood effects." An obvious example is the pollution of a stream. The man who pollutes a stream is in effect forcing others to exchange good water for bad. These others might be willing to make the exchange at a price. But it is not feasible for them, acting individually, to avoid the exchange or to enforce appropriate compensation.

A less obvious example is the provision of highways. In this case, it is technically possible to identify and hence charge individuals for their use of the roads and so to have private operation. However, for general access roads, involving many points of entry and exit, the costs of collection would be extremely high if a charge were to be made for the specific services received by each individual, because of the necessity of establishing toll booths or the equivalent at all entrances. The gasoline tax is a much cheaper method of charging individuals roughly in proportion to their use of the roads. This method, however, is one in which the particular payment cannot be identified closely with the particular use. Hence, it is hardly feasible to have private enterprise provide the service and collect the charge without establishing extensive private monopoly.

These considerations do not apply to long-distance turnpikes with high density of traffic and limited access. For these, the costs of collection are small and in many cases are now being paid, and there are often numerous alternatives, so that there is no serious monopoly problem. Hence, there is every reason why these should be privately owned and operated. If so owned and operated, the enterprise running the highway should receive the gasoline taxes paid on account of travel on it.

Parks are an interesting example because they illustrate the difference between cases that can and cases that cannot be justified by neighborhood effects, and because almost everyone at first sight regards the conduct of National Parks as obviously a valid function of government. In fact, however, neighborhood effects may justify a city park; they do not justify a national park, like Yellowstone National Park or the Grand Canyon. What is the fundamental difference between the two? For the city park, it is extremely difficult to identify the people who benefit from it and to charge them for the benefits which they receive. If there is a park in the middle of the city, the houses on all sides get the benefit of the open space, and people who walk through or by it also benefit. To maintain toll collectors at the gates or to impose annual charges per window overlooking the park would be very expensive and difficult. The entrances to a national park like Yellowstone, on the other hand, are few; most of the people who come stay for a considerable period of time and it is perfectly feasible to set up toll gates and collect admission charges. This is indeed now done, though the charges do not cover the whole costs. If the public wants this kind of an activity enough to pay for it, private enterprises will have every incentive to provide such parks. And, of course, there are many private enterprises of this nature now in existence. I cannot myself conjure up any neighborhood effects or important monopoly effects that would justify governmental activity in this area.

Considerations like those I have treated under the heading of neighborhood effects have been used to rationalize almost every conceivable intervention. In many instances, however, this rationalization is special pleading rather than a legitimate application of the concept of neighborhood effects. Neighborhood effects cut both ways. They can be a reason for limiting the activities of government as well as for expanding them. Neighborhood effects impede voluntary exchange because it is difficult to identify the effects on third parties and to measure their magnitude; but this difficulty is present in governmental activity as well. It is hard to know when neighborhood effects are sufficiently large to justify particular costs in overcoming them and even harder to distribute the costs in an appropriate fashion. Consequently, when government engages in activities to overcome neighborhood effects, it will in part introduce an additional set of neighborhood effects by failing to charge or to compensate individuals properly. Whether the original or the new neighborhood effects are the more serious can only be judged by the facts of the individual case, and even then, only very approximately. Furthermore, the use of government to overcome neighborhood effects itself has an extremely important neighborhood effect which is unrelated to the particular occasion for government action. Every act of government intervention limits the area of individual freedom directly and threatens the preservation of freedom indirectly. [. . . .]

Our principles offer no hard and fast line how far it is appropriate to use government to accomplish jointly what it is difficult or impossible for us to accomplish separately through strictly voluntary exchange. In any particular case of proposed intervention, we must make up a balance sheet, listing separately the advantages and disadvantages. Our principles tell us what items to put on the one side and what items on the other and they give us some basis for attaching importance to the different items. In particular, we shall always want to enter on the liability side of any proposed government intervention, its neighborhood effect in threatening freedom, and give this effect considerable weight. Just how much weight to give to it, as to other items, depends upon the circumstances. If, for example, existing government intervention is minor, we shall attach a smaller weight to the negative effects of additional government intervention. This is an important reason why many earlier liberals, like Henry Simons, writing at a time when government was small by today's standards, were willing to have government undertake activities that today's liberals would not accept now that government has become so overgrown.

Action through Government on Paternalistic Grounds

Freedom is a tenable objective only for responsible individuals. We do not believe in freedom for madmen or children. The necessity of drawing a line between responsible individuals and others is inescapable, yet it means that there is an essential ambiguity in our ultimate objective of freedom. Paternalism is inescapable for those whom we designate as not responsible.

The clearest case, perhaps, is that of madmen. We are willing neither to permit them freedom nor to shoot them. It would be nice if we could rely on voluntary activities of individuals to house and care for the madmen. But I think we cannot rule out the possibility that such charitable activities will be inadequate, if only because of the neighborhood effect involved in the fact that I benefit if another man contributes to the care of the insane. For this reason, we may be willing to arrange for their care through government.

Children offer a more difficult case. The ultimate operative unit in our society is the family, not the individual. Yet the acceptance of the family as the unit rests in considerable part on expediency rather than principle. We believe that parents are generally best able to protect their children and to provide for their development into responsible individuals for whom freedom is appropriate. But we do not believe in the freedom of parents to do what they will with other people. The children are responsible individuals in embryo, and a believer in freedom believes in protecting their ultimate rights.

To put this in a different and what may seem a more callous way, children are at one and the same time consumer goods and potentially responsible members of society. The freedom of individuals to use their economic resources as they want includes the freedom to use them to have children—to buy, as it were, the services of children as a particular form of consumption. But once this choice is exercised, the children have a value in and of themselves and have a freedom of their own that is not simply an extension of the freedom of the parents.

The paternalistic ground for governmental activity is in many ways the most troublesome to a liberal, for it involves the acceptance of a principle—that some shall decide for others—which he finds objectionable in most applications and which he rightly regards as a hallmark of his chief intellectual opponents, the proponents of collectivism in one or another of its guises, whether it be communism, socialism, or a welfare state. Yet there is no use pretending that problems are simpler than in fact they are. There is no avoiding the need for some measure of paternalism. As Dicey wrote in 1914 about an act for the protection of mental defectives, "The Mental Deficiency Act is the first step along a path on which no sane man can decline to enter, but which, if too far pursued, will bring statesmen across difficulties hard to meet without considerable interference with individual liberty."[24] There is no formula that can tell us where to stop. We must, rely on our fallible judgment and, having reached a judgment, on our ability to persuade our fellow men that it is a correct judgment, or their ability to persuade us to modify our views. We must put our faith, here as elsewhere, in a consensus reached by imperfect and biased men through free discussion and trial and error.

Conclusion

A government which maintained law and order, defined property rights, served as a means whereby we could modify property rights and other rules of the economic game, adjudicated disputes about the interpretation of the rules, enforced contracts, promoted competition, provided a monetary framework, engaged in activities to counter technical monopolies and to overcome neighborhood effects widely regarded as sufficiently important to justify government intervention, and which supplemented private charity and the private family in protecting the irresponsible, whether madman or child—such a government would clearly have important functions to perform. The consistent liberal is not an anarchist.

Yet it is also true that such a government would have clearly limited functions and would refrain from a host of activities that are now undertaken by federal and state governments in the United States, and their counterparts in other Western countries. . . . [I]t may help to give a sense of proportion about the role that a liberal would assign government simply to list, in closing this chapter, some activities currently undertaken by government in the U.S., that cannot, so far as I can see, validly be justified in terms of the principles outlined above:

1. Parity price support programs for agriculture.
2. Tariffs on imports or restrictions on exports, such as current oil import quotas, sugar quotas, etc.
3. Governmental control of output, such as through the farm program, or through prorationing of oil as is done by the Texas Railroad Commission.
4. Rent control, such as is still practiced in New York, or more general price and wage controls such as were imposed during and just after World War II.
5. Legal minimum wage rates, or legal maximum prices, such as the legal maximum of zero on the rate of interest that can be paid on demand deposits by commercial banks, or the legally fixed maximum rates that can be paid on savings and time deposits.
6. Detailed regulation of industries, such as the regulation of transportation by the Interstate Commerce Commission. This had some justification on technical monopoly grounds when initially introduced for railroads; it has none now for any means of transport. Another example is detailed regulation of banking.

7. A similar example, but one which deserves special mention because of its implicit censorship and violation of free speech, is control of radio and television by the Federal Communications Commission.

8. Present social security programs, especially the old-age and retirement programs compelling people in effect (*a*) to spend a specified fraction of their income on the purchase of retirement annuity, (*b*) to buy the annuity from a publicly operated enterprise.

9. Licensure provisions in various cities and states which restrict particular enterprises or occupations or professions to people who have a license, where the license is more than a receipt for a tax which anyone who wishes to enter the activity may pay.

10. So-called "public-housing" and the host of other subsidy programs directed at fostering residential construction such as F.H.A. and V.A. guarantee of mortgage, and the like.

11. Conscription to man the military services in peacetime. The appropriate free market arrangement is volunteer military forces; which is to say, hiring men to serve. There is no justification for not paying whatever price is necessary to attract the required number of men. Present arrangements are inequitable and arbitrary, seriously interfere with the freedom of young men to shape their lives, and probably are even more costly than the market alternative. (Universal military training to provide a reserve for war time is a different problem and may be justified on liberal grounds.)

12. National parks, as noted above.

13. The legal prohibition on the carrying of mail for profit.

14. Publicly owned and operated toll roads, as noted above.

This list is far from comprehensive.

NOTES

1. For further reading on protective democracy by a contemporary theorist, see Robert Nozick, *Anarchy, State, and Utopia* (New York: Basic Books, 1974).

2. Harold D. Lasswell, *Politics: Who Gets What, When, How* (New York, 1936).

3. J. A. Schumpeter, *Capitalism, Socialism and Democracy* (New York, 1942; 3rd ed., 1950).

4. Demosthenes, *Against Leptines,* 92, Loeb Classical Library ed., trans. J. H. Vince, 552–53. Cf. also on the episode to which the passage from Xenophon at the head of this chapter refers, Lord Acton, *History of Freedom* (London, 1907), 12:

> On a memorable occasion the assembled Athenians declared it monstrous that they should be prevented from doing whatever they chose; no force that existed could restrain them; they resolved that no duty should restrain them, and that they would be bound by no laws that were not of their own making. In this way the emancipated people of Athens became a tyrant.

5. Aristotle, *Politics, IV, iv,* 7, Loeb Classical Library ed., trans. H. Rackham (Cambridge, Mass., 1932), 304–5.

6. Giovanni Sartori, *Democratic Theory* (New York, 1965), 312.

7. Richard Wollheim, "A Paradox in the Theory of Democracy," in eds. Peter Laslett and W. G. Runciman, *Philosophy, Politics and Society,* 2nd series (Oxford, 1962), 72.

8. Cf. J. L. Talmon, *The Origins of Totalitarian Democracy* (London, 1952) and R. R. Palmer, *The Age of Democratic Revolution* (Princeton, N.J.: Princeton University Press, 1959).

9. Cf. Ludwig von Mises, *Human Action* (Yale University Press, 1949; 3rd ed., Chicago, 1966), 150; also K. R. Popper, *The Open Society and Its Enemies* (London, 1945; 4th ed., Princeton, N.J., 1963), vol. 1, 124; also J. A. Schumpeter, *op. cit., passim*; also the references in my *The Constitution of Liberty* (London, 1960), 444, note 9.

10. Cf. J. A. Schumpeter, *op. cit.*, 258.

11. Cf. *Cato's Letters,* letter no. 60 of 6 January 1721, *op. cit.*, 121.

12. See *Cato's Letters,* letter no. 62 of 20 January 1721, 128.

13. On these matters see particularly R. A. Dahl, *A Preface to Democratic Theory* (Chicago, 1950) and R. A. Dahl and C. E. Lindblom, *Politics, Economics, and Welfare* (New York, 1953).

14. C. A. R. Crossland, *The Future of Socialism* (London, 1956), 205.

15. See E. E. Schattschneider, *Politics, Pressure, and the Tariff* (New York, 1935) and *The Semi-Sovereign People* (New York, 1960).

16. Cf. Mancur Olson Jr., *The Logic of Collective Action* (Harvard, 1965).

17. See in this connection the very relevant discussion of the abstract character of society in K. R. Popper, *op. cit.*, 175.

18. Cf. K. R. Popper, *The Open Society and Its Enemies* (5th ed., London, 1974), vol. 1, 124.

19. John Dewey, "Liberty and Social Control," *Social Frontier,* November 1935, and cf. the fuller comments in my *The Constitution of Liberty*, note 21 to chapter 1.

20. Morris Ginsberg in *Modern Political Thought: The Great Issue ,* ed. W. Ebenstein (New York, 1960).

21. David Miller, *Social Justice* (Oxford, 1976), 17. Cf. also M. Duverger, *The Idea of Politics* (Indianapolis, 1966), 171.

22. D. Miller, *op. cit.*, 23.

23. David Hume, *A Treatise of Human Nature,* book III, section 2, ed. L. A. Selby-Bigge (Oxford, 1958), 495.

24. A. V. Dicey, *Lectures on the Relation between Law and Public Opinion in England during the Nineteenth Century* (2nd ed.; London: Macmillan, 1914), li.

PLURALIST DEMOCRACY

Interests appear in a new guise in pluralist democracy. Rather than appearing as objects of fear or suspicion as they were for civic republicans, many early liberals, and protective democrats, in pluralist theory interests are introduced as natural in the sense that all individuals are said to carry distinct interests that need to be given the opportunity to be expressed politically. Because pluralists hold that any society is composed of individuals with assorted concerns, the good polity will be open to citizens who join with other like-minded individuals to pursue their shared interests. To deny persons the right to pursue their interests, on this account, is to deny them their liberty. For pluralists, free people with similar interests naturally collect together to protect and promote their interests, and in politics this means they form interest groups that seek to be heard and influence policy.

In the first part of this section, we take up Arthur Bentley's arguments about the naturalness of interests, how interest groups form the basis of democratic politics, and how a robust pluralism is said to be able to correct its own mistakes. Bentley's theory of groups signals a fundamental shift in the way much of American democratic theory would view politics in the future. Earlier liberal democratic theory stressed some version of the consent of the governed as expressed through elections and representative institutions. Phrases such as the "will of the people" or the "voice of the people" echo through this creed, calling attention to the primary question of whether "the people" are heard or ignored. But Bentley wants to interrupt the legitimizing relationship between "the people" and government to assert that the basic unit of politics is neither "the people" nor the "individual voter" but instead the group.

Bentley's empiricism is meant to empty political analysis of a normative vocabulary with which to judge policies. No longer are claims to rights, justice, or other normative standards appropriate organizing principles for political analysis. Rather, on Bentley's account, such language should be seen merely as a rhetorical device used to advance group claims. For him, political disagreements represent different interests, and interest is the substance of politics. In this sense, Bentley contradicts the claim by civic republicans and earlier liberals that interests should be suspect in politics. Instead, all societies are said to house different interests, and in democracies, interest groups compete with each other over scarce resources. In his theory, group competition leads to an equilibrium that remains stable until disturbed by the arrival of new groups discontented with the present arrangement. Meeting such a challenge is said to be the automatic response of the group process, which, Bentley thinks, shows that pluralist politics has the capacity to correct its own deficiencies.

The best-known pluralist today is Robert Dahl, whose early works emphasize the naturalness and necessity of groups in an open polity and reject the idea that a small elite governs society. Rather, he sees many competing elites staking out issue-areas that are important to the members of their groups and concentrating the resources of the group on a single or small cluster of issues. He holds that pluralist systems develop and thrive when important resources are widely dispersed throughout society and every potential group is able to gain some leverage in the issue areas that most concern them. With this move, Dahl presents "polyarchy" as the antithesis to closed political systems where political resources are concentrated in the hands of the few in ways that grant them inordinate advantages in obtaining and maintaining most other political resources.

Dahl's early works were met with considerable support as well as criticism. The latter claims he leaves too much out of the story and is unduly optimistic about the ability of the regime to correct for its faults.[1] Dahl's response to his critics is to keep the basic theory of interest groups but simultaneously acknowledge shortcomings as well as paradoxes in the theory. One paradox he reports in his later work stems from his view that although group politics is indispensable to a free, democratic society, these very groups work to freeze inequality and stabilize injustice.[2] Political pluralism has sometimes been criticized because it reinforces conventional arrangements and does not allow for needed changes. Responding to arguments that political pluralism leaves the unorganized and vulnerable unrepresented, pluralists point to the ways new groups, such as racial minorities, women, environmentalists, and a host of others that were politically invisible and inaudible not so long ago have a strong presence in contemporary liberal democracies. The reason, they argue, is that the conservative nature of pluralism is not so extensive as to preclude the arrival of new groups with new demands.

Moreover, Dahl finds that it is important to ask about what can realistically be achieved democratically. He is impatient with idealist accounts of democracy, not only because he believes they are beyond the reach of human beings but also because the regimes that are sometimes presented as ideal, such as the ancient Greek city-states, were deeply flawed and inegalitarian. For this reason, Dahl rejects the ancient republican ideal and turns to what he calls polyarchy, a popularly based regime fitted for the large-scale nations and complex society of today's world. One of the key elements of polyarchy is the important role it assigns to autonomous organizations. Still, Dahl recognizes that interest groups can do harm, particularly in their tendency to stabilize political inequalities.

READINGS

ATHUR BENTLEY, SELECTIONS FROM *THE PROCESS OF GOVERNMENT* (1908)

The term "group" will be used throughout this work in a technical sense. It means a certain portion of the men of a society, taken, however, not as a physical mass cut off from other masses of men, but as a mass activity, which does not preclude the men who participate in it from participating likewise in many other group activities. It is always so many men with all their human quality. It is always so many men, acting, or tending toward action—that is, in various stages of action. Group and group activity are equivalent terms with just a little difference of emphasis, useful only for clearness of expression in different contexts.

It is now necessary to take another step in the analysis of the group. There is no group without its interest. An interest, as the term will be used in this work, is the equivalent of a group. We may speak also of an interest group or of a group interest, again merely for the sake of clearness in expression. The group and the interest are not separate. There exists only the one thing, that is, so many men bound together in or along the path of a certain activity. Sometimes we may be emphasizing the interest phase, sometimes the group phase, but if ever we push them too far apart we soon land in the barren wilderness. There may be a beyond-scientific question as to whether the interest is responsible for the existence of the group, or the group responsible for the existence of the interest. I do not know or care. What we actually find in this world, what we can observe and study, is interested men, nothing more and nothing less. That is our raw material and it is our business to keep our eyes fastened to it.

The word interest in social studies is often limited to the economic interest. There is no justification whatever for such a limitation. I am restoring it to its broader meaning coextensive with all groups whatsoever that participate in the social process. I am at the same time giving it definite, specific content wherever it is used. I shall have nothing to say about "political interest" as such, but very much about the multiform interests that work through the political process.

I am dealing here with political groups and other groups that function in the specifically social process, and not extending the assertion that the words group and interest coincide, over all groups that on any plane can be analyzed out of masses of human beings. One might put the blonde women of the country in one class and the brunettes in another, and call each class a group. It may be that a process of selection of blondes and brunettes is going on, and it may perhaps be—I am taking an extreme case—that it will sometime be found necessary to classify some phase of that process as social and to study it along with other social phenomena. I am not expressing an opinion as to that, and I have no need of forming an opinion. Whether that attitude is taken or not will depend upon practical considerations upon which the investigator himself must pass. I would not say that such a "group" for other than social studies could properly be described as having a blonde or brunette interest in the meaning here given to interest. It would not be a social group, and probably the equivalent of the interest could be better specified without the use of that particular word. But that is neither here nor there. The essential point is that if ever blondes or brunettes appear in political life as such it will be through an interest which they assert, or—what comes in general to the same thing, when the analysis is fully made—which is asserted for them through some group or group leadership which represents them.

In the political world, if we take the interest alone as a psychological quality, what we get is an indefinite, untrustworthy will-o'-the-wisp, which may trick us into any false step whatsoever. Once set it up and we are its slaves, whatever swamp it may lead us to. If we try to take the group without the interest, we have simply nothing at all. We cannot take the first step to define it. The group is activity and the activity is only known to us through its particular type, its value in terms of other activities, its tendency where it is not in the stage which gives manifest results. The interest is just this valuation of the activity, not as distinct from it, but as the valued activity itself.

In using the term interest there are two serious dangers against which we must carefully guard ourselves. One is the danger of taking the interest at its own verbal expression of itself, that is to say, the danger of estimating it as it is estimated by the differentiated activity of speech and written language which reflects it. The other danger is at the far extreme from this. It is that we disregard the group's expressed valuation of itself and that we assign to it a meaning or value that is "objective" in the sense that we regard it as something natural or inevitable or clothed in oughtness. If we should substitute for the actual interest of the activity some "objective utility," to use the economist's term, we should be going far astray, for no such "objective utility" appears in politics at all, however otherwise it may be attributed to the men who compose the society. It is like the undiscovered and unsuspected gold under the mountain, a social nullity. A man who is wise enough may legitimately predict, if he is addicted to the habit of prediction, that a group activity will ultimately form along lines marked out by some objective condition which he thinks he detects. But the interests that we can take into account must lie a good deal closer to the actual existing masses of men than that.

If we cannot take words for our test, and if we cannot take "bed-rock truth," one may say we are left swinging hopelessly in between. Quite the contrary. The political groups are following definite courses. They may appear erratic, but hardly ever to anyone who is in close enough contact with them. The business of the student is to plot the courses. And when he does that—it is the course of only a single step, not of a whole career, that he can plot—he will find that he has all together, the group, the activity, and the interest.

The essential difference between interest as I am defining it and the psychological feeling or desire qualities should be already apparent. I am not introducing any suppositional factor which can be taken in hand, applied to the social activities and used in the pretense of explaining them. I am not taking any mental or other possession which the individual man is supposed to have before he enters society and using it to explain the society. I am not dealing with anything which can be scheduled to any desired extent as a set of abstract general interests, capable of branching out to correspond with the complexity of the activity of the social world. I am not using any interest that can be abstractly stated apart from the whole social background in which it is found at the moment of use.

The interest I put forward is a specific group interest in some definite course of conduct or activity. It is first, last, and all the time strictly empirical. There is no way to find it except by observation. There is no way to get hold of one group interest except in terms of others. A group of slaves for example, is not a group of physical beings who are "slaves by nature," but a social relationship, a specified activity and interest in society. From the interest as a thing by itself no conclusion can be drawn. No fine logic, no calculus of interests will take us a single step forward in the interpreting of society. When we succeed in isolating an interest group the only way to find out what it is going to do, indeed the only way to be sure we have isolated an interest group, is to watch its progress. When we have made sure of one such interest, or group, we shall become more skillful and can make sure of another similar one with less painstaking. When we have compared many sets of groups we shall know better what to expect. But we shall always hold fast to the practical reality, and accept the interests that it offers us as the only interests we can use, studying them as impassively as we would the habits or the organic functions of birds, bees, or fishes.

Such interest groups are of no different material than the "individuals" of a society. They are activity; so are the individuals. It is solely a question of the standpoint from which we look at the activity to define it. The individual stated for himself, and invested with an extra-social unity of his own, is a fiction. But every bit of the activity, which is all we actually know of him, can be stated either on the one side as individual, or on the other side as social group activity. The former statement is in the main of trifling importance in interpreting society; the latter statement is essential, first, last, and all the time. It is common to contrast conditions in India or elsewhere in which "the community is the political unit," with conditions in our own society in which "the individual is the political unit." But in reality such a contrast is highly superficial and limited, made for special purposes of interpretation within the process. From the point of view here taken all such contrasts fade into insignificance except as they are "raw material" when the special processes in connection with which they are made are being studied.

When we have a group fairly well defined in terms of its interests, we next find it necessary to consider the factors that enter into its relative power of dominating other groups and of carrying its tendencies to action through their full course with relatively little check or hindrance. As the interest is merely a manner of stating the value of the group activity, so these factors of dominance are likewise just phases of the statement of the group, not separate from it, nor capable of scientific use as separate things.

First of all, the number of men who belong to the group attracts attention. Number alone may secure dominance. Such is the case in the ordinary American election, assuming corruption and intimidation to be present in such small proportions that they do not affect the result. But numbers notoriously do not decide elections in the former slave states of the South. There is a concentration of interest on political lines which often, and indeed one may say usually, enables a minority to rule a majority. I cannot stop here to discuss the extent to which majorities are represented by minorities under such circumstances, but only to note the fact. Intensity is a word that will serve as well as any other to denote the concentration of interest which gives a group effectiveness in its activity in the face of the opposition of other groups.

This intensity, like interest, is only to be discovered by observation. There is no royal road for scientific workers to take to it. Catchwords like race, ability, education, moral vigor, may serve as tags to indicate its presence, but they are of little or no help to us, and indeed they are more apt to do us positive harm by making us think we have our solutions in advance, and by blinding us to the facts that we should study. Mere vociferation must not be confused with intensity. It is one form of intensity, but very often the intensity of the talk does not correctly reflect the true intensity of the group. This must be allowed for.

Besides number and intensity, there is a technique of group activities which must be taken into account. Blows, bribes, allurements of one kind and another, and arguments also, are characteristic, and to these must be added organization. A group will differentiate under fitting circumstances a special set of activities for carrying on its work. We must learn how these specialized activities vary under different forms of group oppositions, how the technique changes and evolves. We shall find that the change in methods is produced by the appearance of new group interests, directed against the use of the method that is suppressed. If violence gives way to bribery, or bribery to some form of demagogy, or that perhaps to a method called reasoning, it will be possible, if we pursue the study carefully enough, to find the group interest that has worked the change. That group will have its own technique, no more scrupulous probably than the technique it suppresses, but vigorously exerted through the governing institutions of the society, or possibly outside those institutions.

Technique will of course vary with the intensity of interest, as for instance when assassination is adopted by revolutionists who can find no other method to make themselves felt against their opponents. Number also has intimate relations with both technique and intensity. In general it is to be said that there is no rule of thumb which will point out to us any particular lines of activity in which the most powerful groups can inevitably be found. We may sometimes find the greatest intensity over matters that still seem to us trifles, even after we think we have interpreted them in terms of underlying groups, and again we may find slight intensity where we think there ought to be the most determined effort. It is solely a matter for observation. And observation shows, here as before, that no group can be defined or understood save in terms of the other groups of the given time and place. One opposition appears and adjusts itself and another takes its place; and each opposition gets its meaning only in terms of the other oppositions and of the adjustments that have taken place between them. [. . . .]

It is necessary . . . in considering representative government, or democracy, not only past or present, but future as well, to consider it in terms of the various group pressures that form its substance. It is useless to pause with some formal definitions, add on a few theoretical standards, and then try to get the facts straightened out. Instead, at every stage these forms must be considered as they are used by the pressures. As substance, rather than process, they can be taken into account only so far as we gain positive knowledge that they are, in the given state of the group oppositions, used by certain groups in such a way that other groups, reacting against the evil in the situation, are potentially or manifestly tending toward attack upon them.

It does not seem to me necessary here to go back over the analysis of the process. . . . [of] the various agencies of government. Merely to recall them is to point out how the group pressures in the population form themselves on the various discussion levels and organization levels, tending always to express themselves in both ways or in any way, and actually expressing themselves to such degrees as the resistance of the other groups as represented in the government will permit at the given time. But a special reminder is desirable of the district system of representation, which in modern countries as a rule is highly formal when compared with the substance of the interests which are striving to exert themselves through it.

In governments like that of the United States we see these manifold interests gaining representation through many thousands of officials in varying degrees of success, beating some officials down now into delegate activity, intrusting representative activity (in the narrow sense) to other officials at times in high degree, subsiding now and again over great areas while "special interests" make special use of officials, rising in other spots to dominate, using one agency of the government against another, now with stealth, now with open force, and in general moving along the route of time with that organized turmoil which is life where the adjustments are much disturbed. Withal, it is a process which must surprise one more for the trifling proportion of physical violence involved considering the ardent nature of the struggles, than for any other characteristic.

We often hear of "the control of government by the people." The whole process is control. Government is control. Or, in other words, it is the organization of forces, of pressures. In a limited way I might add it is the organization of public opinion, and this indeed is a phrasing which once upon a time I would have put first in the series. But the whole process of control is too deep and vital to be stated as the organization of opinion: the opinion is but one differentiated agency to represent the process, and not at all the most accurate expression of it, at that.

What is usually meant by "control by the people" is only one of the elements in control. It is a generalized statement, poorly representative, indicating certain direct reactions by large masses of men against certain smaller, masses which, as appears in the group oppositions themselves, are controlling the government process to an excessive degree. These oppositions appear, however, on what—to use the terminology of economic theory—may be called the margin of the governmental process. And the reason why the "control by the people" is a poorly representative statement is just because the great underlying masses of control are in existence, much deeper and more fundamental as facts than the contest that is being waged on the margin.

The greater portion of the detail of governmental work, as embodied especially in the law that is being daily sustained, is composed of habitual reactions which are adjustments forced by large, united weak interests upon less numerous, but relatively to the number of adherents, more intense interests. If there is anything that could probably be meant by the phrase "control by the people" just as it stands, it is this. And we may even say that without "control by the people" there would be no government, save in the cases of subjected peoples under foreign masters, with assimilation little advanced. And even here, unless the one weapon of government is the ever-drawn sword, such control is the manifested phenomenon.

There is, be it remembered, the wider field of control, that is of adjustment of group to group, outside the field of government in the narrow sense of the term, and forming the background in which the processes of government are carried on. Often a group interest, developing under some special conditions to an extreme, will give way through this outer control before the operations of government proper are appealed to. Part of this field is a sediment from the process of government itself, involving adjustments so deep set that they are dropped from the ordinary work of the organized government. All of this extra-governmental adjustment, while forming the background for the government process and capable of interpretation by very similar methods, is outside of our immediate field of study.

Now when government, as the representative of the "absent" or quiescent group interests, is distorted from this function to any noticeable extent by the concentrated pressures of smaller group interests, themselves the result of newly opened opportunities in the social mass, and fails to respond as it should, we hear the cry that there is need of "control by the people," and we see the formation of a group interest directly aroused in opposition to the interests which have gained objectionable power. And when the agencies through which the "people," or in other words such large group interests, habitually react fail to work smoothly for them—as is the case with the highly organized parties at times—we find the cry for popular control directed against those very agencies. The mysticism of "the people" is a matter of speech alone. The real facts are to be found by us in the groups as we analyze them out, and there only.

That "pure democracy" often heard of in arguments under similar circumstances and in theories which run to the far extreme from the moving process, may be mentioned in the same connection. It is supposed to be a "government by the people" directly and immediately, but the slightest analysis of the process at any point shows how very poorly representative the phrase is, save as a slogan and rallying cry for some particular groups at special stages of their activity. Freedom, liberty, independence, and other similar rallying cries in the governmental process all need the same kind of interpretation.

If now we take a different point of view and examine the set structure of control in the organized government, including the checks and balances of which American political theory has so much to say, we shall find a great variety of established methods. We have here to do with structures which were set up, and which remain, to prevent special groups, whether "the people" or the "special interests" of current speech, from getting a disproportionate power of functioning through the government. First of all we have, of course, the control of executive by legislature and vice versa, and the control of both by the judiciary. Then we have the control which is arranged by separating local from general issues, a control which in the United States is exerted in three divisions, the federal, the state, and the local governments. Then comes the control involved in the establishment of many independent offices in any one field, each of the offices subject directly to the suffrage. The majority vote on a wide suffrage basis may also be added for controlling all the agencies mentioned. Again we find parties, first as direct group representatives, and then as syndicated agencies for group representation, controlling from their own level, now one, now another, sometimes all, of the more specialized agencies of government, and at times producing a unification, as well as at times a more pronounced splitting, between them. There is also the control of party by party faction, and, of course, of one party by a rival party or by rival parties, that being essential in any party operation. Finally we have the control exerted by groups expressing themselves through public-opinion activities as these are practically analyzed by the controlled agents in the very act of their expression. And all of this controlling process takes at times the appearance of a control of persons and at times of the control of policies, according to the variations of the content that is being functioned through the process.

This structural arrangement of government is that which constitutes representative government, or democracy, whichever term is used. Definitions, or rather descriptions, which state governments in terms of the functioning of the groups through these bits of structure, to whatever extent or in whatever proportions they are present, are something that one can depend on far more than on definitions in terms of artificial men, acting in artificial ways under artificial conditions, and depending entirely on credulity for their claim to mirror rightly the tendencies of the process as it develops in time.

Besides these elements of such government we may also take into account various other methods of control which are now forming themselves as structure to some extent in a great many countries. More of them at once are perhaps to be found in the United States than anywhere else, securing their places on the basis of the actual group force they have behind them; but that is only as it happens. It is no mere accident, but a very normal fact, that the very project of a referendum on ordinary legislation, which is the monopoly of the "friend of the plain people" in the United States is put forth coincidentally by the House of Lords in England for its own official purposes.

We may enumerate here besides the referendum in its various forms, the initiative, the recall, the direct primaries and perhaps also proportional representation and other plans to readjust the organization of the suffrage, where its majorities and minorities seem to work too crudely. This latter bit of structure, proportional representation, at least in the United States, has never had much actual pressure behind it; where it has been introduced it has come as a bit of the poorly representative work of the "wise men" in government; and the group pressures that accompany its use seem to be such that they inevitably break it down instead of sustaining it. [. . . .]

I am perfectly well aware that these various forms of control, as we find them developing, have arguments made for them continually in the name of democracy, and against them continually in the name of representative government, with many criss-cross arguments on both sides. But if there is any way by which theoretically or otherwise they can be shown to be more typical of either democracy or representative government, or more filled with the "spirit" of either of these types of government, than are our present systems, I know not how it is. That is, I know the logic of the arguments, and I know its inutility, but I do not know how the point can be made in terms of the group interests which make up the people.

Group interests there certainly are behind many of these tendencies, and strong ones at that, but they are very concrete, immediate group interests, growing directly out of oppositions which have developed in the developing process. They can be located, most of them, with great exactness as to their strength and meaning in the whole given political system. But they can be located as well on one theory as on another. And the representation that they commonly get on the discussion level, whether from friends or enemies, is very poor indeed, save as so much noise, so much enthusiasm, so much quickening of the flow of blood in the members of the banded group.

ROBERT DAHL, SELECTIONS FROM *DILEMMAS OF PLURALIST DEMOCRACY* (1982)

Independent organizations exist in all democratic countries. Consequently, the problem of democratic pluralism is a universal problem in modern democracy.

Although I believe the first sentence to be true, I doubt whether it can be shown conclusively to be true. [. . . .]

To help the reader see where this chapter is going, let me summarize the gist of it here: *As to democracy:*

1. In the expressions *democratic pluralism* and *pluralist democracy*, the term *democracy* may refer either to an ideal or to a specific type of actual regime. Democracy in the ideal sense is a necessary condition for the best political order. It is not a sufficient condition.
2. Historically, the term *democracy* has been applied to two specific types of actual regimes which, though quite different from one another, have been relatively democratic by comparison with all other regimes. These are the regimes of (a) relatively democratized city-states and (b) relatively democratized nation-states (countries). The first kind of regime can be understood as an attempt to democratize small-scale governments, the second as an attempt to democratize large-scale governments. The second kind of regime may also be called polyarchy.

3. Despite certain inherent limits, nation-states (countries) are, when judged according to the democratic ideal, the largest political units within which relatively democratized regimes will exist in the foreseeable future. Systems smaller than countries would be too ineffective in dealing with many crucial contemporary problems, while systems larger than countries—e.g., international organizations—are almost sure to be far less democratic than the present regimes of democratic countries.

As to pluralism:

4. In the expressions *democratic pluralism* or *pluralist democracy*, the terms *pluralism* and *pluralist* refer to organizational pluralism, that is, to the existence of a plurality of relatively autonomous (independent) organizations (subsystems) within the domain of a state.
5. In all democratic countries, some important organizations are relatively autonomous.
6. A country is a pluralist democracy if (a) it is a democracy in the sense of polyarchy and (b) important organizations are relatively autonomous. Hence all democratic countries are pluralist democracies.

Democracy As Ideal

For the better part of two thousand years, democratic processes were typically held to apply only to very small states, like the city-states of Greece or medieval Italy. The increasing application of democratic ideas to nation-states from the seventeenth century onward required new political institutions radically different from those appropriate to city-states. The new institutions both reflected and fostered changes in ways of thinking about democracy itself. As new forms came to be justified by older ideas, changes in political consciousness occurred that were often subtle, elusive, and confusing. Today the term *democracy* is like an ancient kitchen midden packed with assorted leftovers from twenty-five hundred years of nearly continuous usage.

From a number of possible ways to conceive of democracy, I shall pick two that bear most closely on the problem of democratic pluralism. The first conceives of democracy as an ideal or theoretical system, perhaps at the extreme limit of human possibilities or even beyond. According to this interpretation, an ideal democratic process would satisfy five criteria:

1. Equality in voting: In making collective binding decisions, the expressed preference of each citizen (citizens collectively constitute the *demos*) ought to be taken equally into account in determining the final solution.
2. Effective participation: Throughout the process of collective decision making, including the stage of putting matters on the agenda, each citizen ought to have adequate and equal opportunities for expressing his or her preferences as to the final outcome.
3. Enlightened understanding: In the time permitted by the need for a decision, each citizen ought to have adequate and equal opportunities for arriving at his or her considered judgment as to the most desirable outcome.
4. Final control over the agenda: The body of citizens (the demos) should have the exclusive authority to determine what matters are or are not to be decided by means of

processes that satisfy the first three criteria. (Put in another way, provided the demos does not alienate its final control over the agenda it may delegate authority to others who may make decisions by nondemocratic processes.)

5. Inclusion: The demos ought to include all adults subject to its laws, except transients.

It is hard to see how people could govern themselves if their decision-making processes failed to meet these criteria and equally difficult to understand how they could be said *not* to govern themselves if their political processes were to meet these criteria fully. Since practically all the artifacts uncovered in the kitchen midden of democracy are related to the idea of people governing themselves, it is reasonable to call a process of decision making fully democratic if and only if it meets these criteria (Dahl 1979). [. . . .]

Democracy As Actual Regimes: Small Scale and Large Scale

As attempts were made during the last two centuries to extend democratic processes to the government of an entire country, it became evident that among a people unavoidably numerous and diverse, political conflict would be inescapable and might not be inherently undesirable. Because conflict was inevitable, it would express itself somehow. Is it not better to express it openly rather than stealthily? From assumptions like these it was a short step to the conclusion, which ran counter to the older republican tradition, that in a democratic country organized political parties and interest groups were necessary, normal, and desirable participants in political life.

Thus political institutions developed that, taken together, distinguish the political regimes of modern democratic countries from all other regimes, including those of the relatively democratized city-states. Seven institutions in particular, taken as a whole, define a type of regime that is historically unique:

1. Control over government decisions about policy is constitutionally vested in elected officials.
2. Elected officials are chosen in frequent and fairly conducted elections in which coercion is comparatively uncommon.
3. Practically all adults have the right to vote in the election of officials.
4. Practically all adults have the right to run for elective offices in the government, though age limits may be higher for holding office than for the suffrage.
5. Citizens have a right to express themselves without the danger of severe punishment on political matters broadly defined, including criticism of officials, the government, the regime, the socioeconomic order, and the prevailing ideology.
6. Citizens have a right to seek out alternative sources of information. Moreover, alternative sources of information exist and are protected by law.
7. To achieve their various rights, including those listed above, citizens also have a right to form relatively independent associations or organizations, including independent political parties and interest groups.

Because these statements are meant to characterize actual and not merely nominal rights, institutions, and processes, they can also serve as criteria for distinguishing a special type of modern regime (Dahl 1971). Countries can be classified according to the extent to which their political institutions approximate these criteria. In ordinary usage, countries in which the political institutions most closely approximate these criteria are democratic. In order to emphasize the distinction between regimes like these and democracy in the ideal sense, they may also be called polyarchies. In this book I use several terms interchangeably: modern democratic systems, democratic regimes, democratic countries, large-scale democracy, polyarchy, and so on. None of these terms is meant to imply, of course, that these regimes are democratic in the ideal sense.

Like the regimes of the city-states, modern democratic regimes are far from satisfying the ideal democratic criteria. The gap between ideal and actual is partly the result of factors that are under human control and thus in principle could be remedied by human action. However, to apply democratic processes on a scale as large as a country also runs into certain inherent limits. [. . . .]

To hold that a plurality of important and relatively autonomous organizations exists in democratic countries does not imply that their existence creates a serious problem. If the consequences of organizational pluralism were entirely advantageous, there would be no problem; if, though disadvantages existed, they were minuscule in comparison with the advantages, the problem would not be serious; while if independent organizations could easily be eliminated without doing much harm, the problem could easily be solved. The problem of democratic pluralism is serious, however, precisely because independent organizations are highly desirable and at the same time their independence allows them to do harm. [. . . .]

For Mutual Control

In large political systems independent organizations help to prevent domination and to create mutual control. The main alternative to mutual control in the government of the state is hierarchy. To govern a system as large as a country exclusively by hierarchy is to invite domination by those who control the government of the state. Independent organizations help to curb hierarchy and domination.

Obvious as this conclusion may appear, it stands in fundamental contradiction to the views of social theorists who contend that domination is inevitable. Two bodies of thought portraying domination as inherent in all political systems—up to the present, at least—have been particularly influential. In standard Marxism, a bourgeois society is necessarily dominated by a minority consisting of an exploitative capitalist class. However, in this view domination is not inherent in social existence but is destined to be superseded by freedom and mutuality when capitalism is replaced by socialism. The theories of elite rule developed by Pareto, Mosca, and Michels are far more pessimistic. In their view, domination by a minority—whether a class, an elite, or a social stratum—is inherent in large-scale society. Thus, this trio of elite theorists transformed Marx's profound optimism into an equally profound pessimism.

Whether we choose to accept the view that domination is inherent in social existence, or would vanish under socialism, obviously depends in part on what we understand the term to mean. [Elsewhere] I offered reasons for rejecting one version of domination that depended for its validity more on definition than on observation and analysis. Yet, it would be possible to commit the opposite error of ruling out domination by definition. A tendency toward dominance has been so widely described by social theorists, however, that we cannot dismiss it as groundless or without meaning. Suppose therefore that we try to capture the meaning of this slippery term by adopting something like this: Alpha dominates Beta if Alpha's control (a) is strictly unilateral, (b) persists over a relatively long period of time, (c) extends over a range of actions of great importance to Beta, and (d) compels Beta to act in ways that on balance are costly to her. Now, imagine a system in which rulers dominate their subjects on conditions of work, let us say, or political and religious beliefs and practices, or access to the means of production, or laws defining crime and punishment, or the conditions of access to an education, or all of these things and more. The question arises: Could subjects possibly transform such a system of domination into a system of mutual (though not necessarily equal, fair, or democratic) controls with respect to important matters like these?

Views of domination like those found in standard Marxism and Italian elite theory are surely correct in emphasizing the strength and universality of tendencies toward domination. Where these views go wrong is in underestimating the strength of tendencies toward political autonomy and mutual control. Throughout history, relatively autonomous organizations have developed around certain universal human situations that generate common experiences, identifications, and values: we and they, insider and outsider, friend and enemy, sacred and profane, true believer and infidel, civilized man and barbarian. Kinship, language, birthplace, residence, religion, occupation, everywhere stimulate a thrust toward organization and independence. Alongside Michels' famous iron law of oligarchy—"Who says organization says oligarchy"—stands another: Every organization develops an impulse toward its own independence. The two universal tendencies are alloyed; and in the alloy, the law of oligarchy bends more easily than iron.

Less metaphorically, subjects can sometimes gain a degree of independence from their rulers on matters of importance to themselves if they can make the costs of domination so high that domination no longer looks worthwhile to the rulers. Resources are not infinite after all, and exercising control nearly always requires an outlay of resources. Domination, it is fair to say, always does. Thus, control is almost always to some extent costly to the ruler; and domination is sure to be—though it may be cheap, it does not come free. Rulers therefore have to decide when and whether the game of domination is worth the candle. Sometimes it is not.

In describing how this might come about, it is useful to imagine that the ruler is at least moderately rational. A ruler whose actions were directed only to maximizing his own goals and were rationally calculated would not commit his resources beyond the point at which the value of the benefits he expected to gain were exceeded by the costs. The value of control might be defined as the excess of expected benefits over expected costs. If the costs of control exceed the benefits, then effective control in that range or domain has no value to the ruler. Confronted by the prospect that the costs of control were going to exceed the benefits, even rulers with great but finite resources would rationally forego the full attainment of their goals in order to exercise control within the limits of their resources. Rational rulers would allocate their finite resources among goals so as to maximize the net benefits (as evaluated from the perspective of their goals). Wherever the costs of control exceeded the benefits, it would be rational for these rulers to reduce costs by leaving some actions beyond their control, leaving some matters outside their control, or accepting a higher level of unreliability and unpredictability in their control. For the subjects, of course, the trick is to raise the costs of domination and thus reduce its value to the rulers.

Fine in theory, one might object, but what about the poor devil whose neck is squarely under the ruler's heel? To contend that subjects can always escape domination would be witless. Nonetheless, a variety of factors do, at times, enable subjects to raise the costs of domination. To begin with, it is virtually impossible for a single actor or a unified team to acquire a complete monopoly over all resources. Consequently, subjects nearly always have access to *some* resources, however pitiful they may be. Moreover, subjects can sometimes cooperate, combine their resources, and thus increase the costs of control. In addition, rulers are rarely a solidary group. Although each member of a dominant elite may have an interest in maintaining the elite's domination over the rest of the society, and so too an interest in walling off internal disputes from outsiders, security around the wall is not always perfectly tight and traffic through it may be mutually profitable. If some outsiders have resources that might be thrown into the struggle, their help could be crucial to the victory of a faction within the walls.

For reasons like these, subjects can sometimes push the costs of control over certain matters to a point where rulers no longer find it worthwhile to try to dominate their subjects on these particular questions. Subjects thus acquire a degree of political autonomy. The change toward religious toleration in Europe after the bloody and destructive religious conflicts of the sixteenth and seventeenth centuries reflected an appreciation by monarchs that the gains from enforced religious conformity were very much smaller than had been supposed, the costs were very much greater, and on balance, the costs greatly exceeded the gains. In the sixteenth and seventeenth centuries, neither emperor nor pope succeeded in dominating all the city states of northern Italy. In their desire for independence, the city-states made outside domination too costly, despite the superior resources—in gross—of the two main contenders. In Britain, Sweden, Norway, and the Netherlands, parliaments gained independence from domination by centralized monarchies. In the eighteenth century, the growing acceptance of organized political oppositions in Britain reflected a fundamentally changed perspective in which—as with religion earlier—the costs expected from tolerating political opponents declined while the costs expected from repression increased. In the nineteenth and early twentieth centuries, workers combined their meager resources in trade unions and successfully overthrew the unilateral domination of employers over wages, hours, and working conditions.

One could endlessly multiply historical examples showing how members of a weaker group have combined their resources, raised the costs of control, overcome domination on certain matters important to them, and acquired some measure of political autonomy. Often what results is a system of mutual controls. Thus, after parliament gained independence from the monarch, for a long time neither could dominate the other; each partly controlled the other in important ways. Later, mutual controls developed between cabinet and parliament; later still, between parliament and electorate. And even later, the rise of independent trade unions helped to bring about mutual controls between unions and employers.

Thus domination can be transformed into a system of mutual controls. Lest one exaggerate the possibility, however, let me sound several cautionary notes. While domination is not inherent in social existence, subjects cannot always bring domination to an end: ask prisoners in concentration camps whether they can overthrow their jailers. Moreover, while Michels exaggerated the strength of the iron law, the tendency toward oligarchy is always there. An organization that successfully prevents domination by outsiders may provide the means, as Michels rightly saw, by which its own leaders now dominate its members. Nor is mutual control equivalent to equitable control, much less to equal or democratic control. To say, then, that independent organizations help to prevent domination and bring about mutual control is not to say that they guarantee justice, equality, or democracy. A political system can be pluralist and yet lack democratic institutions. Nondemocratic systems can contain important organizations that are relatively autonomous vis-à-vis the government of the state; some authoritarian countries do.

For Democracy on a Large Scale

Yet, while relatively autonomous organizations are not sufficient for democracy per se, they are a necessary element in a large-scale democracy, both as a prerequisite for its operation and as an inevitable consequence of its institutions.

The rights required for democracy on a large scale make relatively autonomous organizations simultaneously possible and necessary. For example, elections cannot be contested in a large system without organizations. To forbid political parties would make it impossible for citizens to coordinate their efforts in order to nominate and elect their preferred candidates and thus would violate the criteria of voting equality and effective participation. To forbid all political parties save one would be to grant exceptional opportunities to the members of the one party in comparison with other citizens. To prohibit citizens from organizing freely in order to make their views known to legislators and to other citizens would violate the criteria of effective participation and enlightened understanding and it would mock the idea of final control over the agenda by the citizen body. Thus the introduction of democratic processes into the government of a country and the enforcement of the rights required if democratic procedures are to be effectively protected make it both possible and advantageous for various groups to form autonomous organizations. Because organizations are possible and advantageous, they are also inevitable.

From the perspective of the previous section, the institutions of polyarchy make organizations possible in a democratic country, because they impose very high costs on efforts to destroy the relative autonomy of organizations that are formed to contest the government's conduct. Where the institutions have gained widespread support, as they generally have in countries with long-established systems of polyarchy, the costs of suppression far outstrip the likely gains even for the most influential actors with the greatest access to political resources, that is, the political elites. If the institutions of polyarchy in a country make it possible for groups to form autonomous organizations, they also make it advantageous to do so—not least for the political elites themselves. In particular, as elites discovered comparatively early in the development of polyarchal institutions, in order to exert maximum influence on the conduct, policies, personnel, and structure of government by competing for office in elections or by affecting the chances that a legislator (or a popularly elected executive) will be reelected, it is highly advantageous to organize political parties and pressure groups. Once parties and pressure groups exist, no elite groups can suppress them without destroying the institutions that distinguish polyarchy from more authoritarian regimes. Indeed, one of the first acts of a new authoritarian regime is generally to suppress all opposition parties; one of the first acts of a regime formed to institute democracy is to allow parties to exist. [. . . .]

Defects in Pluralist Democracy

Desirable as independent organizations are for these reasons, they also appear to be implicated in . . . [several] problems of democratic pluralism: [one is] they may help to stabilize injustices.

Even when the institutional guarantees of polyarchy exist and the political system of a country is democratic to this extent, organizational pluralism is perfectly consistent with extensive inequalities.[3] Moreover, the influence and power of organizations does more than simply register existing inequalities in other resources. Organization is itself a resource. It confers advantage directly on its leaders and often indirectly on at least some members. Although organization is indispensable for offsetting the universal tendency toward domination, the pattern of pluralism in a particular country even while checking domination may help to sustain inequalities of various kinds, including inequality in control over the government of the state. For example, when organizations are not broadly inclusive in their membership, political inequality is a likely consequence, for, other things being equal, the organized are more influential than an equivalent number of unorganized citizens.

The inequalities to which organizational pluralism contributes would be less consequential if pluralism were invariably a dynamic force with a more or less steady thrust toward the reduction of inequalities. No theoretical reasoning I know of has ever been advanced to demonstrate that such a dynamic exists. There are grounds for thinking instead that in some democratic countries, organizational pluralism develops a self-sustaining pattern over fairly long periods. In this respect, the dynamic of organizational pluralism may have rather different consequences for polyarchies than for authoritarian regimes. Because these differences in consequences may partly account for conflicting views about the values of pluralism, a brief digression may be helpful.

Like polyarchies, authoritarian regimes exist in countries with varying amounts of diversity. In some countries, notably in the Soviet Union, social and cultural diversity is enormous. Potential cleavages appear to exist along almost every kind of difference that is familiar in democratic countries: language, region, ethnic group, race, religion, status, occupation, ideology . . . An extraordinary concentration of resources in the hands of the central leadership, extremely severe sanctions against opponents, and an overwhelming (if not invariably successful) effort to eliminate all forms of organizational autonomy are necessary to prevent these differences from appearing in public conflicts. One can readily imagine that a plurality of interests and organizations would mushroom if extensive liberalization were to occur in the Soviet Union. What is true of the USSR in extreme form because of its great size and diversity holds true, though often in less extreme form, in many other countries with authoritarian regimes. Liberalization always poses a serious danger to authoritarian regimes; in some it threatens the territorial unity of the country itself.

A demand for greater personal and organizational autonomy and a lowering of the barriers to oppositions is one major point that the various internal critics of an authoritarian regime are likely to agree on—witness Sakharov, the Westernizer and liberal democrat; Solzhenitsyn, the Christian Slavophile; and Medvedev, the neoLeninist. But because liberalization would undermine the capacity of the current rulers to dominate the government of the state, and through it much of society, it is a demand that rulers are quite likely to see, with justification, as revolutionary. Even in a comparatively liberalized hegemonic order like Yugoslavia's, a threshold exists beyond which demands for further liberalization are viewed by leaders as subversive, because any further lowering of the barriers would lead inevitably to organized political oppositions, which would threaten to undermine the dominant position of the party, its leaders, and possibly the unity of the country itself.

The situation is different in democratic countries. As a result of the comparatively low barriers to organizational autonomy, organizations tend to exist around the most salient cleavages. Given no drastic constitutional changes, if the same cleavages persist over an extended period and if the pattern of political conflict remains more or less stable, then a specific pattern of organizational pluralism may persist. The major organizations—political parties and trade unions, for example—reach the particular limits of their followings, which may be considerably short of the total numbers of hypothetically available followers but near the effective maximum set by the attitudes and expectations of organizational leaders, members, and nonmembers. Disputes become more routinized as the techniques of negotiation and conciliation are institutionalized and each antagonist grows aware of the rough limits to which the others will go. In systems of "corporate pluralism," to use Rokkan's term (Rokkan 1966, 105), the consequences of a genuine breakdown in negotiations may take on the proportions of a nearly unthinkable national disaster. The leaders in all the major organizations may conclude that a "politics of accommodation," as Lijphart has called the Dutch system (Lijphart 1975), is necessary for the very survival of the country itself.

Even in countries where the major economic organizations are less comprehensive and centralized than in the Netherlands or the Scandinavian countries, organizations involved in important conflicts often reach an accommodation with others. In practice if not in propaganda, each accepts the existence of the others and even concedes, if sometimes grudgingly, their legitimacy as spokesmen for the interests of their followers. Thereafter, none seeks seriously to destroy the others; in any case, each has enough resources to make the costs far too high. Although such a system is sometime said to be in equilibrium, it would be more accurate to say that among the major organized interests there is a mutual accommodation or détente. When this happens, organized pluralism is a stabilizing force that is highly conservative in the face of demands for innovative structural change. Each of the major organized forces in a country prevents the others from making changes that might seriously damage its perceived interests. As a consequence, structural reforms that would significantly and rapidly redistribute control, status, income, wealth, and other resources are impossible to achieve—unless, ironically, they are made at the expense of the unorganized. In this way, a powerful social force that in authoritarian countries carries with it the unmistakable odor of revolution can in democratic countries strongly reinforce the status quo.

References

Dahl, Robert A. 1971. *Polyarchy: Participation and opposition*. New Haven, Conn.: Yale University Press.
———. 1979. "Procedural Democracy." In *Philosophy, politics and society*, edited by Peter Laslett and James Fishkin. 5th Series. New Haven, Conn.: Yale University Press.
Lijphart, Arend. 1975. *The politics of accommodation: Pluralism and democracy in the Netherlands*. 2nd ed. Berkeley: University of California Press.
Rokkan, Stein. 1966. Norway: Numerical democracy and corporate pluralism. In Robert Dahl, *Political oppositions in western democracies*, 70–115. New Haven, Conn.: Yale University Press.

NOTES

1. For example, see Peter Bachrach and Morton Baratz, "Two Faces of Power," *American Political Science Review* LVI (December, 1962). Also see Theodore Lowi, *The End of Liberalism* (New York: Norton, 1969).

2. For a restatement of his pluralism, see Dahl, *Dilemmas of Pluralist Democracy* (New Haven, Conn.: Yale University Press, 1982) as well as his *Democracy and Its Critics* (New Haven, Conn.: Yale University Press, 1989) and *On Democracy* (New Haven, Conn.: Yale University Press, 1998).

3. Although critics often attribute to "pluralist theory" the assertion that groups are equal in their influence over decisions, it is doubtful that anyone who might be described as a theorist of pluralism has ever made such an assertion.

PERFORMANCE DEMOCRACY

The republican concern about the common good and citizens who are civically virtuous seems difficult to sustain in the modern world. Voters are asking less about how policies affect *us* and more how they affect *me*. According to the performance model of democracy, this move from the collective conception of politics to the individual one is the mark of modern democratic politics and realistically illustrates the way that both voters and candidates understand themselves today.

Joseph Schumpeter offers an influential revision of classical democratic thought with what we call performance democracy. In place of the republican standard of a common good to judge democratic politics, Schumpeter finds voters asking first and foremost about their own good. If government performs well, that is, serves their immediate well-being, then they retain it; if not, then they vote to replace it. At election time, Schumpeter sees voters choosing between competing elites who offer their own products to voters who treat alternative policies as consumer products. As Schumpeter understands matters, this kind of assessment has been developing for several centuries as society has become more secularized and ideas about a common good have become demythologized. Today, he argues, people think in instrumental terms, and it is no surprise that they bring personal, utilitarian standards to politics. In this setting, voters do not pay attention to what they share with other citizens or to the long-term good of the polity or even to their own long-term good.

The social fragmentation and political disarray that communitarians trace to liberalism is something that Schumpeter attributes to the kind of democracy he sees developing in the West. For him, these changes weigh against self-moderating impulses and shared agreements about the common good and replace them with narrow, short-term self-interests. Tocqueville's "self-interests rightly understood" does not make an appearance in Schumpeter's account of democratic citizens who focus on their immediate, tangible concerns.

Schumpeter finds that politics has become a vast marketplace where parties offer competitive products and victory goes to the one that is able to attract a winning coalition of political consumers. The question candidates ask themselves in this theory is not what is best for the country but what will attract enough voters to win. With this in mind, Schumpeter holds that voters are subject to manipulation and frequently get something they do not really want.

Although no common good is possible in democratic politics, according to Schumpeter, competing parties and candidates often put forward proposals they claim will serve something like a common good. Even when candidates put forward proposals in the name of the good of the whole, in reality they are appealing to a diverse collection of voters in order to construct a winning coalition. For Schumpeter, once elections are held in modern, mass democracy then successful elites govern with an eye to sustaining their winning coalitions, and citizens are rendered relatively inactive. And once officials have been elected, Schumpeter wants voters to leave them alone. Too much democracy can, on his account, create problems for democracy. Here, the answer to the shortcomings of democracy is not more democracy as participatory democrats insist, but the efficient stewardship of government. One of the things this means for Schumpeter is that a professional bureaucracy must be allowed to do its work unimpeded.

An important variation of performance democracy appears in the work of Anthony Downs who is even more reliant on economic analysis to theorize about democracy than Schumpeter. Downs works with many of the assumptions that guide Schumpeter's analysis: namely that voters reference politics to their own well-being and that leaders search not for a common good but a strategy that will get them elected or reelected. For Downs, politics is guided by the same kind of reasoning found in economic markets. Acting as political consumers, citizens try to get the best deal they can for themselves. They do this by recognizing that they cannot get everything they want and that it is better to concentrate on what is most important to them and not on their secondary interests. What this means, according to Downs, is that voters discount their consumer interests, that is, the way they spend their money, in order to concentrate on their income or what Downs calls their producer interests.

In an environment of limited time and information resources, persuasion takes center stage in the political process and enhances the role of the successful persuader to that of an invaluable intermediary between the citizenry and the state. Downs follows this economic logic to explain why special interest groups have enjoyed such legislative success and public interest groups have not faired as well. Given the limited political resources available to ordinary citizens, they show themselves to be perfectly rational when they allow themselves to be exploited regarding their consumer interests since this affords them the opportunity to optimize their more immediately pressing producer interests. Taken a step further, this model suggests that the ratio of expended resources necessary even to educate oneself to one's best interest in a political contest, in relation to the possibility that a single vote would influence the outcome of the election, weighs against the logic of participation, informed or otherwise. Contrary to conventional wisdom, then, Downs reasons that under such conditions voter apathy is the logical response of any rational actor.

What Schumpeter and Downs describe is a political dynamic in which citizens have come to expect their government to be responsive to their individual interests. In such an environment, Schumpeter and Downs insist that references to a common good appear as nostalgic remnants of a political past that ought to be dispensed with if we are to engage in sober political analysis. In their accounts of democracy, we are given a market model where political discourse is not meant to enlighten citizens but to mobilize preferences. Accordingly, competing policy proposals become commodities, and the most attractive will carry the day. Voters, for their part, are expected to be pragmatic rather than civic. For all of the criticisms mounted against this model of democracy, those attracted to it insist that it represents the way existing modern democratic governments and their citizens and leaders really do behave.

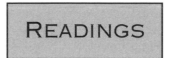

READINGS

JOSEPH A. SCHUMPETER, SELECTIONS FROM *CAPITALISM, SOCIALISM, AND DEMOCRACY* (1942)

The Classical Doctrine of Democracy

The Common Good and the Will of the People

The eighteenth-century philosophy of democracy may be couched in the following definition: the democratic method is that institutional arrangement for arriving at political decisions which realizes the common good by making the people itself decide issues through the election of individuals who are to assemble in order to carry out its will. Let us develop the implications of this.

It is held, then, that there exists a Common Good, the obvious beacon light of policy, which is always simple to define and which every normal person can be made to see by means of rational argument. There is hence no excuse for not seeing it and in fact no explanation for the presence of people who do not see it except ignorance—which can be removed—stupidity and anti-social interest. More over, this common good implies definite answers to all questions so that every social fact and every measure taken or to be taken can unequivocally be classed as "good" or "bad." All people having therefore to agree, in principle at least, there is also a Common Will of the people (= will of all reasonable individuals) that is exactly coterminous with the common good or interest or welfare or happiness. The only thing, barring stupidity and sinister interests, that can possibly bring in disagreement and account for the presence of an opposition is a difference of opinion as to the speed with which the goal, itself common to nearly all, is to be approached. Thus every member of the community, conscious of that goal, knowing his or her mind, discerning what is good and what is bad, takes part, actively and responsibly, in furthering the former and fighting the latter and all the members taken together control their public affairs.

It is true that the management of some of these affairs requires special aptitudes and techniques and will therefore have to be entrusted to specialists who have them. This does not affect the principle, however, because these specialists simply act in order to carry out the will of the people exactly as a doctor acts in order to carry out the will of the patient to get well. It is also true that in a community of any size, especially if it displays the phenomenon of division of labor, it would be highly inconvenient for every individual citizen to have to get into contact with all the other citizens on every issue in order to do his part in ruling or governing. It will be more convenient to reserve only the most important decisions for the individual citizens to pronounce upon—say by referendum—and to deal with the rest through a committee appointed by them—an assembly or parliament whose members will be elected by popular vote. This committee or body of delegates, as we have seen, will not represent the people in a legal sense but it will do so in a less technical one—it will voice, reflect or represent the will of the electorate. Again as a matter of convenience, this committee, being large, may resolve itself into smaller ones for the various departments of public affairs. Finally, among these smaller committees there will be a general-purpose committee, mainly for dealing with current administration, called cabinet or government, possibly with a general secretary or scapegoat at its head, a so-called prime minister.[1]

As soon as we accept all the assumptions that are being made by this theory of the polity—or implied by it—democracy indeed acquires a perfectly unambiguous meaning and there is no problem in connection with it except how to bring it about. Moreover we need only forget a few logical qualms in order to be able to add that in this case the democratic arrangement would not only be the best of all conceivable ones, but that few people would care to consider any other. It is no less obvious however that these assumptions are so many statements of fact every one of which would have to be proved if we are to arrive at that conclusion. And it is much easier to disprove them.

There is, first, no such thing as a uniquely determined common good that all people could agree on or be made to agree on by the force of rational argument. This is due not primarily to the fact that some people may want things other than the common good but to the much more fundamental fact that to different individuals and groups the common good is bound to mean different things. This fact, hidden from the utilitarian by the narrowness of his outlook on the world of human valuations, will introduce rifts on questions of principle which cannot be reconciled by rational argument because ultimate values—our conceptions of what life and what society should be—are beyond the range of mere logic. They may be bridged by compromise in some cases but not in others. Americans who say, "We want this country to arm to its teeth and then to fight for what we conceive to be right all over the globe" and Americans who say, "We want this country to work out its own problems which is the only way it can serve humanity" are facing irreducible differences of ultimate values which compromise could only maim and degrade.

Secondly, even if a sufficiently definite common good—such as for instance the utilitarian's maximum of economic satisfaction[2]—proved acceptable to all, this would not imply equally definite answers to individual issues. Opinions on these might differ to an extent important enough to produce most of the effects of "fundamental" dissension about ends themselves. The problems centering in the evaluation of present versus future satisfactions, even the case of socialism versus capitalism, would be left still open, for instance, after the conversion of every individual citizen to utilitarianism. "Health" might be desired by all, yet people would still disagree on vaccination and vasectomy. And so on.

The utilitarian fathers of democratic doctrine failed to see the full importance of this simply because none of them seriously considered any substantial change in the economic framework and the habits of bourgeois society. They saw little beyond the world of an eighteenth-century ironmonger.

But, third, as a consequence of both preceding propositions, the particular concept of the will of the people or the *volonté générale* that the utilitarians made their own vanishes into thin air. For that concept presupposes the existence of a uniquely determined common good discernible to all. Unlike the romanticists, the utilitarians had no notion of that semi-mystic entity endowed with a will of its own—that "soul of the people" which the historical school of jurisprudence made so much of. They frankly derived their will of the people from the wills of individuals. And unless there is a center, the common good, toward which, in the long run at least, *all* individual wills gravitate, we shall not get that particular type of "natural" *volonté générale*. The utilitarian center of gravity, on the one hand unifies individual wills, tends to weld them by means of rational discussion into the will of the people and, on the other hand, confers upon the latter the exclusive ethical dignity claimed by the classic democratic creed. *This creed does not consist simply in worshiping the will of the people as such* but rests on certain assumptions about the "natural" object, of that will which object is sanctioned by utilitarian reason. Both the existence and the dignity of this kind of *volonté générale* are gone as soon as the idea of the common good fails us. And both the pillars of the classical doctrine inevitably crumble into dust. [. . . .]

Human Nature in Politics

In the ordinary run of often repeated decisions the individual is subject to the salutary and rationalizing influence of favorable and unfavorable experience. He is also under the influence of relatively simple and unproblematical motives and interests which are but occasionally interfered with by excitement. Historically, the consumers' desire for shoes may, at least in part, have been shaped by the action of producers offering attractive footgear and campaigning for it; yet at any given time it is a genuine want, the definiteness of which extends beyond "shoes in general" and which prolonged experimenting clears out much of the irrationalities that may originally have surrounded it.[3] Moreover under the stimulus of those simple motives consumers learn to act upon unbiased expert advice about some things (houses, motorcars) and themselves become experts in others. It is simply not true that housewives are easily fooled in the matter of foods, *familiar* household articles, wearing apparel. And, as every salesman knows to his cost, most of them have a way of insisting on the exact article they want.

This of course holds true still more obviously on the producers' side of the picture. No doubt, a manufacturer may be indolent, a bad judge of opportunities or otherwise incompetent; but there is an effective mechanism that will reform or eliminate him. Again Taylorism rests on the fact that man may perform simple handicraft operations for thousands of years and yet perform them inefficiently. But neither the intention to act as rationally as possible nor a steady pressure toward rationality can seriously be called into question at whatever level of industrial or commercial activity we choose to look.[4]

And so it is with most of the decisions of daily life that lie within the little field which the individual citizen's mind encompasses with a full sense of its reality. Roughly, it consists of the things that directly concern himself, his family, his business dealings, his hobbies, his friends and enemies, his township or ward, his class, church, trade union or any other social group of which he is an active member—the things under his personal observation, the things which are familiar to him independently of what his newspaper tells him, which he can directly influence or manage and for which he develops the kind of responsibility that is induced by a direct relation to the favorable or unfavorable effects of a course of action.

Once more: definiteness and rationality in thought and action[5] are not guaranteed by this familiarity with men and things or by that sense of reality or responsibility. Quite a few other conditions which often fail to be fulfilled would be necessary for that. For instance, generation after generation may suffer from irrational behavior in matters of hygiene and yet fail to link their sufferings with their noxious habits. As long as this is not done, objective consequences, however regular, of course do not produce subjective experience. Thus it proved unbelievably hard for humanity to realize the relation between infection and epidemics: the facts pointed to it with what to us seems unmistakable clearness; yet to the end of the eighteenth century, doctors did next to nothing to keep people afflicted with infectious disease, such as measles or smallpox, from mixing with other people. And things must be expected to be still worse whenever there is not only inability but reluctance to recognize causal relations or when some interest fights against recognizing them.

Nevertheless and in spite of all the qualifications that impose themselves, there is for everyone, within a much wider horizon, a narrower field—widely differing in extent as between different groups and individuals and bounded by a broad zone rather than a sharp line—which is distinguished by a sense of reality or familiarity or responsibility. And this field harbors relatively definite individual volitions. These may often strike us as unintelligent, narrow, egotistical; and it may not be obvious to everyone why, when it comes to political decisions, we should worship at their shrine, still less why we should feel bound to count each of them for one and none of them for more than one. If, however, we do choose to worship we shall at least not find the shrine empty.[6]

Now this comparative definiteness of volition and rationality of behavior does not suddenly vanish as we move away from those concerns of daily life in the home and in business which educate and discipline us. In the realm of public affairs there are sectors that are more within the reach of the citizen's mind than others. This is true, first of local affairs. Even there we find a reduced power of discerning facts, a reduced preparedness to act upon them, a reduced sense of responsibility. We all know the man—and a very good specimen he frequently is—who says that the local administration is not his business and callously shrugs his shoulders at practices which he would rather die than suffer in his own office. High-minded citizens in a hortatory mood who preach the responsibility of the individual voter or taxpayer invariably discover the fact that this voter does not feel responsible for what the local politicians do. Still, especially in communities not too big for personal contacts, local patriotism may be a very important factor in "making democracy work." Also, the problems of a town are in many respects akin to the problems of a manufacturing concern. The man who understands the latter also understands, to some extent, the former. The manufacturer, grocer or workman need not step out of his world to have a rationally defensible view (that may of course be right or wrong) on street cleaning or town halls.

Second, there are many national issues that concern individuals and groups so directly and unmistakably as to evoke volitions that are genuine and definite enough. The most important instance is afforded by issues involving immediate and personal pecuniary profit to individual voters and groups of voters, such as direct payments, protective duties, silver policies and so on. Experience that goes back to antiquity shows that by and large voters react promptly and rationally to any such chance. But the classical doctrine of democracy evidently stands to gain little from displays of rationality of this kind. Voters thereby prove themselves bad and indeed corrupt judges of such issues,[7] and often they even prove themselves bad judges of their own long-run interests, for it is only the short-run promise that tells politically and only short-run rationality that asserts itself effectively.

However, when we move still farther away from the private concerns of the family and the business office into those regions of national and international affairs that lack a direct and unmistakable link with those private concerns, individual volition, command of facts and method of inference soon cease to fulfill the requirements of the classical doctrine. What strikes me most of all and seems to me to be the core of the trouble is the fact that the sense of reality is so completely lost. Normally, the great political questions take their place in the psychic economy of the typical citizen with those leisure-hour interests that have not attained the rank of hobbies, and with the subjects of irresponsible conversation. These things seem so far off; they are not at all like a business proposition; dangers may not materialize at all and if they should they may not prove so very serious; one feels oneself to be moving in a fictitious world.

This reduced sense of reality accounts not only for a reduced sense of responsibility but also for the absence of effective volition. One has one's phrases, of course, and one's wishes and daydreams and grumbles; especially, one has one's likes and dislikes. But ordinarily they do not amount to what we call a will—the psychic counterpart of purposeful responsible action. In fact, for the private citizen musing over national affairs there is no scope for such a will and no task at which it could develop. He is a member of an unworkable committee, the committee of the whole nation, and this is why he expends less disciplined effort on mastering a political problem than he expends on a game of bridge.[8]

The reduced sense of responsibility and the absence of effective volition in turn explain the ordinary citizen's ignorance and lack of judgment in matters of domestic and foreign policy which are if anything more shocking in the case of educated people and of people who are successfully active in non-political walks of life than it is with uneducated people in humble stations. Information is plentiful and readily available. But this does not seem to make any difference. Nor should we wonder at it. We need only compare a lawyer's attitude to his brief and the same lawyer's attitude to the statements of political fact presented in his newspaper in order to see what is the matter. In the one case the lawyer has qualified for appreciating the relevance of his facts by years of purposeful labor done under the definite stimulus of interest in his professional competence; and under a stimulus that is no less powerful he then bends his acquirements, his intellect, his will to the contents of the brief. In the other case, he has not taken the trouble to qualify; he does not care to absorb the information or to apply to it the canons of criticism he knows so well how to handle; and he is impatient of long or complicated argument. All of this goes to show that without the initiative that comes from immediate responsibility, ignorance will persist in the face of masses of information however complete and correct. It persists even in the face of the meritorious efforts that are being made to go beyond presenting information and to teach the use of it by means of lectures, classes, discussion groups. Results are not zero. But they are small. People cannot be carried up the ladder.

Thus, the typical citizen drops down to a lower level of mental performance as soon as he enters the political field. He argues and analyzes in a way which he would readily recognize as infantile within the sphere of his real interests. He becomes a primitive again. His thinking becomes associative and affective. And this entails two further consequences of ominous significance.

First, even if there were no political groups trying to influence him, the typical citizen would in political matters tend to yield to extra-rational or irrational prejudice and impulse. The weakness of the rational processes he applies to politics and the absence of effective logical control over the results he arrives at would in themselves suffice to account for that. Moreover, simply because he is not "all there," he will relax his usual moral standards as well and occasionally give in to dark urges which the conditions of private life help him to repress. But as to the wisdom or rationality of his inferences and conclusions, it may be just as bad if he gives in to a burst of generous indignation. This will make it still more difficult for him to see things in their correct proportions or even to see more than one aspect of one thing it a time. Hence, if for once he does emerge from his usual vagueness and does display the definite will postulated by the classical doctrine of democracy, he is as likely as not to become still more unintelligent and irresponsible than he usually is. At certain junctures, this may prove fatal to his nation.

Second, however the weaker the logical element in the processes of the public mind and the more complete the absence of rational criticism and of the rationalizing influence of personal experience and responsibility, the greater are the opportunities for groups with an ax to grind. These groups may consist of professional politicians or of exponents of an economic interest or of idealists of one kind or another or of people simply interested in staging and managing political shows. The sociology of such groups is immaterial to the argument in hand. The only point that matters here is that, Human Nature in Politics being what it is, they are able to fashion and, within very wide limits, even to create the will of the people. What we are confronted with in the analysis of political processes is largely not a genuine but a manufactured will. And often this artifact is all that in reality corresponds to the *volonté générale* of the classical doctrine. So far as this is so, the will of the people is the product and not the motive power of the political process.

The ways in which issues and the popular will on any issue are being manufactured is exactly analogous to the ways of commercial advertising. We find the same attempts to contact the subconscious. We find the same technique of creating favorable and unfavorable associations which are the more effective the less rational they are. We find the same evasions and reticences and the same trick of producing opinion by reiterated assertion that is successful precisely to the extent to which it avoids rational argument and the danger of awakening the critical faculties of the People. And so on. Only, all these arts have infinitely more scope in the sphere of public affairs than they have in the sphere of private and professional life. The picture of the prettiest girl that ever lived will in the long run prove powerless to maintain the sales of a bad cigarette. There is no equally effective safeguard in the case of political decisions. Many decisions of fateful importance are of a nature that makes it impossible for the public to experiment with them at its leisure and at moderate cost. Even if that is possible, however, judgment is as a rule not so easy to arrive at as it is in the case of the cigarette, because effects are less easy to interpret.

But such arts also vitiate, to an extent quite unknown in the field of commercial advertising, those forms of political advertising that profess to address themselves to reason. To the observer, the anti-rational or, at all events, the extra-rational appeal and the defenselessness of the victim stand out more and not less clearly when cloaked in facts and arguments. We have seen above why it is so difficult to impart to the public unbiased information about political problems and logically correct inferences from it and why it is that information and arguments in political matters will "register" only if they link up with the citizen's preconceived ideas. As a rule, however, these ideas are not definite enough to determine particular conclusions. Since they can themselves be manufactured, effective political argument almost inevitably implies the attempt to twist existing volitional premises into a particular shape and not merely the attempt to implement them or to help the citizen to make up his mind.

Thus information and arguments that are really driven home are likely to be the servants of political intent. Since the first thing man will do for his ideal or interest is to lie, we shall expect, and as a matter of fact we find, that effective information is almost always adulterated or selective[9] and that effective reasoning in politics consists mainly in trying to exalt certain propositions into axioms and to put others out of court; it thus reduces to the psycho-technics mentioned before. The reader who thinks me unduly pessimistic need only ask himself whether he has never heard—or said himself—that this or that awkward fact must not be told publicly, or that a certain line of reasoning, though valid, is undesirable. If men who according to any current standard are perfectly honorable or even high-minded reconcile themselves to the implications of this, do they not thereby show what they think about the merits or even the existence of the will of the people?

There are of course limits to all this.[10] And there is truth in Jefferson's dictum that in the end the people are wiser than any single individual can be, or in Lincoln's about the impossibility of "fooling all the people all the time." But both dicta stress the long-run aspect in a highly significant way. It is no doubt possible to argue that given time the collective psyche will evolve opinions that not infrequently strike us as highly reasonable and even shrewd. History however consists of a succession of short-run situations that may alter the course of events for good. If all the people can in the short run be "fooled" step by step into something they do not really want, and if this is not an exceptional case which we could afford to neglect, then no amount of retrospective common sense will alter the fact that in reality they neither raise nor decide issues but that the issues that shape their fate are normally raised and decided for them. More than anyone else the lover of democracy has every reason to accept this fact and to clear his creed from the aspersion that it rests upon make-believe. [. . . .]

Another Theory of Democracy

Competition for Political Leadership

I think that most students of politics have by now come to accept the criticisms leveled at the classical doctrine of democracy in the preceding chapter. I also think that most of them agree, or will agree before long, in accepting another theory which is much truer to life and at the same time salvages much of what sponsors of the democratic method really mean by this term. Like the classical theory, it may be put into the nutshell of a definition.

It will be remembered that our chief troubles about the classical theory centered in the proposition that "the people" hold a definite and rational opinion about every individual question and that they give effect to this opinion—in a democracy—by choosing "representatives" who will see to it that that opinion is carried out. Thus the selection of the representatives is made secondary to the primary purpose of the democratic arrangement which is to vest the power of deciding political issues in the electorate. Suppose we reverse the roles of these two elements and make the deciding of issues by the electorate secondary to the election of the men who are to do the deciding. To put it differently, we now take the view that the role of the people is to produce a government, or else an intermediate body which in turn will produce a national executive[11] or government. And we define: the democratic method is that institutional arrangement for arriving at political decisions in which individuals acquire the power to decide by means of a competitive struggle for the people's vote.

Defense and explanation of this idea will speedily show that, as to both plausibility of assumptions and tenability of propositions, it greatly improves the theory of the democratic process.

First of all, we are provided with a reasonably efficient criterion by which to distinguish democratic governments from others. We have seen that the classical theory meets with difficulties on that score because both the will and the good of the people may be, and in many historical instances have been, served just as well or better by governments that cannot be described as democratic according to any accepted usage of the term. Now we are in a somewhat better position partly because we are resolved to stress a *modus procedendi* the presence or absence of which it is in most cases easy to verify. [. . . .]

Second, the theory embodied in this definition leaves all the room we may wish to have for a proper recognition of the vital fact of leadership. The classical theory did not do this but, as we have seen, attributed to the electorate an altogether unrealistic degree of initiative which practically amounted to ignoring leadership. But collectives act almost exclusively by accepting leadership—this is the dominant mechanism of practically any collective action which is more than a reflex. Propositions about the working and the results of the democratic method that take account of this are bound to be infinitely more realistic than propositions which do not. They will not stop at the execution of a *volonté générale* but will go some way to showing how it emerges or how it is substituted or faked. What we have termed Manufactured Will is no longer outside the theory, an aberration for the absence of which we piously pray; it enters on the ground floor as it should.

Third, however, so far as there are genuine group-wise volitions at all—for instance the will of the unemployed to receive unemployment benefit or the will of other groups to help—our theory does not neglect them. On the contrary we are now able to insert them in exactly the role they actually play. Such volitions do not as a rule assert themselves directly. Even if strong and definite, they remain latent, often for decades, until they are called to life by some political leader who turns them into political factors. This he does, or else his agents do it for him, by organizing these volitions, by working them up and by including eventually appropriate items in his competitive offering. The interaction between sectional interests and public opinion and the way in which they produce the pattern we call the political situation appear from this angle in a new and much clearer light.

Fourth, our theory is of course no more definite than is the concept of competition for leadership. This concept presents similar difficulties as the concept of competition in the economic sphere, with which it may be usefully compared. In economic life competition is never completely lacking, but hardly ever is it perfect. Similarly, in political life there is always some competition, though perhaps only a potential one, for the allegiance of the people. To simplify matters we have restricted the kind of competition for leadership which is to define democracy, to free competition for a free vote. The justification for this is that democracy seems to imply a recognized method by which to conduct the competitive struggle, and that the electoral method is practically the only one available for communities of any size. But though this excludes many ways of securing leadership which should be excluded, such as competition by military insurrection, it does not exclude the cases that are strikingly analogous to the economic phenomena we label "unfair" or "fraudulent" competition or restraint of competition. And we cannot exclude them because if we did we should be left with a completely unrealistic ideal.[12] Between this ideal case which does not exist and the cases in which all competition with the established leader is prevented by force, there is a continuous range of variation within which the democratic method of government shades off into the autocratic one by imperceptible steps. But if we wish to understand and not to philosophize, this is as it should be. The value of our criterion is not seriously impaired thereby.

Fifth, our theory seems to clarify the relation that subsists between democracy and individual freedom. If by the latter we mean the existence of a sphere of individual self-government the boundaries of which are historically variable—*no* society tolerates absolute freedom even of conscience and of speech, *no* society reduces that sphere to zero—the question clearly becomes a matter of degree. We have seen that the democratic method does not necessarily guarantee a greater amount of individual freedom than another political method would permit in similar circumstances. It may well be the other way round. But there is still a relation between the two. If, on principle at least, everyone is free to compete for political leadership[13] by presenting himself to the electorate, this will in most cases though not in all mean a considerable amount of freedom of discussion *for all.* In particular it will normally mean a considerable amount of freedom of the press. This relation between democracy and freedom is not absolutely stringent and can be tampered with. But, from the standpoint of the intellectual, it is nevertheless very important. At the same time, it is all there is to that relation.

Sixth, it should be observed that in making it the primary function of the electorate to produce a government (directly or through an intermediate body) I intended to include in this phrase also the function of evicting it. The one means simply the acceptance of a leader, or a group of leaders, the other means simply the withdrawal of this acceptance. This takes care of an element the reader may have missed. He may have thought that the electorate controls as well as installs. But since electorates normally do not control their political leaders in any way except by refusing to reelect them or the parliamentary majorities that support them, it seems well to reduce our ideas about this control in the way indicated by our definition. Occasionally, spontaneous revulsions occur which upset a government or an individual minister directly or else enforce a certain course of action. But they are not only exceptional, they are, as we shall see, contrary to the spirit of the democratic method.

Seventh, our theory sheds much-needed light on an old controversy. Whoever accepts the classical doctrine of democracy and in consequence believes that the democratic method is to guarantee that issues be decided and policies framed according to the will of the people must be struck by the fact that, even if that will were undeniably real and definite, decision by simple majorities would in many cases distort it rather than give effect to it. Evidently the will of the majority is the will of the majority and not the will of "the people." The latter is a mosaic that the former completely fails to "represent." To equate both by definition is not to solve the problem. Attempts at real solutions have however been made by the authors of the various plans for Proportional Representation.

These plans have met with adverse criticism on practical grounds. It is in fact obvious not only that proportional representation will offer opportunities for all sorts of idiosyncrasies to assert themselves but also that it may prevent democracy from producing efficient governments and thus prove a danger in times of stress. But before concluding that democracy becomes unworkable if its principle is carried out consistently, it is just as well to ask ourselves whether this principle really implies proportional representation. As a matter of fact it does not. If acceptance of leadership is the true function of the electorate's vote, the case for proportional representation collapses because its premises are no longer binding. The principle of democracy then merely means that the reins of government should be handed to those who command more support than do any of the competing individuals or teams. And this in turn seems to assure the standing of the majority system within the logic of the democratic method, although we might still condemn it on grounds that lie outside of that logic. [. . . .]

The Principle Applied

We may sum up as follows. In observing human societies we do not as a rule find it difficult to specify, at least in a rough commonsense manner, the various ends that the societies under

study struggle to attain. These ends may be said to provide the rationale or meaning of corresponding individual activities. But it does not follow that the social meaning of a type of activity will necessarily provide the motive power, hence the explanation of the latter. If it does not,
a theory that contents itself with an analysis of the social end or need to be served cannot be
accepted as an adequate account of the activities that serve it. For instance, the reason why
there is such a thing as economic activity is of course that people want to eat, to clothe themselves and so on. To provide the means to satisfy those wants is the social end or meaning of
production. Nevertheless we all agree that this proposition would make a most unrealistic starting point for a theory of economic activity in commercial society and that we shall do much
better if we start from propositions about profits. Similarly, the social meaning or function of
parliamentary activity is no doubt to turn out legislation and, in part, administrative measures.
But in order to understand how democratic politics serve this social end, we must start from
the competitive struggle for power and office and realize that the social function is fulfilled, as
it were, incidentally—in the same sense as production is incidental to the making of profits.

Finally, as to the role of the electorate, only one additional point need be mentioned. We
have seen that the wishes of the members of a parliament are not the ultimate data of the
process that produces government. A similar statement must be made concerning the electorate. Its choice—ideologically glorified into the Call from the People—does not flow from
its initiative but is being shaped, and the shaping of it is an essential part of the democratic
process. Voters do not decide issues. But neither do they pick their members of parliament
from the eligible population with a perfectly open mind. In all normal cases the initiative lies
with the candidate who makes a bid for the office of member of parliament and such local
leadership as that may imply. Voters confine themselves to accepting this bid in preference to
others or refusing to accept it. Even most of those exceptional cases in which a man is *genuinely* drafted by the electors come into the same category for either of two reasons: naturally
a man need not bid for leadership if he has acquired leadership already; or it may happen that
a local leader who can control or influence the vote but is unable or unwilling to compete for
election himself designates another man who then may seem to have been sought out by the
voters acting on their own initiative.

But even as much of electoral initiative as acceptance of one of the competing candidates
would in itself imply is further restricted by the existence of parties. A party is not, as classical doctrine (or Edmund Burke) would have us believe, a group of men who intend to promote public welfare "upon some principle on which they are all agreed." This rationalization
is so dangerous because it is so tempting. For all parties will of course, at any given time, provide themselves with a stock of principles or planks and these principles or planks may be as
characteristic of the party that adopts them and as important for its success as the brands of
goods a department store sells are characteristic of it and important for its success. But the department store cannot be defined in terms of its brands and a party cannot be defined in terms
of its principles. A party is a group whose members propose to act in concert in the competitive struggle for political power. If that were not so it would be impossible for different parties to adopt exactly or almost exactly the same program. Yet this happens as everyone
knows. Party and machine politicians are simply the response to the fact that the electoral
mass is incapable of action other than a stampede, and they constitute an attempt to regulate
political competition exactly similar to the corresponding practices of a trade association. The
psycho-technics of party management and party advertising, slogans and marching tunes, are
not accessories. They are of the essence of politics. So is the political boss. [. . . .]

Some Implications of the Preceding Analysis

Exactly as there is no case for or against socialism at all times and in all places, so there is no absolutely general case for or against the democratic method. And exactly as with socialism, this makes it difficult to argue by means of a *ceteris paribus* clause, for "other things" *cannot* be equal as between situations in which democracy is a workable, or the only workable, arrangement and situations in which it is not. Democracy thrives in social patterns that display certain characteristics and it might well be doubted whether there is any sense in asking how it would fare in others that lack those characteristics—or how the people in those other patterns would fare with it. The conditions which I hold must be fulfilled for the democratic method to be a success[14]—in societies in which it is possible for it to work at all—I shall group under four headings; and I shall confine myself to the great industrial nations of the modern type.

The first condition is that the human material of politics—the people who man the party machines, are elected to serve in parliament, rise to cabinet office—should be of sufficiently high quality. This means more than that individuals of adequate ability and moral character must exist in sufficient numbers. As has been pointed out before, the democratic method selects not simply from the population but only from those elements of the population that are available for the political vocation or, more precisely, that offer themselves for election. All methods of selection do this of course. All of them therefore may, according to the degree to which a given vocation attracts talent and character, produce in it a level of performance that is above or below the national average. But the competitive struggle for responsible office is, on the one hand, wasteful of personnel and energy. On the other hand, the democratic process may easily create conditions in the political sector that, once established, will repel most of the men who can make a success at anything else. For both these reasons, adequacy of material is particularly important for the success of democratic government. It is not true that in a democracy people always have the kind and quality of government they want or merit.

There may be many ways in which politicians of sufficiently good quality can be secured. Thus far however, experience seems to suggest that the only effective guarantee is in the existence of a social stratum, itself a product of a severely selective process, that takes to politics as a matter of course. If such a stratum be neither too exclusive nor too easily accessible for the outsider and if it be strong enough to assimilate most of the elements it currently absorbs, it not only will present for the political career products of stocks that have successfully passed many tests in other fields—served, as it were, an apprenticeship in private affairs—but it will also increase their fitness by endowing them with traditions that embody experience, with a professional code and with a common fund of views. [. . . .]

The second condition for the success of democracy is that the effective range of political decision should not be extended too far. How far it can be extended depends not only on the general limitations of the democratic method which follow from the analysis presented in the preceding section but also on the particular circumstances of each individual case. To put this more concretely: the range does not only depend, for instance, on the kind and quantity of matters that can be successfully handled by a government subject to the strain of an incessant struggle for its political life; it also depends, at any given time and place, on the quality of the men who form that government and on the type of political machine and the pattern of public opinion they have to work with. From the standpoint of our theory of democracy it is not necessary to require, as it would be from the standpoint of the classical theory, that only such matters should be dealt with by the political apparatus which the people at large can fully understand and have a serious opinion about. But a less exacting requirement of the same nature still imposes itself. [. . . .]

As a third condition, democratic government in modern industrial society must be able to command, for all purposes the sphere of public activity is to include—no matter whether this be much or little—the services of a well-trained bureaucracy of good standing and tradition, endowed with a strong sense of duty and a no less strong *esprit de corps*. Such a bureaucracy is the main answer to the argument about government by amateurs. Potentially it is the only answer to the question so often heard in this country: democratic politics has proved itself unable to produce decent city government; how can we expect the nation to fare if everything, eventually including the whole of the productive process, is to be handed over to it? And finally, it is also the principal answer to the question about how our second condition can be fulfilled whenever the sphere of public control is wide.

ANTHONY DOWNS, SELECTIONS FROM "AN ECONOMIC THEORY OF POLITICAL ACTION IN A DEMOCRACY" (1957)

In spite of the tremendous importance of government decisions in every phase of economic life, economic theorists have never successfully integrated government with private decision-makers in a single general equilibrium theory. Instead they have treated government action as an exogenous variable, determined by political considerations that lie outside the purview of economics. This view is really a carry-over from the classical premise that the private sector is a self-regulating mechanism and that any government action beyond maintenance of law and order is "interference" with it rather than an intrinsic part of it.[15]

However, in at least two fields of economic theory, the centrality of government action has forced economists to formulate rules that indicate how government "should" make decisions. [. . . .]

[O]vert statements of a decision rule to guide government action are extremely rare in economic theory. However, it does not unduly distort reality to state that most welfare economists and many public finance theorists implicitly assume that the "proper" function of government is to maximize social welfare. Insofar as they face the problem of government decision-making at all, they nearly all subscribe to some approximation of this normative rule.

The use of this rule has led to two major difficulties. First, it is not clear what is meant by "social welfare," nor is there any agreement about how to "maximize" it. In fact, a long controversy about the nature of social welfare in the "new welfare economics" led to Kenneth Arrow's conclusion that no rational method of maximizing social welfare can possibly be found unless strong restrictions are placed on the preference orderings of the individuals in society.[16]

The complexities of this problem have diverted attention from the second difficulty raised by the view that government's function is to maximize social welfare. Even if social welfare could be defined, and methods of maximizing it could be agreed upon, what reason is there to believe that the men who run the government would be motivated to maximize it? To state that they "should" do so does not mean that they will. [. . . .]

In light of this reasoning, any attempt to construct a theory of government action without discussing the motives of those who run the government must be regarded as inconsistent with the main body of economic analysis. Every such attempt fails to face the fact that governments are concrete institutions run by men, because it deals with them on a purely normative level. As a result, these attempts can never lead to an integration of government with other decision-makers in a general equilibrium theory. Such integration demands a positive approach that explains how the governors are led to act by their own selfish motives. In the following sections, I present a model of government decision-making based on this approach.

In building this model, I shall use the following definitions:

1. *Government* is that agency in the division of labor which has the power to coerce all other agents in society; it is the locus of "ultimate" power in a given area.[17]
2. A *democracy* is a political system that exhibits the following characteristics:
    a) Two or more parties compete in periodic elections for control of the governing apparatus.
    b) The party (or coalition of parties) winning a majority of votes gains control of the governing apparatus until the next election.
    c) Losing parties never attempt to prevent the winners from taking office, nor do winners use the powers of office to vitiate the ability of losers to compete in the next election.
    d) All sane, law-abiding adults who are governed are citizens, and every citizen has one and only one vote in each election.

Though these definitions are both somewhat ambiguous, they will suffice for present purposes. Next I set forth the following axioms:

1. Each political party is a team of men who seek office solely in order to enjoy the income, prestige, and power that go with running the governing apparatus.
2. The winning party (or coalition) has complete control over the government's actions until the next election. There are no votes of confidence between elections either by a legislature or by the electorate, so the governing party cannot be ousted before the next election. Nor are any of its orders resisted or sabotaged by an intransigent bureaucracy.
3. Government's economic powers are unlimited. It can nationalize everything, hand everything over to private interests, or strike any balance between these extremes.
4. The only limit on government's powers is that the incumbent party cannot in any way restrict the political freedom of opposition parties or of individual citizens, unless they seek to overthrow it by force.
5. Every agent in the model—whether an individual, a party or a private coalition—behaves rationally at all times; that is, it proceeds toward its goals with a minimal use of scarce resources and undertakes only those actions for which marginal return exceeds marginal cost.[18]

From these definitions and axioms springs my central hypothesis: political parties in a democracy formulate policy strictly as a means of gaining votes. They do not seek to gain office in order to carry out certain preconceived policies or to serve any particular interest groups; rather they formulate policies and serve interest groups in order to gain office. Thus their social function—which is to formulate and carry out policies when in power as the government—is accomplished as a by-product of their private motive—which is to attain the income, power, and prestige of being in office.

This hypothesis implies that, in a democracy, the government always acts so as to maximize the number of votes it will receive. In effect, it is an entrepreneur selling policies for votes instead of products for money. Furthermore, it must compete for votes with other parties, just as two or more oligopolists compete for sales in a market. [. . . .]

Lack of complete information on which to base decisions is a condition so basic to human life that it influences the structure of almost every social institution. In politics especially, its effects are profound. [. . . .]

In this model, imperfect knowledge means (1) that parties do not always know exactly what citizens want; (2) that citizens do not always know what the government or its opposition has done, is doing, or should be doing to serve their interests; and (3) that the information needed to overcome both types of ignorance is costly—in other words, that scarce resources must be used to procure and assimilate it. Although these conditions have many effects upon the operation of government in the model, I concentrate on only three: persuasion, ideologies, and rational ignorance.

As long as we retain the assumption of perfect knowledge, no citizen can possibly influence another's vote. Each knows what would benefit him most, what the government is doing, and what other parties would do if they were in power. Therefore, the citizen's political taste structure, which I assume to be fixed, leads him directly to an unambiguous decision about how he should vote. If he remains rational, no persuasion can change his mind.

But, as soon as ignorance appears, the clear path from taste structure to voting decision becomes obscured by lack of knowledge. Though some voters want a specific party to win because its policies are clearly the most beneficial to them, others are highly uncertain about which party they prefer. They are not sure just what is happening to them or what would happen to them if another party were in power. They need more facts to establish a clear preference. By providing these facts, persuaders can become effective.

Persuaders are not interested per se in helping people who are uncertain become less so; they want to produce a decision that aids their cause. Therefore, they provide only those facts which are favorable to whatever group they are supporting. Thus, even if we assume that no erroneous or false data exist, some men are able to influence others by presenting them with a biased selection of facts.

This possibility has several extraordinarily important consequences for the operation of government. First, it means that some men are more important than others politically, because they can influence more votes than they themselves cast. Since it takes scarce resources to provide information to hesitant citizens, men who command such resources are able to wield more than proportional political influence, *ceteris paribus*. The government, being rational, cannot overlook this fact in designing policy. As a result, equality of franchise no longer assures net equality of influence over government action. In fact, it is irrational for a democratic government to treat its citizens with equal deference in a world in which knowledge is imperfect.

Second, the government is itself ignorant of what its citizens want it to do. Therefore it must send out representatives (1) to sound out the electorate and discover their desires and (2) to persuade them it should be re-elected. In other words, lack of information converts democratic government into representative government because it forces the central planning board of the governing party to rely upon agents scattered throughout the electorate. [. . . .]

This reasoning implies that a democratic government in a rational world will always be run on a quasi-representative, quasi-decentralized basis, no matter what its formal constitutional structure, as long as communication between the voters and the governors is less than perfect. Another powerful force working in the same direction is the division of labor. To be efficient, a nation must develop specialists in discovering, transmitting, and analyzing popular opinion, just as it develops specialists in everything else. These specialists are the representatives. They exercise more power, and the central planning board exercises less, the less efficient are communication facilities in society.

The third consequence of imperfect knowledge and the resulting need for persuasion is really a combination of the first two. Because some voters can be influenced, specialists in influencing them appear. And, because government needs intermediaries between it and the people, some of these influencers pose as "representatives" of the citizenry. On one hand, they attempt to convince the government that the policies they stand for—which are of direct benefit to themselves—are both good for and desired by a large portion of the electorate. On the other hand, they try to convince the electorate that these policies are in fact desirable. Thus one of their methods of getting government to believe that public opinion supports them is to create favorable opinion through persuasion. Though a rational government will discount their claims, it cannot ignore them altogether. It must give the influencers more than proportional weight in forming policy, because they may have succeeded in creating favorable opinions in the silent mass of voters and because their vociferousness indicates a high intensity of desire. Clearly, people with an intense interest in some policy are more likely to base their votes upon it alone than are those who count it as just another issue; hence government must pay more attention to the former than the latter. To do otherwise would be irrational.

Finally, imperfect knowledge makes the governing party susceptible to bribery. In order to persuade voters that its policies are good for them, it needs scarce resources, such as television time, money for propaganda, and pay for precinct captains. One way to get such resources is to sell policy favors to those who can pay for them, either by campaign contributions, favorable editorial policies, or direct influence over others. Such favor buyers need not even pose as representatives of the people. They merely exchange their political help for policy favors—a transaction eminently rational for both themselves and the government.

Essentially, inequality of political influence is a necessary result of imperfect information, given an unequal distribution of wealth and income in society. When knowledge is imperfect, effective political action requires the use of economic resources to meet the cost of information. Therefore, those who command such resources are able to swing more than their proportional weight politically. This outcome is not the result of irrationality or dishonesty. On the contrary, lobbying in a democracy is a highly rational response to the lack of perfect information, as is government's submission to the demands of lobbyists. To suppose otherwise is to ignore the existence of information costs—that is, to theorize about a mythical world instead of the real one. Imperfect knowledge allows the unequal distributions of income, position, and influence—which are all inevitable in any economy marked by an extensive division of labor—to share sovereignty in a realm where only the equal distribution of votes is supposed to reign.

Since the parties in this model have no interest per se in creating any particular type of society, the universal prevalence of ideologies in democratic politics appears to contradict my hypothesis. But this appearance is false. In fact, not only the existence of ideologies, but also many of their particular characteristics, may be deduced from the premise that parties seek office solely for the income, power, and prestige that accompany it.[19] Again, imperfect knowledge is the key factor.

In a complex society the cost in time alone of comparing all the ways in which the policies of competing parties differ is staggering. Furthermore, citizens do not always have enough information to appraise the differences of which they are aware. Nor do they know in advance what problems the government is likely to face in the coming election period.

Under these conditions many a voter finds party ideologies useful because they remove the necessity for relating every issue to his own conception of "the good society." Ideologies help him focus attention on the differences between parties; therefore, they can be used as samples of all the differentiating stands. Furthermore, if the voter discovers a correlation between each party's ideology and its policies, he can rationally vote by comparing ideologies rather than policies. In both cases he can drastically reduce his outlay on political information by informing himself only about ideologies instead of about a wide range of issues.

Thus lack of information creates a demand for ideologies in the electorate. Since political parties are eager to seize any method of gaining votes available to them, they respond by creating a supply. Each party invents an ideology in order to attract the votes of those citizens who wish to cut costs by voting ideologically.[20]

This reasoning does not mean that parties can change ideologies as though they were disguises, putting on whatever costume suits the situation. Once a party has placed its ideology "on the market," it cannot suddenly abandon or radically alter that ideology without convincing the voters that it is unreliable. Since voters are rational, they refuse to support unreliable parties; hence no party can afford to acquire a reputation for dishonesty. Furthermore, there must be some persistent correlation between each party's ideology and its subsequent actions; otherwise voters will eventually eschew ideological voting as irrational. Finally, parties cannot adopt identical ideologies, because they must create enough product differentiation to make their output distinguishable from that of their rivals, so as to entice voters to the polls. However, just as in the product market, any markedly successful ideology is soon imitated, and differentiation takes place on more subtle levels. [. . . .]

When information is costly, no decision maker can afford to know everything that might possibly bear on his decision before he makes it. He must select only a few data from the vast supply in existence and base his decision solely upon them. This is true even if he can procure data without paying for them, since merely assimilating them requires time and is therefore costly.

The amount of information it is rational for a decision-maker to acquire is determined by the following economic axiom: It is always rational to perform any act if its marginal return is larger than its marginal cost. The marginal cost of a "bit" of information is the return foregone by devoting scarce resources—particularly time—to getting and using it. The marginal return from a "bit" is the increase in utility income received because the information enabled the decision maker to improve his decision. In an imperfectly informed world, neither the precise cost nor the precise return is usually known in advance; but decision makers can nevertheless employ the rule just stated by looking at expected costs and expected returns.

This reasoning is as applicable to politics as it is to economics. Insofar as the average citizen is concerned, there are two political decisions that require information. The first is deciding which party to vote for; the second is deciding on what policies to exercise direct influence on government policy formation (that is, how to lobby). Let us examine the voting decision first. [. . . .]

The marginal return on information acquired for voting purposes is measured by the expected gain from voting "correctly" instead of "incorrectly." In other words, it is the gain in utility a voter believes he will receive if he supports the party which would really provide him with the highest utility income instead of supporting some other party. However, unless his vote actually decides the election, it does not cause the "right" party to be elected instead of a "wrong" party; whether or not the "right" party wins does not depend on how he votes. Therefore, voting "correctly" produces no gain in utility whatsoever; he might as well have voted "incorrectly."

This situation results from the insignificance of any one voter in a large electorate. Since the cost of voting is very low, hundreds, thousands, or even millions of citizens can afford to vote. Therefore, the probability that any one citizen's vote will be decisive is very small indeed. It is not zero, and it can even be significant if he thinks the election will be very close; but, under most circumstances, it is so negligible that it renders the return from voting "correctly" infinitesimal. This is true no matter how tremendous a loss in utility income the voter would experience if the "wrong" party were elected. And if that loss is itself small—as it may be when parties resemble each other closely or in local elections—then the incentive to become well informed is practically nonexistent.

Therefore, we reach the startling conclusion that it is irrational for most citizens to acquire political information for purposes of voting. As long as each person considers the behavior of others as given, it is simply not worthwhile for him to acquire information so as to vote "correctly" himself. The probability that his vote will determine which party governs is so low that even a trivial cost of procuring information outweighs its return. Hence ignorance of politics is not a result of unpatriotic apathy; rather it is a highly rational response to the facts of political life in a large democracy.

This conclusion does not mean that every citizen who is well informed about politics is irrational. A rational man can become well informed for four reasons: (1) he may enjoy being well informed for its own sake, so that information as such provides him with utility; (2) he may believe the election is going to be so close that the probability of his casting the decisive vote is relatively high; (3) he may need information to influence the votes of others so that he can alter the outcome of the election or persuade government to assign his preferences more weight than those of others; or (4) he may need information to influence the formation of government policy as a lobbyist. Nevertheless, since the odds are that no election will be close enough to render decisive the vote of any one person, or the votes of all those he can persuade to agree with him, the rational course of action for most citizens is to remain politically uninformed. Insofar as voting is concerned, any attempt to acquire information beyond that furnished by the stream of "free" data is for them a sheer waste of resources.

The disparity between this conclusion and the traditional conception of good citizenship in a democracy is indeed striking. How can we explain it? The answer is that the benefits which a majority of citizens would derive from living in a society with a well-informed electorate are indivisible in nature. When most members of the electorate know what policies best serve their interests, the government is forced to follow those policies in order to avoid defeat (assuming that there is a consensus among the informed). This explains why the proponents of democracy think citizens should be well informed. But the benefits of these policies accrue to each member of the majority they serve, regardless of whether he has helped bring them about. In other words, the individual receives these benefits whether or not he is well informed, so long as most people are well informed and his interests are similar to those of the majority. On the other hand, when no one else is well informed, he cannot produce these benefits by becoming well informed himself, since a collective effort is necessary to achieve them.

Thus, when benefits are indivisible, each individual is always motivated to evade his share of the cost of producing them. If he assumes that the behavior of others is given, whether or not he receives any benefits does not depend on his own efforts. But the cost he pays does depend on his efforts; hence the most rational course for him is to minimize that cost—in this case, to remain politically ignorant. Since every individual reasons in the same way, no one bears any costs, and no benefits are produced.

The usual way of escaping this dilemma is for all individuals to agree to be coerced by a central agency. Then each is forced to pay his share of the costs, but he knows all others are likewise forced to pay. Thus everyone is better off than he would be if no costs were borne, because everyone receives benefits which (I here assume) more than offset his share of the costs. This is a basic rationale for using coercion to collect revenues for national defense and for many other government operations that yield indivisible benefits.[21]

But this solution is not feasible in the case of political information. The government cannot coerce everyone to be well informed, because "well-informedness" is hard to measure, because there is no agreed-upon rule for deciding how much information of what kinds each citizen "should" have, and because the resulting interference in personal affairs would cause a loss of utility that would probably outweigh the gains to be had from a well-informed electorate. The most any democratic government has done to remedy this situation is to compel young people in schools to take courses in civics, government, and history.

Consequently, it is rational for every individual to minimize his investment in political information, in spite of the fact that most citizens might benefit substantially if the whole electorate were well informed. As a result, democratic political systems are bound to operate at less than maximum efficiency. Government does not serve the interests of the majority as well as it would if they were well informed, but they never become well informed. It is collectively rational, but individually irrational, for them to do so; and, in the absence of any mechanism to insure collective action, individual rationality prevails.

When we apply the economic concept of rationality to the second political use of information, lobbying, the results are similarly incompatible with the traditional view of democracy. In order to be an effective lobbyist, a citizen must persuade the governing party that the policies he wants either are already desired by a large number of other citizens or are sufficiently beneficial to the rest of the electorate so that it will, at worst, not resent the enactment of these policies. To be persuasive, the would-be lobbyist must be extremely well informed about each policy area in which he wishes to exert influence. He must be able to design a policy that benefits him more than any other would, to counter any arguments advanced by opposing lobbyists, and to formulate or recognize compromises acceptable to him. Therefore, being a lobbyist requires much more information than voting, since even well-informed voters need only compare alternatives formulated by others.

For this reason, the cost of acquiring enough information to lobby effectively is relatively high. A lobbyist must be an expert in the policy areas in which he tries to exert influence. Since few men can afford the time or money necessary to become expert in more than one or two policy areas (or to hire those already expert), most citizens must specialize in a very few areas. Such behavior is rational even though policies in many areas affect them to some extent. Conversely, only a few specialists will actively exert pressure on the government in any one policy area. As a result, each need not heavily discount his own impact because of the large number of other persons influencing the decision, as he does in regard to voting. On the contrary, for those few lobbyists who specialize in any given area, the potential return from political information may be very high—precisely because they are so few.

The men who can best afford to become lobbyists in any policy area are those whose incomes stem from that area. This is true because nearly every citizen derives all his income from one or two sources; hence any government policy affecting those sources is of vital interest to him. In contrast, each man spends his income in a great many policy areas, so that a change in any one of them is not too significant to him. Therefore, men are much more likely to exert direct influence on government policy formation in their roles as producers than in their roles as consumers. In consequence, a democratic government is usually biased in favor of producer interests and against consumer interests, even though the consumers of any given product usually outnumber its producers. Tariff legislation provides a notorious example of this bias.

It should be stressed that such systematic exploitation of consumers by producers acting through government policy is not a result of foolish apathy on the part of consumers. In fact, just the opposite is true. Government's anticonsumer bias occurs because consumers rationally seek to acquire only that information which provides a return larger than its cost. The saving a consumer could make by becoming informed about how government policy affects any one product he purchases simply does not recompense him for the cost of informing himself—particularly since his personal influence on government policy would probably be slight. Since this is true of almost every product he buys, he adopts a course of rational ignorance, thereby exposing himself to extensive exploitation. Yet it would be irrational for him to act otherwise. In other words, lobbying is effective in a democracy *because* all the agents concerned—the exploiters, the exploited, and the government—behave rationally.

Clearly, rational behavior in a democracy is not what most normative theorists assume it to be. Political theorists in particular have often created models of how the citizens of a democracy ought to behave without taking into account the economics of political action. Consequently, much of the evidence frequently cited to prove that democratic politics are dominated by irrational (non-logical) forces in fact demonstrates that citizens respond rationally (efficiently) to the exigencies of life in an imperfectly informed world.[22]

NOTES

1. The official theory of the functions of a cabinet minister holds in fact that he is appointed in order to see to it that in his department the will of the people prevails.

2. The very meaning of "greatest happiness" is open to serious doubt. But even if this doubt could be removed and definite meaning could be attached to the sum total of economic satisfaction of a group of people, that maximum would still be relative to given situations and valuations, which it may be impossible to alter, or compromise on, in a democratic way.

3. In the above passage irrationality means failure to act rationally upon a given wish. It does not refer to the reasonableness of the wish itself in the opinion of the observer. This is important to note because economists in appraising the extent of consumers' irrationality sometimes exaggerate it by confusing the two things. Thus, a factory girl's finery may seem to a professor an indication of irrational behavior for

which there is no other explanation but the advertiser's arts. Actually, it may be all she craves for. If so her expenditure on it may be ideally rational in the above sense.

4. This level differs of course not only as between epochs and places but also, at a given time and place, as between different industrial sectors and classes. There is no such thing as a universal pattern of rationality.

5. Rationality of thought and rationality of action are two different things. Rationality of thought does not always guarantee rationality of action. And the latter may be present without any conscious deliberation and irrespective of any ability to formulate the rationale of one's action correctly. The observer, particularly the observer who uses interview and questionnaire methods, often overlooks this and hence acquires an exaggerated idea of the importance of irrationality in behavior. This is another source of those overstatements which we meet so often.

6. It should be observed that in speaking of definite and genuine volitions I do not mean to exalt them into ultimate data for all kinds of social analysis. Of course they are themselves the product of the social process and the social environment. All I mean is that they may serve as data for the kind of special-purpose analysis which the economist has in mind when he derives prices from tastes or wants that are "given" at any moment and need not be further analyzed each time. Similarly we may for our purpose speak of genuine and definite volitions that at any moment are given independently of attempts to manufacture them, although we recognize that these genuine volitions themselves are the result of environmental influences in the past, propagandist influences included. This distinction between genuine and manufactured will . . . is a difficult one and cannot be applied in all cases and for all purposes. For our purpose however it is sufficient to point to the obvious common-sense case which can be made for it.

7. The reason why the . . . [utilitarians] so completely overlooked this is that they did not consider the possibilities of mass corruption in modern capitalism. Committing in their political theory the same error which they committed in their economic theory, they felt no compunction about postulating that "the people" were the best judges of their own individual interests and that these must necessarily coincide with the interests of all the people taken together. Of course this was made easier for them because actually though not intentionally they philosophized in terms of bourgeois interests which had more to gain from a parsimonious state than from any direct bribes.

8. It will help to clarify the point if we ask ourselves why so much more intelligence and clear-headedness show up at a bridge table than in, say, political discussion among non-politicians. At the bridge table we have a definite task; we have rules that discipline us; success and failure are clearly defined; and we are prevented from behaving irresponsibly because every mistake we make will not only immediately tell but also be immediately allocated to us. These conditions, by their failure to be fulfilled for the political behavior of the ordinary citizen, show why it is that in politics he lacks all the alertness and the judgment he may display in his profession.

9. Selective information, if in itself correct, is an attempt to lie by speaking the truth.

10. Possibly they might show more clearly if issues were more frequently decided by referendum. Politicians presumably know why they are almost invariably hostile to that institution.

11. The insincere word "executive" really points in the wrong direction. It ceases however to do so if we use it in the sense in which we speak of the "executives" of a business corporation who also do a great deal more than "execute" the will of the stockholders.

12. As in the economic field, *some* restrictions are implicit in the legal and moral principles of the community.

13. Free, that is, in the same sense in which everyone is free to start another textile mill.

14. By "success" I mean no more than that the democratic process reproduce itself steadily without creating situations that enforce resort to non-democratic methods and that it cope with current problems in a way which all interests that count politically find acceptable in the long run. I do not mean that every observer, from his own individual standpoint, need approve of the results.

15. See Gerhard Colm, *Essays in Public Finance and Fiscal Policy* (New York: Oxford University Press, 1955), 6–8.

16. *Social Choice and Individual Values* (New York: Wiley, 1951).

17. This definition is taken from Robert A. Dahl and Charles E. Lindblom, *Politics, Economics, and Welfare* (New York: Harper, 1953), 42. However, throughout most of my analysis the word "government" refers to the governing party rather than the institution as here defined.

18. The term "rational" in this article is synonymous with "efficient." This economic definition must not be confused with the logical definition (i.e., pertaining to logical propositions) or the psychological definition (i.e., calculating or unemotional).

19. I define "ideologies" as verbal images of "the good society" and of the chief policies to be used in creating it.

20. In reality, party ideologies probably stem originally from the interests of those persons who found each party. But, once a political party is created, it takes on an existence of its own and eventually becomes relatively independent of any particular interest group. When such autonomy prevails, my analysis of ideologies is fully applicable.

21. See Paul A. Samuelson, "The Pure Theory of Public Expenditures," *Review of Economics and Statistics* XXXVI (November, 1954), 387–89.

22. In this sentence the word "irrational" is not the opposite of the word "rational," as the synonyms in parentheses show. Admittedly, such dual usage may cause confusion. However, I have employed the word "rational" instead of its synonym "efficient" throughout this article because I want to emphasize the fact that an intelligent citizen always carries out any act whose marginal return exceeds its marginal cost. In contrast, he does not always make use of logical thinking, because, under some conditions, the marginal return from thinking logically is smaller than its marginal cost. In other words, it is sometimes rational (efficient) to act irrationally (non-logically), in which case an intelligent man eschews rationality in the traditional sense so as to achieve it in the economic sense.

6

PARTICIPATORY DEMOCRACY

E very democrat subscribes to the idea that some degree of popular participation is necessary to guarantee government by consent, if only to re-ratify the continued desirability of the current regime. But like so many concepts in the democratic tradition, participation carries with it a broad interpretative latitude, both in terms of its proper scope and its normative value. What distinguishes participatory thinkers from other democrats is their fundamental belief that the real benefits of democracy can only be appreciated and sustained by a society that is characterized by relatively high levels of citizen intervention in the tasks of governing. Variants of participatory politics have gone under such labels as radical or direct democracy, but the core concept that unites these doctrines is the same; namely the idea that free and fair voting procedures are not sufficient to ensure that the democratic ideal will be realized in political practice.[1]

Participatory theorists want to move beyond voting and other conventional ways of formal democratic expression to make room for additional modes of political activity that can help to retrieve the substantive promise of democratic life. In this way, many proponents of participatory democracy want to bring the lessons of an expanded idea of political activity to what has conventionally been nonpolitical areas of social life, such as the workplace, bureaucracies, the home, and schools.[2] For these democrats, voting and similar modes of political activity are too confining, particularly in a complex, mass society. Voices are said to be lost, and the concerns of the most vulnerable members of society are overwhelmed by two-party competition and interest group politics. On their account, the formal political mechanisms of liberal democracy reduce the role of citizenship to registering approval or disapproval of a simplified set of partisan proposals. In the end, according to participatory democrats, such a model inevitably turns citizens into increasingly disinterested spectators.

John Dewey complains about the very thing that Schumpeter and Downs see as the essence of modern democracy—that it is, in Dewey's words, "a competitive open market."

The problem for Dewey is that this does not leave room for discourse or meaningful avenues of popular input. For him, the tension between practices that promote freedom and autocratic methods is evidenced by the fact that both are at work in our society. With this in mind, he notes that while the threat to freedom by kings and aristocrats has been extinguished, the democratic principle has now come under attack by a new intellectual aristocracy. Here, expert opinion has replaced public opinion as the source of authority in public life in ways that usurp the prerogative of citizen influence in key processes of decisionmaking. As he sees matters, voters need not decide on the specifics of policy but they should determine its general direction. They are qualified to do so, he argues, not because they have some specialized training but because they possess sufficient common sense. Against those who claim that the many are not suited to such important deliberations, either from weakness of intellect or a flawed moral capacity, Dewey argues that these disabilities can be overcome if ordinary people have opportunities to educate themselves on the findings of experts and then to act responsibly.

The success of democracy depends upon other conditions as well. One that Dewey emphasizes is the need to devise expanded avenues of participation. He asserts that only by reclaiming public arenas for the practice of localized self-government can citizens hope to govern themselves freely and wisely. He thus urges the expansion of opportunities for discussion and persuasion throughout society as a means of retrieving what he takes to be the defining principle of democracy. But such discussions must also proceed with the understanding that democratic objectives can never be realized without a commitment to democratic means and attitudes, that is, without tolerance, inclusiveness, and the protection of freedom.

Benjamin Barber offers us "strong democracy" as a desirable alternative to purely representative or "weak" models of democracy, which look to remote forms of representation to solve organizational problems as well as to the collectivistic tendencies of a unitary, direct democracy with its emphasis on conformity and consensus. Through "strong democracy," he promotes local self-determination, which, he believes, will transform isolated individuals into community-based, participatory citizens. Here, he draws upon a tradition of small-scale political organization in the form of neighborhood-assemblies to envision credible, participatory arenas that complement representative institutions in important ways without replacing them at every level. Meaningful participation does not take place in the quiet corners of private life for Barber. Rather, he ties it to the processes of community-building and the education of citizenship. From this perspective, if popular preferences are to guide government policies and if the terms of debate are to remain open to diverse voices and changing perspectives, then decisionmaking must begin at the bottom of the representative ladder instead of at the top.

Like Dewey, Barber works with the idea that it is democratic deliberation and action that create democratic citizens. In this sense, democracy provides its own education, as participants are empowered to fulfill their roles as democratic actors at the same time as they come to appreciate the heavy responsibilities of self-governance. As Dewey and Barber see matters, participation brings people together in common projects where they develop not only new skills but more importantly construct a strong civic sense that they use both in their local settings as well as in the larger world of national politics. To the extent that the complexities of mass society complicate the coordinating tasks of a democratic society, Barber sees the electronic media as a partial solution to the problems of scale when deliberation must involve large numbers of citizens.

READINGS

JOHN DEWEY, "DEMOCRATIC ENDS NEED DEMOCRATIC METHODS FOR THEIR REALIZATION" (1939)

Unforeseen commitments out of town have prevented me from attending the meeting at Town Hall to which I have looked forward with such great interest. I am proud of the work of the Committee for Cultural Freedom, and its efforts to defend and advance the integrity of cultural and intellectual life.

As we listen to accounts of the repression of cultural freedom in countries which have been swept by totalitarian terror, let us bear in mind that our chief problems are those within our own culture. In the modern world, every country under some circumstances becomes fertile soil for seeds out of which grow fanatical conflict, intolerance, racial oppression.

The attitude which prevails in some parts of our country towards Negroes, Catholics and Jews is spiritually akin to the excesses that have made a shambles of democracy in other countries of the world.

The conflict between the methods of freedom and those of totalitarianism, insofar as we accept the democratic ideals to which our history commits us, is within our own institutions and attitudes. It can be won only by extending the application of democratic methods, methods of consultation, persuasion, negotiation, cooperative intelligence in the task of making our own politics, industry, education—our culture generally—a servant and an evolving manifestation of democratic ideas.

Resort to military force is a first sure sign that we are giving up the struggle for the democratic way of life, and that the Old World has conquered morally as well as geographically.

If there is one conclusion to which human experience unmistakably points, it is that democratic ends demand democratic methods for their realization. Authoritarian methods now offer themselves to us in new guises. They come to us claiming to serve the ultimate ends of freedom by immediate, and allegedly temporal, techniques of suppression.

Or they recommend adoption of a totalitarian regime in order to fight totalitarianism. In whatever form they offer themselves, they owe their seductive power to their claim to serve ideal ends.

Our first defense is to realize that democracy can be served only by the slow day by day adoption and contagious diffusion in every phase of our common life of methods that are identical with the ends to be reached.

There is no substitute for intelligence and integrity in cultural life. Anything else is a betrayal of human freedom no matter in what guise it presents itself.

An American democracy can serve the world only as it demonstrates in the conduct of its own life the efficacy of plural, partial, and experimental methods in securing and maintaining an ever-increasing release of the powers of human nature, in service of a freedom which is cooperative and a cooperation which is voluntary.

We cannot sit back in complacent optimism. History will not do our work for us. Neither is there any call for panic or pessimism.

We, members and friends of the Committee for Cultural Freedom, must dedicate our-selves to the task of securing and widening cultural freedom with eyes open and minds alert to every danger which threatens it. We must always remember that the dependence of ends upon means is such that the only ultimate result is the result that is attained today, tomorrow, the next day, and day after day, in the succession of years and generations.

Only thus can we be on guard against those who paint a rosy future which has no date in order to cover up their theft of our existing liberties. Only thus can we be sure that we face our problems in details one by one as they arise, and with all the resources provided by col-lective intelligence operating in cooperative action.

JOHN DEWEY, SELECTION FROM *THE PUBLIC AND ITS PROBLEMS* (1927)

A negative phase of the earlier argument for political democracy has largely lost its force. For it was based upon hostility to dynastic and oligarchic aristocracies, and these have largely been reft of power. The oligarchy which now dominates is that of an economic class. It claims to rule, not in virtue of birth and hereditary status, but in virtue of ability in management and of the burden of social responsibilities which it carries, in virtue of the position which supe-rior abilities have conferred upon it. At all events, it is a shifting, unstable oligarchy, rapidly changing its constituents, who are more or less at the mercy of accidents they cannot control and of technological inventions. Consequently, the shoe is now on the other foot. It is argued that the check upon the oppressive power of this particular oligarchy lies in an intellectual aristocracy, not in appeal to an ignorant, fickle mass whose interests are superficial and triv-ial, and whose judgments are saved from incredible levity only when weighted down by heavy prejudice.

It may be argued that the democratic movement was essentially transitional. It marked the passage from feudal institutions to industrialism, and was coincident with the transfer of power from landed proprietors, allied to churchly authorities, to captains of industry, under conditions which involved an emancipation of the masses from legal limitations which had previously hemmed them in. But, so it is contended in effect, it is absurd to convert this legal liberation into a dogma which alleges that release from old oppressions confers upon those emancipated the intellectual and moral qualities which fit them for sharing in regulation of the affairs of state. The essential fallacy of the democratic creed, it is urged, is the notion that a historic movement which effected an important and desirable release from restrictions is ei-ther a source or a proof of capacity in those thus emancipated to rule, when in fact there is no factor common in the two things. The obvious alternative is rule by those intellectually qualified, by expert intellectuals.

This revival of the Platonic notion that philosophers should be kings is the more taking because the idea of experts is substituted for that of philosophers, since philosophy has be-come something of a joke, while the image of the specialist, the expert in operation, is ren-dered familiar and congenial by the rise of the physical sciences and by the conduct of in-dustry. A cynic might indeed say that the notion is a pipe dream, a revery entertained by the intellectual class in compensation for an impotence consequent upon the divorce of theory and practice, upon the remoteness of specialized science from the affairs of life: the gulf being bridged, not by the intellectuals but by inventors and engineers hired by captains of industry. One approaches the truth more nearly when one says that the argument proves too much for its own cause. If the masses are as intellectually irredeemable as its premise implies, they at all events have both too many desires and too much power to permit rule by experts to obtain. The very ignorance, bias, frivolity, jealousy, instability, which are alleged to incapacitate them from share in political affairs, unfit them still more for passive submission to rule by intellectuals. Rule by an economic class may be disguised from the masses; rule by experts could not be covered up. It could be made to work only if the intellectuals became the willing tools of big economic interests. Otherwise they would have to ally themselves with the masses, and that implies, once more, a share in government by the latter.

A more serious objection is that expertness is most readily attained in specialized technical matters, matters of administration and execution which postulate that general policies are already satisfactorily framed. It is assumed that the policies of the experts are in the main both wise and benevolent, that is, framed to conserve the genuine interests of society. The final obstacle in the way of any aristocratic rule is that in the absence of an articulate voice on the part of the masses, the best do not and cannot remain the best, the wise cease to be wise. It is impossible for highbrows to secure a monopoly of such knowledge as must be used for the regulation of common affairs. In the degree in which they become a specialized class, they are shut off from knowledge of the needs which they are supposed to serve.

The strongest point to be made in behalf of even such rudimentary political forms as democracy has already attained, popular voting, majority rule and so on, is that to some extent they involve a consultation and discussion which uncover social needs and troubles. This fact is the great asset on the side of the political ledger. De Tocqueville wrote it down almost a century ago in his survey of the prospects of democracy in the United States. Accusing a democracy of a tendency to prefer mediocrity in its elected rulers, and admitting its exposure to gusts of passion and its openness to folly, he pointed out in effect that popular government is educative as other modes of political regulation are not. It forces a recognition that there are common interests, even though the recognition of *what* they are is confused; and the need it enforces of discussion and publicity brings about some clarification of what they are. The man who wears the shoe knows best that it pinches and where it pinches, even if the expert shoemaker is the best judge of how the trouble is to be remedied. Popular government has at least created public spirit even if its success in informing that spirit has not been great.

A class of experts is inevitably so removed from common interests as to become a class with private interests and private knowledge, which in social matters is not knowledge at all. The ballot is, as often said, a substitute for bullets. But what is more significant is that counting of heads compels prior recourse to methods of discussion, consultation and persuasion, while the essence of appeal to force is to cut short resort to such methods. Majority rule, just as majority rule, is as foolish as its critics charge it with being. But it never is *merely* majority rule. As a practical politician, Samuel J. Tilden, said a long time ago: "The means by which a majority comes to be a majority is the more important thing": antecedent debates, modification of views to meet the opinions of minorities, the relative satisfaction given the latter by the fact that it has had a chance and that next time it may be successful in becoming a majority. Think of the meaning of the "problem of minorities" in certain European states, and compare it with the status of minorities in countries having popular government. It is true that all valuable as well as new ideas begin with minorities, perhaps a minority of one. The important consideration is that opportunity be given that idea to spread and to become the possession of the multitude. No government by experts in which the masses do not have the chance to inform the experts as to their needs can be anything but an oligarchy managed in the interests of the few. And the enlightenment must proceed in ways which force the administrative specialists to take account of the needs. The world has suffered more from leaders and authorities than from the masses.

The essential need, in other words, is the improvement of the methods and conditions of debate, discussion and persuasion. That is *the* problem of the public. We have asserted that this improvement depends essentially upon freeing and perfecting the processes of inquiry and of dissemination of their conclusions. Inquiry, indeed, is a work which devolves upon experts. But their expertness is not shown in framing and executing policies, but in discovering and making known the facts upon which the former depend. They are technical experts in the sense that scientific investigators and artists manifest *expertise*. It is not necessary that the many should have the knowledge and skill to carry on the needed investigations; what is required is that they have the ability to judge of the bearing of the knowledge supplied by others upon common concerns.

It is easy to exaggerate the amount of intelligence and ability demanded to render such judgments fitted for their purpose. In the first place, we are likely to form our estimate on the basis of present conditions. But indubitably one great trouble at present is that the data for good judgment are lacking; and no innate faculty of mind can make up for the absence of facts. Until secrecy, prejudice, bias, misrepresentation, and propaganda as well as sheer ignorance are replaced by inquiry and publicity, we have no way of telling how apt for judgment of social policies the existing intelligence of the masses may be. It would certainly go much further than at present. In the second place, *effective* intelligence is not an original, innate endowment. No matter what are the differences in native intelligence (allowing for the moment that intelligence can be native), the actuality of mind is dependent upon the education which social conditions effect. Just as the specialized mind and knowledge of the past is embodied in implements, utensils, devices and technologies which those of a grade of intelligence which could not produce them can now intelligently use, so it will be when currents of public knowledge blow through social affairs.

The level of action fixed by *embodied* intelligence is always the important thing. In savage culture a superior man will be superior to his fellows, but his knowledge and judgment will lag in many matters far behind that of an inferiorly endowed person in an advanced civilization. Capacities are limited by the objects and tools at hand. They are still more dependent upon the prevailing habits of attention and interest which are set by tradition and institutional customs. Meanings run in the channels formed by instrumentalities of which, in the end, language, the vehicle of thought as well as of communication, is the most important. A mechanic can discourse of ohms and amperes as Sir Isaac Newton could not in his day. Many a man who has tinkered with radios can judge of things which Faraday did not dream of. It is aside from the point to say that if Newton and Faraday were now here, the amateur and mechanic would be infants beside them. The retort only brings out the point: the difference made by different objects to think of and by different meanings in circulation. A more intelligent state of social affairs, one more informed with knowledge, more directed by intelligence, would not improve original endowments one whit, but it would raise the level upon which the intelligence of all operates. The height of this level is much more important for judgment of public concerns than are differences in intelligence quotients. As Santayana has said: "Could a better system prevail in our lives a better order would establish itself in our thinking. It has not been for want of keen senses, or personal genius, or a constant order in the outer world, that mankind has fallen back repeatedly into barbarism and superstition. It has been for want of good character, good example, and good government." The notion that intelligence is a personal endowment or personal attainment is the great conceit of the intellectual class, as that of the commercial class is that wealth is something which they personally have wrought and possess.

A point which concerns us in conclusion passes beyond the field of intellectual method, and trenches upon the question of practical re-formation of social conditions. In its deepest and richest sense a community must always remain a matter of face-to-face intercourse. This is why the family and neighborhood, with all their deficiencies, have always been the chief agencies of nurture, the means by which dispositions are stably formed and ideas acquired which laid hold on the roots of character. The Great Community, in the sense of free and full intercommunication, is conceivable. But it can never possess all the qualities which mark a local community. It will do its final work in ordering the relations and enriching the experience of local associations. The invasion and partial destruction of the life of the latter by outside uncontrolled agencies is the immediate source of the instability, disintegration and restlessness which characterize the present epoch. Evils which are uncritically and indiscriminately laid at the door of industrialism and democracy might, with greater intelligence, be referred to the dislocation and unsettlement of local communities. Vital and thorough attachments are bred only in the intimacy of an intercourse which is of necessity restricted in range.

Benjamin Barber, Selection from *Strong Democracy* (1984)

A well-known adage has it that under a representative government the voter is free only on the day he casts his ballot. Yet even this act may be of dubious consequence in a system where citizens use the franchise only to select an executive or judicial or legislative elite that in turn exercises every other duty of civic importance. To exercise the franchise is unhappily also to renounce it. The representative principle steals from individuals the ultimate responsibility for their values, beliefs, and actions. And it is far less hospitable to such primary Western values as freedom, equality, and social justice than weak democrats might wish.

Representation is incompatible with freedom because it delegates and thus alienates political will at the cost of genuine self-government and autonomy. As Rousseau warned, "The instant a people allows itself to be represented it loses its freedom."[3] Freedom and citizenship are correlates; each sustains and gives life to the other. Men and women who are not directly responsible through common deliberation, common decision, and common action for the policies that determine their common lives are not really free at all, however they enjoy security, private rights, and freedom from interference.

Representation is incompatible with equality because, in the astute words of the nineteenth-century French Catholic writer Louis Veuillot, "when I vote my equality falls into the box with my ballot, they disappear together."[4] Equality, construed exclusively in terms of abstract personhood or of legal and electoral equity, omits the crucial economic and social determinants that shape its real-life incarnation. In the absence of community, equality is a fiction that not merely divides as easily as it unites but that raises the specter of a mass society made up of indistinguishable consumer clones.

Representation, finally, is incompatible with social justice because it encroaches on the personal autonomy and self-sufficiency that every political order demands, because it impairs the community's ability to function as a regulating instrument of justice, and because it precludes the evolution of a participating public in which the idea of justice might take root.[5]

Freedom, equality, and justice are in fact all *political* values that depend for their theoretical coherence and their practical efficacy on self-government and citizenship. They cannot be apprehended or practiced except in the setting of citizenship. They are not conterminous with the condition of politics, they are aspects of a satisfactory response to the condition of politics. They cannot be externally defined and then appropriated for political use; rather, they must be generated and conditioned by politics.

This point relates directly to the problem of the independent ground. In . . . weak democracy, the banished independent ground (in whose place a mode of politics is supposed to operate) is covertly reintroduced in the guise of such notions as noblesse oblige (the wisdom of an authoritative elite), or the free market (the absolute autonomy of the individual as an irrefutable premise of pluralist market and contract relations). Yet the definition of the political condition developed above would suggest that it is precisely such notions as "wisdom," "rights," and "freedom" that need to be given meaning and significance within the setting of democratic politics. These terms and others like them are essentially contestable: their meaning is subject to controversy at a fundamental level and cannot be discovered by abstract reasoning or by an appeal to external authority.[6] This is why they become the focus of discourse in democratic politics: they do not define but are defined by politics.

Representative democracy suffers, then, both from its reliance on representative principle and from its vulnerability to seduction by an illicit rationalism—from the illusion that metaphysics can establish the meaning of debatable political terms. By permitting, even encouraging, the reintroduction of independent grounds, representative modes of democracy subvert the very political process that was supposed to meet and overcome the absence of such grounds. By subordinating the will and judgment of citizens to abstract norms about which there can be no real consensus, these modes demean citizenship itself and diminish correspondingly the capacities of a people to govern itself. And by allowing heteronomous notions of right to creep into the politics of self-legislation, they fatally undermine the autonomy on which all real political freedom depends. Citizens become subject to laws they did not truly participate in making; they become the passive constituents of representatives who, far from reconstituting the citizens' aims and interests, usurp their civic functions and deflect their civic energies.

To the extent that these criticisms apply, thin democracy is not very democratic, nor even convincingly political. For all the talk about politics in Western democratic regimes, it is hard to find in all the daily activities of bureaucratic administration, judicial legislation, executive leadership, and party policy-making anything that resembles citizen engagement in the creation of civic communities of public ends. Politics has become what politicians do; what citizens do (when they do anything) is vote for the politicians.

Two alternative forms of democracy seem to hold out some hope that these difficulties can be alleviated through the activation of citizenship and community. The first, which I call *unitary democracy,* is motivated by the need for consensus but ultimately betrays the democratic impulse—particularly when it is separated from the small-scale institutions out of which it arose. The second, *strong democracy,* seems able to remedy a number of the shortcomings of weak democracy without failing prey to the excesses of unitary democracy. It is the argument of this book that the strong form of democracy is the only form that is genuinely and completely democratic. It may also be the only one capable of preserving and advancing the political form of human freedom in a world that grows ever more hostile to traditional liberal democracy.

Unitary Democracy. The unitary form of democracy is defined by politics in the consensual mode and seems at first glance to eschew representation (if not politics itself) in pursuit of its central norm, unity. It calls for all divisive issues to be settled unanimously through the organic will of a homogeneous or even monolithic community often identified symbolically as a race or nation or people or communal will. The government posture here is centralized and active, while the posture of the citizenry is ambiguous, since the individual citizen achieves his civic identity through merging his self with the collectivity, that is to say, through self-abandonment. Although this surrender assures a certain equality (another characteristic norm of unitary and strong democracy), it is obviously corrupting to autonomy and thus ultimately to citizenship itself.

The institutional bias of unitary democracy is symbolic, i.e., government is associated with the symbolic entity in which the community will is embodied. In subordinating participation in a greater whole to identification with that whole and autonomy and self-legislation to unity and group self-realization, unitary democracy becomes conformist, collectivist, and often even coercive. In small face-to-face communities it is relatively benign, and it has historically served both equality and citizenship reasonably well in places where they might otherwise not have been served at all.[7] In such settings, unitary democracy relies on voluntary self-identification with the group, peer pressure, social conformism, and a willing acceptance of group norms—mechanisms that, to be sure, have their own perils but that are for the most part well immunized against the virulent modern strains of infectious totalism.[8]

In larger settings, however, where the community becomes an impersonal abstraction and individuals relate anonymously and anomically with masses of strangers, unitary democracy can turn malevolent, can be perilous to freedom and citizenship and ruinous to democracy. In its final phase, the French Revolution seemed to aspire to the unitary ideal in its most obnoxious form. Thus Hyppolyte Castille glorified the reign of terror in these startling words: "The most perfect community would be where tyranny was an affair of the whole community. That proves fundamentally that the most perfect society would be one where there is the least freedom in the satanic [i.e., individualist] meaning of this word."[9] It is this unitary perversion of "direct" democracy that has aroused so many liberals to condemn participation and community as well as the arguments for "political freedom" with which their proponents justify these ideals.

To bring it into our typology, we may give unitary democracy, considered as a response to the dilemmas of the political condition, the following formal definition: *democracy in the unitary mode resolves conflict in the absence of an independent ground through community consensus as defined by the identification of individuals and their interests with a symbolic collectivity and its interests.*

As I have suggested, whether the consensual community is large and abstract (as in the case of fascism in its pure, national form) or small and face-to-face (as in the case of the homogeneous eighteenth century New England town or the rural Swiss commune will determine whether unitary democracy becomes vicious or merely irrelevant.[10] But in neither case is it consistently participatory (since it undermines self-legislation) or genuinely political (since it "wills" away conflict). For the identification of individual with collectivity—which permits a government in the unitary mode to speak not only for but *as* "The People"—conceals and obscures the representative relationship that actually obtains between citizens and governing organs. Moreover, the symbolic collectivity denoted by such abstract terms as *the nation* or *the Aryan Race* or *the communal will*—since it is no longer circumscribed by the actual wills (or choices) of individual citizens acting in concert—usually turns out to be a cipher for some surreptitious set of substantive norms. It turns out, in other words, to be camouflage for the reintroduction of independent grounds, a stalking horse for Truth in the midst of politics, a Trojan Horse carrying Philosophers, Legislators, and other seekers of Absolute Certainty into the very inner sanctum of democracy's citadel. And so, in the place where we expect finally to hear the voices of active citizens determining their own common destiny through discourse and deliberation, we hear instead the banished voice of hubris, of would-be-truth and of could-be-right, which were unable to get a hearing on their own merits. Had they done so, the occasion for politics, democratic or otherwise, would never have arisen.

Thus does the promise of unitary democracy fade: unable to escape weak democracy's dependency on representation and the covert independent ground, it adds to them all the grave risks of monism, conformism, and coercive consensualism. No wonder that liberal democrats cringe at the prospect of "benevolent" direct democratic alternatives. With the perils of unitary democracy in mind, they justifiably fear the remedy for representation more than its ills.

The central question for the future of democracy thus becomes: Is there an alternative to liberal democracy that does not resort to the subterfuges of unitary democracy? In the absence of a safe alternative, it is the better part of prudence to stick by the representative forms of democracy, deficiencies and all.

Strong Democracy: Politics in the Participatory Mode

The future of democracy lies with strong democracy—with the revitalization of a form of community that is not collectivistic, a form of public reasoning that is not conformist, and a set of civic institutions that is compatible with modern society. Strong democracy is defined by politics in the participatory mode: literally, it is self-government by citizens rather than representative government in the name of citizens. Active citizens govern themselves directly here, not necessarily at every level and in every instance, but frequently enough and in particular when basic policies are being decided and when significant power is being deployed. Self-government is carried on through institutions designed to facilitate ongoing civic participation in agenda-setting, deliberation, legislation, and policy implementation (in the form of "common work"). Strong democracy does not place endless faith in the capacity of individuals to govern themselves, but it affirms with Machiavelli that the multitude will on the whole be as wise as or even wiser than princes and with Theodore Roosevelt that "the majority of the plain people will day in and day out make fewer mistakes in governing themselves than any smaller body of men will make in trying to govern them."[11]

Considered as a response to the dilemmas of the political condition, strong democracy can be given the following formal definition: *strong democracy in the participatory mode resolves conflict in the absence of an independent ground through a participatory process of ongoing, proximate self-legislation and the creation of a political community capable of transforming dependent private individuals into free citizens and partial and private interests into public goods.*

The crucial terms in this strong formulation of democracy are *activity, process, self-legislation, creation,* and *transformation.* Where weak democracy eliminates conflict (the anarchist disposition), represses it (the realist disposition), or tolerates it (the minimalist disposition), strong democracy *transforms conflict*. It turns dissensus into an occasion for mutualism and private interest into an epistemological tool of public thinking.

Participatory politics deals with public disputes and conflicts of interest by subjecting them to a never-ending process of deliberation, decision, and action. Each step in the process is a flexible part of ongoing procedures that are embedded in concrete historical conditions and in social and economic actualities. In place of the search for a prepolitical independent ground or for an immutable rational plan, strong democracy relies on participation in an evolving problem-solving community that creates public ends where there were none before by means of its own activity and of its own existence as a focal point of the quest for mutual solutions. In such communities, public ends are neither extrapolated from absolutes nor "discovered" in a preexisting "hidden consensus." They are literally forged through the act of public participation, created through common deliberation and common action and the effect that deliberation and action have on interests, which change shape and direction when subjected to these participatory processes.

Strong democracy, then, seems potentially capable of transcending the limitations of representation and the reliance on surreptitious independent grounds without giving up such defining democratic values as liberty, equality, and social justice. Indeed, these values take on richer and fuller meanings than they can ever have in the instrumentalist setting of liberal democracy. For the strong democratic solution to the political condition issues out of a self-sustaining dialectic of participatory civic activity and continuous community-building in which freedom and equality are nourished and given political being. Community grows out of participation and at the same time makes participation possible; civic activity educates individuals how to think publicly as citizens even as citizenship informs civic activity with the required sense of publicness and justice. Politics becomes its own university, citizenship its own training ground, and participation its own tutor. Freedom is what comes out of this process, not what goes into it. Liberal and representative modes of democracy make politics an activity of specialists and experts whose only distinctive qualification, however, turns out to be simply that they engage in politics that they encounter others in a setting that requires action and where they have to find a way to act in concert. Strong democracy is the politics of amateurs, where every man is compelled to encounter every other man without the intermediary of expertise.

This universality of participation—every citizen his own politician—is essential, because the "Other" is a construct that becomes real to an individual only when he encounters it directly in the political arena. He may confront it as an obstacle or approach it as an ally, but it is an inescapable reality in the way of and on the way to common decision and common action. *We* also remains an abstraction when individuals are represented either by politicians or as symbolic wholes. The term acquires a sense of concreteness and simple reality only when individuals redefine themselves as citizens and come together directly to resolve a conflict or achieve a purpose or implement a decision. Strong democracy creates the very citizens it depends upon *because* it depends upon them, because it permits the representation neither of *me* nor of *we*, because it mandates a permanent confrontation between the *me* as citizen and the "Other" as citizen, forcing *us* to think in common and act in common. The citizen is by definition a *we*-thinker, and to think of the *we* is always to transform how interests are perceived and goods defined.

This progression suggests how intimate the ties are that bind participation to community.

Citizenship is not a mask to be assumed or shed at will. It lacks the self-conscious mutability of a modern social "role" as Goffman might construe it. In strong democratic politics, participation is a way of defining the self, just as citizenship is a way of living. The old liberal notion, shared even by radical democrats such as Tom Paine, was that a society is "composed of distinct, unconnected individuals [who are] continually meeting, crossing, uniting, opposing, and separating from each other, as accident, interest, and circumstances shall direct."[12] Such a conception repeats the Hobbesian error of setting participation and civic activity apart from community. Yet participation without community, participation in the face of deracination, participation by victims or bondsmen or clients or subjects, participation that is uninformed by an evolving idea of a "public" and unconcerned with the nurturing of self-responsibility, participation that is fragmentary, part-time, halfhearted, or impetuous—these are all finally sham, and their failure proves nothing.

It has in fact become a habit of the shrewder defenders of representative democracy to chide participationists and communitarians with the argument that enlarged public participation in politics produces no great results. Once empowered, the masses do little more than push private interests, pursue selfish ambitions, and bargain for personal gain, the liberal critics assert. Such participation is the work of prudent beasts and is often less efficient than the ministrations of representatives who have a better sense of the public's appetites than does the public itself. But such a course in truth merely gives the people all the insignia and none of the tools of citizenship and then convicts them of incompetence. Social scientists and political elites have all too often indulged themselves in this form of hypocrisy. They throw referenda at the people without providing adequate information, full debate, or prudent insulation from money and media pressures and then pillory them for their lack of judgment. They overwhelm the people with the least tractable problems of mass society—busing, inflation, tax structures, nuclear safety, right-to-work legislation, industrial waste disposal, environmental protection (all of which the representative elites themselves have utterly failed to deal with)—and then carp at their uncertainty or indecisiveness or the simple-mindedness with which they muddle through to a decision. But what general would shove rifles into the hands of civilians, hurry them off to battle, and then call them cowards when they are overrun by the enemy?

Strong democracy is not government by "the people" or government by "the masses," because a people are not yet a citizenry and masses are only nominal freemen who do not in fact govern themselves. Nor is participation to be understood as random activity by maverick cattle caught up in the same stampede or as minnow school movement by clones who wiggle in unison. As with so many central political terms, the idea of participation has an intrinsically normative dimension—a dimension that is circumscribed by citizenship. Masses make noise, citizens deliberate; masses behave, citizens act; masses collide and intersect, citizens engage, share, and contribute. At the moment when "masses" start deliberating, acting, sharing, and contributing, they cease to be masses and become citizens. Only then do they "participate."

Or, to come at it from the other direction, to be a citizen *is* to participate in a certain conscious fashion that presumes awareness of and engagement in activity with others. This consciousness alters attitudes and lends to participation that sense of the *we* I have associated with community. To participate *is* to create a community that governs itself, and to create a self-governing community *is* to participate. Indeed, from the perspective of strong democracy, the two terms *participation* and *community* are aspects of one single mode of social being: citizenship. Community without participation first breeds unreflected consensus and uniformity, then nourishes coercive conformity, and finally engenders unitary collectivism of a kind that stifles citizenship and the autonomy on which political activity depends. Participation without community breeds mindless enterprise and undirected, competitive interest-mongering. Community without participation merely rationalizes collectivism, giving it an aura of legitimacy. Participation without community merely rationalizes individualism, giving it the aura of democracy.

This is not to say that the dialectic between participation and community is easily institutionalized. Individual civic activity (participation) and the public association formed through civic activity (the community) call up two strikingly different worlds. The former is the world of autonomy, individualism, and agency; the latter is the world of sociability, community, and interaction. The world views of individualism and communalism remain at odds; and institutions that can facilitate the search for common ends without sabotaging the individuality of the searchers, and that can acknowledge pluralism and conflict as starting points of the political process without abdicating the quest for a world of common ends, may be much more difficult to come by than a pretty paragraph about the dialectical interplay between individual participation and community. Yet it is just this dialectical balance that strong democracy claims to strike.

NOTES

1. See Carole Pateman, *Participation and Democratic Theory* (Cambridge: Cambridge University Press, 1970), particularly chap. 1.

2. For a discussion of workplace democracy, see Pateman as well as Carol Gould, *Rethinking Democracy: Freedom and Social Co-operation in Politics, Economy and Society* (Cambridge: Cambridge University Press, 1988). See also Peter Bachrach and Aryeh Botwinick. *Power and Empowerment: A Radical Theory of Participatory Democracy* (Philadelphia: Temple University Press, 1992).

3. Jean-Jacques Rousseau, *The Social Contract*, book 3, chap. 15. A later philosopher writing in the same vein insists upon "the logical impossibility of the 'representative' system." Since "the will of the people is not transferable, nor even the will of single individual, the first appearance of professional leadership marks the beginning of the end" (Robert Michels, *Political Parties: A Sociological Study of the Oligarchical Tendencies of Modern Democracy* [Glencoe, Ill.: Free Press, 1915; reprinted, 1949], 33–34).

4. Cited by Michels, *Political Parties,* 39; my translation.

5. Court-ordered busing programs, which are "right" by every legal standard, nonetheless manage to remedy the effects of public prejudice only by destroying public responsibility and activity in a realm (schooling) that is traditionally associated with vigorous neighborhood civic activity. Here the principle of right collides with the principle of participation, and the damage done to the latter imperils, in the long run, the possibility of sustaining the former by democratic means.

6. The idea of "essential contestability," first developed in a philosophical setting by W. B. Gallie, has been given an illuminating political context by William Connolly in *The Terms of Political Discourse* (Lexington, Mass.: Heath, 1974).

7. Peter Laslett provides the "face-to-face" society with a sociology and a history in his seminal work *The World We Have Lost* (London: Methuen, 1965).

8. I have tried to give an account of the strengths and the dangers of face-to-face democracy in the Swiss German Alps in my *The Death of Communal Liberty* (Princeton, N.J.: Princeton University Press, 1974). Readers may refer to this work for a fuller discussion.

9. Hippoyte Castille, *History of the Second Republic,* cited by Eduard Bernstein, *Evolutionary Social-*

ism, ed. Sidney Hook (New York: Schocken Books, 1961).

10. Even in such benign settings as the Vermont town meeting or an urban crisis cooperative, direct democracy can be problematic. See for example Jane J. Mansbridge's sociologically astute study *Beyond Adversary Democracy* (New York: Basic Books, 1980).

11. "The People are wiser and more constant than Princes," writes Machiavelli in his *Discourses on Livy,* book 1, chap. 58. Roosevelt is cited in R. A. Allen, "The National Initiative Proposal: A Preliminary Analysis," *Nebraska Law Review* 58, 4 (1979): 1011.

12. Thomas Paine, "Dissertation on First Principles of Government," in *Writings*, vol. 3, ed. N. D. Conway (New York: Putnam, 1894–1896), 268.

III

CRITIQUES OF CONTEMPORARY DEMOCRATIC THEORY AND PRACTICE

I n this section, we take up several arguments about the crisis and the promise of contemporary liberal democracy in order to explore some of the prominent debates driving democratic thought today. Our goal in presenting these works is to highlight the continuities and discontinuities that characterize current critiques of democracy and to call attention to those voices that identify certain key democratic objectives that they believe remain unfulfilled.

For many realists and neorealists, contemporary models hide too much, particularly the pervasiveness of power, and rob politics of any purpose beyond satisfying interests. Departing from the empirical realism of pluralism and performance democracy, realists and neorealists propose to reintroduce power as a central feature of democracy and show how it can be used and abused. Realists hold that power is an inescapable feature of any politics, including democratic politics, and they urge democratic citizens to remain vigilant to the risks and limits involved in the use of power.

A more sweeping criticism comes from postmodernists who question the premises of both traditional and contemporary theories and find our ideas about power and politics to be myopic and dangerous. They see a process of normalization and formalism at work in current theories and practices, which hides the many forms of domination they detect in the postmodern world. What is postmodern about our time, many of them argue, is that the internal logic of modernity has destroyed its own foundations, such as its faith in reason and progress. For these authors, these are ideological constructions designed to serve some at the expense of the rest. Yet they do not see domination stemming from a single source, such as the state, class, race, or gender, although each carries its own forms of subordination. Rather they find multiple locations of power, each working to normalize inegalitarian practices and delegitimize alternative ways of thinking, speaking, and acting. To confront this situation, some postmodernists turn to a reconceptualized pluralism. This is not the interest-driven pluralism proposed by Bentley and Dahl but one that strives to account for the diversity, complexity, and ambiguity of contemporary identities.

The problem is different for those who hold that modern democratic politics has debased language to such an extent that it cannot play the role originally assigned to it: to inform, to expose, and to enable citizens to reason together and to find a common ground to settle their differences. These critics, whom we call discursive democrats, find that political rhetoric has become a weapon employed by contending sides, not for the purpose of enlightening but as a potent means of mobilizing supporters and embarrassing opponents. They also hold that political language is being replaced by the language of experts, robbing citizens of their democratic rights to challenge and revise public policy.

Another set of criticisms revolves around issues of equality and inclusion. In a world impatient with many of the forms of nonpolitical hierarchy that have long marked liberal democratic societies, justifications of current practices of inequality are no longer acceptable. The reason for controversy is that some find that equality cannot simply mean investing persons who had been previously excluded with the same formal rights that had been available to other citizens, such as the franchise. For these critics, full citizenship means looking at the various artificial exclusions that have marked civil society and correcting them.

Many non-Western democrats find that there is a danger in borrowing too much from Western theory. Here, the issue is not that Western democracy has nothing to say to the political challenges they face in their parts of the world. Rather, these critics find it necessary to speak in their own vernacular and work with their own tradition and cultural resources. For some, the danger of contemporary Western democracy is its penchant for uniformity. From their perspective, the issue has less to do with competitive elections and majority rule than with the tendency of contemporary Western democracy to remake every culture in its own image: secular, interest-attentive, market-driven, and disdainful of tradition. On this account, the globalization of Western democracy is meant not to ensure a variety of democratic expressions but to assure a world that is made safe for Western versions of politics, economics, and culture. Many non-Western theories of democracy also emphasize something that is taken for granted in the West, namely human rights, and make it a central feature of a responsive government. In the process, they also place more emphasis on eliminating great disparities of wealth and power.

THE REALIST AND NEOREALIST CRITIQUES

The realist critiques discussed in this section make power the central issue for understanding politics. They find that power is unavoidable and inescapable and that it can undermine the very goals it serves. For this reason, they insist that it is essential to be continually attuned to the nature, sources, and expressions of power as both a constructive and potentially self-destructive force. They are unimpressed with a crude realism which holds that politics is simply about winning.

Max Weber finds that power is an unavoidable fact of political life, and when we attempt to ignore power or distance ourselves from it, we only delude ourselves. As such, politics requires us to be alert to how our own best efforts fall short and how our best intentions often conceal unintended and unexpected costs. Writing at the turn of the twentieth century, Weber sees the old order of Europe giving way to new modes of knowledge (science), politics (democracy), and organization (bureaucracy). For him, the traditional patterns of belief and action have become demythologized.

Weber is considered by many to have introduced a modern realism into political analysis by refusing to allow revolutionary or conservative idealism to drive politics in a changing world. For him, the underlying consideration of politics is power and its ability to do both good and evil. Moreover, he believes that in politics, no act can be purely ethical. As he put matters in *Politics as a Vocation,* "in numerous instances, the attainment of good ends is bound to the fact that one must be willing to pay the price of using morally dubious means or at least dangerous ones." Anyone who is serous about politics, he insists, must realize its "ethical paradoxes." And these paradoxes do not disappear when politics becomes democratic.[1]

For Weber, one of the great problems facing contemporary democracy is bureaucracy—something he believes can arise only in mass democracy. Modern bureaucracy has replaced earlier forms of administration because of its vast superiority, efficiency, and productivity. Traditional methods of government recruitment, so reliant on favoritism, privilege, or nepotism, have been replaced by an openness based on competency. One of the paradoxes of modern democratic politics, then, is seen in the fact that the perfection of those bureaucratic methods has become indispensable to delivering the public policies demanded in mass democracy. At the same time, this very success has depleted the elected government of its capacity for popular accountability. Because the new bureaucratic structures have their own rules and procedures that often circumvent the voice of the demos, mass democracy and bureaucracy form a critical tension with one another. Ultimately, Weber sees humanity as condemned to increasingly regimented forms of existence and argues that efforts to institute an alternative to bureaucracy must be viewed as utopian and dangerous.

The Italian neorealist, Norberto Bobbio, looks at what he takes to be the essential link between freedom and popular rule, that is, between liberalism and democracy. As he sees matters, liberalism holds up claims against the state, whether it is democratic or not; the democratic state invests sovereignty with the majority, and it can interfere with liberty. For those who want to preserve rights by weakening or abandoning democracy as well as those who want to preserve democracy by discarding rights, Bobbio argues that liberalism and democracy unavoidably require each other. No society can be democratic without being free (and vice versa); but the mutual dependence between liberty and democracy does not mean they are always compatible.

An important problem that Bobbio addresses is whether democracy has carried out its promises, and he finds that it has not. He notices that oligarchy has not disappeared with democracy, that power often remains "hidden," that citizens are often "uneducated," that technicians often rule, and that bureaucracy is frequently beyond the reach of public accountability.

For Bobbio, some of "the broken promises" of democracy are unavoidable but others are not. This conclusion leads him to argue against both a perfectionist view of democracy, where some sort of final harmony might be installed, as well as an accommodating view that holds that conventional democratic arrangements are sufficient to ensure democratic justice. Bobbio finds that democracy is about struggle, not only among competing groups in society but also between citizens and organized power, whether public or private. For this reason, he wants democrats to challenge secretive and exclusionary practices that diminish the role of the public in public affairs, without being seduced by utopian visions of ultimate political solutions to human problems.

READINGS

MAX WEBER, SELECTIONS FROM *ECONOMY AND SOCIETY* (1922)

We are primarily interested in "domination" insofar as it is combined with "administration." Every domination both expresses itself and functions through administration. Every administration, on the other hand, needs domination, because it is always necessary that some powers of command be in the hands of somebody. Possibly the power of command may appear in a rather innocent garb; the ruler may be regarded as their "servant" by the ruled, and he may look upon himself in that way. [. . . .]

The decisive reason for the advance of bureaucratic organization has always been its purely *technical* superiority over any other form of organization. The fully developed bureaucratic apparatus compares with other organizations exactly as does the machine with the non-mechanical modes of production. Precision, speed, unambiguity, knowledge of the files, continuity, discretion, unity, strict subordination, reduction of friction and of material and personal costs—these are raised to the optimum point in the strictly bureaucratic administration, and especially in its monocratic form. As compared with all collegiate, honorific, and avocational forms of administration, trained bureaucracy is superior on all these points. And as far as complicated tasks are concerned, paid bureaucratic work is not only more precise but, in the last analysis, it is often cheaper than even formally unremunerated honorific service. [   ]

Today, it is primarily the capitalist market economy which demands that the official business of public administration be discharged precisely, unambiguously, continuously, and with as much speed as possible. Normally, the very large modern capitalist enterprises are themselves unequaled models of strict bureaucratic organization. Business management throughout rests on increasing precision, steadiness, and, above all, speed of operations. This, in turn, is determined by the peculiar nature of the modern means of communication, including, among other things, the news service of the press. The extraordinary increase in the speed by which public announcements, as well as economic and political facts, are transmitted exerts a steady and sharp pressure in the direction of speeding up the tempo of administrative reaction towards various situations. The optimum of such reaction time is normally attained only by a strictly bureaucratic organization. (The fact that the bureaucratic apparatus also can, and indeed does, create certain definite impediments for the discharge of business in a manner best adapted to the individuality of each case does not belong into the present context.)

Bureaucratization offers above all the optimum possibility for carrying through the principle of specializing administrative functions according to purely objective considerations. Individual performances are allocated to functionaries who have specialized training and who by constant practice increase their expertise. "Objective" discharge of business primarily means a discharge of business according to *calculable rules* and "without regard for persons."

"Without regard for persons," however, is also the watchword of the market and, in general, of all pursuits of naked economic interests. Consistent bureaucratic domination means the leveling of "status honor." Hence, if the principle of the free market is not at the same time restricted, it means the universal domination of the "class situation." That this consequence of bureaucratic domination has not set in everywhere proportional to the extent of bureaucratization is due to the differences between possible principles by which polities may supply their requirements. However, the second element mentioned, calculable rules, is the most important one for modern bureaucracy. The peculiarity of modern culture, and specifically of its technical and economic basis, demands this very "calculability" of results. When fully developed, bureaucracy also stands in a specific sense, under the principle of *sine ira ac studio*. Bureaucracy develops the more perfectly, the more it is "dehumanized," the more completely it succeeds in eliminating from official business love, hatred, and all purely personal, irrational, and emotional elements which escape calculation. This is appraised as its special virtue by capitalism. [. . . .]

For the field of administrative activity proper, that is, for all state activities that fall outside the field of law creation and court procedure, one has become accustomed to claims for the freedom and the paramountcy of individual circumstances. General norms are held to play primarily a negative role, as barriers to the official's positive and "creative" activity which should never be regulated. The bearing of this thesis may be disregarded here. Decisive is that this "freely" creative administration (and possibly judicature) would not constitute a realm of *free*, arbitrary action and discretion, of *personally* motivated favor and valuation, such as we shall find to be the case among pre-bureaucratic forms. The rule and the rational pursuit of "objective" purposes, as well as devotion to these, would always constitute the norm of conduct. Precisely those views which most strongly glorify the "creative" discretion of the official accept, as the ultimate and highest lodestar for his behavior in public administration, the specifically modern and strictly "objective" idea of *raison d'etat*. Of course, the sure instincts of the bureaucracy for the conditions of maintaining its own power in the home state (and through it, in opposition to other states) are inseparably fused with this canonization of the abstract and "objective" idea of "reasons of state." Most of the time, only the power interests of the bureaucracy give a concretely exploitable content to this by no means unambiguous ideal; in dubious cases, it is always these interests which tip the balance. We cannot discuss this further here. The only decisive point for us is that in principle a system of rationally debatable "reasons" stands behind every act of bureaucratic administration, namely, either subsumption under norms, or a weighing of ends and means.

In this context, too, the attitude of all "democratic" currents, in the sense of currents that would minimize "domination," is necessarily ambiguous. "Equality before the law" and the demand for legal guarantees against arbitrariness demand a formal and rational "objectivity" of administration, as opposed to the personal discretion flowing from the "grace" of the old patrimonial domination. If, however, an "ethos"—not to speak of other impulses—takes hold of the masses on some individual question, its postulates of *substantive* justice, oriented toward some concrete instance and person, will unavoidably collide with the formalism and the rule-bound and cool "matter-of-factness" of bureaucratic administration. Emotions must in that case reject what reason demands.

The propertyless masses especially are not served by the formal "equality before the law" and the "calculable" adjudication and administration demanded by bourgeois interests. Naturally, in their eyes justice and administration should serve to equalize their economic and social life-opportunities in the face of the propertied classes. Justice and administration can fulfill this function only if they assume a character that is informal because "ethical" with respect to substantive content. . . . Not only any sort of "popular justice"—which usually does not ask for reasons and norms—but also any intensive influence on the administration by so-called "public opinion"—that is, concerted action born of irrational "sentiments" and usually staged or directed by party bosses or the press—thwarts the rational course of justice just as strongly, and under certain circumstances far more so, as the "star chamber" proceedings of absolute rulers used to be able to do. [. . . .]

In spite of its indubitable technical superiority, bureaucracy has everywhere been a relatively late development. A number of obstacles have contributed to this, and only under certain social and political conditions have they definitely receded into the background.

Bureaucratic organization has usually come into power on the basis of a leveling of economic and social differences. This leveling has been at least relative, and has concerned the significance of social and economic differences for the assumption of administrative functions.

Bureaucracy inevitably accompanies modern *mass democracy,* in contrast to the democratic self-government of small homogeneous units. This results from its characteristic principle: the abstract regularity of the exercise of authority, which is a result of the demand for "equality before the law" in the personal and functional sense—hence, of the horror of "privilege," and the principled rejection of doing business "from case to case." Such regularity also follows from the social preconditions of its origin. Any non-bureaucratic administration of a large social structure rests in some way upon the fact that existing social, material, or honorific preferences and ranks are connected with administrative functions and duties. This usually means that an economic or a social exploitation of position, which every sort of administrative activity provides to its bearers, is the compensation for the assumption of administrative functions.

Bureaucratization and democratization within the administration of the state therefore signify an increase of the cash expenditures of the public treasury, in spite of the fact that bureaucratic administration is usually more "economical" in character than other forms. . . . Mass democracy which makes a clean sweep of the feudal, patrimonial, and—at least in intent— the plutocratic privileges in administration unavoidably has to put paid professional labor in place of the historically inherited "avocational" administration by notables.

This applies not only to the state. For it is no accident that in their own organizations the democratic mass parties have completely broken with traditional rule by notables based upon personal relationships and personal esteem. Such personal structures still persist among many old conservative as well as old liberal parties, but democratic mass parties are bureaucratically organized under the leadership of party officials, professional party and trade union secretaries, etc. [. . . .]

The progress of bureaucratization within the state administration itself is a phenomenon paralleling the development of democracy, as is quite obvious in France, North America, and now in England. Of course, one must always remember that the term "democratization" can be misleading. The *demos* itself, in the sense of a shapeless mass, never "governs" larger associations, but rather is governed. What changes is only the way in which the *demos,* or better, which social circles from its midst are able to exert upon the content and the direction of administrative activities by means of "public opinion." "Democratization," in the sense here intended, does not necessarily mean an increasingly active share of the subjects in government. This may be a result of democratization, but it is not necessarily the case.

We must expressly recall at this point that the political concept of democracy, deduced from the "equal rights" of the governed, includes these further postulates: (1) prevention of the development of a closed status group of officials in the interest of a universal accessibility of office, and (2) minimization of the authority of officialdom in the interest of expanding the sphere of influence of "public opinion" as far as practicable. Hence, wherever possible, political democracy strives to shorten the term of office through election and recall, and to be relieved from a limitation to candidates with special expert qualifications. Thereby democracy inevitably comes into conflict with the bureaucratic tendencies which have been produced by its very fight against the notables. The loose term "democratization" cannot be used here, in so far as it is understood to mean the minimization of the civil servants' power in favor of the greatest possible "direct" rule of the *demos,* which in practice means the respective party leaders of the *demos.* The decisive aspect here—indeed it is rather exclusively so—is the *leveling of the governed* in face of the governing and bureaucratically articulated group, which in turn may occupy a quite autocratic position, both in fact and in form. [. . . .]

Once fully established, bureaucracy is among those social structures which are the hardest to destroy. Bureaucracy is *the* means of transforming social action into rationally organized action. Therefore, as an instrument of rationally organizing authority relations, bureaucracy was and is a power instrument of the first order for one who controls the bureaucratic apparatus. Under otherwise equal conditions, rationally organized and directed action is superior to every kind of collective behavior and also social action opposing it. Where administration has been completely bureaucratized, the resulting system of domination is practically indestructible.

The individual bureaucrat cannot squirm out of the apparatus into which he has been harnessed. In contrast to the "notable" performing administrative tasks as a honorific duty or as a subsidiary occupation (avocation), the professional bureaucrat is chained to his activity in his entire economic and ideological existence. In the great majority of cases he is only a small cog in a ceaselessly moving mechanism which prescribes to him an essentially fixed route of march. The official is entrusted with specialized tasks, and normally the mechanism cannot be put into motion or arrested by him, but only from the very top. The individual bureaucrat is, above all, forged to the common interest of all the functionaries in the perpetuation of the apparatus and the persistence of its rationally organized domination.

The ruled, for their part, cannot dispense with or replace the bureaucratic apparatus once it exists, for it rests upon expert training, a functional specialization of work, and an attitude set on habitual virtuosity in the mastery of single yet methodically integrated functions. If the apparatus stops working, or if its work is interrupted by force, chaos results, which it is difficult to master by improvised replacements from among the governed. This holds for public administration as well as for private economic management. Increasingly the material fate of the masses depends upon the continuous and correct functioning of the ever more bureaucratic organizations of private capitalism, and the idea of eliminating them becomes more and more utopian.

Increasingly, all order in public and private organizations is dependent on the system of files and the discipline of officialdom, that means, its habit of painstaking obedience within its wonted sphere of action. The latter is the more decisive element, however important in practice the files are. The naive idea . . . of destroying the basis of "acquired rights" together with "domination" by destroying the public documents overlooks that the settled orientation of *man* for observing the accustomed rules and regulations will survive independently of the documents. Every reorganization of defeated or scattered army units, as well as every restoration of an administrative order destroyed by revolts, panics, or other catastrophes, is effected by an appeal to this conditioned orientation, bred both in the officials and in the subjects, of obedient adjustment to such [social and political] orders. If the appeal is successful it brings, as it were, the disturbed mechanism to "snap into gear" again.

The objective indispensability of the once-existing apparatus, in connection with its peculiarly "impersonal" character, means that the mechanism—in contrast to the feudal order based upon personal loyalty—is easily made to work for anybody who knows how to gain control over it. [. . . .]

The democratization of society in its totality, and in the *modern* sense of the term, whether actual or perhaps merely formal, is an especially favorable basis of bureaucratization, but by no means the only possible one. After all, bureaucracy has merely the [limited] striving to level those powers that stand in its way in those concrete areas that, in the individual case, it seeks to occupy. We must remember the fact which we have encountered several times and which we shall have to discuss repeatedly: that "democracy" as such is opposed to the "rule" of bureaucracy, in spite and perhaps because of its unavoidable yet unintended promotion of bureaucratization. Under certain conditions, democracy creates palpable breaks in the bureaucratic pattern and impediments to bureaucratic organization. Hence, one must in every individual historical case analyze in which of the special directions bureaucratization has there developed. [. . . .]

The power position of a fully developed bureaucracy is always great, under normal conditions overpowering. The political "master" always finds himself, vis-à-vis the trained official, in the position of a dilettante facing the expert. This holds whether the "master," whom the bureaucracy serves, is the "people" equipped with weapons of legislative initiative, referendum, and the right to remove officials; or a parliament elected on a more aristocratic or more democratic basis and equipped with the right or the *de facto* power to vote a lack of confidence; or an aristocratic collegiate body, legally or actually based on self-recruitment; or a popularly elected president or an "absolute" or "constitutional" hereditary monarch. [. . . .]

Given the basic fact of the irresistible advance of bureaucratization, the question about the future forms of political organization can only be asked in the following way:

1. How can one possibly save *any remnants* of "individualist" freedom in any sense? After all, it is a gross self-deception to believe that without the achievements of the age of the Rights of Man any one of us, including the most conservative, can go on living his life. [. . . .]
2. In view of the growing indispensability of the state bureaucracy and its corresponding increase in power, how can there be any guarantee that any powers will remain which can check and effectively control the tremendous influence of this stratum? How will democracy even in this limited sense be *at all possible*? [. . . .]

In a modern state the actual ruler is necessarily and unavoidably the bureaucracy, since power is exercised neither through parliamentary speeches nor monarchical enunciations but through the routines of administration. This is true of both the military and civilian officialdom. Even the modern higher-ranking officer fights battles from the "office" just as the so-called progress toward capitalism has been the unequivocal criterion for the modernization of the economy since medieval times, so the progress toward bureaucratic officialdom—characterized by formal employment, salary, pension, promotion, specialized training and functional division of labor, well-defined areas of jurisdiction, documentary procedures, hierarchical sub- and super-ordination—has been the equally unambiguous yardstick for the modernization of the state, whether monarchic or democratic; at least if the state is not a small canton with rotating administration, but comprises masses of people. The democratic state no less than the absolute state eliminates administration by feudal, patrimonial, patrician or other notables holding office in honorary or hereditary fashion, in favor of employed civil servants. It is they who decide on all our everyday needs and problems. [. . . .]

Sociologically speaking, the modern state is an "enterprise" just like a factory: this exactly is its historical peculiarity. [. . . .]

This all-important economic fact: the "separation" of the worker from the material means of production, destruction, administration, academic research, and finance in general is the common basis of the modern state, in its political, cultural and military sphere, and of the private capitalist economy. In both cases the disposition over these means is in the hands of that power whom the *bureaucratic apparatus* (of judges, officials, officers, supervisors, clerks, and noncommissioned officers) directly obeys or to whom it is available in case of need. This apparatus is nowadays equally typical of all those organizations; its existence and function are inseparably cause and effect of this concentration of the means of operation—in fact, the apparatus is its very form. Increasing public ownership in the economic sphere today unavoidably means increasing bureaucratization.

NORBERTO BOBBIO, SELECTION FROM "THE FUTURE OF DEMOCRACY" (1984)

A Minimal Definition of Democracy

My premise is that the only way a meaningful discussion of democracy, as distinct from all forms of autocratic government, is possible is to consider it as characterized by a set of rules (primary or basic) which establish *who* is authorized to take collective decisions and which *procedures* are to be applied. Every social group needs to take decisions binding on all members of the group so as to ensure its own survival, both internally and externally. But even group decisions are made by individuals (the group as such does not decide anything). As a result, for a decision, taken by individuals (one, several, many, all together) to be accepted as a collective decision, it is necessary for it to be taken on the basis of rules (whether written or customary) which lay down who are the individuals authorized to take the decisions binding on all the members of the group and what procedures are to be used. As for the persons called upon to take (or collaborate in the taking of) collective decisions, a democracy is characterized by conferring this power (which, in so far as it is authorized by the basic law of the constitution, becomes a right) to a large number of members of the group. I realize the phrase 'a large number' is vague. But, apart from the fact that political pronouncements issue forth from the realm of the 'nearly' and 'mostly,' it is wrong to say all, because even in the most perfect democratic system, individuals cannot vote until they have reached a certain age. 'Omnicracy,' or the rule of everyone, is an ideal upper limit. What number of individuals must have the vote before it is possible to start talking of a democracy cannot be established in terms of an abstract principle, i.e., leaving out of account historical circumstances and the need for a yardstick to make any judgement. All that can be said is that a society in which the ones to have the vote are adult male citizens is more democratic than one in which only property owners have the vote, and less democratic than one in which women also have the vote. The statement that in the last century there occurred in some countries a continuous process of democratization means that the number of those entitled to vote steadily increased.

As for the mode in which decisions are arrived at, the basic rule of democracy is the rule of the majority, in other words the rule according to which decisions are considered collective, and thus binding on the whole group, if they are approved by at least the majority of those entrusted with taking the decision. If a majority decision is valid, a unanimous decision is all the more valid. But unanimity is possible only in a limited or homogenous group and can be demanded only in two extreme and diametrically opposed cases: either when a very serious decision is involved, so that everyone taking part has the right of veto; or when the decision has negligible implications, so that someone who does not expressly disagree acquiesces (the case of tacit consent). Naturally unanimity is required when only two people are to decide. This provides a clear distinction between a decision based on genuine agreement and one taken according to the law (which usually involves only majority approval).

Moreover, even a minimal definition of democracy, like the one I adopt, requires more than just conferring the right to participate directly or indirectly in the making of collective decisions on a substantial number of citizens, and more than the existence of procedural rules like majority rule (or in extreme cases unanimity). There is a third condition involved, namely that those called upon to take decisions, or to elect those who are to take decisions, must be offered real alternatives and be in a position to choose between these alternatives. For this condition to be realized those called upon to take decisions must be guaranteed the so-called basic rights: freedom of opinion, of expression, of speech, of assembly, of association, etc. These are the rights on which the liberal state has been founded since its inception, giving rise to the doctrine of the *Rechtsstaat, or* juridical state, in the full sense of the term, i.e., the state which not only exercises power *sub lege,* but exercises it within limits derived from the constitutional recognition of the so-called 'inviolable' rights of the individual. Whatever may be the philosophical basis of these rights, they are the necessary precondition for the mainly procedural mechanisms, which characterize a democratic system, to work properly. The constitutional norms which confer these rights are not rules of the game as such: they are preliminary rules which allow the game to take place.

From this it follows that the liberal state is not only the historical but the legal premise of the democratic state. The liberal state and the democratic state are doubly interdependent: if liberalism provides those liberties necessary for the proper exercise of democratic power, democracy guarantees the existence and persistence of fundamental liberties. In other words: an illiberal state is unlikely to ensure the proper workings of democracy, and conversely an undemocratic state is unlikely to be able to safeguard basic liberties. The historical proof of this interdependence is provided by the fact that when both liberal and democratic states fall they fall together.

Ideals and Brute Facts

Having outlined the basic principles I am now in a position to get down to the subject at issue and offer some observations on the present state of democracy. We are dealing with a topic which is usually debated under the heading 'the transformations of democracy.' A collection of everything that has been written about the transformations of democracy would fill a library. But the word 'transformation' is so vague that it allows radically different assessments. For the Right (I have in mind for example the book *The Transformation of Democracy* by V. Pareto, founding father of a long and continuous tradition of laments about the crisis of civilization), democracy has been transformed into a semi-anarchic regime which will bring about the 'disintegration' of the state. For the Left (I am thinking of a book like the one by J. Agnoli, *Die Transformation der Demokratie* typical of 'extra-parliamentary' criticism), parliamentary democracy is progressively turning into an autocratic regime. Rather than concentrate on the notion of transformation, I believe it is more useful for our purposes to reflect on the gap between democratic ideals and 'actually existing democracy' (an expression I am using in the same sense as when people talk of 'actually existing socialism'). Someone in a lecture once drew my attention to the concluding words which Pasternak puts in the mouth of Gordon, the friend of Doctor Zhivago. 'This has happened several times in the course of history. A thing which has been conceived in a lofty, ideal manner is transformed into brute facts. Thus Rome came out of Greece and the Russian Revolution came out of the Russian Enlightenment.' In a similar way, I will add, the liberal and democratic thought of Locke, Rousseau, Tocqueville, Bentham, or John Stuart Mill turned into the actions of . . . (you can fill in yourselves any name you see fit—you will easily be able to find more than one). It is precisely these 'brute facts' and not what has been conceived as 'noble and lofty ideals' which are at issue here, or, put another way, what is at issue here is the contrast between what was promised and what has actually come about. I will single out six of these broken promises.

The Birth of the Pluralist Society

Democracy was born of an individualistic conception of society, at variance with the organic conception which prevailed in classical times and in the intervening period and according to which the whole has primacy over its parts. Instead it conceives every form of society, especially political society, as an artificial product formed by the will of individuals. The emergence of the individualistic conception of society and the state and the decline of the organic conception can be accounted for by the interaction of three events in the history of ideas which are characteristic of social philosophy in the modern age.

(1) The contractarian theories of the seventeenth and eighteenth centuries whose initial hypothesis that civil society is preceded by a state of nature in which sovereign power is exercised by free and equal individuals who agree among themselves to bring into existence a communal power entrusted with the function of guaranteeing their life and liberty (as well as their property).

(2) The birth of political economy, that is to say of an analysis of society and of social relations whose subject is once again the individual human being, *homo oeconomicus*, not the *politikon zoon* of traditional thought, who is considered not in his own right but as the member of a community. This individual, according to Adam Smith, 'in pursuing his own interest, often promotes the interests of society more effectively than if he set out to actually promote them.' (Indeed, according to Macpherson's interpretation, the state of nature conceived by Hobbes and Locke is a prefiguration of a market society).[2]

(3) The utilitarian philosophy of Bentham and Mill, for which only one criterion can serve as the basis of an objective ethical system, and hence distinguish good from evil, without resorting to vague concepts such as 'nature' and the like. This criterion takes as its starting point the consideration of essentially personal states of mind, such as pleasure and pain, and thus resolves the traditional problem of the common good by defining it as the sum of individual good, or, in Bentham's formula, as the happiness of the greatest number.

By adopting the hypothesis of the sovereignty of the individual, who, by reaching agreement with other individuals who are equally sovereign, creates political society, democratic doctrine imagined a state without the intermediary bodies which characterize the corporatist society of medieval cities, or the state composed of various ranks and estates which necessarily preceded the institution of absolute monarchies. It envisaged a political society without any subsidiary associations of particular interests intervening between the sovereign people made up of so many individuals (one man one vote) and its representatives. There would be none of the factions so hated by Rousseau, and deprived of legal influence by the law of Le Chapelier (rescinded in France as late as 1887). What has actually happened in democratic states is the exact opposite: increasingly it is less and less the individual who is the most influential factor in politics and more and more it is the group: large organizations, associations of all kinds, trade unions of every conceivable profession, political parties of widely differing ideologies. Groups and not individuals are the protagonists of political life in a democratic society: there is no longer one sovereign power, namely the people or nation, composed of individuals who have acquired the right to participate directly or indirectly in government, the people conceived as an ideal (or mystical) unit. Instead the people are divided into opposing and conflicting groups, all relatively autonomous in relation to central government (an autonomy which individual human beings have lost or have never had, except in an ideal model of government which has always been refuted by the facts).

The ideal model of democratic society was a centripetal society. The reality is a centrifugal society, which has not just one centre of power (the 'general will' envisaged by Rousseau), but a plethora of them, and which deserves the name, as political scientists agree, of poly-centric society or polyarchy (or, put more strongly but not altogether incorrectly, a 'poly-cracy'). The model of the democratic state, based on popular sovereignty, was conceived in the image of, and as analogous to, the sovereignty of the prince, and hence was a monist model of society. The real society underlying democratic government is pluralist.

The Renewed Vigour of Particular Interests

This primary transformation of democracy (primary in the sense that it concerns the distribution of power) gives rise to the second which concerns the nature of representation. Modern democracy, which came into being as representative democracy, was meant, in contrast to the democracy of classical times, to be epitomized by a system of political representation, i.e. a form of representation in which the representative who is called on to pursue the interests of the nation cannot be subject to a binding mandate. The principle on which political representation is based is the exact antithesis of the one underlying the representation of particular interests, where the representative, having to support the cause of the person represented, is subject to a binding mandate (a feature of private law which makes provisions for the contract being revoked in cases where the mandate has been exceeded). One of the most famous and historically significant debates held in the French Constituent Assembly, which gave birth to the Constitution of 1791, witnessed the victory of those who maintained that the deputy, once elected, became the representative of the nation and no longer of the electorate: as such he was no longer bound by any mandate. The unrestricted mandate had previously been a prerogative of the king who, on convening the *états généraux* had claimed that the delegates of the estates had not been sent to the assembly with *pourvoirs restrictifs.* As an overt expression of sovereignty, unrestricted mandate was transferred from the sovereignty of the king to the sovereignty of the assembly elected by the people. Ever since then, the veto on binding mandates has become an axiomatic rule in all constitutions based on democratic representation, and where democracy has had to fight for survival it has always found convinced supporters in those who defended representative democracy against attempts to replace it by, or integrate it with, representation of particular interests.

No constitutional norm has ever been more violated than the veto on binding mandates. No principle has been more disregarded than that of political representation. But in a society composed of relatively autonomous groups competing to gain supremacy, to assert their own interests over those of other groups, could such a norm, such a principle, ever be realized in practice? Apart from the fact that every group tends to identify the national interest with its own, is there any general criterion which would enable us to distinguish the common interest from the particular interest of this or that group, or from the combination of particular interests of groups which come to an arrangement among themselves at the expense of others? Whoever represents particular interests always has a binding mandate. And where can we find a representative who does not represent particular interests? Certainly not in trade unions, for the drawing up of wage agreements depends on them as do national agreements concerning the organization and cost of labour, all of which have an enormous political impact. In parliament? But what does party discipline signify if not an open violation of the veto on restricted mandates? Every now and then some deputies take advantage of the secret ballot to give party discipline the slip, but are they not branded in Italy as 'snipers,' that is as renegades to be singled out for public disapproval? The veto on restricted mandates, when all is said and done, is a rule without any sanctions attached. On the contrary, the only sanction feared by the deputy, whose re-election depends on the continued support of his party, is the one applied if he transgresses the opposite principle of toeing the official line, thus obliging him to consider himself bound by the mandate given to him by his party.

Confirmation of the victory—I would dare to say a definitive one of the representation of interests over impartial political representation—is provided by the type of relationship, which is coming to be the norm in most democratic states in Europe, between opposed interest groups (representatives of industrialists and workers respectively) and parliament. This relationship has brought about a new type of social system which is called, rightly or wrongly, 'neo-corporatism,' and is characterized by a triangular arrangement in which the government, ideally the representative of national interests, intervenes only as a mediator between the two sides and at most can act as guarantor (generally an impotent one) to ensure that any agreement reached is honoured. Those who some ten years ago thought out this model, which is now at the centre of the debate on the 'transformations' of democracy, defined a neo-corporatist society as offering a solution to social conflicts involving a procedure, that of agreement between large organizations, which has nothing to do with political representation but instead is the typical expression of the representation of particular interests.

The Survival of Oligarchies

The third unfulfilled promise of democracy concerns its failure to put an end to oligarchical power. I have no need to dwell on this point because the subject has been extensively dealt with and is uncontroversial, at least since the end of the last century when Gaetano Mosca propounded his theory of the political class which, due to Pareto's influence, came to be known as the theory of elites. The guiding principle of democratic thought has always been liberty, understood in the sense of autonomy, that is, the ability to be governed by one's own laws (according to Rousseau's famous definition). This should lead to the perfect identification between the person who lays down a rule of conduct and the one who submits to it, and hence to the elimination of the traditional distinction, which is the basis of all political thinking, between the governed and those who govern. Representative democracy, which is after all the only form of democracy which actually exists and is operative, is by its very nature a renunciation of the principle of liberty as autonomy. The hypothesis that the future 'computer-ocracy,' as it has been called, might make direct democracy possible, by giving all citizens the possibility of transmitting their votes to an electronic brain, is puerile. To judge by the number of laws which are tabled every year in Italy, responsible citizens would have to be called upon to cast their vote at least once a day. Such an excess of participation, which produces the phenomenon which Dahrendorf has pejoratively called that of the 'total citizen,' only results in the political satiety and increasing apathy of the electorate. The price which has to be paid for the commitment of the few is often the indifference of the many. Nothing risks killing off democracy more effectively than an excess of democracy.

Naturally the fact that elites are present in the power structure does not eliminate the difference between democratic and autocratic regimes. Even Mosca realized this, though he was a conservative who professed to be a liberal but not a democrat, and who worked out a complex typology of forms of government with a view to demonstrating that, while oligarchies will always be found in power, distinctions can be made between different forms of government on the basis of the different ways they are formed and organized. As my starting point was a largely procedural definition of democracy, it should not be forgotten that one of the advocates of this interpretation, Joseph Schumpeter, struck the nail on the head when he argued that the defining characteristic of a democratic regime is not the absence of elites but the presence of several elites in competition with each other for the votes of the public. In C. B. Macpherson's book, *The Life and Times of Liberal Democracy*,[4] four phases are identified in the development of democracy from the last century to the present: the current phase, which he defines as 'democracy of equilibrium,' corresponds to Schumpeter's definition. An Italian elitist who is an expert on Mosca and Pareto, made a concise but, in my view, telling distinction between elites which *impose* themselves and elites which *propose* themselves.

Limited Space

If democracy has been unsuccessful in completely defeating oligarchical power, it has been even less successful in penetrating all the spaces in which the power to make decisions binding on an entire social group is exercised. In this context the relevant distinction is no longer between the power of the few and of the many, but between ascending and descending power. Moreover, it is more appropriate in this matter to speak of inconsistency than of broken promises, since modern democracy came into being as a method for legitimizing and regulating political decisions in the strict sense of the term, or of the 'government' as such, whether national or local, where individuals are taken into account in their general role as citizens, and not in their many particular roles as members of a religious faith, as workers, as soldiers, as consumers, as invalids etc. Once universal suffrage has been achieved, if it is possible to speak of the process of democratization being extended this should manifest itself less in the transition from representative to direct democracy, as is often maintained, than in the transition from political to social democracy. The issue is less a question of 'who votes?' than of 'where does one vote?.' In other words, when people want to know if a development towards greater democracy has taken place in a certain country, what should be looked for is an increase, not in the number of those who have the right to participate in making the decisions which concern them, but in the number of contexts or spaces in which they can exercise this right. As long as the process of democratization has not made inroads into the two great blocks of power from above which exist in developed societies, big business and bureaucracy—leaving aside whether this would be desirable even if it were possible—the process of democratization cannot be said to be complete.

However I am intrigued to observe that in those spaces which are, in traditional terms, non-political, for example in the factory, there has been a declaration of certain liberties within that specific power system analogous to the declaration of the rights of the citizen *vis à vis* the political power system. I am thinking of, for example, the Italian Workers' Statute of 1970, and of the current efforts to draw up a charter of patients' rights. Even where the prerogatives of the citizen vis á vis the state are concerned, the concession of the right to certain liberties preceded the granting of political rights. As I said when talking about the relationship of the liberal state to the democratic state, the concession of political rights has been a natural consequence of the concession of basic liberties; the only guarantee that the right to liberties will be respected consists in the fight to control in the last instance the power which underwrites this guarantee.

Invisible Power

The fifth promise unfulfilled by the reality of democracy when compared to the ideal is the elimination of invisible power. While the literature on the relationship between democracy and oligarchical power is immense, the subject of invisible power has so far remained largely neglected (partly because it cannot be researched using the techniques usually employed by sociologists, such as interviews, opinion polls, etc.). It may be that I am particularly influenced by what happens in Italy, where the presence of invisible power (mafia, camorra, anomalous Masonic lodges, secret services which are a law unto themselves, authorities who ought to be keeping a check on subversive elements but instead are protecting them) is, if you pardon the play on words, highly conspicuous. The fact remains, however, that the most extensive research on this subject I have come across so far is a book by an American scholar, Alan Wolfe, *The Limits of Legitimacy*,[5] which dedicates a well-documented chapter to what he calls the 'double state,' double in the sense that according to him there exists an invisible state alongside the visible state. It is well known that democracy, when it first appeared, held out the prospect of ridding human society for ever of invisible power, so as to give birth to a form of government which would have carried on its business in public, 'au grand jour' (as Maurice Joly put it). Modern democracy made the democracy of the Ancient World as its model, and in particular the halcyon days of the tiny city of Athens, when the people assembled in the *agora* and freely took their decisions in the clear light of day, having heard the orators illustrating the various points of view. Plato denigrated it (but Plato was anti-democratic) by calling it 'theatrocracy' (a word found, significantly enough, in Nietzsche). One of the reasons for the superiority of democracy over the absolute states which had reasserted the value of *arcana imperii,* the secrets of authority, and defended with historical and political arguments the need for major political decisions to be made in secret cabinet meetings, far from the indiscreet gaze of the public, was based on the conviction that democratic government could finally bring about the transparency of power, 'power without masks.'

In the Appendix to *Perpetual Peace* Kant formulated and illustrated the basic principle according to which 'All actions relating to the rights of other men are wrong, if the maxims from which they follow are inconsistent with publicity.'[6] This means that an action which I am forced to keep secret is certainly an action not only unjust, but one which if it were made public would provoke such a strong reaction that carrying it out would be impossible. Which state, to give the example Kant uses himself, could declare publicly, in the actual moment of signing an international treaty, that it will not honour it? Which civil servant can declare in public that he will use public money for private purposes? What results from framing the problem in these terms is that the principle that all acts of government must be open to public scrutiny is important not only, as is usually said, to permit the citizen to be aware of the acts of those in power and hence control them, but also because public scrutiny is itself a form of control, is a device which allows distinctions to be made between what is permissible and what is not. It is no coincidence that politics based on the *arcana imperii* went hand in hand with theories of *raison d'état*, i.e., with theories according to which the state is permitted what is denied to private citizens and thus the state is forced to act in secret so as not to cause an outrage. (To give some idea of the exceptional power of the tyrant, Plato says that only the tyrant is allowed to perform in public scandalous acts which ordinary mortals imagine performing only in their dreams).[7] Needless to say public accountability of power is all the more necessary in a state like ours, in which technological progress has increasingly given the authorities a practically unlimited power to monitor everything citizens are doing, down to the

last detail. If I earlier expressed reservations about whether the 'computer-ocracy' is of benefit to those governed in a democracy, I have no doubt about the service it can perform to
those who govern. The ideal of the powerful has always been to see every gesture and to listen to every word of their subjects (if possible without being seen or heard): nowadays this
ideal is realizable. No despot in antiquity, no absolute monarch of the modern age, even if
surrounded by a thousand informers, has ever succeeded in having all the information on his
subjects that the most democratic governments can obtain using electronic brains. The old
question running through the history of political thought: 'Who guards the guards?,' can now
be reformulated as 'Who controls the controllers?' If no adequate answer can be found to this
question, democracy, in the sense of visible government, is lost. In this case we are dealing
not so much with a broken promise but with a trend which actually contradicts the basic
premises of democracy, a trend not towards the greatest possible control of those in power
by the citizens, but towards the greatest control of the subjects by those in power.

The Uneducated Citizen

The sixth broken promise concerns the education of the citizen. All the apologias made on
behalf of democracy over the last two centuries have included the argument that the only way
of making a citizen out of a subject is to confer on him or her those rights which writers on
public law in the nineteenth century termed *activae civitatis*. Education for democracy takes
place as an integral part of the operation of democracy in practice. It is not a precondition of
it: it was not conceived as a precondition even in the Jacobin model, according to which the
revolutionary dictatorship comes first and only subsequently the reign of virtue. No, for the
good democrat the reign of virtue (which for Montesquieu constituted the basic principle of
democracy as opposed to fear, the basis of despotism) is equated with democracy, which not
only cannot do without virtue, understood in terms of love of the *res publica,* but at the same
time promotes it, feeds it and reinforces it.

One of the classic expressions of this notion can be found in the chapter on ideal government in John Stuart Mill's *Considerations on Representative Government*. He distinguishes active from passive citizens, and specifies that while, in general, rulers prefer the
latter, because it is so much easier to keep docile or apathetic subjects in their place,
democracy needs the former. He deduces from this that if passive citizens were to pre-
dominate rulers would gladly turn their subjects into a flock of sheep, interested only in
grazing next to each other (and who are not to complain, I might add, even when there
are meagre supplies of grass).[8] This led him to propose the enlargement of suffrage to include the lower classes, on the principle that one of the remedies to the tyranny of the majority is precisely to involve in elections not only the well-off, who always constitute a minority of the population and tend naturally to serve their own exclusive interests, but the
lower classes as well. He said participation in elections has a great educative value; it is via
political discussion that the worker transcends his repetitive work within the narrow confines of the factory, and is able to understand the relationship between distant events and
his own interests, and have contact with citizens different from those he has dealings with
in everyday life and thus consciously become a member of a community.[9] Education for
citizenship was one of the favourite subjects (treated under the heading 'political culture')
of American political science in the 1950s, and rivers of ink flowed on the subject which
rapidly dried and faded. Among the many categories they created I remember the distinction they made between a 'society of subjects,' i.e., geared to the outputs of the system,

that is to the benefits which the electorate hopes to derive from the political system, and a 'society of participants,' i.e., geared to inputs, which is formed by voters who consider themselves potentially involved in articulating demands and formulating decisions.

Taking stock of the present situation, the most well-established democracies are impotent before the phenomenon of increasing political apathy, which has overtaken about half of those with the right to vote. In terms of political culture these are people without any orientation, either to outputs or inputs of the system. They are simply unconcerned by what is being done by bureaucrats at the local town hall, which is neatly called in Italian *il palazzo*, 'the palace.' I am aware that political apathy admits of more benign interpretations. But even the most benign interpretations cannot make me forget that all the great democratic theorists would find it difficult to see the renunciation of the right to vote as the beneficial outcome of education to citizenship. In democratic regimes, like the Italian one, in which the percentage of voters is still very high (but is declining with every election that passes), there are good reasons to believe that the use of the vote as an expression of opinion is declining, while what is increasing is the use of the vote as a means of exchange. Thus in the ascetic terminology of the political scientist, the vote is becoming geared towards outputs; or, to use a cruder but less obscurantist phrase, is being 'bought,' a type of *clientelismo* based on the often illusory principle of *do ut des* (political support in exchange for personal favours). But I cannot help thinking of Tocqueville who, in a speech to the Chamber of Deputies (27 January 1848) complained about the degeneration of the tenor of public life which meant that 'commonly held opinions, feelings, ideas are being increasingly replaced by particular interests.' Turning to his colleagues, he wondered 'whether the number of those who vote for reasons of vested interest has not increased and the vote of those who decide on the basis of political opinion has not decreased'; he deplored this tendency as the expression of a 'base and vulgar morality,' which produces the principle that 'those who have political rights think of using them solely in their own interest.'

The Rule of Technicians

Broken promises. But were they promises that could ever have been kept? I would say not. Leaving aside the natural gulf which I alluded to at the outset between the lofty nobility of the ideal and the brute facts which its realization have brought about, the project of political democracy was conceived for a society much less complex than the one that exists today. The promises were not kept because of obstacles which had not been foreseen or which cropped up unexpectedly as a result of 'transformations' (in this case I believe the term 'transformations' to be appropriate) in the nature of civil society. I will point out three of them.

First, as societies gradually change from a family economy to a market economy, from a market economy to an economy which is protected, regulated, and planned, there is an increase in the number of political problems whose solution requires technical expertise. Technical problems require experts, an expanding team of specialized personnel. This had already been noticed over a century ago by Saint-Simon, who had predicted the substitution of the government of jurists by the government of scientists. With the progress of statistical techniques, which outstrip anything which Saint-Simon could have remotely imagined and which only experts are able to use, the need for the so-called 'rule of the technicians' has increased out of all proportion.

Technocracy and democracy are antithetical: if the expert plays a leading role in industrial society he cannot be considered as just any citizen. The hypothesis which underlies democracy is that all are in a position to make decisions about everything. The technocracy claims, on the contrary, that the only ones called on to make decisions are the few who have the relevant expertise. In the time of absolute states, as I have already said, the common people had to be kept at bay from the *arcana imperii* because they were considered too ignorant. Now the common people are certainly less ignorant. But are not the problems to be resolved, problems like the struggle against inflation, securing full employment, ensuring the fair distribution of incomes, becoming increasingly complicated? Do not these problems, by their very nature, require scientific and technical knowledge which are no less arcane for the man or woman in the street (no matter how well educated)?

The Growth of the Bureaucratic Apparatus

The second unforeseen obstacle to emerge is the continued increase in the scale of bureaucracy, i.e., of a power apparatus arranged hierarchically from top to bottom, and hence diametrically opposed to the system of democratic power. Assuming that grades of power exist in any society, a political system can be visualized as a pyramid; but whereas in a democratic society power is transmitted from the base upwards, in a bureaucratic society power descends from the top.

The democratic state and the bureaucratic state have historically been much more interconnected than might be thought from contrasting them so starkly. All states which have become more democratic have simultaneously become more bureaucratic, because the process of bureaucratization is to a great extent the consequence of the process of democratization. Proof of this is the fact that today the dismantling of the Welfare State, which had necessitated an unprecedented bureaucratic apparatus, conceals the proposal, if not to dismantle democratic power, then certainly to reduce it to within clearly circumscribed limits. The reasons why democratization should have gone hand in hand with bureaucratization, which is after all something Max Weber clearly envisaged, are generally understood. When those who had the right to vote were just property owners, it was natural that they should ask the public authority to perform a single basic function: the protection of private property. This gave rise both to the doctrine of the limited state, the night-watchman state, or, as it is known now, the minimal state, and to the constitution of the state as an association of property owners for the defence of that natural right which was for Locke precisely the right to property. From the moment the vote was extended to the illiterate it was inevitable that they would ask the state to set up free schools, and so take on board a responsibility unknown to the states of traditional oligarchies and of the first bourgeois oligarchy. When the right to vote was also extended to non-property owners, to the have-nots, to those whose only property was their labour, it resulted in them asking the state for protection from unemployment, and in due course for state insurance schemes against illness and old age, for maternity benefits, for subsidized housing, etc. So it was that the Welfare State came about, like it or not, as the response to demands emanating from below, demands which were, in the fullest sense of the word, democratic.

The Inability to Satisfy Demand

The third obstacle is intimately bound up with the question of the overall ability of a democratic system to 'deliver the goods': a problem that in the last few years has provoked debate over the so-called 'ungovernability' of democracy. In essence the central issue is this: first the liberal state, and then by extension the democratic state, have contributed to the emancipation of civil society from the political system. This process of emancipation has created a situation where civil society has increasingly become an inexhaustible source of demands on government, which in order to carry out its functions properly must make adequate responses. But how can government respond if the demands generated by a free society are increasingly numerous, pressing and onerous? As I have said, the necessary precondition for any democratic government is the guarantee of civil liberties: well, freedom of the press, freedom of assembly and association are all channels via which the citizen can appeal to those in government to ask for advantages, benefits, special terms, a more equal distribution of resources. The quantity and rapid turnover of these demands are such that no political system, however efficient, is able to cope with them. This results in the so-called 'overloading' of government and the necessity for the political system to make drastic choices. But one choice excludes another, and not making certain choices produces dissatisfaction.

It does not stop there. The speed with which demands are made of government by citizens is in marked contrast to the slowness with which the complex procedures of a democratic political system allow the political elite to make adequate decisions. As a result the mechanism for inserting demands into the system and the one for extracting responses are increasingly out of phase, the first working at an ever faster rate while the second slows down more and more. This is precisely the opposite of what happens in an autocratic system, which is capable of controlling demand, having previously stifled the autonomy of civil society, and is in practice quicker to make appropriate decisions since it is freed from the obligation to observe complex decision-making procedures like those peculiar to a parliamentary system. In short, democracy is good at generating demands and bad at satisfying them. Autocracy, on the other hand, is in a position to stifle demands and is better placed to meet them.

In Spite of Everything

After all I have said so far someone could be excused for expecting a catastrophic vision of the future of democracy. I offer nothing of the kind. Compared with the inter-war years, which were called *L'ère des tyrannies* in the famous book by Elie Halévy, democratic regimes have continually enlarged their territory. Juan Linz's book, *The Breakdown of Democracy*, draws mainly on material to do with the aftermath of the First World War. The contrasting book by Julian Santamaria, *The Transition to Democracy in Southern Europe and Latin America*, concentrates on the events following the Second World War. Once the First World War had finished it only took a few years in Italy, and ten in Germany, for the parliamentary state to be overthrown. After the Second World War, where democracy was restored it has not been overthrown, and in other states authoritarian governments have been overthrown. Even in a country like Italy, where democracy is not the ruling force and works inadequately, it is not seriously at risk, even if I utter these words with a certain trepidation.

Let us be clear on this: I am speaking about internal dangers, dangers which could arise from the extreme Right or extreme Left. In Eastern Europe, where democratic regimes were suffocated at birth or are unable to see the light of day, the reason for this has been and continues to be external. In this analysis I have concentrated on the internal difficulties of democracy and not the external ones, which derive from the way different countries work together in the international system. Well, my conclusion is that the broken promises and the unforeseen obstacles which I have surveyed here are not sufficient to 'transform' a democratic regime into an autocratic one. The essential difference between the first and the second has been preserved. The minimal content of the democratic state has not been impaired: guarantees of the basic liberties, the existence of competing parties, periodic elections with universal suffrage, decisions which are collective or the result of compromise (as in consociational democracies or in the neo-corporatist system) or made on the basis of the majority principle, or in any event as the outcome of open debate between the different factions or allies of a government coalition. Some democracies are more unstable, more vulnerable than others and there are different degrees of approximation to the ideal model, but even one which is far removed from the model can in no way be confused with an autocratic state and even less with a totalitarian one.

I have not referred to external threats, because the subject I am addressing is the future of democracy and not the future of humanity. On the latter, I must confess, I am not inclined to place any bets. Parodying the title of our convention: 'The Future Has Already Begun,' someone in humourous vein could wonder 'And what if instead the future had already finished?'

However I think I am able to offer a final observation, even if I admit it is a risky one to make: no war has yet broken out between states established as democratic regimes. This does not mean democratic states have not fought wars, but so far they have never fought them *with each other*.[10] This is, as I have said, a bold assertion, but I challenge someone to refute it. Could Kant have been right when he proclaimed that the first definitive clause in a hypothetical treaty to ensure perpetual peace should read 'The constitution of every state should be republican?'[11] Certainly the concept of 'republic' Kant refers to does not coincide with the present concept of 'democracy,' but the notion that a safeguard against war would be the internal constitution of states has proved to be the powerful, fertile, inspiring idea behind the many pacifist projects which have succeeded one another over the last two centuries, even if in practice they remained still born. The objections raised against Kant's principle have always stemmed from a failure to understand that since it involves a universal principle it holds only if *all,* and not just a few or several, adopt the form of government required to achieve perpetual peace.

The Appeal to Values

To conclude, an answer must be given to the fundamental question, the one I have heard repeated often, especially by the young, so vulnerable to illusions and disappointments. If democracy is mainly a set of procedural rules, how can it claim to rely on 'active citizens'? To have active citizens are not perhaps ideals necessary? Of course ideals are necessary. But how can anyone ignore the great struggles over ideals which have produced these rules? Shall we try to enumerate them?

First and foremost, the ideal of toleration emerges only after centuries of cruel wars of religion. If today there is a threat to world peace this is once again due to fanaticism, in other words to blind belief in having a monopoly of truth and having the requisite force to impose it on others. It is useless to cite examples: they are right in front of our eyes every day. Second, there is the ideal of nonviolence: I have never forgotten Karl Popper's dictum according to which the essential distinction between a democratic state and a non-democratic one is that only in the former can citizens get rid of their government without bloodshed.[12] The formal rules of democracy, which are so frequently derided, have introduced for the first time into history techniques for coexistence designed to resolve social conflict without recourse to violence. Only where these rules are respected is the adversary no longer an enemy (to be destroyed), but an opponent who tomorrow may be in our shoes. Third, there is the ideal of the gradual renewal of society via the free debate of ideas and the modification of attitudes and ways of life: only democracy allows silent revolutions to take shape and spread, as has happened in the case of the relationship between the sexes in the last few decades, which is probably the greatest revolution of our age. Finally there is the idea of brotherhood (the *fraternité* of the French Revolution). The bulk of human history is the history of fratricide. In his *Philosophy of History* (and in this way I can break off the discussion at the point where I came in) Hegel defined history as an 'immense slaughterhouse.'[13] Can we disagree? In no country in the world can the democratic method last without becoming a habit. But can it become a habit without recognition of the bonds of kinship which unite all human beings in a common destiny? This recognition is all the more necessary now that every day we are made more aware of this common destiny. We ought, by the dim light of reason which still lights our path, to act accordingly.

NOTES

1. Max Weber, *From Max Weber: Essays in Sociology*, eds. H. H. Gerth and C. Wright Mills (New York: Oxford University Press, 1958), 121, 125.

2. C. B. Macpherson, *The Political Theory of Possessive Individualism* (Oxford: Clarendon Press, 1973).

3. I am referring to R. Dahrendorf, "Citizenship and Beyond: The Social Dynamics of an Idea," *Social Research* 41 (1974): 673–701.

4. C. B. Macpherson, *The Life and Times of Liberal Democracy* (Oxford: Oxford University Press, 1977).

5. A. Wolfe, *The Limits of Legitimacy: Political Contradictions of Contemporary Capitalism* (New York: Free Press, 1977).

6. I. Kant, "Perpetual Peace. A Philosophical Essay," in *Kant's Political Writings*, trans. H. B. Nisbet (Cambridge: Cambridge University Press, 1970), 126.

7. *The Republic of Plato*, trans. F. M. Carnford (Oxford: Oxford University Press, 1941), ix 571cd, 296–7.

8. J. S. Mill, "Considerations on Representative Government," in *Collected Papers of John Stuart Mill*, vol. XIX (Toronto: University of Toronto Press, 1977), 406.

9. J. S. Mill, "Considerations on Representative Government," 470.

10. This thesis has been defended recently using theoretical and historical arguments by M. W. Doyle, "Kant, Liberal Legacies and Foreign Affairs," *Philosophy and Public Affairs* XII (1983): 205–35, 323–53.

11. I. Kant, "Perpetual Peace," 99.

12. K. Popper, *The Open Society and Its Enemies* (London: Routledge and Kegan Paul, 1962), 124.

13. G. W. F. Hegel, *Lectures on the Philosophy of World History*, trans. H. B. Nibet (Cambridge: Cambridge University Press, 1975), cf. 69.

8

POSTMODERNIST CRITIQUES

Postmodern political thinkers come forward to challenge some of the basic premises of the Enlightenment project, including its commitment to universal rationalism, its belief in the neutrality of knowledge, and its conceptualization of equality. These authors argue that reason is a human construction, and like all constructions is subject to competing interpretations. Moreover, postmodernists find that the Enlightenment celebration of rights and formal democratic procedure disguises the ways in which contemporary practices perpetuate a variety of forms of domination and control, which function to subvert modern conceptions of dignity and self-determination.

While not speaking directly to the conventional concerns of most democratic thinkers, Michel Foucault has a great deal to say about the most political of concepts: power. Unlike more traditional accounts, which situate power in easily identified institutions, procedures, or mechanisms of force, Foucault conceives of power as something that is "irreducibly plural" and located throughout society.[1] This means, among other things, that it is not something that rests only with the "state" or the "sovereign." In *Power/Knowledge*, he attempts to show how all forms of knowledge bear the stamp of power, especially where they claim to be purely objective modes of understanding. But beyond calling attention to this "secret" connection between power and knowledge, Foucault hopes to liberate those voices and experiences that have been excluded or extinguished by the practices of the dominant regimes of knowledge. His call for an "insurrection of subjected knowledge" seeks to create a space in which those languages that "have been disqualified as inadequate to their task or insufficiently elaborated" can be allowed to speak and challenge the dominant forms of knowledge and their claims as to what constitutes legitimate behavior.

From this standpoint, Foucault sets aside questions concerning sovereignty or the state-centered model of institutional power and focuses his attention on what he calls disciplinary power. For him, disciplinary power permeates actions that attempt to normalize hierarchical relationships and make them appear as resting on something other than power.[2] As Foucault understands matters, disciplinary power is not centralized but is constituted by multiple components and techniques that are never wholly contained by institutional arrangements. With this reasoning, he finds that modern society has created the most comprehensive mechanisms of power and control ever known.

Many postmodernists are pessimistic about the future, particularly the possibility of achieving the kind of harmony envisaged by the Enlightenment project. Others, such as William Connolly and Chantal Mouffe, call for a politics of skepticism that also seeks to challenge present configurations of power. What they have in mind is a strategy for decentering dominant ways of thinking and acting in order to approach politics with a healthy suspicion about its totalizing claims, particularly those that impose order and discipline by stigmatizing difference as a form of deviance.

Connolly finds modern politics operating under an "ontology of concord," which envisions a harmonious design for society and the persons who inhabit it. For him, such an ideal model does not and cannot exist. Instead, he sees a world where social structures and identities are complex, ambiguous, and in many ways incongruous. Connolly holds that our dominant political doctrines and practices give rise to a pervasive "normalizing pressure," which condemns those individuals who fail to conform to prescribed norms. Against these tendencies, he promotes an "ontology of discordance," which acknowledges the necessity of social order while calling for greater appreciation of the discordant features that persist in every society and every self. Unlike the conventional model of tolerance, which asks citizens merely to ignore each other where differences are identified, Connolly hopes to promote an enhanced reciprocity and even a sense of generosity between distinct identities that remain inevitably joined in a common condition.

Like Connolly, Mouffe's work retains several key modern objectives, such as freedom and equality, while offering a postmodern critique of rationality. Also like Connolly, she argues that many of the theoretical orientations we have inherited contain dangerous flaws, especially those involved in our understanding of what it means to be political. In an effort to salvage a progressive alternative, she reaches for tools that one might have thought discarded by postmodernists, but does so in her own way. For example, she calls upon tradition as communitarians do and rights as liberals do. In her hands, tradition is the liberal–democratic tradition that offers us a shared vocabulary to reaffirm and reconfigure democratic ideals. And rights mean "democratic rights," which become essential to the kind of politics Mouffe promotes. But in acknowledging a debt to republicanism and liberalism, she insists that their current influence has become an obstacle to "deepening the democratic revolution." From her perspective, the indeterminate character of all democratic agreements underscores the necessity of diversity and conflict in democratic life. This emphasis on flexibility, openness, and the democratic prerogative for reevaluation finds expression in a radicalized pluralism that seeks to displace the prominence of individualism in liberal–democratic society in order to make space for new types of citizen identities, which are said to extend democratic practices into new spheres of institutional and social experience.

READINGS

MICHEL FOUCAULT, SELECTION FROM *POWER/KNOWLEDGE* (1972)

[W]hat are these various contrivances of power, whose operations extend to such differing levels and sectors of society and are possessed of such manifold ramifications? What are their mechanisms, their effects and their relations? The issue here can, I believe, be crystallized essentially in the following question: is the analysis of power or of powers to be deduced in one way or another from the economy? Let me make this question and my reasons for posing it somewhat clearer. It is not at all my intention to abstract from what are innumerable and enormous differences; yet despite, and even because of these differences, I consider there to be a certain point in common between the juridical, and let us call it, liberal, conception of political power (found in the *philosophes* of the eighteenth century) and the Marxist conception, or at any rate a certain conception currently held to be Marxist. I would call this common point an economism in the theory of power. By that I mean that in the case of the classic, juridical theory, power is taken to be a right, which one is able to possess, like a commodity, and which one can in consequence transfer or alienate, either wholly or partially, through a legal act or through some act that establishes a right, such as takes place through cession or contract. Power is that concrete power which every individual holds, and whose partial or total cession enables political power or sovereignty to be established. This theoretical construction is essentially based on the idea that the constitution of political power obeys the model of a legal transaction involving a contractual type of exchange (hence the clear analogy that runs through all these theories between power and commodities, power and wealth). In the other case—I am thinking here of the general Marxist conception of power—one finds none of all that. Nonetheless, there is something else inherent in this latter conception, something which one might term an economic functionality of power. This economic functionality is present to the extent that power is conceived primarily in terms of the role it plays in the maintenance simultaneously of the relations of production and of a class domination which the development and specific forms of the forces of production have rendered possible. On this view, then, the historical *raison d'être* of political power is to be found in the economy. Broadly speaking, in the first case we have a political power whose formal model is discoverable in the process of exchange, the economic circulation of commodities; in the second case, the historical *raison d'être* of political power and the principle of its concrete forms and actual functioning, is located in the economy. Well then, the problem involved in the researches to which I refer can, I believe, be broken down in the following manner: in the first place, is power always in a subordinate position relative to the economy? Is it always in the service of, and ultimately answerable to, the economy? Is its essential end and purpose to serve the economy? Is it destined to realise, consolidate, maintain and reproduce the relations appropriate to the economy and essential to its functioning? In the second place, is power modeled upon the commodity? Is it something that one possesses, acquires, cedes through force or contract, that one alienates or recovers, that circulates, that voids this or that region? Or, on the contrary, do we need to employ varying tools in its analysis—even, that is, when we allow that it effectively remains the case that the relations of power do indeed remain profoundly enmeshed in and with economic relations and participate with them in a common circuit? If that is the case, it is not the models of functional subordination or formal isomorphism that will characterise the interconnection between politics and the economy. Their indissolubility will be of a different order, one that will be our task to determine.

What means are available to us today if we seek to conduct a non-economic analysis of power? Very few, I believe. We have in the first place the assertion that power is neither given, nor exchanged, nor recovered, but rather exercised, and that it only exists in action. Again, we have at our disposal another assertion to the effect that power is not primarily the maintenance and reproduction of economic relations, but is above all a relation of force. The questions to be posed would then be these: if power is exercised, what sort of exercise does it involve? In what does it consist? What is its mechanism? There is an immediate answer that many contemporary analyses would appear to offer: power is essentially that which represses. Power represses nature, the instincts, a class, individuals. Though one finds this definition of power as repression endlessly repeated in present day discourse, it is not that discourse which invented it—Hegel first spoke of it, then Freud and later Reich. In any case, it has become almost automatic in the parlance of the times to define power as an organ of repression. So should not the analysis of power be first and foremost an analysis of the mechanisms of repression?

Then again, there is a second reply we might make: if power is properly speaking the way in which relations of forces are deployed and given concrete expression, rather than analysing it in terms of cession, contract or alienation, or functionally in terms of its maintenance of the relations of production, should we not analyse it primarily in terms of *struggle, conflict* and *war?* One would then confront the original hypothesis, according to which power is essentially repression, with a second hypothesis to the effect that power is war, a war continued by other means. This reversal of Clausewitz's assertion that war is politics continued by other means has a triple significance: in the first place, it implies that the relations of power that function in a society such as ours essentially rest upon a definite relation of forces that is established at a determinate, historically specifiable moment, in war and by war. Furthermore, if it is true that political power puts an end to war, that it installs, or tries to install, the reign of peace in civil society, this by no means implies that it suspends the effects of war or neutralises the disequilibrium revealed in the final battle. The role of political power, on this hypothesis, is perpetually to re-inscribe this relation through a form of unspoken warfare; to re-inscribe it in social institutions, in economic inequalities, in language, in the bodies themselves of each and everyone of us.

So this would be the first meaning to assign to the inversion of Clausewitz's aphorism that war is politics continued by other means. It consists in seeing politics as sanctioning and upholding the disequilibrium of forces that was displayed in war. But there is also something else that the inversion signifies, namely, that none of the political struggles, the conflicts waged over power, with power, for power, the alterations in the relations of forces, the favouring of certain tendencies, the reinforcements etc., etc., that come about within this 'civil peace'—that none of these phenomena in a political system should be interpreted except as the continuation of war. They should, that is to say, be understood as episodes, factions and displacements in that same war. Even when one writes the history of peace and its institutions, it is always the history of this war that one is writing. The third, and final, meaning to be assigned to the inversion of Clausewitz's aphorism, is that the end result can only be the outcome of war, that is, of a contest of strength, to be decided in the last analyses by recourse to arms. The political battle would cease with this final battle. Only a final battle of that kind would put an end, once and for all, to the exercise of power as continual war.

So, no sooner do we attempt to liberate ourselves from economistic analyses of power, than two solid hypotheses offer themselves: the one argues that the mechanisms of power are those of repression. For convenience sake, I shall term this Reich's hypothesis. The other argues that the basis of the relationship of power lies in the hostile engagement of forces. Again for convenience, I shall call this Nietzsche's hypothesis.

These two hypotheses are not irreconcilable; they even seem to be linked in a fairly convincing manner. After all, repression could be seen as the political consequence of war, somewhat as oppression, in the classic theory of political right, was seen as the abuse of sovereignty in the juridical order.

One might thus contrast two major systems of approach to the analysis of power: in the first place, there is the old system as found in the *philosophes* of the eighteenth century. The conception of power as an original right that is given up in the establishment of sovereignty, and the contract, as matrix of political power, provide its points of articulation. A power so constituted risks becoming oppression whenever it over-extends itself, whenever—that is—it goes beyond the terms of the contract. Thus we have contract-power, with oppression as its limit, or rather as the transgression of this limit. In contrast, the other system of approach no longer tries to analyse political power according to the schema of contract-oppression, but in accordance with that of war-repression, and, at this point, repression no longer occupies the place that oppression occupies in relation to the contract, that is, it is not abuse, but is, on the contrary, the mere effect and continuation of a relation of domination. On this view, repression is none other than the realisation, within the continual warfare of this pseudopeace, of a perpetual relationship of force.

Thus we have two schemes for the analysis of power. The contract-oppression schema, which is the juridical one, and the domination-repression or war-repression schema for which the pertinent opposition is not between the legitimate and illegitimate, as in the first schema, but between struggle and submission.

It is obvious that all my work in recent years has been couched in the schema of struggle–repression, and it is this—which I have hitherto been attempting to apply—which I have now been forced to reconsider, both because it is still insufficiently elaborated at a whole number of points, and because I believe that these two notions of repression and war must themselves be considerably modified if not ultimately abandoned. In any case, I believe that they must be submitted to closer scrutiny.

I have always been especially diffident of this notion of repression: it is precisely with reference to those genealogies . . . of the history of penal right, of psychiatric power, of the control of infantile sexuality, etc.—that I have tried to demonstrate to you the extent to which the mechanisms that were brought into operation in these power formations were something quite other, or in any case something much more, than repression. The need to investigate this notion of repression more thoroughly springs therefore from the impression I have that it is wholly inadequate to the analysis of the mechanisms and effects of power that it is so pervasively used to characterise today.

*   *   *

The course of study that I have been following until now roughly since 1970/71—has been concerned with the *how* of power. I have tried, that is, to relate its mechanisms to two points of reference, two limits: on the one hand, to the rules of right that provide a formal delimitation of power; on the other, to the effects of truth that this power produces and transmits, and which in their turn reproduce this power. Hence we have a triangle: power, right, truth.

Schematically, we can formulate the traditional question of political philosophy in the following terms: how is the discourse of truth, or quite simply, philosophy as that discourse which *par excellence* is concerned with truth, able to fix limits to the rights of power? That is the traditional question. The one I would prefer to pose is rather different. Compared to the traditional, noble and philosophic question it is much more down to earth and concrete. My problem is rather this: what rules of right are implemented by the relations of power in the production of discourses of truth? Or alternatively, what type of power is susceptible of producing discourses of truth that in a society such as ours are endowed with such potent effects? What I mean is this: in a society such as ours, but basically in any society, there are manifold relations of power which permeate, characterise and constitute the social body, and these relations of power cannot themselves be established, consolidated nor implemented without the production, accumulation, circulation and functioning of a discourse. There can be no possible exercise of power without a certain economy of discourses of truth which operates through and on the basis of this association. We are subjected to the production of truth through power and we cannot exercise power except through the production of truth. This is the case for every society, but I believe that in ours the relationship between power, right and truth is organised in a highly specific fashion. If I were to characterise, not its mechanism itself, but its intensity and constancy, I would say that we are forced to produce the truth of power that our society demands, of which it has need, in order to function: we *must* speak the truth; we are constrained or condemned to confess or to discover the truth. Power never ceases its interrogation, its inquisition, its registration of truth: it institutionalises, professionalises and rewards its pursuit. In the last analysis, we must produce truth as we must produce wealth, indeed we must produce truth in order to produce wealth in the first place. In another way, we are also subjected to truth in the sense in which it is truth that makes the laws, that produces the true discourse which, at least partially, decides, transmits and itself extends upon the effects of power. In the end, we are judged, condemned, classified, determined in our undertakings, destined to a certain mode of living or dying, as a function of the true discourses which are the bearers of the specific effects of power.

So, it is the rules of right, the mechanisms of power, the effects of truth or if you like, the rules of power and the powers of true discourses, that can be said more or less to have formed the general terrain of my concern, even if, as I know full well, I have traversed it only partially and in a very zig-zag fashion. I should like to speak briefly about this course of research, about what I have considered as being its guiding principle and about the methodological imperatives and precautions which I have sought to adopt. As regards the general principle involved in a study of the relations between right and power, it seems to me that in Western societies since Medieval times it has been royal power that has provided the essential focus around which legal thought has been elaborated. It is in response to the demands of royal power, for its profit and to serve as its instrument or justification, that the juridical edifice of our own society has been developed. Right in the West is the King's right. Naturally everyone is familiar with the famous, celebrated, repeatedly emphasised role of the jurists in the organisation of royal power. We must not forget that the re-vitalisation of Roman Law in the twelfth century was the major event around which, and on whose basis, the juridical edifice which had collapsed after the fall of the Roman Empire was reconstructed. This resurrection of Roman Law had in effect a technical and constitutive role to play in the establishment of the authoritarian, administrative, and, in the final analysis, absolute power of the monarchy. And when this legal edifice escapes in later centuries from the control of the monarch, when, more accurately, it is turned against that control, it is always the limits of this sovereign power that are put in question, its prerogatives that are challenged. In other words, I believe that the King remains the central personage in the whole legal edifice of the West. When it comes to the general organisation of the legal system in the West, it is essentially with the King, his rights, his power and its eventual limitations, that one is dealing. Whether the jurists were the King's henchmen or his adversaries, it is of royal power that we are speaking in every case when we speak of these grandiose edifices of legal thought and knowledge.

There are two ways in which we do so speak. Either we do so in order to show the nature of the juridical armoury that invested royal power, to reveal the monarch as the effective embodiment of sovereignty, to demonstrate that his power, for all that it was absolute, was exactly that which befitted his fundamental right. Or, by contrast, we do so in order to show the necessity of imposing limits upon this sovereign power, of submitting it to certain rules of right, within whose confines it had to be exercised in order for it to remain legitimate. The essential role of the theory of right, from medieval times onwards, was to fix the legitimacy of power; that is the major problem around which the whole theory of right and sovereignty is organised.

When we say that sovereignty is the central problem of right in Western societies, what we mean basically is that the essential function of the discourse and techniques of right has been to efface the domination intrinsic to power in order to present the latter at the level of appearance under two different aspects: on the one hand, as the legitimate rights of sovereignty, and on the other, as the legal obligation to obey it. The system of right is centred entirely upon the King, and it is therefore designed to eliminate the fact of domination and its consequences.

My general project over the past few years has been, in essence, to reverse the mode of analysis followed by the entire discourse of right from the time of the Middle Ages. My aim, therefore, was to invert it, to give due weight, that is, to the fact of domination, to expose both its latent nature and its brutality. I then wanted to show not only how right is, in a general way, the instrument of this domination which scarcely needs saying—but also to show the extent to which, and the forms in which, right (not simply the laws but the whole complex of apparatuses, institutions and regulations responsible for their application) transmits and puts in motion relations that are not relations of sovereignty, but of domination. Moreover, in speaking of domination I do not have in mind that solid and global kind of domination that one person exercises over others, or one group over another, but the manifold forms of domination that can be exercised within society. Not the domination of the King in his central position, therefore, but that of his subjects in their mutual relations: not the uniform edifice of sovereignty, but the multiple forms of subjugation that have a place and function within the social organism.

The system of right, the domain of the law, are permanent agents of these relations of domination, these polymorphous techniques of subjugation. Right should be viewed, I believe, not in terms of a legitimacy to be established, but in terms of the methods of subjugation that it instigates.

The problem for me is how to avoid this question, central to the theme of right, regarding sovereignty and the obedience of individual subjects in order that I may substitute the problem of domination and subjugation for that of sovereignty and obedience. Given that this was to be the general line of my analysis, there were a certain number of methodological precautions that seemed requisite to its pursuit. In the very first place, it seemed important to accept that the analysis in question should not concern itself with the regulated and legitimate forms of power in their central locations, with the general mechanisms through which they operate, and the continual effects of these. On the contrary, it should be concerned with power at its extremities, in its ultimate destinations, with those points where it becomes capillary, that is, in its more regional and local forms and institutions. Its paramount concern, in fact, should be with the point where power surmounts the rules of right which organise and delimit it and extends itself beyond them, invests itself in institutions, becomes embodied in techniques, and equips itself with instruments and eventually even violent means of material intervention. To give an example: rather than try to discover where and how the right of punishment is founded on sovereignty, how it is presented in the theory of monarchical right or in that of democratic right, I have tried to see in what ways punishment and the power of punishment are effectively embodied in a certain number of local, regional, material institutions, which are concerned with torture or imprisonment, and to place these in the climate—at once institutional and physical, regulated and violent—of the effective apparatuses of punishment. In other words, one should try to locate power at the extreme points of its exercise, where it is always less legal in character.

A second methodological precaution urged that the analysis should not concern itself with power at the level of conscious intention or decision; that it should not attempt to consider power from its internal point of view and that it should refrain from posing the labyrinthine and unanswerable question: 'Who then has power and what has he in mind? What is the aim of someone who possesses power?' Instead, it is a case of studying power at the point where its intention, if it has one, is completely invested in its real and effective practices. What is needed is a study of power in its external visage, at the point where it is in direct and immediate relationship with that which we can provisionally call its object, its target, its field of application, there—that is to say—where it installs itself and produces its real effects.

Let us not, therefore, ask why certain people want to dominate, what they seek, what is their overall strategy. Let us ask, instead, how things work at the level of on-going subjugation, at the level of those continuous and uninterrupted processes which subject our bodies, govern our gestures, dictate our behaviours, etc. In other words, rather than ask ourselves how the sovereign appears to us in his lofty isolation, we should try to discover how it is that subjects are gradually, progressively, really and materially constituted through a multiplicity of organisms, forces, energies, materials, desires, thoughts, etc. We should try to grasp subjection in its material instance as a constitution subjects. This would be the exact opposite of Hobbes project in *Leviathan,* and of that, I believe, of all jurists for whom the problem is the distillation of a single will—or rather, the constitution of a unitary, singular body animated by the spirit of sovereignty—from the particular wills of a multiplicity of individuals. Think of the scheme of Leviathan: insofar as he is a fabricated man, Leviathan is no other than the amalgamation of a certain number of separate individualities, who find themselves reunited by the complex of elements that go to compose the State; but at the heart of the State, or rather, at its head, there exists something which constitutes it as such, and this is sovereignty, which Hobbes says is precisely the spirit of Leviathan. Well, rather than worry about the problem of the central spirit, I believe that we must attempt to study the myriad of bodies which are constituted as peripheral *subjects* as a result of the effects of power.

A third methodological precaution relates to the fact that power is not to be taken to be a phenomenon of one individual's consolidated and homogeneous domination over others, or that of one group or class over others. What, by contrast, should always be kept in mind is that power, if we do not take too distant a view of it, is not that which makes the difference between those who exclusively possess and retain it, and those who do not have it and submit to it. Power must by analysed as something which circulates, or rather as something which only functions in the form of a chain. It is never localised here or there, never in anybody's hands, never appropriated as a commodity or piece of wealth. Power is employed and exercised through a net-like organisation. And not only do individuals circulate between its threads; they are always in the position of simultaneously undergoing and exercising this power. They are not only its inert or consenting target; they are always also the elements of its articulation. In other words, individuals are the vehicles of power, not its points of application.

The individual is not to be conceived as a sort of elementary nucleus, a primitive atom, a multiple and inert material on which power comes to fasten or against which it happens to strike, and in so doing subdues or crushes individuals. In fact, it is already one of the prime effects of power that certain bodies, certain gestures, certain discourses, certain desires, come to be identified and constituted as individuals. The individual, that is, is not the *vis-à-vis* of power; it is, I believe, one of its prime effects. The individual is an effect of power, and at the same time, or precisely to the extent to which it is that effect, it is the element of its articulation. The individual which power has constituted is at the same time its vehicle.

There is a fourth methodological precaution that follows from this: when I say that power establishes a network through which it freely circulates, this is true only up to a certain point. In much the same fashion we could say that therefore we all have a fascism in our heads, or, more profoundly, that we all have a power in our bodies. But I do not believe that one should conclude from that that power is the best distributed thing in the world, although in some sense that is indeed so. We are not dealing with a sort of democratic or anarchic distribution of power through bodies. That is to say, it seems to me—and this then would be the fourth methodological precaution—that the important thing is not to attempt some kind of deduction of power starting from its centre and aimed at the discovery of the extent to which it permeates into the base, of the degree to which it reproduces itself down to and including the most molecular elements of society. One must rather conduct an *ascending* analysis of power, starting, that is, from its infinitesimal mechanisms, which each have their own history, their own trajectory, their own techniques and tactics, and then see how these mechanisms of power have been—and continue to be—invested, colonised, utilised, involuted, transformed, displaced, extended etc., by ever more general mechanisms and by forms of global domination. It is not that this global domination extends itself right to the base in a plurality of repercussions: I believe that the manner in which the phenomena, the techniques and the procedures of power enter into play at the most basic levels must be analysed, that the way in which these procedures are displaced, extended and altered must certainly be demonstrated; but above all what must be shown is the manner in which they are invested and annexed by more global phenomena and the subtle fashion in which more general powers or economic interests are able to engage with these technologies that are at once both relatively autonomous of power and act as its infinitesimal elements. In order to make this clearer, one might cite the example of madness. The descending type of analysis, the one of which I believe one ought to be wary, will say that the bourgeoisie has, since the sixteenth or seventeenth century, been the dominant class; from this premise, it will then set out to deduce the internment of the insane. One can always make this deduction, it is always easily done and that is precisely what I would hold against it. It is in fact a simple matter to show that since lunatics are precisely those persons who are useless to industrial production, one is obliged to dispense with them. One could argue similarly in regard to infantile sexuality—and several thinkers, including Wilhelm Reich have indeed sought to do so up to a certain point. Given the domination of the bourgeois class, how can one understand the repression of infantile sexuality? Well, very simply—given that the human body had become essentially a force of production from the time of the seventeenth and eighteenth century, all the forms of its expenditure which did not lend themselves to the constitution of the productive forces—and were therefore exposed as redundant—were banned, excluded and repressed. These kinds of deduction are always possible. They are simultaneously correct and false. Above all they are too glib, because one can always do exactly the opposite and show, precisely by appeal to the principle of the dominance of the bourgeois class, that the forms of control of infantile sexuality could in no way have been predicted. On the contrary, it is equally plausible to suggest that what was needed was sexual training, the encouragement of a sexual precociousness, given that what was fundamentally at stake was the constitution of a labour force whose optimal state, as we well know, at least at the beginning of the nineteenth century, was to be infinite: the greater the labour force, the better able would the system of capitalist production have been to fulfil and improve its functions.

I believe that anything can be deduced from the general phenomenon of the domination of the bourgeois class. What needs to be done is something quite different. One needs to investigate historically, and beginning from the lowest level, how mechanisms of power have been able to function. In regard to the confinement of the insane, for example, or the repression and interdiction of sexuality, we need to see the manner in which, at the effective level of the family, of the immediate environment, of the cells and most basic units of society, these phenomena of repression or exclusion possessed their instruments and their logic, in response to a certain number of needs. We need to identify the agents responsible for them, their real agents (those which constituted the immediate social *entourage*, the family, parents, doctors, etc.), and not be content to lump them under the formula of a generalised bourgeoisie. We need to see how these mechanisms of power, at a given moment, in a precise conjuncture and by means of a certain number of transformations, have begun to become economically advantageous and politically useful. I think that in this way one could easily manage to demonstrate that what the bourgeoisie needed, or that in which its system discovered its real interests, was not the exclusion of the mad or the surveillance and prohibition of infantile masturbation (for, to repeat, such a system can perfectly well tolerate quite opposite practices), but rather, the techniques and procedures themselves of such an exclusion. It is the mechanisms of that exclusion that are necessary, the apparatuses of surveillance, the medicalisation of sexuality, of madness, of delinquency, all the micro-mechanisms of power, that came, from a certain moment in time, to represent the interests of the bourgeoisie. Or even better, we could say that to the extent to which this view of the bourgeoisie and of its interests appears to lack content, at least in regard to the problems with which we are here concerned, it reflects the fact that it was not the bourgeoisie itself which thought that madness had to be excluded or infantile sexuality repressed. What in fact happened instead was that the mechanisms of the exclusion of madness, and of the surveillance of infantile sexuality, began from a particular point in time, and for reasons which need to be studied, to reveal their political usefulness and to lend themselves to economic profit, and that as a natural consequence, all of a sudden, they came to be colonised and maintained by global mechanisms and the entire State system. It is only if we grasp these techniques of power and demonstrate the economic advantages or political utility that derives from them in a given context for specific reasons, that we can understand how these mechanisms come to be effectively incorporated into the social whole.

To put this somewhat differently: the bourgeoisie has never had any use for the insane; but the procedures it has employed to exclude them have revealed and realised—from the nineteenth century onwards, and again on the basis of certain transformations—a political advantage, on occasion even a certain economic utility, which have consolidated the system and contributed to its overall functioning. The bourgeoisie is interested in power, not in madness, in the system of control of infantile sexuality, not in that phenomenon itself. The bourgeoisie could not care less about delinquents, about their punishment and rehabilitation, which economically have little importance, but it is concerned about the complex of mechanisms with which delinquency is controlled, pursued, punished and reformed, etc.

As for our fifth methodological precaution: it is quite possible that the major mechanisms of power have been accompanied by ideological productions. There has, for example, probably been an ideology of education, an ideology of the monarchy, an ideology of parliamentary democracy, etc.; but basically I do not believe that what has taken place can be said to be ideological. It is both much more and much less than ideology. It is the production of effective instruments for the formation and accumulation of knowledge—methods of observation, techniques of registration, procedures for investigation and research, apparatuses of control. All this means that power, when it is exercised through these subtle mechanisms, cannot but evolve, organise and put into circulation a knowledge, or rather apparatuses of knowledge, which are not ideological constructs.

By way of summarising these five methodological precautions, I would say that we should direct our researches on the nature of power not towards the juridical edifice of sovereignty, the State apparatuses and the ideologies which accompany them, but towards domination and the material operators of power, towards forms of subjection and the inflections and utilisations of their localised systems, and towards strategic apparatuses. We must eschew the model of Leviathan in the study of power. We must escape from the limited field of juridical sovereignty and State institutions, and instead base our analysis of power on techniques and tactics of domination.

This, in its general outline, is the methodological course that I believe must be followed, and which I have tried to pursue in the various researches that we have conducted over recent years on psychiatric power, on infantile sexuality, on political systems, etc. Now as one explores these fields of investigation, observing the methodological precautions I have mentioned, I believe that what then comes into view is a solid body of historical fact, which will ultimately bring us into confrontation with the problems of which I want to speak this year.

This solid, historical body of fact is the juridical-political theory of sovereignty of which I spoke a moment ago, a theory which has had four roles to play. In the first place, it has been used to refer to a mechanism of power that was effective under the feudal monarchy. In the second place, it has served as instrument and even as justification for the construction of the large scale administrative monarchies. Again, from the time of the sixteenth century and more than ever from the seventeenth century onwards, but already at the time of the wars of religion, the theory of sovereignty has been a weapon which has circulated from one camp to another, which has been utilised in one sense or another, either to limit or else to re-inforce royal power: we find it among Catholic monarchists and Protestant anti-monarchists, among Protestant and more-or-less liberal monarchists, but also among Catholic partisans of regicide or dynastic transformation. It functions both in the hands of aristocrats and in the hands of parliamentarians. It is found among the representatives of royal power and among the last feudatories. In short, it was the major instrument of political and theoretical struggle around systems of power of the sixteenth and seventeenth centuries. Finally, in the eighteenth century, it is again this same theory of sovereignty, re-activated through the doctrine of Roman Law, that we find in its essentials in Rousseau and his contemporaries, but now with a fourth role to play: now it is concerned with the construction, in opposition to the administrative, authoritarian and absolutist monarchies, of an alternative model, that of parliamentary democracy. And it is still this role that it plays at the moment of the Revolution.

Well, it seems to me that if we investigate these four roles there is a definite conclusion to be drawn: as long as a feudal type of society survived, the problems to which the theory of sovereignty was addressed were in effect confined to the general mechanisms of power, to the way in which its forms of existence at the higher level of society influenced its exercise at the lowest levels. In other words, the relationship of sovereignty, whether interpreted in a wider or a narrower sense, encompasses the totality of the social body. In effect, the mode in which power was exercised could be defined in its essentials in terms of the relationship sovereign–subject. But in the seventeenth and eighteenth centuries, we have the production of an important phenomenon, the emergence, or rather the invention, of a new mechanism of power possessed of highly specific procedural techniques, completely novel instruments, quite different apparatuses, and which is also, I believe, absolutely incompatible with the relations of sovereignty.

This new mechanism of power is more dependent upon bodies and what they do than upon the Earth and its products. It is a mechanism of power which permits time and labour, rather than wealth and commodities, to be extracted, from bodies. It is a type of power which is constantly exercised by means of surveillance rather than in a discontinuous manner by means of a system of levies or obligations distributed over time. It presupposes a tightly knit grid of material coercions rather than the physical existence of a sovereign. It is ultimately dependent upon the principle, which introduces a genuinely new economy of power, that one must be able simultaneously both to increase the subjected forces and to improve the force and efficacy of that which subjects them.

This type of power is in every aspect the antithesis of that mechanism of power which the theory of sovereignty described or sought to transcribe. The latter is linked to a form of power that is exercised over the Earth and its products, much more than over human bodies and their operations. The theory of sovereignty is something which refers to the displacement and appropriation on the part of power, not of time and labour, but of goods and wealth. It allows discontinuous obligations distributed over time to be given legal expression but it does not allow for the codification of a continuous surveillance. It enables power to be founded in the physical existence of the sovereign, but not in continuous and permanent systems of surveillance. The theory of sovereignty permits the foundation of an absolute power in the absolute expenditure of power. It does not allow for a calculation of power in terms of the minimum expenditure for the maximum return.

This new type of power, which can no longer be formulated in terms of sovereignty, is, I believe, one of the great inventions of bourgeois society. It has been a fundamental instrument in the constitution of industrial capitalism and of the type of society that is its accompaniment. This non-sovereign power, which lies outside the form of sovereignty, is disciplinary power. Impossible to describe in the terminology of the theory of sovereignty from which it differs so radically, this disciplinary power ought by rights to have led to the disappearance of the grand juridical edifice created by that theory. But in reality, the theory of sovereignty has continued not only to exist as an ideology of right, but also to provide the organising principle of the legal codes which Europe acquired in the nineteenth century, beginning with the Napoleonic Code.

Why has the theory of sovereignty persisted in this fashion as an ideology and an organising principle of these major legal codes? For two reasons, I believe. On the one hand, it has been, in the eighteenth and again in the nineteenth century, a permanent instrument of criticism of the monarchy and of all the obstacles that can thwart the development of disciplinary society. But at the same time, the theory of sovereignty, and the organisation of a legal code centred upon it, have allowed a system of right to be superimposed upon the mechanisms of discipline in such a way as to conceal its actual procedures, the element of domination inherent in its techniques, and to guarantee to everyone, by virtue of the sovereignty of the State, the exercise of his proper sovereign rights. The juridical systems—and this applies both to their codification and to their theorisation—have enabled sovereignty to be democratised through the constitution of a public right articulated upon collective sovereignty, while at the same time this democratisation of sovereignty was fundamentally determined by and grounded in mechanisms of disciplinary coercion.

To put this in more rigorous terms, one might say that once it became necessary for disciplinary constraints to be exercised through mechanisms of domination and yet at the same time for their effective exercise of power to be disguised, a theory of sovereignty was required to make an appearance at the level of the legal apparatus, and to re-emerge in its codes. Modern society, then, from the nineteenth century up to our own day, has been characterised on the one hand, by a legislation, a discourse, an organisation based on public right, whose principle of articulation is the social body and the delegative status of each citizen; and, on the other hand, by a closely linked grid of disciplinary coercions whose purpose is in fact to assure the cohesion of this same social body. Though a theory of right is a necessary companion to this grid, it cannot in any event provide the terms of its endorsement. Hence these two limits, a right of sovereignty and a mechanism of discipline, which define, I believe, the arena in which power is exercised. But these two limits are so heterogeneous that they cannot possibly be reduced to each other. The powers of modern society are exercised through, on the basis of, and by virtue of, this very heterogeneity between a public right of sovereignty and a polymorphous disciplinary mechanism. This is not to suggest that there is on the one hand an explicit and scholarly system of right which is that of sovereignty, and, on the other hand, obscure and unspoken disciplines which carry out their shadowy operations in the depths, and thus constitute the bedrock of the great mechanism of power. In reality, the disciplines have their own discourse. They engender, for the reasons of which we spoke earlier, apparatuses of knowledge (*savoir*) and a multiplicity of new domains of understanding. They are extraordinarily inventive participants in the order of these knowledge-producing apparatuses. Disciplines are the bearers of a discourse, but this cannot be the discourse of right. The discourse of discipline has nothing in common with that of law, rule, or sovereign will. The disciplines may well be the carriers of a discourse that speaks of a rule, but this is not the juridical rule deriving from sovereignty, but a natural rule, a norm. The code they come to define is not that of law but that of normalisation. Their reference is to a theoretical horizon which of necessity has nothing in common with the edifice of right. It is human science which constitutes their domain, and clinical knowledge their jurisprudence.

In short, what I have wanted to demonstrate in the course of the last few years is not the manner in which at the advance front of the exact sciences the uncertain, recalcitrant, confused dominion of human behaviour has little by little been annexed to science: it is not through some advancement in the rationality of the exact sciences that the human sciences are gradually constituted. I believe that the process which has really rendered the discourse of the human sciences possible is the juxtaposition, the encounter between two lines of approach, two mechanisms, two absolutely heterogeneous types of discourse: on the one hand there is the re-organisation of right that invests sovereignty, and on the other, the mechanics of the coercive forces whose exercise takes a disciplinary form. And I believe that in our own times power is exercised simultaneously through this right and these techniques and that these techniques and these discourses, to which the disciplines give rise invade the area of right so that the procedures of normalisation come to be ever more constantly engaged in the colonisation of those of law. I believe that all this can explain the global functioning of what I would call a *society of normalisation*. I mean, more precisely, that disciplinary normalisations come into ever greater conflict with the juridical systems of sovereignty: their incompatibility with each other is ever more acutely felt and apparent; some kind of arbitrating discourse is made ever more necessary, a type of power and of knowledge that the sanctity of science would render neutral. It is precisely in the extension of medicine that we see, in some sense, not so much the linking as the perpetual exchange or encounter of mechanisms of discipline with the principle of right. The developments of medicine, the general medicalisation of behaviours, conducts, discourses, desires, etc., take place at the point of intersection between the two heterogeneous levels of discipline and sovereignty. For this reason, against these usurpations by the disciplinary mechanisms, against this ascent of a power that is tied to scientific knowledge, we find that there is no solid recourse available to us today, such being our situation, except that which lies precisely in the return to a theory of right organised around sovereignty and articulated upon its ancient principle. When today one wants to object in some way to the disciplines and all the effects of power and knowledge that are linked to them, what is it that one does, concretely, in real life, what do the Magistrates Union[3] or other similar institutions do, if not precisely appeal to this canon of right, this famous, formal right, that is said to be bourgeois, and which in reality is the right of sovereignty? But I believe that we find ourselves here in a kind of blind alley: it is not through recourse to sovereignty against discipline that the effects of disciplinary power can be limited, because sovereignty and disciplinary mechanisms are two absolutely integral constituents of the general mechanism of power in our society.

If one wants to look for a non-disciplinary form of power, or rather, to struggle against disciplines and disciplinary power, it is not towards the ancient right of sovereignty that one should turn, but towards the possibility of a new form of right, one which must indeed be anti-disciplinarian, but at the same time liberated from the principle of sovereignty. It is at this point that we once more come up against the notion of repression, whose use in this context I believe to be doubly unfortunate. On the one hand, it contains an obscure reference to a certain theory of sovereignty, the sovereignty of the sovereign rights of the individual, and on the other hand, its usage introduces a system of psychological reference points borrowed from the human sciences, that is to say, from discourses and practices that belong to the disciplinary realm. I believe that the notion of repression remains a juridical-disciplinary notion whatever the critical use one would make of it. To this extent the critical application of the notion of repression is found to be vitiated and nullified from the outset by the two-fold juridical and disciplinary reference it contains to sovereignty on the one hand and to normalisation on the other.

WILLIAM CONNOLLY, "DEMOCRACY AND NORMALIZATION" (1987)

The Ambiguity of Democracy

Democracy is the pride and the hope of modernity. It also contains danger. The danger does not flow merely from forces hostile to democratic institutions. It resides within the ideal itself.

Democracy makes the state accountable to the people; it reduces unwarranted privilege; it protects the rights of citizens; it fosters allegiance to the public good by implicating its members in common projects; it encourages a healthy skepticism toward rules, authority, laws, experts, and regulations; it enables skeptical citizens to curtail governmental officials bent upon a destructive course.

Other types of state do some of these things to some degree. But democracy combines them and balances the oppositions among them in distinctive ways. For, when it functions in accord with its essential purpose, a democracy treats its members as citizens; more significantly, it fosters institutions and traditions that encourage individuals to expect this treatment as a matter of course. Periodic elections, due process, constitutional protection of basic rights, the publication of laws and policies, public dialogue over the wisdom of alternative programs and candidates—these practices infuse respect for persons into the public realm. And people treated with respect and dignity in one realm of life are, first, more likely to insist upon respect in other areas, and, second, better equipped to wrest that dignity from people and institutions reluctant to bestow it.[4] Democratic institutions foster a robust, skeptical citizenry who give allegiance to the order partly because it nourishes these qualities in them; and the citizens in turn provide the institutions with the creative energies essential to a vibrant public life.

The democratic citizen, I am suggesting, is less willing than members of other societies to be a mere stone in an edifice. The democratic citizen is more likely to weigh fateful public decisions to ascertain their effects on the common good today or tomorrow. He or she is more likely to dissent from or protest or resist or organize to overturn arbitrary treatment and policies. The unwillingness to be a stone in an edifice contributes over the long term to the health of democratic society. That, anyway, is the faith that makes democracy the pride and hope of modernity.

There is a large gap between this idealization and the actual practice of democratic states. We notice the gap because we are pulled by the ideal. Or, better, we define the difference as a discrepancy when we are pulled by that dimension of democracy idealized here.

For if citizens are unsuited to serve merely as role bearers in a large enterprise, an opposing element in the democratic ideal nonetheless functions to grind them into material for use. The hope and the danger reside inside the same ideal; they are not neatly separable into two competing "conceptions of democracy."

Perhaps the briefest way to discern this connection is to recall that Rousseau, seeking freedom for all citizens, found it necessary to implicate each morally in the laws governing all.

Only in this way, he thought, could laws be experienced not as impediments to one's freedom but as expressions of one's citizenship. This idea continues to have an important presence in modern understandings of citizenship, freedom, and democracy. And once Rousseau's strictures against size, commercialism, gender equality, and foreign involvement have been lifted, the area of life covered by regulations in which the citizen is to be implicated can be seen to expand magnificently.

The best-known interpretations of Rousseau emphasize the connection between his ideal of communal freedom and his insistence that the individual identify with the standards of the polity. This emphasis, congenial to individualists who seek to differentiate their views of freedom and democracy from Rousseauian theory, is not false; but it does ignore a feature of Rousseau's thought shared with his modern critics: his recognition that the customs and norms constituting a way of life are not natural but artificial, not discovered but formed conventions. "But the social order is a sacred right," Rousseau says, "that serves as a basis for all others. However that right does not come from nature; it is therefore based on conventions."[5]

If a form of life is known by its participants to be conventional, then established traditions will be experienced as hateful restraints unless they are submitted to the will either of the individual or the collectivity. Enhancement of the willful and conventional character of life—an enhancement that helps to define the character of modernity itself—can thereby also deepen the experience of unfreedom among participants. Modern democracy seeks to make life more free, more the result of willed convention than tradition unreflectively followed or behavior disconnected from will. It thus draws a larger portion of life into the fold of thematized norms. And by thereby enlarging the field of potential conduct deemed to be abnormal, it exerts internal pressure on participants to identify with established norms in order to establish themselves as free agents. In this setting one is unfree to the extent that (a) one is governed by traditions unthematized publicly; (b) one is governed by conventions undemocratically established; (c) one is governed by democratically established conventions at odds with one's will; (d) one falls below the threshold of normality needed to qualify as an agent capable of free or autonomous conduct. The close relation between modernity and the experience of alienation is bound up with this more fundamental set of connections among the conventionalization of life, democratization, free agency, and the enlargement of the sphere of commonality.

Democratic theory and practice thus contain an ambiguous space in which individuality and commonality are simultaneously differentiated and pressed to harmonize more closely. The periodic drive to expand the scope of democratic participation can be seen as an attempt to resolve this ambiguity with respect to norms recently drawn into the sphere of thematized conventions. The conversion of traditions governing gender relations, sexuality, education, child rearing, and work into contestable conventions encourages the effort to foster identification with them through participation in their creation. The ambiguity is to be dissolved either by changing the will of participants to foster identification or by changing the conventions to conform to the will. But the ways in which structural limits inhibit the restructuring of conventions tend to skew the process toward the first pole of this continuum. And participation seldom seems to bring the dividends it promises for freedom: one constellation of hostile and resentful citizens is spawned by that action which temporarily satisfies the other's sense of justice in the established order of things. The tenacity of the ambiguity is underplayed by those who believe that participation is its solution.

Democratic theorists also tend to try to dissolve an issue that is inherently indissoluble, and these attempts blind them to one set or another of the normalizing pressures inherent in democracy. The individualist seeks resolution by stating formal conditions for individual agency while hesitating to acknowledge the drive within democracy itself to close the gap between the identity of the self as a free agent and the social roles and norms with which the self is to identify. Any normalizing pressures observed are then projected onto features of modern life alien to democracy. Advocates of the politics of the common good obscure the ambiguity by insisting that, when properly institutionalized, individuality and commonality harmonize nicely. The individual is to be "situated" within a common good which realizes the essential good in the self.[6]

The debate between individualists and communalists, I want to say, enables each to identify blind spots in the other while it disables each side from discerning them in itself. This is so because each side thinks that this is an ambiguity to be resolved rather than acknowledged and expressed in the institutional life. So where normalization proceeds relentlessly, the individualist will tend to convert certain of its results into elements appropriate to the very identity of the healthy, normal agent, and the communalist will select others to be ingredients in the good life we seek in common. Together they screen out too much of the politics of normalization. [. . . .]

If, as I have suggested, contemporary democratic theory tends to obscure normalizing tendencies built into modern democratic practice, where are the disciplines which foster and maintain these norms? They are located below the threshold of practices incorporated into the logic of democratic legitimization, or, perhaps, they are experienced more as ontological and social preconditions of democratic life than as elements built into the extension of normalization in a democratic world. The proliferation of dualities of normality (normal/abnormal, healthy/sick, rational/irrational, responsible/irresponsible, stable/unstable) correlates with the enlargement of those areas of life into which bureaucratically enforced norms have penetrated. The growth of the latter has been dramatic. By comparison, for instance, to a hundred years ago a much larger portion of the American population today is either employed in institutions whose primary purpose is to observe, control, correct, confine, reform, cure, or regulate other people (e.g., the police, the military, intelligence agencies, polling centers, reform schools, therapeutic centers, halfway houses, prisons, welfare agencies, nursing homes, juridical institutions) or is the object of these operations (e.g., illegal aliens, prisoners, tax evaders, dissidents, welfare recipients, delinquents, the mentally disturbed, the retarded, nursing-home clients, divorcees).

These institutional complexes are governed by diverse purposes. But, first (in line with [Carl] Friedrich's injunction to achieve "appropriate discipline or perish"), each operationalizes standards through which a target population is defined, judged, helped, corrected, or punished; second, the dualities of normality each constitutes are in need of redemption by theories of rationality, agency, and responsibility; and, third, the complex of theoretically redeemed practices functions to enclose the normal individual within parameters of stability, responsibility, innocence, and merit. These disciplines help to constitute the contemporary self as an individual. And conduct severely out of sync with the standards of normal individuality is seen to reflect an incapacity in the self or a defect in its supporting social conditions. In either case the interpretation calls for new disciplines that establish greater harmony between the self and conventions governing the order.

I wish to say that the modern urge to establish airtight philosophies of rationality and subjectivity is the wish to harmonize these two elements in the democratic ideal, to show how the extension of commonality can coalesce with the encouragement of individuality. But the desire to establish the appearance of harmony in actual democracies or the possibility of it in ideal democracies suppresses the ambiguity in democracy itself. And the suppression of this ambiguity tends to license the insidious extension of normalization into new corners of life. We need a theory and practice of democracy that appreciates this element of disharmony. One that understands harmonization to be normalization. One that insists that normalization, while unavoidable and desirable to some degree, also inflicts wounds on life. When the wounds are exposed we are in a better position to reconsider the appropriate scope of normalization and to attain a more critical perspective on those characteristics of the order that propel its extension. But to say these things it is necessary to reconsider the ontological frame within which modern democratic theory has been located.

Democracy and Discordance

The politics of modern democracies revolve not so much around the extent to which life should be normalized as around the question as to which norms shall govern the extension of normalization. In these struggles the participation of those already defined as severely abnormal tends to be discredited or disallowed. The irony of a normalizing democracy is that its projection of participation (or consent, or even sometimes rights) into new areas tends to be accompanied by the marginalization of new sectors of the population or newly defined sectors of the self.

The modern effort to redeem standards of normality encourages those in pursuit of redemption to support a social ontology that converts boundaries and standards central to modern life into precepts of rationality, morality, or self-realization. These recipes for secular redemption cover up ambiguities inside democratic life. By making disciplines appear to be natural or rational or fulfilling they suppress the element of artificiality, unreason, and arbitrariness contained within them. They contribute in this way to the de-democratization of democracy.

By "social ontology" I mean a set of fundamental understandings about the relations of humans to themselves, to others, and to the world. An Aristotelian ontology understands the world to be a place where human beings can, when their common life is properly constituted, realize the telos appropriate to them. A Christian view construes the world and its "creatures" to be created by God; it defines the issues of life in terms of the proper relation of creatures to their creator.

The social ontology sustaining modern democracy has a trunk with two main branches. The trunk is formed by the principle of a subject realizing its essence in a larger world. The principle of subjectivity expresses the double faith that knowledge, action, and moral standards flow from a privileged center of agency and that this center can be redeemed by a transcendental argument showing it to be a necessary presupposition of life. The individualist branch locates subjectivity in the self; its medium is the interests, rights, responsibilities, and knowledge of individual subjects. The communal branch privileges the community or the intersubjective background in which life is situated; its medium is those virtues and identifications linking the individual to the larger whole. Hobbes, Locke, Kant, and Rawls represent powerful proponents of the first position, though most of them find it necessary to give some place to features in the second. Rousseau, Marx, Dewey, and Habermas give primacy to the second, though most of them incorporate significant elements from the first into their theories. Debates between them consist largely in each side trying to show how the other necessarily presupposes elements of the opposing theory to sustain itself. The current debate between civic republicans such as Charles Taylor, Michael Sandel, and Alasdair MacIntyre and individualists such as Ronald Dworkin and John Rawls exhibits these characteristics, though each side incorporates more features from the other than was the case with the majority of their classic predecessors. Having participated in such debates, I do not wish to discount their importance. But the terms of the established debate do obscure affinities between the adversaries in need of attention.

Each theory gravitates toward an ontology of concord. That is, each assumes that when properly constituted and situated the individual or collective subject achieves harmony with itself and with the other elements of social life. Thus any otherness discerned in the actual world becomes a sign that the selves in which it is located are incapacitated or that there is unintegrated material in need of assimilation or that the community needs to be broadened to internalize that which is now external to it. Otherness, the opponents agree, is something to be corrected, eliminated, punished, or integrated. The issue between them is how normalization is to proceed. Otherness—that which does not fit neatly into the form assumed by self or society—is not treated as that which might not fit because even a good order (or self) must itself produce elements that do not synchronize with its structure. It is never defined as worthy of respect in its very difference from the identity or good given primacy by the order or the theory in question.

A theory that must constantly define otherness as incapacity or a need requiring communal response or a sign that the communal terms of integration must be reformed lends too much ontological significance to the politics of normalization.

This characterization of commonality between two contending theories exaggerates. I mean to point to complementary tendencies linking opposing parties rather than to a monolithic drive uniting secret allies. The tendencies reside within texts and practices; they are less often explicit themes defended by them. And, as we shall see, there are also subversive tendencies in these same texts and practices to which I propose to give greater legitimacy. These subversive tendencies deserve greater prominence because they provide a counter to the politics of de-democratization built into the normalizing practices of democracy.

The relation between modern democratic theory and an ontology of concord is best brought out by contrasting the latter to an ontology of discordance or necessary dissonance within concord. The philosophy of discordance allows a place for the pursuit of personal and common identity while it strives to subdue the politics of normalization.

The latter philosophy refuses to postulate actual or potential identity among the elements constituting the self or the society. It expects discordance to be lodged in every unity achieved or discovered. And it discerns within the modern quest for identity the secularization of traditional religious impulses: devout secularists convert the creationist ontology into one which relocates unity and creativity in individual or collective subjects or in a pluralism which harmonizes these interdependent dimensions.

An ontology of discordance identifies some forms of otherness as the unavoidable effect of socially engendered harmonics. That which is recalcitrant or subjugated or excluded may be a sign that any human construct worthy of admiration must spawn that which does not fit. When we conclude that otherness (dirt, things out of place, unreason, mystery, eccentricity, instability) is itself produced by the artifices through which we complete ourselves, we are in a position to reconsider politically established orientations to these deformations. We place ourselves in a position to discern and combat that side of democratic idealism which tends to equate good citizenship with normalization or to identify radical critique of an existing order with the aspiration to propel more inclusive forms of selfhood and community into being. We open ourselves to a philosophy that seeks, even in its commitment to the common good, to establish more space for otherness to be. And that sensibility better prepares us to uncover the pressures to normalize built into the structure of contemporary political economies.

The first question a normalizing democrat (or rationalist or moralist) poses when confronted with the ontology of discordance is, "How could it validate itself if its own formulation corrodes every ethic and theory of truth?" And the first and last answer the questioner typically accepts, "It cannot and therefore it is a self-refuting theory to be eliminated from the ranks of viable candidates for consideration." I do not now intend to respond in detail to this all too familiar question and answer, though I have dealt with them elsewhere.[7] I think, indeed, that the charge of incoherence itself expresses a contestable faith in the sufficiency of the knowing enterprise; it presumes that since cognitive orientations to communication presuppose the redeemability of truth claims, no rhetorical strategy operating on the edge of this circle of cognition could call this faith into question. Here, however, we will consider two different questions. First, what philosophers have articulated an ontology of discordance and what effect does it have on the appearance presented by democratic practice? Second, is it possible to defend democratic institutions while endorsing such a philosophy and, if so, what alterations in the theory and practice of democracy are suggested by resituating them in this setting?

It may appear that Hobbesian philosophy expresses an appreciation of discordance. The self is at war with itself and often at odds with the dictates of reason and order. But every move Hobbes makes in his theory of self to support such a perspective is redefined in the theories of reason, sovereignty, and God. Hobbesian political theology grounds itself upon faith in divine providence in the last instance. It counsels humans limited by sinful dispositions and by partiality in their reasoning to treat the mysteries of life as signs of the omnipotence of their creator. There is a modest effort in Hobbes's thought to give space to difference when it does not interfere with the dictates of order. But the doctrine of reason as the human window onto God's will and commands absorbs the initial appearance of discordance into a higher concordance imposed upon humans through reason. Though resistance will persist in the rational order, it is always a sign of sin or irrationality in need of correction. Hobbes is a theorist of political conflict but not of discordance lodged within order and rationality.

Nietzsche is the modern thinker of significance who first explores such a perspective relentlessly. William James articulates some of its characteristics in his philosophy of radical empiricism. And Michel Foucault gives it a contemporary expression. But the first saw democracy only as a vehicle of weakness and resentment; the second did not explore the political implication's of his thought; and the third was wary of its contribution to normalization.

We can glimpse the idea of discordance in this formulation by Nietzsche: "What alone can our teaching be? That no one *gives* a human being his qualities: not God, not society, not his parents, not his ancestors, not he himself. . . . He is not the result of a special design, a will, a purpose."[8] The human is the incomplete animal, completed only within the frame of social form. But since humans were not designed to fit neatly into any social form, and since no ideal form has been predesigned to mesh with every drive and stirring within the self, every particular form of completion subjugates even while it realizes something in us, does violence to selves even while enabling them to be. It is this ambiguous relation between our need for completion and the arbitrary element within any actual completion that leads Nietzsche to characterize the human as "the sick animal." Our resentment against discordance and finitude encourages us to create compensatory philosophies of concordance. And the quest for concordance through the containment or assimilation or conquest of otherness exacerbates this sickness.

The politics of insidious assimilation flows most dramatically from the effort to improve the self by drawing it closer to its true self or final essence. Foucault, the genealogist of modernity as the normalizing society, states this theme in the following way: "One might say that the ancient right to *take* life or *let* live was replaced by a power to *foster* life or disallow it to the point of death." Power in the old regimes "was essentially a right of seizure: of things, time, bodies, and ultimately life itself; it culminated in the privilege to seize life in order to suppress it." Much of life existed outside or on the margins of power, and power entered into life whenever it overstepped its prescribed limits. As power shifts from protecting sovereign prerogatives to enabling life to realize its potentialities within a well-ordered society, power becomes more constitutive (more "productive") in character. It now works to "incite, reinforce, control, optimize, and organize the forces under it: a power bent on generating forces, making them grow, and ordering them, rather than one dedicated to impeding them, making them submit or destroying them."[9]

While modern philosophies of self and society compete to give the right purposes to these optimizing forces, they coalesce to obscure the way in which optimizing power normalizes. Normalization is further abetted by the modern shift in the locus of sovereignty from the ruler to the people. For power now serves the people itself. This tightening of the web of power culminates in the new shape of war. "Wars are no longer waged in the name of a sovereign who must be defended; they are waged on behalf of the existence of everyone. . . . The atomic situation is now at the end point of this process: the power to expose a whole population to death is the underside of the power to guarantee an individual's continued existence."[10]

Foucault is ambivalent about democracy, suggesting that since every order requires boundaries and limits, democratic procedures may be the best way to establish them after all. But Nietzsche's hostility contains no apparent ambivalence. Democracy is the triumph of weakness over strength; it expresses the triumph of resentment over the affirmation of life in its discordance and finitude; it gives the "herd" hegemony over that which would deviate from it. But I believe Foucault and Nietzsche overlooked certain ingredients in democratic practice expressive of the essential tension between the need for commonality and the need to respond to the ways in which commonality subjugates. Perhaps they did so because the dimension of democracy most attuned to the element of discordance within concord has periodically found a more robust expression in America than in Europe.

A political theory attuned to discordance lodged within the concordance between thought and unthought, word and thought, word and thing, mood and its articulation, common good and the good of particular selves, personal identities socially redeemed and that in the self subdued by such redemption, the imperatives of the present and the needs of the future, the desire for transcendental reassurance and the indifference of the world to that desire—a political theory attentive to such discordance will find a highly congenial strain within the ambiguous legacy of democracy. This strain will be given its due only when the strife, recalcitrance, and dissimulation within democratic politics is treated as part of the affirmation of life itself, and that orientation will be possible only to the degree that the imperatives of modern political economies are relaxed to establish more space for discordance to be, without disrupting the necessary limits of order.

Thus Spoke Zarathustra can be read as a series of dialogues between Zarathustra and his animals, the soothsayer, the ugliest man, the old woman, the higher men, etc.; it can also be read as a plurality of voices in Zarathustra jostling for a hearing. It is a book for "everyone and no one" because each of us contains disturbing voices within the plurality available to us and few of us are willing to allow these disturbances to find expression. Because we yearn for a world in which our finitude is redeemed and in which suffering is shown to serve some higher purpose, we are inclined to give hegemony to these voices of reassurance. To be weak is to close off the voices of discordance within the self; it is *also* to demand punishment of those whose discordant articulations create disturbance in oneself.

Democracy, when it is not enveloped in the ontological tissue of concordance or bound by the chains of economic rationality, is a medium through which these voices of otherness can find expression in the self and the public world.

Democratic life is, first, the medium through which any self can wage *its* own struggle between weakness and strength. If the self is the locus of strife between the quest for transcendental purpose in life and the affirmation of life without such purpose, between revenge against temporality and affirmation of finitude, between silencing the disturbance of otherness and accepting it as a spur to the self, and if economic class, birth, gender, or formal education do not suffice to differentiate weakness from strength, then democratic turbulence— the politics that settles the settled—enables this struggle to be waged within anyone and everyone. It exposes any self to the possibility of affirming life amidst its discordances; it thus encourages greater acceptance of otherness in oneself and other selves. There should be, indeed, ample space for debate between alternative interpretations of what the struggle is and how to wage it. For many would revise the definitions of "weakness" and "strength" endorsed here. But as long as the definitions advanced here have some presence in the public life, democratic practice still emerges as the best medium through which each can confront the disturbance posed by otherness to the self.

Democratic practice is, second, the best way, particularly when a range of citizens acknowledges this internal strife, to define the limits, norms, and ends appropriate to the common life. If any self is incomplete without social form and if any good social form realizes some things in the self by subordinating others, democratic politics allows a common good to be defined while also enabling the dirt within it to find expression. Democratic politics of the sort endorsed here does not eliminate the need for norms. It insists upon it. But when conditions are right, and when a sufficient number of citizens have affirmed discordance as part of the human condition, democratic turbulence subdues the politics of normalization. It supports the ambiguous relation to public life essential to freedom. It—again when it is freed from the shackles of concordant ontology—expresses the ambiguity lodged in its own mode of politics without giving too much ontological weight to the social requirements of normalization.

This, again, is a radical idealization of democracy. Rather, it is a double idealization. It accentuates tendencies in democratic practice worthy of glorification and then dissociates them from ontologies of concordance that obscure the violence in normalization. It concentrates attention on the persistent ambiguity between the democratic appreciation of individuality and its drive to extend popular control over common areas of life, between its appreciation of agency and its tendency to convert social norms into definitional preconditions of agency, between the human drive to have settled expectations and the need to expose the dirt buried within them. By enabling its own ambiguity to become more overt it encourages us to be wary of doctrines that glorify normalization by defining it as harmonization; it encourages us to treat normalization as an ambiguous good to be qualified, countered, and politicized.

A theory of democracy located in an ontology of discordance will idealize politics. Politics, at its best, is the medium through which essential ambiguities can be expressed and given some redress. It is simultaneously the best way to establish or confirm commonalities and expose uncertainties, repressed voices, exclusions, and injuries lodged within them. Politics, again at its best, calls into question settlements sedimented into moral consensus, economic rationality, administrative procedure, legal propriety, psychiatric judgment, and ontological necessity. It enables cherished media of harmonization such as the self as subject, economic growth as a fundamental component of the good life, and the indispensability of political authority to be experienced simultaneously as mechanisms of normalization and as vehicles of realization.

Under the right conditions, then, democracy politicizes and politics democratizes. The problem is to identify the right conditions and to recognize those features of contemporary life that now militate against their consolidation. That, at least, is an agenda for those of us who wish to situate democracy within a philosophy of dissonant holism.

Chantal Mouffe, "Radical Democracy: Modern or Postmodern?" (1988)

What does it mean to be on the left today? In the twilight years of the twentieth century is it in any way meaningful to invoke the Enlightenment ideals that lay behind the project of the transformation of society? We are undoubtedly living through the crisis of the Jacobin imaginary, which has, in diverse ways, characterized the revolutionary politics of the last two hundred years. It is unlikely that Marxism will recover from the blows it has suffered; not only the discredit brought upon the Soviet model by the analysis of totalitarianism, but also the challenge to class reductionism posed by the emergence of new social movements. But the fraternal enemy, the social democratic movement, is not in any better shape. It has proved incapable of addressing the new demands of recent decades, and its central achievement, the welfare state, has held up badly under attack from the right, because it has not been able to mobilize those who should have interests in defending its achievements.

As for the ideal of socialism, what seems to be in question is the very idea of progress that is bound up with the project of modernity. In this respect, discussion of the postmodern, which until now had focused on culture, has taken a political turn. Alas, the debate all too quickly petrified around a set of simplistic and sterile positions. Whereas Habermas accuses of conservatism all those who criticize the universalist ideal of the Enlightenment,[11] Lyotard declares with pathos that after Auschwitz the project of modernity has been eliminated. Richard Rorty rightly remarks that one finds on both sides an illegitimate assimilation of the political project of the Enlightenment and its epistemological aspects. This is why Lyotard finds it necessary to abandon political liberalism in order to avoid a universalist philosophy, whereas Habermas, who wants to defend liberalism, holds on, despite all of its problems, to this universalist philosophy.[12] Habermas indeed believes that the emergence of universalist forms of morality and law is the expression of an irreversible collective process of learning, and that to reject this implies a rejection of modernity, undermining the very foundations of democracy's existence. Rorty invites us to consider Blumenberg's distinction, in *The Legitimacy of the Modern Age,* between two aspects of the Enlightenment, that of "self-assertion" (which can be identified with the political project) and that of "self-foundation" (the episte-mological project). Once we acknowledge that there is no necessary relation between these two aspects, we are in the position of being able to defend the political project while aban-doning the notion that it must be based on a specific form of rationality.

Rorty's position, however, is problematic because of his identification of the political proj-ect of modernity with a vague concept of "liberalism," which includes both capitalism and democracy. For, at the heart of the very concept of political modernity, it is important to dis-tinguish two traditions, liberal and democratic, both of which, as Macpherson has shown, are articulated only in the nineteenth century and are thus not necessarily related in any way. Moreover, it would be a mistake to confuse this "political modernity" with "social modernity," the process of modernization carried out under the growing domination of relations of capi-talist production. If one fails to draw this distinction between democracy and liberalism, be-tween political liberalism and economic liberalism; if, as Rorty does, one conflates all these notions under the term *liberalism,* then one is driven, under the pretext of defending moder-nity, to a pure and simple apology for the "institutions and practices of the rich North Atlantic democracies,"[13] which leaves no room for a critique (not even an immanent critique[14]) that would enable us to transform them.

Confronted by this "postmodernist bourgeois liberalism" that Rorty advocates, I would like to show how the project of a "Radical and Plural Democracy," one that Ernesto Laclau and I have already sketched out in our book *Hegemony and Socialist Strategy: Towards a Radical Democratic Politics,*[15] proposes a reformulation of the socialist project that avoids the twin pitfalls of marxist socialism and social democracy, while providing the left with a new imaginary, an imaginary that speaks to the tradition of the great emancipatory strug-gles but that also takes into account recent theoretical contributions by psychoanalysis and philosophy. In effect, such a project could be defined as being both modern and post-modern. It pursues the "unfulfilled project of modernity," but, unlike Habermas, we be-lieve that there is no longer a role to be played in this project by the epistemological per-spective of the Enlightenment. Although this perspective did play an important part in the emergence of democracy, it has become an obstacle in the path of understanding those new forms of politics, characteristic of our societies today, which demand to be ap-proached from a nonessentialist[16] perspective. Hence the necessity of using the theoretical tools elaborated by the different currents of what can be called the postmodern in philos-ophy and of appropriating their critique of rationalism and subjectivism.[17]

The Democratic Revolution

Different criteria have been suggested for defining modernity. They vary a great deal de-pending on the particular levels or features one wants to emphasize. I, for one, think that modernity must be defined at the political level, for it is there that social relations take shape and are symbolically ordered. Insofar as it inaugurates a new type of society, modernity can be viewed as a decisive point of reference. In this respect the fundamental characteristic of modernity is undoubtedly the advent of the democratic revolution. As Claude Lefort has shown, this democratic revolution is at the origin of a new kind of institution of the social, in which power becomes an "empty place." For this reason, modern democratic society is con-stituted as "a society in which power, law and knowledge are exposed to a radical indetermi-nation, a society that has become the theatre of an uncontrollable adventure, so that what is instituted never becomes established, the known remains undetermined by the unknown, the present proves to be undefinable."[18] The absence of power embodied in the person of the prince and tied to a transcendental authority preempts the existence of a final guarantee or source of legitimation; society can no longer be defined as a substance having an organic identity. What remains is a society without clearly defined outlines, a social structure that is impossible to describe from the perspective of a single, or universal, point of view. It is in this way that democracy is characterized by the "dissolution of the landmarks of certainty."[19] I think that such an approach is extremely suggestive and useful because it allows us to put many of the phenomena of modern societies in a new perspective. Thus, the effects of the democratic revolution can be analyzed in the arts, theory, and all aspects of culture in general, enabling one to formulate the question of the relation between modernity and postmodernity in a new and more productive way. Indeed, if one sees the democratic revolution as Lefort portrays it, as the distinctive feature of modernity, it then becomes clear that what one means when one refers to postmodernity in philosophy is to recognize the impossibility of any ultimate foundation or final legitimation that is constitutive of the very advent of the democratic form of society and thus of modernity itself. This recognition comes after the failure of several attempts to replace the traditional foundation that lay within God or Nature with an alternative foundation lying in Man and his Reason. These attempts were doomed to failure from the start because of the radical indeterminacy that is characteristic of modern democracy. Nietzsche had already understood this when he proclaimed that the death of God was inseparable from the crisis of humanism.

Therefore the challenge to rationalism and humanism does not imply the rejection of modernity but only the crisis of a particular project within modernity, the Enlightenment project of self-foundation. Nor does it imply that we have to abandon its political project, which is its achievement of equality and freedom for all. In order to pursue and deepen this aspect of the democratic revolution, we must ensure that the democratic project takes account of the full breadth and specificity of the democratic struggles in our times. It is here that the contribution of the so-called postmodern critique comes into its own.

How, in effect, can we hope to understand the nature of these new antagonisms if we hold on to an image of the unitary subject as the ultimate source of intelligibility of its actions? How can we grasp the multiplicity of relations of subordination that can affect an individual if we envisage social agents as homogeneous and unified entities? What characterizes the struggles of these new social movements is precisely the multiplicity of subject-positions, which constitutes a single agent and the possibility for this multiplicity to become the site of an antagonism and thereby politicized. Thus the importance of the critique of the rationalist concept of a unitary subject, which one finds not only in poststructuralism but also in psychoanalysis, in the philosophy of language of the late Wittgenstein, and in Gadamer's hermeneutics.

To be capable of thinking politics today, and understanding the nature of these new struggles and the diversity of social relations that the democratic revolution has yet to encompass, it is indispensable to develop a theory of the subject as a decentered, detotalized agent, a subject constructed at the point of intersection of a multiplicity of subject-positions between which there exists no a priori or necessary relation and whose articulation is the result of hegemonic practices. Consequently, no identity is ever definitively established, there always being a certain degree of openness and ambiguity in the way the different subject-positions are articulated. What emerges are entirely new perspectives for political action, which neither liberalism—with its idea of the individual who only pursues his or her own interest—nor Marxism—with its reduction of all subject-positions to that of class—can sanction, let alone imagine.

It should be noted, then, that this new phase of the democratic revolution, while it is, in its own way, a result of the democratic universalism of the Enlightenment, also puts into question some of its assumptions. Many of these new struggles do in fact renounce any claim to universality. They show how in every assertion of universality there lies disavowal of the particular and a refusal of specificity. Feminist criticism unmasks the particularism hiding behind those so-called universal ideals which, in fact, have always been mechanisms of exclusion. Carole Pateman, for example, has shown how classical theories of democracy were based upon the exclusion of women:

> The idea of universal citizenship is specifically modern, and necessarily depends on the emergence of the view that all individuals are born free and equal, or are naturally free and equal to each other. No individual is naturally subordinate to another, and all must thus have public standing as citizens, that upholds their self-governing status. Individual freedom and equality also entails that government can arise only through agreement or consent. We are all taught that the "individual" is a universal category that applies to anyone or everyone, but this is not the case. "The individual" is a man.[20]

The reformulation of the democratic project in terms of radical democracy requires giving up the abstract Enlightenment universalism of an undifferentiated human nature. Even though the emergence of the first theories of modern democracy and of the individual as a bearer of rights was made possible by these very concepts, they have today become a major obstacle to the future extension of the democratic revolution. The new rights that are being claimed today are the expression of differences whose importance is only now being asserted, and they are no longer rights that can be universalized. Radical democracy demands that we acknowledge difference—the particular, the multiple, the heterogeneous—in effect, everything that had been excluded by the concept of Man in the abstract. Universalism is not rejected but particularized; what is needed is a new kind of articulation between the universal and the particular.

Practical Reason: Aristotle Versus Kant

This increasing dissatisfaction with the abstract universalism of the Enlightenment explains the rehabilitation of the Aristotelian concept of *phronesis*. This "ethical knowledge," distinct from knowledge specific to the sciences (*episteme*), is dependent on the ethos, the cultural and historical conditions current in the community, and implies a renunciation of all pretense to universality.[21] This is a kind of rationality proper to the study of human praxis, which excludes all possibility of a "science" of practice but which demands the existence of a "practical reason," a region not characterized by apodictic statements, where the reasonable prevails over the demonstrable. Kant brought forth a very different notion of practical reason, one that required universality. As Ricoeur observes: "By elevating to the rank of supreme principle the rule of universalisation, Kant inaugurated one of the most dangerous ideas which was to prevail from Fichte to Marx; that the practical sphere was to be subject to a scientific kind of knowledge comparable to the scientific knowledge required in the theoretical sphere."[22] So, too, Gadarner criticizes Kant for having opened the way to positivism in the human sciences and considers the Aristotelian notion of *phronesis* to be much more adequate than the Kantian analysis of judgment to grasp the kind of relation existing between the universal and the particular in the sphere of human action.[23]

The development of the postempiricist philosophy of science converges with hermeneutics to challenge the positivistic model of rationality dominant in the sciences. Theorists such as Thomas Kuhn and Mary Hesse have contributed a great deal to this critique by pointing to the importance of rhetorical elements in the evolution of science. It is agreed today that we need to broaden the concept of rationality to make room for the "reasonable" and the "plausible" and to recognize the existence of multiple forms of rationality.

Such ideas are crucial to the concept of a radical democracy in which judgment plays a fundamental role that must be conceptualized appropriately so as to avoid the false dilemmas between, on the one hand, the existence of some universal criterion and, on the other, the rule of arbitrariness. That a question remains unanswerable by science or that it does not attain the status of a truth that can be demonstrated does not mean that a reasonable opinion cannot be formed about it or that it cannot be an opportunity for a rational choice. Hannah Arendt was absolutely right to insist that in the political sphere one finds oneself in the realm of opinion, or "doxa," and not in that of truth, and that each sphere has its own criteria of validity and legitimacy.[24] There are those, of course, who will argue that such a position is haunted by the specter of relativism. But such an accusation makes sense only if one remains in the thrall of a traditional problematic, which offers no alternative between objectivism and relativism.

Affirming that one cannot provide an ultimate rational foundation for any given system of values does not imply that one considers all views to be equal. As Rorty notes, "the real issue is not between people who think one view as good as any other and people who do not. It is between people who think our culture, our purpose or institutions cannot be supported except conversationally and people who still hope for other sorts of support."[25] It is always possible to distinguish between the just and the unjust, the legitimate and the illegitimate, but this can only be done from within a given tradition, with the help of standards that this tradition provides; in fact, there is no point of view external to all tradition from which one can offer a universal judgment. Furthermore, to give up the distinction between logic and rhetoric to which the postmodern critique leads—and where it parts with Aristotle—does not mean that "might makes right" or that one sinks into nihilism. To accept with Foucault that there cannot be an absolute separation between validity and power (since validity is always relative to a specific regime of truth, connected to power) does not mean that we cannot distinguish within a given regime of truth between those who respect the strategy of argumentation and its rules, and those who simply want to impose their power.

Finally, the absence of foundation "leaves everything as it is," as Wittgenstein would say, and obliges us to ask the same questions in a new way. Hence the error of a certain kind of apocalyptical postmodernism which would like us to believe that we are at the threshold of a radically new epoch, characterized by drift, dissemination, and by the uncontrollable play of significations. Such a view remains captive of a rationalistic problematic, which it attempts to criticize. As Searle has pointed out to Derrida: "The real mistake of the classical metaphysician was not the belief that there were metaphysical foundations, but rather the belief that somehow or other such foundations were necessary, the belief that unless there are foundations something is lost or threatened or undermined or just in question."[26]

Tradition and Democratic Politics

Because of the importance it accords to the particular, to the existence of different forms of rationality, and to the role of tradition, the path of radical democracy paradoxically runs across some of the main currents of conservative thinking. One of the chief emphases of conservative thought does indeed lie in its critique of the Enlightenment's rationalism and universalism, a critique it shares with postmodernist thought; this proximity might explain why certain postmodernists have been branded as conservative by Habermas. In fact, the affinities can be found not on the level of the political but in the fact that, unlike liberalism and marxism, both of which are doctrines of reconciliation and mastery, conservative philosophy is predicated upon human finitude, imperfection, and limits. This does not lead unavoidably to a defense of the status-quo and to an antidemocratic vision, for it lends itself to various kinds of articulation.

The notion of tradition, for example, has to be distinguished from that of traditionalism. Tradition allows us to think our own insertion into historicity, the fact that we are constructed as subjects through a series of already existing discourses, and that it is through this tradition which forms us that the world is given to us and all political action made possible. A conception of politics like that of Michael Oakeshott, who attributes a central role to the existing "traditions of behavior" and who sees political action as "the pursuit of an intimation," is very useful and productive for the formulation of radical democracy. Indeed, for Oakeshott,

> Politics is the activity of attending to the general arrangement's of a collection of people who, in respect of their common recognition of a manner of attending to its arrangements, compose a single community. . . . This activity, then, springs neither from instant desires, nor from general principles, but from the existing traditions of behavior themselves. And the form it takes, because it can take no other, is the amendment of existing arrangements by exploring and pursuing what is intimated in them.[27]

If one considers the liberal democratic tradition to be the main tradition of behavior in our societies, one can understand the extension of the democratic revolution and development of struggles for equality and liberty in every area of social life as being the pursuit of these "intimations" present in the liberal democratic discourse. Oakeshott provides us with a good example, while unaware of the radical potential of his arguments. Discussing the legal status of women, he declares that

> the arrangements which constitute a society capable of political activity, whether these are customs or institutions or laws or diplomatic decisions, are at once coherent and incoherent; they compose a pattern and at the same time they intimate a sympathy for what does not fully appear. Political activity is the exploration of that sympathy; and consequently, relevant political reasoning will be convincing exposure of a sympathy, present but not yet followed up, and the convincing demonstration that now is the appropriate moment for recognizing it.[28]

He concludes that it is in this way that one is capable of recognizing the legal equality of women. It is immediately apparent how useful reasoning of this kind can be as a justification of the extension of democratic principles.

This importance afforded to tradition is also one of the principal themes of Gadamer's philosophical hermeneutics, which offers us a number of important ways of thinking about the construction of the political subject. Following Heidegger, Gadamer asserts the existence of a fundamental unity between thought, language, and the world. It is through language that the horizon of our present is constituted; this language bears the mark of the past; it is the life of the past in the present and thus constitutes the movement of tradition. The error of the Enlightenment, according to Gadamer, was to discredit "prejudices" and to propose an ideal of understanding which requires that one transcend one's present and free oneself from one's insertion into history. But it is precisely these prejudices that define our hermeneutical situation and constitute our condition of understanding and openness to the world. Gadamer also rejects the opposition drawn up by the Enlightenment between tradition and reason because for him

> tradition is constantly an element of freedom and of history itself. Even the most genuine and solid tradition does not persist by nature because of the inertia of what once existed. It needs to be affirmed, embraced, cultivated. It is, essentially, preservation such as is active in all historical change. But preservation is an act of reason, though an unconspicuous one. For this reason, only what is new, or what is planned, appears as the result of reason. But this is an illusion. Even where life changes violently, as in ages of revolution, far more of the old is preserved in the supposed transformation of everything than anyone knows, and combines with the new to create a new value.[29]

This conception of tradition, as borne through language found in Gadamer, can be made more specific and complex if reformulated in terms of Wittgenstein's "language games." Seen in this light, tradition becomes the set of language games that make up a given community. Since for Wittgenstein language games are an indissoluble union between linguistic rules, objective situations, and forms of life,[30] tradition is the set of discourses and practices that form us as subjects. Thus we are able to think of politics as the pursuit of intimations, which in a Wittgensteinian perspective can be understood as the creation of new usages for the key terms of a given tradition, and of their use in new language games that make new forms of life possible.

To be able to think about the politics of radical democracy through the notion of tradition, it is important to emphasize the composite, heterogeneous, open, and ultimately indeterminate character of the democratic tradition. Several possible strategies are always available, not only in the sense of the different interpretations one can make of the same element, but also because of the way in which some parts or aspects of tradition can be played against others. This is what Gramsci, perhaps the only Marxist to have understood the role of tradition, saw as a process of disarticulation and rearticulation of elements characteristic of hegemonic practices.[31]

Recent attempts by neoliberals and neoconservatives to redefine concepts such as liberty and equality and to disarticulate the idea of liberty from that of democracy demonstrate how within the liberal democratic tradition different strategies can be pursued, making available different kinds of intimations. Confronted by this offensive on the part of those who want to put an end to the articulation that was established in the nineteenth century between liberalism and democracy and who want to redefine liberty as nothing more than an absence of coercion, the project of radical democracy must try to defend democracy and to expand its sphere of applicability to new social relations. It aims to create another kind of articulation between elements of the liberal democratic tradition, no longer viewing rights in an individualist framework but as "democratic rights." This will create a new hegemony, which will be the outcome of the articulation of the greatest possible number of democratic struggles.

What we need is a hegemony of democratic values, and this requires a multiplication of democratic practices, institutionalizing them into ever more diverse social relations, so that a multiplicity of subject-positions can be formed through a democratic matrix. It is in this way—and not by trying to provide it with a rational foundation—that we will be able not only to defend democracy but also to deepen it. Such a hegemony will never be complete, and anyway, it is not desirable for a society to be ruled by a single democratic logic. Relations of authority and power cannot completely disappear, and it is important to abandon the myth of a transparent society, reconciled with itself, for that kind of fantasy leads to totalitarianism. A project of radical and plural democracy, on the contrary, requires the existence of multiplicity, of plurality, and of conflict, and sees in them the *raison d'être* of politics.

Radical Democracy, a New Political Philosophy

If the task of radical democracy is indeed to deepen the democratic revolution and to link together diverse democratic struggles, such a task requires the creation of new subject-positions that would allow the common articulation, for example, of antiracism, antisexism, and anticapitalism. These struggles do not spontaneously converge, and in order to establish democratic equivalences, a new "common sense" is necessary, which would transform the identity of different groups so that the demands of each group could be articulated with those of others according to the principle of democratic equivalence. For it is not a matter of establishing a mere alliance between given interests but of actually modifying the very identity of these forces. In order that the defense of workers' interests is not pursued at the cost of the rights of women, immigrants, or consumers, it is necessary to establish an equivalence between these different struggles. It is only under these circumstances that struggles against power become truly democratic.

Political philosophy has a very important role to play in the emergence of this common sense and in the creation of these new subject-positions, for it will shape the "definition of reality" that will provide the form of political experience and serve as a matrix for the construction of a certain kind of subject. Some of the key concepts of liberalism, such as rights, liberty, and citizenship, are claimed today by the discourse of possessive individualism, which stands in the way of the establishment of a chain of democratic equivalences.

I have already referred to the necessity of a concept of democratic rights, rights which, while belonging to the individual, can only be exercised collectively and presuppose the existence of equal rights for others. But radical democracy also needs an idea of liberty that transcends the false dilemma between the liberty of the ancients and the moderns and allows us to think individual liberty and political liberty together. On this issue, radical democracy shares the preoccupations of various writers who want to redeem the tradition of civic republicanism. This trend is quite heterogeneous, and it is therefore necessary to draw distinctions among the so-called communitarians who, while they all share a critique of liberal individualism's idea of a subject existing prior to the social relations that form it, have differing attitudes toward modernity. On the one hand, there are those like Michael Sandel and Alasdair MacIntyre, inspired mainly by Aristotle, who reject liberal pluralism in the name of a politics of the common good; and, on the other hand, those like Charles Taylor and Michael Walzer, who, while they criticize the epistemological presuppositions of liberalism, try to incorporate its political contribution in the area of rights and pluralism.[32] The latter hold a perspective closer to that of radical democracy, whereas the former maintain an extremely ambiguous attitude toward the advent of democracy and tend to defend premodern conceptions of politics, drawing no distinctions between the ethical and the political which they understand as the expression of shared moral values.

It is probably in the work of Machiavelli that civic republicanism has the most to offer us, and in this respect the recent work of Quentin Skinner is of particular interest. Skinner shows that in Machiavelli one finds a conception of liberty that, although it does not postulate an objective notion of the good life (and therefore is, according to Isaiah Berlin, a "negative" conception of liberty), nevertheless includes ideals of political participation and civic virtue (which, according to Berlin, are typical of a "positive" conception of liberty). Skinner shows that the idea of liberty is portrayed in the *Discourses* as the capacity for individuals to pursue their own goals, their "humors" (*humori*). This goes together with the affirmation that in order to ensure the necessary conditions for avoiding coercion and servitude, thereby rendering impossible the use of this liberty, it is indispensable for individuals to fulfill certain public functions and to cultivate required virtues. For Machiavelli, if one is to exercise civic virtue and serve the common good, it is in order to guarantee oneself a certain degree of personal liberty which permits one to pursue one's own ends.[33] We encounter in this a very modern conception of individual liberty articulated onto an old conception of political liberty, which is fundamental for the development of a political philosophy of radical democracy.

But this appeal to a tradition of civic republicanism, even in the privileging of its Machiavellian branch, cannot wholly provide us with the political language needed for an articulation of the multiplicity of today's democratic struggles. The best it can do is provide us with elements to fight the negative aspects of liberal individualism while it remains inadequate to grasp the complexity of politics today. Our societies are confronted with the proliferation of political spaces which are radically new and different and which demand that we abandon the idea of a unique constitutive space of the constitution of the political, which is particular to both liberalism and civic republicanism. If the liberal conception of the "unencumbered self" is deficient, the alternative presented by the communitarian defenders of civic republicanism is unsatisfactory as well. it is not a question of moving from a "unitary unencumbered self" to a "unitary situated self"; the problem is with the very idea of the unitary subject. Many communitarians seem to believe that we belong to only one community, defined empirically and even geographically, and that this community could be unified by a single idea of the common good. But we are in fact always multiple and contradictory subjects, inhabitants of a diversity of communities (as many, really, as the social relations in which we participate and the subject-positions they define), constructed by a variety of discourses and precariously and temporarily sutured at the intersection of those subject-positions. Thus the importance of the postmodern critique for developing a political philosophy aimed at making possible a new form of individuality that would be truly plural and democratic. A philosophy of this sort does not assume a rational foundation for democracy, nor does it provide answers, in the way of Leo Strauss, to questions concerning the nature of political matters and the best regime. On the contrary, it proposes to remain within the cave and, as Michael Walzer puts it, "to interpret to one's fellow citizens the world of meanings that we share."[34] The liberal democratic tradition is open to many interpretations, and the politics of radical democracy is but one strategy among others. Nothing guarantees its success, but this project has set out to pursue and deepen the democratic project of modernity. Such a strategy requires us to abandon the abstract universalism of the Enlightenment, the essentialist conception of a social totality, and the myth of a unitary subject. In this respect, far from seeing the development of postmodern philosophy as a threat, radical democracy welcomes it as an indispensable instrument in the accomplishment of its goals.

NOTES

1. *Politics, Philosophy, Culture: Interviews and Other Writings, 1977–1984,* trans. Lawrence Kritzman (New York: Routledge, 1988), 104.

2. *Discipline and Punish* (New York: Pantheon, 1977), 183.

3. This Union, established after 1968, has adopted a radical line on civil rights, the law, and the prisons.

4. The ways in which citizenship helps to foster individuality are nicely developed by George Kateb in "The Moral Distinctiveness of Representative Democracy," *Ethics* (April 1981). My disagreement with Kateb revolves around his depreciation of normalizing tendencies built into the ideal of democracy and into the structure of the American political economy. A thoughtful critique/appreciation of Kateb's essay is developed by Morton Schoolman in "Liberalism's Ambiguous Legacy: Individuality and Technological Constraints," *Research in Philosophy and Technology* 7 (1984): 229–54.

5. *On the Social Contract,* ed. Roger Masters, trans. Judith Masters (New York: St. Martin's Press, 1978), 47.

6. I have in mind the recent work by Charles Taylor, *Philosophical Papers,* vols. 1 and 2 (Cambridge: Cambridge University Press, 1982); Michael Sandel, *Liberalism and the Limits of Justice* (Cambridge: Cambridge University Press, 1982); and Alasdair MacIntyre, *After Virtue* (South Bend: University of Notre Dame Press, 1981).

7. See "Taylor, Truth and Otherness," in *Political Theory* (August 1985) and chapter 10 of *Politics and Ambiguity.*

8. *Twilight of the Idols,* trans. R. J. Hollingdale (New York: Penguin Books, 1968), 54.

9. *The History of Sexuality,* vol. 1, trans. Robert Hurley (New York: Vintage Press, 1980), 38, 136.

10. *The History of Sexuality,* vol. 1, 136.

11. Jürgen Habermas, "Modernity—An Incomplete Project," in *The Anti-Aesthetic: Essays on Postmodern Culture,* ed. Hal Foster (Port Townsend, Wash.: Bay Press, 1983).

12. Richard Rorty, "Habermas and Lyotard on Postmodernity," in *Habermas and Modernity,* ed. Richard J. Bernstein (Oxford: Polity Press, 1985), 161–75.

13. Richard Rorty, "Postmodernist Bourgeois Liberalism," *Journal of Philosophy* 80 (October 1983), 585.

14. That is a critique that draws from principles that are already established. *Eds.*

15. Ernesto Laclau and Chantal Mouffe, *Hegemony and Socialist Strategy: Towards a Radical Democratic Politics* (London: Verso, 1985).

16. Nonessentialism is a doctrine that rejects the idea that there are fundamental qualities that define the inherent character of an individual or social construct. *Eds.*

17. I am referring not only to poststructuralism but also to other trends like psychoanalysis, post-Heideggerian hermeneutics, and the philosophy of language of the second Wittgenstein, which all converge in a critique of rationalism and subjectivism.

18. Claude Lefort, *The Political Forms of Modern Society* (Oxford: Polity Press, 1986), 305.

19. Claude Lefort, *Essais sur le Politique* (Paris: Editions du Seuil, 1986), 29 (English translation, see *Democracy and Political Theory,* trans. David Macey, Cambridge: Polity in association with Basil Blackwell, 1988).

20. Carole Pateman, "Removing Obstacles to Democracy" (Paper presented to the International Political Science Association meeting, Ottawa, Canada, October 1986, mimeographed).

21. Recent interpretations of Aristotle try to dissociate him from the tradition of natural law and to underline the differences between him and Plato on this issue. See, for instance, Hans-Georg Gadamer's remarks in *Truth and Method* (New York: Crossroad, 1984), 278–89.

22. Paul Ricoeur, *Du texte à l'action* (Paris: Editions du Seuil, 1986), 248–51 (English translation, see *From Text to Action,* trans. Kathleen Blamey and John B. Thompson, Evanston, Ill.: Northwestern University Press, 1991).

23. Gadamer, *Truth and Method*, 33–39.

24. Hannah Arendt, *Between Past and Future* (New York: Viking Press, 1968).

25. Richard Rorty *Consequences of Pragmatism* (Minneapolis: University of Minnesota Press, 1982), 167.

26. John R. Searle, "The Word Turned Upside Down," *The New York Review of Books* 27 (October 1983): 78.

27. Michael Oakeshott, *Rationalism in Politics* (London: Methuen, 1967), 123.

28. Michael Oakeshott, 124.

29. Gadamer, *Truth and Method*, 250.

30. Ludwig Wittgenstein, *Philosophical Investigations* (Oxford: Blackwell, 1953).

31. On this issue see my article "Hegemony and Ideology in Gramsci," in *Gramsci and Marxist Theory*, ed. Chantal Mouffe (London: Routledge and Kegan Paul, 1979), 168–204.

32. I refer here to the following studies: Michael Sandel, *Liberalism and the Limits of Justice* (Cambridge: Cambridge University Press, 1982); Alasdair MacIntyre, *After Virtue* (Notre Dame, Ind.: University of Notre Dame Press, 1984); Charles Taylor, *Philosophy and the Human Sciences,* Philosophical Papers, 2 (Cambridge: Cambridge University Press, 1985); Michael Walzer, *Spheres of Justice* (New York: Basic Books, 1983).

33. Quentin Skinner, "The Idea of Negative Liberty: Philosophical and Historical Perspectives," in *Philosophy in History,* eds. R. Rorty, J. B. Schneewind, and Q. Skinner (Cambridge: Cambridge University Press, 1984).

34. Walzer, *Spheres of Justice*, xiv.

DISCOURSE AND DEMOCRACY

The ancient Greeks claim that they are governed by speech while non-Greeks are governed by force and are, therefore, barbarians. As they see themselves, the Greeks obey laws only after deliberation and not because it comes from those who are more powerful. This approach remains important to many democrats who find it is necessary to express our own ideas about what is good and bad for ourselves and our community. We want to tell others about what matters to us. However, some democrats expect more from speech: they want citizens who not only speak but also listen and whose political orientations and priorities are subject to modification through a rational exchange of ideas with others. Like Aristotle, discursive democrats hold that democracy should enable citizens to speak freely, and they also want citizens who listen to different positions and learn from an open debate. For this to happen, discursive democrats expect citizens to employ their reason when they speak and listen in order to identify ways they can live together in freedom.[1]

Many critics of discursive democracy find that such a communicative task is beyond democratic practice, which, they hold, is open to manipulation. Some, such as Schumpeter, find that speech is vulnerable in a democracy because of the propensity of its citizens to be preoccupied with their immediate concerns and fears. In such a milieu, people respond to those who promise or frighten them the most. Today, much political language is shallow and manipulative and appears to confirm Schumpeter's observations. Rather than enlightening citizens and inviting collective negotiation, many critics find that contemporary political rhetoric seems diversionary, myopic, and self-serving.

Jürgen Habermas seeks to embolden democratic speech through a theory of language he calls communicative action. For him, the Enlightenment's emphasis on rational discourse remains vital today, in spite of what many postmodernist critics argue.[2] Habermas recognizes that participants in a conversation begin with their own subjective views, but he holds that language itself harbors a logic of consensual understanding between competent parties. He offers his theory of political language as an optimistic light on the possibility of identifying rationally grounded convictions worthy of collective endorsement.[3] Habermas's communicative project, then, describes the potential for a rational foundation for public deliberation through speech acts that are backed up by good reasons.

But it is precisely this critical capacity for collective evaluation that is jeopardized today, according to Habermas. In its place, he sees the steering mechanisms of money and power as distorting the outcome of public preferences. To combat this threat, he reaches for what he takes to be one of the richest legacies of the Enlightenment, that is, reason and the capacity to test arguments through public speech. For him, communicative action provides a foundation for a democratic society capable of completing the promise of universal justice put forth by the Enlightenment.[4]

Habermas joins the liberal tradition by preserving distinctions between the state and civil society and the critical role of constitutional safeguards in structuring the space of political action. At the same time he also draws from the republican tradition to emphasize the role of public deliberation in the maintenance of free societies. For him, self-interested choices based on a market model of politics are an impoverished vision of political life. Yet he objects to the ethical component of the republican model, promoting instead a discourse theory that provides a rational rather than an ethical understanding of collective decisionmaking. The republican presumption of a homogeneous and civically virtuous identity, which makes possible the collective perception of common good, asks too much of citizens in pluralistic societies and neglects the unifying possibilities inherent in honest and open public reasoning. By acknowledging that politics involves a type of bargaining and compromise between competing interests while also attending to the need to work with universal principles, Habermas offers his deliberative model as a means of returning to the normative component of politics without making any single normative stance trump all of the others.

Sheldon Wolin finds a different problem regarding speech in contemporary liberal democracy. Efforts to make some matters so important that they are not subject to democratic scrutiny drains democracy of its commitment to public debate. With this in mind, Wolin has charged John Rawls with offering a theory of justice that fails to appreciate the role of discourse in democracy. According to Wolin, the core of democracy rests on its openness and readiness to hear new voices and concerns as well as to reevaluate existing policies. For this reason, no grand narrative—whether from Rawls or others—can be welcomed in democratic politics. If a regime is to remain democratic, he insists that it cannot allow the political encounters of citizens with all of their disagreements to be replaced by a formula. However, Wolin finds that what should be arguable, and hence contestable, is too often placed beyond the reach of democratic discourse today. Although not a participatory democrat as are Dewey and Barber, Wolin shares with them the commitment to keep democracy open and fluid and resists efforts to close out the public from scrutinizing positions that should be contestable.

READINGS

JÜRGEN HABERMAS, "THREE NORMATIVE MODELS OF DEMOCRACY" (1966)

I would like to sketch a proceduralist view of democracy and deliberative politics that differs in relevant aspects from both the liberal and the republican paradigm. Let me delineate the opposing features of these two established models. I will then introduce a new proceduralist conception by way of a critique of the "ethical overload" of the republican view. The last part of the essay further elaborates the three normative models of democracy by comparing their corresponding images of state and society.

The Two Received Views of Democratic Politics

According to the "liberal" or Lockean view, the democratic process accomplishes the task of programming the government in the interest of society, where the government is represented as an apparatus of public administration, and society as a market-structured network of interactions among private persons. Here politics (in the sense of the citizens' political will-formation) has the function of bundling together and pushing private interests against a government apparatus specializing in the administrative employment of political power for collective goals. On the "republican" view, however, politics involves more than this mediating function, it is rather constitutive for the processes of society as a whole. "Politics" is conceived as the reflective form of substantial ethical life, namely as the medium in which the members of somehow solitary communities become aware of their dependence on one another and, acting with full deliberation as citizens, further shape and develop existing relations of reciprocal recognition into an association of free and equal consociates under law. With this, the liberal architectonic of government and society undergoes an important change: in addition to the hierarchical regulations of the state and the decentralized regulations of the market, that is, besides administrative power and individual personal interests, *solidarity* and the orientation to the common good appear as a *third source* of social integration. In fact, this horizontal political will-formation aimed at mutual understanding or communicatively achieved consensus is even supposed to enjoy priority, both in a genetic and a normative sense. An autonomous basis in civil society, a basis independent of public administration and market-mediated private commerce, is assumed as a precondition for the praxis of civic self-determination. This basis preserves political communication from being swallowed up by the government apparatus or assimilated to market structures. In the republican conception, the political public sphere acquires, along with its base in civil society, a strategic significance. These competing approaches yield two contrasting images of the citizen.

According to the liberal view, the citizen's status is determined primarily according to negative rights they have vis-à-vis the state and other citizens. As bearers of these rights they enjoy the protection of the government, as long as they pursue their private interests within the boundaries drawn by legal statutes—and this includes protection against government interventions. Political rights, such as voting rights and free speech, have not only the same structure but also a similar meaning as civil rights that provide a space within which legal subjects are released from external compulsion. They give citizens the opportunity to assert their private interests in such a way that by means of elections, the composition of parliamentary bodies, and the formation of a government, these interests are finally aggregated into a political will that makes an impact on the administration.

According to the republican view, the status of citizens is not determined by the model of negative liberties to which these citizens can lay claim *as* private persons. Rather, political rights—preeminently rights of political participation and communication—are positive liberties. They guarantee not freedom from external compulsion but the possibility of participation in a common praxis, through the exercise of which citizens can first make themselves into what they want to be—politically autonomous authors of a community of free and equal persons. To this extent, the political process does not just serve to keep government activity under the surveillance of citizens who have already acquired a prior social autonomy in the exercise of their private rights and prepolitical liberties. Just as little does it act as a hinge between state and society, for administrative authority is not at all an autochthonous authority; it is not something given. Rather, this authority emerges from the citizens' power produced communicatively in the praxis of self-legislation, and it finds its legitimation in the fact that it protects this praxis by institutionalizing public liberty. So, the state's *raison d'etre* lies not primarily in the protection of equal private rights but in the guarantee of an inclusive opinion- and will-formation in which free and equal citizens reach an understanding on which goals and norms lie in the equal interest of all.

The polemic against the classical concept of the legal person as bearer of private rights reveals a controversy about the concept of law itself. While in the liberal view the point of a legal order is to make it possible to determine in each case which individuals are entitled to which rights, in the republican view these "subjective" rights owe their existence to an "objective" legal order that both enables and guarantees the integrity of an autonomous life in common based on mutual respect: "For republicans rights ultimately are nothing but determinations of the prevailing political will, while for liberals some rights are always grounded in a 'higher law' of . . . reason."[5] Finally, the different ways of conceptualizing the role of citizen and of law express a deeper disagreement about the *nature of the political process*. In the liberal view, the political process of opinion- and will-formation in the public sphere and in parliament is determined by the competition of strategically acting collectivities trying to maintain or acquire positions of power. Success is measured by the citizens' approval, quantified as votes, of persons and programs. In their choices at the polls, voters give expression to their preferences. Their voting decisions have the same structure as the acts of choice made by participants in a market. They license access to the positions of power that political parties fight over in the same success-oriented attitude.

According to the republican view, the political opinion- and will-formation occurring in the public sphere and in parliament obeys not the structures of market processes but the obstinate structures of a public communication oriented to mutual understanding. For politics, in the sense of a praxis of civic self-legislation, the paradigm is not the market but dialogue. This dialogic conception imagines politics as contestation over questions of value and not simply questions of preference.

Proceduralist Versus Communitarian Views of Politics

The republican model as compared to the liberal one has the advantage of preserving the original meaning of democracy in terms of the institutionalization of a public use of reason jointly exercised by autonomous citizens. This model accounts for those communicative conditions that confer legitimating force on political opinion- and will-formation. These are precisely the conditions under which the political process can be presumed to generate reasonable results. A contest for power, if represented according to the liberal model of market competition, is determined by the rational choice of optimal strategies. Given an indissoluble pluralism of prepolitical values and interests that are at best aggregated with equal weight in the political process, politics loses all reference to the normative core of a public use of reason. The republican trust in the force of political discourses stands in contrast to the liberal skepticism about reason. Such discourses are meant to allow one to discuss value orientations and interpretations of needs and wants, and then to change these in an *insightful way*.

But contemporary republicans tend to give this public communication a communitarian reading. It is precisely this move toward an *ethical constriction* of *political discourse* that I call into question. Politics may not be assimilated to a hermeneutical process of self-explication of a shared form of life or collective identity. Political questions may not be reduced to the type of ethical questions where we, as members of a community, ask who we are and who we would like to be. In its communitarian interpretation the republican model is too idealistic even within the limits of a purely normative analysis. On this reading, the democratic process is dependent on the virtues of citizens devoted to the public weal. This expectation of virtue already led Rousseau to split the citizen oriented to the common good from the private man, who cannot be ethically overburdened. The unanimity of the political legislature was supposed to be secured in advance by a substantive ethical consensus. In contrast, a discourse-theoretic interpretation insists on the fact that democratic will-formation draws its legitimating force not from a previous convergence of settled ethical convictions but both from the communicative presuppositions that allow the better arguments to come into play in various forms of deliberation and from the procedures that secure fair bargaining processes. Discourse theory breaks with a purely ethical conception of civic autonomy.

According to the communitarian view, there is a necessary connection between the deliberative concept of democracy and the reference to a concrete, substantively integrated ethical community. Otherwise one could not explain, in this view, how the citizens' orientation to the common good would be at all possible. The individual, so the argument goes, can become aware of her co-membership in a collective form of life, and therewith become aware of a prior social bond, only in a practice exercised with others in common. The individual can get a clear sense of commonalities and differences, and hence a sense of who she is and who she would like to be, only in the public exchange with others who owe their identities to the same traditions and similar formation processes. This assimilation of political discourses to the clarification of a collective ethical self-understanding does not sit well with the function of the legislative processes they issue in. Legal statutes no doubt also contain teleological elements, but these involve more than just the hermeneutic explication of shared value orientations. By their very structure laws are determined by the question of which norms citizens want to adopt for regulating their living together. To be sure, discourses aimed at achieving self-understanding—discourses in which the participants want to get a clear understanding of themselves as members of a specific nation, as members of a locale or a state, as inhabitants of a region, and so on; in which they want to determine which traditions they will continue; in which they strive to determine how they will treat one another, and how they will treat minorities and marginal groups; in short, discourses in which they want to get clear about the kind of society they want to live in—such discourses are also an important part of politics. But these questions are subordinate to moral questions and connected with pragmatic questions. Moral questions in the narrow sense of the Kantian tradition are questions of justice. The question having *priority* in legislative politics concerns how a matter can be regulated in the equal interest of all. The making of norms is primarily a justice issue and is gauged by principles that state what is equally good for all. And unlike ethical questions, questions of justice are not related from the outset to a specific collective and its form of life. The politically enacted law of a concrete legal community must, if it is to be legitimate, at least be compatible with moral tenets that claim universal validity going beyond the legal community.

Moreover, compromises make up the bulk of political processes. Under conditions of religious, or in any way cultural and societal pluralism, politically relevant goals are often selected by interests and value orientations that are by no means constitutive for the identity of the community at large, hence for the whole of an intersubjectively shared form of life. The political interests and values that stand in conflict with each other without prospects of consensus are in need of a balancing that cannot be achieved through ethical discourses—even if the outcomes of bargaining processes are subject to the proviso that they must not violate a culture's agreed-upon basic values. The required balance of competing interests comes about as a compromise between parties that may rely on mutual threats. A legitimate kind of bargaining certainly depends on a prior regulation of fair terms for achieving results, which are acceptable for all parties on the basis of their differing preferences. While debates on such regulations should assume the forms of practical discourse that neutralize power, bargaining itself well allows for strategic interactions. The deliberative mode of legislative practice is not intended just to ensure the ethical validity of laws. Rather, one can understand the complex validity claim of legal norms as the claim, on the one hand, to compromise competing interests in a manner compatible with the common good and, on the other hand, to bring universalistic principles of justice into the horizon of the specific form of life of a particular community.

In contrast to the ethical constriction of political discourse, the concept of deliberative politics acquires empirical reference only when we take account of the multiplicity of communicative forms of rational political will-formation. It is not discourse of an ethical type that could grant on its own the democratic genesis of law. Instead, deliberative politics should be conceived as a syndrome that depends on a network of fairly regulated bargaining processes and of various forms of argumentation, including pragmatic, ethical, and moral discourses, each of which relies on different communicative presuppositions and procedures. In legislative politics the supply of information and the rational choice of strategies are interwoven with the balancing of interests, with the achievement of ethical self-understanding and the articulation of strong preferences, with moral justification and tests of legal coherence. Thus "dialogical" and "instrumental" politics, the two ideal-types that Frank Michelman has opposed in a polarizing fashion,[6] do in fact interpenetrate in the medium of deliberations of various kinds.

Images of State and Society

If we start from this proceduralist concept of deliberative politics, this reading of democracy has implications for the concept of society. Both the liberal and the republican model presuppose a view of society as centered in the state—be it the state as guardian of a market-society or the state as the self-conscious institutionalization of an ethical community.

According to the *liberal view,* the democratic process takes place in the form of compromises between competing interests. Fairness is supposed to be granted by the general and equal right to vote, the representative composition of parliamentary bodies, by decision rules, and so on. Such rules are ultimately justified in terms of liberal basic rights. According to the *republican view,* democratic will-formation takes place in the form of an ethical-political discourse; here deliberation can rely on a culturally established background consensus shared by the citizenry. Discourse theory takes elements from both sides and integrates these in the concept of an ideal procedure for deliberation and decision-making. Weaving together pragmatic considerations, compromises, discourses of self-understanding, and justice, this democratic procedure grounds the presumption that reasonable or fair results are obtained. According to this proceduralist view, practical reason withdraws from universal human rights, or from the concrete ethical substance of a specific community, into the rules of discourse and forms of argumentation. In the final analysis, the normative content arises from the very structure of communicative actions. These descriptions of the democratic process set the stage for different conceptualizations of state and society.

According to the republican view, the citizens' political opinion- and will-formation forms the medium through which society constitutes itself as a political whole. Society is, from the very start, political society—*societas civilis*. Hence democracy becomes equivalent to the political self-organization of society as a whole. This leads to a *polemic understanding of politics directed against the state apparatus*. In Hannah Arendt's political writings one can see where republican argumentation directs its salvos: in opposition to the privatism of a depoliticized population and in opposition to the acquisition of legitimation through entrenched parties, the public sphere should be revitalized to the point where a regenerated citizenry can, in the forms of a decentralized self-governance, (once again) appropriate the power of pseudo-independent state agencies. From this perspective, society would finally develop into a political totality.

Whereas the separation of the state apparatus from society elicits a polemical reaction from the republican side, according to the liberal view it cannot be eliminated but only bridged by the democratic process. The regulated balancing of power and interests has need of constitutional channeling, of course. The democratic will-formation of self-interested citizens is laden with comparatively weak normative expectations. The constitution is supposed to tame the state apparatus through normative constraints (such as basic rights, separation of powers, etc.) and to force it, through the competition of political parties on the one hand and that between government and opposition on the other, to take adequate account of competing interests and value orientations. This *state-centered understanding of politics* can forego the unrealistic assumption of a citizenry capable of collective action. Its focus is not so much the input of a rational political will-formation but the output of sensible and effective administrative accomplishments. Liberal argumentation aims its salvos against the potential disturbance of an administrative power that interferes with the spontaneous forces of a self-regulating society. The liberal model hinges not on the democratic self-determination of deliberating citizens but on the legal institutionalization of an economic society that is supposed to guarantee an essentially nonpolitical common good by the satisfaction of private preferences.

Discourse theory invests the democratic process with normative connotations stronger than those found in the liberal model but weaker than those of the republican model. Once again, it takes elements from both sides and fits them together in a new way. In agreement with republicanism, it gives center stage to the process of political opinion- and will-formation, but without understanding the constitution as something secondary; rather it conceives the principles of the constitutional state as a consistent answer to the question of how the demanding communicative forms of a democratic opinion- and will-formation can be institutionalized. Discourse theory has the success of deliberative politics depend not on a collectively acting citizenry but on the institutionalization of the corresponding procedures and conditions of communication. Proceduralized popular sovereignty and a political system tied in to the peripheral networks of the political public sphere go hand-in-hand with the image of a *decentered society*. This concept of democracy no longer needs to operate with the notion of a social whole centered in the state and imagined as a goal-oriented subject writ large. Just as little does it represent the whole in a system of constitutional norms mechanically regulating the interplay of powers and interests in accordance with the market model.

Discourse theory altogether jettisons certain premises of the *philosophy of consciousness.* Either these premises invite us to ascribe the praxis of civic self-determination to one encompassing macrosubject, or they have us apply the rule of law to many isolated private subjects. The former approach views the citizenry as a collective actor that reflects the whole and acts for it; in the latter, individual actors function as dependent variables in system processes that move along blindly. Discourse theory works instead with the *higher-level intersubjectivity* of communication processes that flow through both the parliamentary bodies and the informal networks of the public sphere. Within and outside the parliamentary complex, these subjectless forms of communication constitute arenas in which a more or less rational opinion- and will-formation can take place.

Informal public opinion-formation generates "influence"; influence is transformed into "communicative power" through the channels of political elections; and communicative power is again transformed into "administrative power" through legislation. As in the liberal model, the boundaries between "state" and "society" are respected; but in this case, civil society provides the social basis of autonomous public spheres that remain as distinct from the economic system as from the administration. This understanding of democracy suggests a new balance between the three resources of money, administrative power, and solidarity, from which modern societies meet their needs for integration. The normative implications are obvious: the integrative force of "solidarity," which can no longer be drawn solely from sources of communicative action, should develop through widely expanded and differentiated public spheres as well as through legally institutionalized procedures of democratic deliberation and decision-making. It should gain the strength to hold its own against the two other mechanisms of social integration—money and administrative power.

This view has implications for how one understands legitimation and popular sovereignty.

On the liberal view, democratic will-formation has the exclusive function of *legitimating* the exercise of political power. Election results are the license to assume governmental power, whereas the government must justify the use of power to the public. On the republican view, democratic will-formation has the significantly stronger function of *constituting* society as a political community and keeping the memory of this founding act alive with each election. The government is not only empowered to exercise a largely open mandate but also programmatically committed to carry out certain policies. It remains bound to a self-governing political community. Discourse theory brings a third idea into play: the procedures and communicative presuppositions of democratic opinion- and will-formation function as the most important sources for the discursive rationalization of the decisions of an administration constrained by law and statute. Rationalization means more than mere legitimation but less than the constitution of political power. The power available to the administration changes its aggregate condition as soon as it emerges from a public use of reason and a communicative power that do not just monitor the exercise of political power in a belated manner but more or less program it as well. Notwithstanding this discursive rationalization, only the administrative system itself can "act." The administration is a subsystem specialized for collectively binding decisions, whereas the communicative structures of the public sphere comprise a far-flung network of sensors that in the first place react to the pressure of societywide problematics and stimulate influential opinions. The public opinion that is worked up via democratic procedures into communicative power cannot "rule" of itself, but can only point the use of administrative power in specific directions.

The concept of popular sovereignty stems from the republican appropriation and revaluation of the early modern notion of sovereignty initially associated with absolutist regimes.

The state, which monopolizes all the means for a legitimate implementation of force, is seen as an overpowering concentrate of power—as the Leviathan. This idea was transferred by Rousseau to the will of the united people. He fused the strength of the Leviathan with the classical idea of the self-rule of free and equal citizens and combined it with his modern concept of autonomy. Despite this sublimation, the concept of sovereignty remained bound to the notion of an embodiment in the assembled, physically present people. According to the republican view, the people are the bearers of a sovereignty that in principle cannot be delegated: in their sovereign character the people cannot have others represent them. Liberalism opposes this with the more realistic view that in the constitutional state any authority originating from the people is exercised only "by means of elections and voting and by specific legislative, executive, and judicial organs."[7]

These two views would exhaust the alternatives only if we had to conceive state and society in terms of the whole and its parts—where the whole is constituted either by a sovereign citizenry or by a constitution. To the discourse theory of democracy corresponds, however, the image of a decentered society. To be sure, with the political public sphere the proceduralist model sets off an arena for the detection, identification, and interpretation of those problems that affect society as a whole. But the "self" of the self-organizing legal community here disappears in the subjectless forms of communication that regulate the flow of deliberations in such a way that their fallible results enjoy the presumption of rationality. This is not to denounce the intuition connected with the idea of popular sovereignty but to interpret it in intersubjective terms. Popular sovereignty, even if it becomes anonymous, retreats into democratic procedures and the legal implementation of their demanding communicative presuppositions only in order to make itself felt as communicatively generated power. Strictly speaking, this communicative power springs from the interactions between legally institutionalized will-formation and culturally mobilized publics. The latter, for their part, find a basis in the associations of a civil society quite distinct from both state and economy alike.

Read in procedural terms, the idea of popular sovereignty refers to a context that, while enabling the self-organization of a legal community, is not at the disposal of the citizens' will in any way. Deliberation is certainly supposed to provide the medium for a more or less conscious integration of the *legal community;* but this mode does not extend to the whole of society in which the political system is *embedded* as only one among several subsystems. Even in its own proceduralist self-understanding, deliberative politics remains a component of a complex society, which as a whole resists the normative approach practiced in legal theory. In this regard the discourse-theoretic reading of democracy has a point of contact with a detached sociological approach that considers the political system neither the peak nor the center, nor even the formative model of society in general, but just one action system among others. On the other hand, politics must still be able to communicate, through the medium of law, with all the other legitimately ordered spheres of action, however these happen to be structured and steered.

SHELDON WOLIN, SELECTIONS FROM "THE LIBERAL/DEMOCRATIC DIVIDE" (1996)

Despite the political setbacks of the last two decades, American liberals could console themselves that liberalism retains intellectual superiority over its critics. During those same decades, analytic philosophers in Britain and America put aside their prejudices and began gingerly to practice "political philosophy." Insofar as it is possible to attribute to one man and one book the principal responsibility for both developments, John Rawls incontestably would be that man and his *A Theory of Justice* (Harvard University Press, 1971) would be that book. His accomplishment is nothing less than to have set the terms of liberal discourse in the English-speaking countries.

Beyond his professional accomplishments, there is much to admire in the man: honesty, lucidity, moral and professional seriousness, and a remarkable receptiveness to criticism and suggestion. Rawls is truly the virtuous philosopher whose great personal achievement is to have rejected celebrity status.

Although *Justice* provided a comprehensive theory of rights and of the moral principles appropriate to a liberal society, its political and constitutional principles were sketched only briefly. Now, in *Political Liberalism* (Columbia University Press, 1993), he has attempted to remedy these and other deficiencies and to connect his proposals with cultural and historical traditions to a far greater degree than was previously the case.

The avowedly political focus of *Liberalism* invites some critical lines of questioning that were closed in *Justice* or were, at best, tangential to that enterprise. One such line is suggested by the remark of a reviewer who congratulated Rawls for putting "the 'political' back into 'political philosophy.'"[8]

Accordingly, in what follows, I explore Rawls's notion of the political by asking what kind of politics it promotes or encourages. I do this by raising what is for Rawls a nonquestion of the status of democracy within his version of liberalism. And because *Liberalism* is a work of political philosophy, I want to say something about its conception of that vocation and its relation to a democratic politics. Although that too may appear to be another non-Rawlsian question, it goes to the difference between liberalism and democracy and to the question of how it is possible to theorize democracy without resorting to anti- or undemocratic impositions; or, if it is possible, whether Rawlsian constructivism and its sovereign theorist are the way to do it.

The idea of democracy that I employ runs roughly like this. Democracy should not depend on elites making a one-time gift to the demos of a predesigned framework of equal rights. This does not mean that rights do not matter a great deal, but rights in a democracy depend on the demos winning them, extending them substantively, and, in the process, acquiring experience of the political, that is, of participating in power, reflecting on the consequences of its exercise, and struggling to sort out the common well-being amid cultural differences and socioeconomic disparities. The presence of democracy is not signified by paying deference to a formal principle of popular sovereignty but by ensuring continuing political education, nor is democracy nurtured by stipulating that reasonable principles of justice be in place from the beginning. Democracy requires that the experiences of justice and injustice serve as moments for the demos to think, to reflect, perchance to construct themselves as actors. Democracy is about the continuing self-fashioning of the demos. [. . . .]

The scope of *Liberalism* is dictated by its purpose: to provide a guide to deliberations about basic "political values"—about "constitutional essentials and questions of basic justice" and how these connect with culture, tradition, and other "background" conditions. These values "alone" are meant "to settle such fundamental questions" as voting, religious toleration, equality of opportunity, and ownership of property. Rawls expects his citizens or, more precisely, their representatives at a constitutional convention to be able to decide these matters, and he wants to ensure that they will be decided properly and openly.

Accordingly, he proposes—an earlier age would have said legislates—a hegemonic mode of discourse, "public reason," which citizens are to accept and employ in their discussions of basics. It applies broadly to "public advocacy in the public forum," to elections, to citizens, to candidates, and even to political groups whenever essentials are at issue (*PL*, 215). Otherwise, Rawls warns, citizens will be "hypocritical," saying one thing and doing another (*PL*, 214–15). Thus public reason is to be the discourse of a transparent political society earnestly seeking the public good in public (*PL*, 213).

Rawls's assumption throughout is that a politics of reason is a neutral instead of a neutralizing principle, which works against those who have not had the leisure to adopt it as the governing ideal of human conduct. Its model is neither demotic nor pluralistic but a discourse of the authoritative: "To check whether we are following public reason we might ask: how would our argument strike us presented in the form of a supreme court opinion? Reasonable? Outrageous?" (*PL*, 254).

Public reason has moral as well as discursive imperatives, for in addition to incorporating a political conception of justice (which includes basic rights and opportunities, the priority of rights over the good, and ensuring all citizens of "adequate all-purpose means" to make use of their liberties), public reason is constrained by "guidelines of inquiry that specify ways of reasoning and criteria for the kinds of information relevant for political questions." Public reason is to conform, therefore, to preestablished rules of evidence, inference, and reason (*PL*, 223–26). Citizens have "a moral, not a legal, duty" to explain to others how the principles and policies they espouse find support in public reason (*PL*, 217). The condition that makes possible this lofty level of public discourse is that the topic of "social and economic inequalities" is ruled out of order even though those inequalities are acknowledged to be "political" in nature (*PL*, 229–30).

Rawlsian democracy might be likened to a hermetically sealed condition of deliberation that allows rationality to rule by suppressing certain topics and historical grievances and excluding diverse languages of protest from public councils. Inadvertently, the limitations of Rawlsian reason are exposed: it cannot make sense of, much less function within, a setting of sharp conflicts, whether doctrinal, economic, political, or rhetorical.

Public reason, we might say, is the general will in the age of academic liberalism. And like the general will, it is haunted by the specter of differences. Unlike Rousseau, Rawls will not banish certain groups (although he will come perilously close to doing so) but will seek their incorporation, a solution rendered easier because of the politically trivial character of the differences with which Rawls is concerned.

Rawls proposes a "reasonable pluralism." It is not designed to obstruct and mediate State power (the discourse of *Liberalism* is innocent of the idea of the State), nor is it driven, like Madisonian pluralism, by interests, primarily economic. "Reasonable pluralism" converts differences from a threat to an accomplice of stability, co-opting them so that in the end they are eviscerated, absorbed into a consensus that requires smoothing off the rough, possibly irrational edges of differences. The crucial move is where Rawls locates differences and how he represents them.

Rawls introduces *Liberalism* as the remedy for the "unrealistic" aspect of his classic *Justice* and the restatement of its theory in the narrower form of a "political" rather than a "moral" conception (*PL*, xvi–xvii). As a moral theory, *Justice* belonged to the category of "comprehensive doctrines," which *Liberalism* now regards as the source of the political problem rather than the solution. A comprehensive doctrine is defined as covering "all recognized values and virtues within one rather precisely articulated system" (*PL*, xvi, 152, note 17). Although he notes that such doctrines may be philosophical, religious, or moral, the only doctrines he pauses over are the moral philosophies of utilitarianism and Kantianism. There is little or no allusion to the likes of democratic localists, socialists, radical feminists, Christian fundamentalists, Black Muslims, or Jewish Hasidim. Given his narrow representation of comprehensive doctrines, Rawls might have marginalized those doctrines that aim at imposing their comprehensive beliefs on society as a whole; instead he proceeds, first, by defining the problem as one of finding the proper basis for a "profoundly divided" liberal political society (*PL*, xxv). Liberal freedom is alleged to have spawned comprehensive belief systems that not only are in "doctrinal conflict" with one another but have "no prospect of resolution" (*PL*, xxviii). Fortunately, they are also "reasonable." The question then becomes, how to make a pluralism of comprehensive doctrines work so as to create a consensus that will ensure a stable cooperative society?

Rawls's solution to a problem whose contours are left vague and whose political importance is underdescribed is to exploit an alleged element of "reasonableness" common to some or most comprehensive doctrines and to declare that the sum of the parts equals an "overlapping consensus" of the whole. This is said to solve the problem of "how a well-ordered society can be unified and stable" (*PL*, 133–34). A consensus that appeals to all reasonable comprehensive doctrines will enable their adherents to share in the common rights and freedoms of equal citizens and, as we shall see, to become acculturated in the allegedly noncomprehensive doctrine of political liberalism.

Because it embodies the reasonable, liberalism is recommended as a noncomprehensive doctrine that is uniquely qualified to unify a doctrinally divided society. However, there appears to be a price exacted of some doctrines. As Rawls unfolds his conception of a society based on a consensus of reasonable doctrinaires, it seems less a theory than a strategy for establishing a liberal political hegemony. Citizens may expect "limits [on] their freedom to advance certain ways of life" (*PL*, 209). At the same time, their support of an overlapping consensus composed of reasonable comprehensive doctrines confirm not only that they have "sustained ways of life fully worthy of citizens' devoted allegiance" (*PL*, 209) but "this fact" should reassure them that the society is allowing space to worthy ways of life (*PL*, 210). Despite that space, however, those who subscribe to such doctrines are warned that they may have to allow some "leeway" so as to accommodate their teachings to the conclusions of public reason. A "reasonable and effective public conception" will eventually "bend comprehensive doctrines toward itself, shaping them if need be from unreasonable to reasonable" (*PL*, 246–47). At the same time that citizens are thus being pressed toward conformity, they are expected, if incongruously, to strive always to express "sincerity of opinion" (*PL*, 241–42).

The deeper significance of this formulation is that it reveals how a liberal society creates cultural pressures to restrain the individualism that forms so fundamental a part of *Liberalism*. In *Justice*, Rawls tried to juggle a concern for distributive justice with a severe conception of individual autonomy. "Each person," he wrote, "possesses an inviolability founded on justice that even the welfare of society as a whole cannot override" (*TJ*, 3). Although that position is reaffirmed in *Liberalism*, primarily as the priority of liberty and individual rights, Rawls wants nonetheless to combine that conception of a rights-sensitive, individualistic being with a stronger, more active civic being. This requires that he temper liberal egoism—"free and rational persons concerned to further their own interests" (*TJ*, 11)—which *Justice* used as a departure point. To make civic beings of those who were liberals before they were citizens requires that Rawls relax the inviolability of his individuals to render them permeable to, and malleable by, the influences of "tradition" and "culture."

How should a political theorist distribute his concern between the political and the theoretical? The obvious answer is, of course, to both. But it is not so easy to look inward and contemplate an order one is creating and then, looking outward, ponder not only its relationship to the public world but one's interpretation of that world. What is easy is to follow the "logic" of the inner order to a satisfactory conclusion and then, in ad hoc fashion, point to the contacts it establishes with one's representations of the external world.

Liberalism is described by Rawls as preoccupied with "a few long-standing classical problems" of "the grounds of the basic religious and political liberties and the basic rights of citizens in civil society" (*PL*, xxviii). He defends the omission of questions such as "democracy in the firm and the workplace . . . retributive justice . . . the environment," gender, or family by asserting that solutions to "the classical problems" can furnish an "outline" for addressing more recent questions (*PL*, xxviii–xxix). It does not turn on its potential for enabling us to see unsuspected connections in the world or to see familiar things in a new light but rather to see new things in a familiar light. The problems that attract Rawls are "internal" to his own theory rather than in the world; his concern is to fill in "the few missing pieces" in the earlier work. "Justice as fairness . . . [uses] a fundamental organizing idea within which all ideas and principles can be systematically related and connected" (*PL*, 9). His theory is preoccupied with its own theoreticalness, with looking inward.

But what are the implications of pursuing the ideal of theoretical completeness while looking outward and admitting that a liberal society will be plagued continuously by inequalities—inequalities that are inevitably translated into injustices? How does theory encompass simultaneously the contraries of an ideally just whole and a dirempted reality?

Rawls defends the character of his theory by saying that it "is abstract in the same way that the conception of a perfectly competitive market, or of general economic equilibrium, is abstract, that is, it singles out certain aspects as especially significant from the standpoint of political justice and leaves others aside" (*PL*, 154–55; see also 20). The issue is not, however, the uncontroversial point that a theorist may omit matters but whether the "standpoint" justifies omissions so damaging to the theory that they cannot afford to be included. Assuming that abstractness is not dictated solely by theoretical economies, decisions about what is to be excluded might represent a strategy for resolving what Rawls takes as his fundamental concern, "the conflicts implicit in the fact of reasonable pluralism." Or, it may be that his remark, "I don't think I really know why I took the course I did," is as much a tribute to his honesty as it is a revelation of liberalism unable to comprehend the political world it claims to address (*PL*, xxx). Political matters omitted from *Liberalism* include class structures, bureaucracy, military power in a liberal order that is constitutionalist and capitalist, economic institutions and their powers, the great question of how to limit drastically the control over public discourse exercised by corporate and governmental bodies, and the compatibility of the ethics and culture of capitalism with the ethics and culture of Rawlsian citizenship, let alone with democracy.

Given these excluded topics and the genuine divisiveness they imply, it is formulaic and empty to proclaim that in a democracy political power, which is always coercive power, is the power of the public, that is, "of free and equal citizens as a collective body" (*PL*, 216). If we ask how citizens actually exercise that awesome power, we are told, anticlimactically, "by voting and in other ways" (*PL*, 217–18). In fact, Rawls is interested not in the exercise of coercive power by the citizens but in the construction of a civics class in which all "should be ready to explain the basis of their actions to one another in terms each could reasonably expect the others might endorse as consistent with their freedom and equality" (*PL*, 218).

However, it is not merely contentious political problems that are omitted. Comprehensive doctrines that are deemed "unreasonable" are to be cordoned off. Thus, if there are "unreasonable and irrational doctrines," the recommended response is "to contain them so that they do not undermine the unity and justice of society" (*PL*, xvii).

That rationale could justify repressiveness, but the truly repressive elements are in Rawls's positive prescriptions rather than in his negative injunctions. The Rawlsian ideal is of a reasonable person who can accept reasonable disagreements "between persons who have realized their two moral powers to a degree sufficient to be free and equal citizens . . . and who have an enduring desire to know fair terms of cooperation and to be fully cooperating members of society" (*PL*, 55). But to modulate such a formulation by saying it is an ideal is either to say that it is politically problematic or to give a shocking response to the "real" pluralism of ghettoized populations, to the escapees who are enraged at being lumped with those they have left behind as well as at the bestowal of liberal "advantages," and to the remnants of the working class who see no place for themselves in a society where the liberal boast is that all are "in." To impose the bland ideal of reasonableness and to posit a "nonhistorical" original position from which to stipulate basic principles is to lobotomize the historical grievances of the desperate.

If that should seem too harsh, consider the following formulation in which Rawls attempts to fill in his principle that not all conceptions of the good should be allowed to be pursued but only those "ways of life worthy of citizens' devoted support." "Strong feelings" and "zealous aspirations," Rawls declares, do not justify a claim to "resources" or reshaping institutions to achieve "certain goals." "Desires and wants, however intense, are not in themselves reasons in matters of constitutional essentials and basic justice" (*PL*, 190).

Rawls does not pause over the possibility that "strong feelings" and "zealous aspirations" might be directly related to frustration on the part of those social classes and groups for whom the rhetoric and processes of "reasonable pluralism" have been least responsive. Instead, he seems to look forward to the elimination of the passions generated by oppression and neglect, apparently forgetting his own insight into the intractable existence of significant inequalities. Thus, by guaranteeing "primary goods" (basic rights and liberties, fair equality of opportunity, and minimum economic needs), "reasons of justice" can be detached "not only from the ebb and flow of primary wants and desires but even from sentiments and commitments" (*PL*, 190). Rawls would even impose an additional norm on public reason, the "burden of judgment." It emphasizes the difficulties that citizens face "in the ordinary course of political life." It reminds us that evidence is often conflicting and of uncertain weight, that our concepts are often vague and inadequate, and that our experiences are different (*PL*, 55–57).

Clearly, such considerations matter, but they are not neutral. The rhetoric of the desperate is likely to be a simplifying one, reflective of a condition reduced to essentials. A rhetoric of complexity, ever since Burke, has found favor with those whose expectations are secure. [. . . .]

Despite its numerous references to a concept of "the political," what is most wanting in *Liberalism* is an analysis of the current condition of the political and of the political prospects of liberalism itself. *Liberalism* needs a departure point such as the opening question of Emerson's essay *Experience*: "Where do we find ourselves?"

In the context of political philosophy and of a book with the title *Political Liberalism,* it is not tendentious to read Emerson's question as a political question: Where do we find ourselves politically? The question might then induce a philosopher to say whether his undertaking is intended primarily as a contribution to formal philosophy, whether formal philosophy means contextless (except for philosophy itself) and what sense it makes to talk about the contextless political, whether it will help us find who and where we are politically, and why we are where we are and why that is or is not importantly different from where and who we were.

It would not do for the philosopher to excuse himself, as Rawls does, saying that he has set aside questions of "gender and the family" because "the same equality of the Declaration of Independence that Lincoln invoked to condemn slavery can be invoked to condemn the inequality and oppression of women" (*PL,* xxix). Rawls might have felt sufficiently prodded by the Emerson protocol to reflect on why his particular formulations are at all responsive to the lapsed political condition of a society that has publicly endorsed those values for a very long time while disregarding or rejecting them in practice. Or, he might wonder what would be analogous to slavery in today's advanced economies of low wages, coerced overtime, and a permanent underclass.

By honoring Emerson's question, the political philosopher might help us to find our political selves or, at least, to find ourselves politically. To be able to do that would mean recognizing that, by itself, philosophy does not equip the philosopher to make his way around politics. Or, stated differently, philosophy does not become "political" simply because it treats political topics in a philosophical way; it becomes political when it gives evidence of grasping what is happening to the political world. Specifically, it would mean that the starting point for even a minimalist democrat should be the recognition that, considered broadly as a political project, democracy is out of synch with or opposed by virtually every dominant tendency in the American economy, cultural life, and politics.

In rebuttal, of course, the political philosopher can reject the Emersonian counsel to present a picture not of where we are politically but of what he wishes us to be politically (e.g., a "constitutional democracy"), and he may do it not by addressing us directly as actors but by constructing us as homunculi in an original position, reprogrammed to respond so that the philosopher may speak formally to other philosophers, seeking their approval of his "device of representation" rather than our gratitude for illuminating our condition.

The philosopher might justify his practice by saying that he is not in the business of empirical analysis or policy prescriptions but seeks instead a theoretical justification of the main principles that constitute the political. As Stuart Hampshire explains defensively in a review of *Liberalism,* the liberal philosopher "is not called upon to propose some general method of resolving casuistical problems of public policy."[9] That objection, perhaps licit under the conventions of philosophy, should be considered an evasion for the same reason that moves Hampshire's mild complaint that "the noise and muddle of actual politics are altogether absent" from *Liberalism.*[10]

To satisfy the Emersonian prerequisite, a political philosopher would be expected to provide not a detailed empirical analysis but rather an informed and thoughtful estimate of a condition. A model is available in Sir Thomas More's *Utopia,* the first part of which consists of a condensed critique of economic, social, and political practices of England; the second part, "Utopia" proper, details the institutional background and political and moral principles that were offered as remedies for the unjust condition exposed in the first part. Ironically, although utopia literally means "nowhere" and More playfully locates it in no specific part of the world, it is firmly grounded in a critical analysis.

For his part, Rawls postulates a nowhere that is oxymoronic, a "well-ordered democratic society." His society "is to be viewed as a complete and closed social system . . . [with no] relations with other societies . . . [and] where we will lead a complete life" (*PL*, 40–41). Without a gesture acknowledging the human beings streaming across our southern borders, Rawls adopts a starting point, although imaginary, that is harsh, even claustrophobic: "It is also closed . . . in that entry into it is only by birth and exit from it is only by death. We have no prior identity before being in society" (*PL*, 40–41).

Although it may serve the purposes of a formal theory to posit a closed society with *a* tradition and a citizenry informed by *the* public political culture, these erasive monochromes are not hospitable to democracy. In Rawls's closed polity, all of politics seems centered in one abstract public space whose vast dimensions are never a problem. The result is a curious asymmetry. For Rawls, those spatial dimensions preclude, without argument, participatory democracy as a serious alternative, but they do not prevent Rawls from levying a series of stringent moral demands and ideals of reasonableness that presuppose closer, more intimate relationships of the kind that localized democracy might well foster but surely a highly bureaucratized, market-driven society would not.

Where Rawls most resembles More is to the credit of neither. His ideal world is the realized yearning for a frictionless polity. If the constitutional guarantees are "secure," Rawls assures us, no basic conflict "is likely to arise" that would justify opposition to his political conception as a whole. Institutions should be framed, he opines, "so that intractable conflicts are unlikely to arise" (*PL*, 154–56). While claiming that his concern is not with the actual world, Rawls repeatedly invokes the practices commonly identified with his own society.

The result is a construction that claims merely to be that of a free-standing society but is, in actuality, a utopia in the pejorative sense, an ideological project whose author is unaware that he has fashioned a disguisement instead of a solution.

Notes

1. For a discussion on the importance of reason and speech in democratic politics, see Thomas Spragens, *Reason and Democracy* (Durham: Duke University Press, 1990).

2. See *The Philosophical Discourse of Modernity: Twelve Lectures* (Cambridge, Mass.: MIT Press, 1987), chap. 1.

3. See *Reason and the Rationalization of Society*, trans. Thomas McCarthy (Boston: Beacon Press, 1984), 10–11.

4. For an effort to apply discursive democracy, see John Dryzek, *Democracy in Capitalist Times* (New York: Oxford University Press, 1996).

5. F. I. Michelman, "Conceptions of Democracy in American Constitutional Argument: Voting Rights," *Florida Law Review* 41, no. 3 (July 1989): 446f.

6. F. I. Michelman, 446f.

7. Cf. *The Basic Law of the Federal Republic of Germany,* article 20, sec. 2.

8. Jeremy Waldron, "Justice Revisited: Rawls Turns Towards Political Philosophy," *Times Literary Supplement* (No. 4707), 18 June 1983, 5–6, at 5.

9. Stuart Hampshire, "Liberalism: The New Twist," *New York Review of Books,* 12 August 1993, 43–47, at 44–45.

10. Stuart Hampshire, 46.

10

PUSHING FOR INCLUSION

For the ancient Greeks, democracy means the rule of the many as opposed to the rule of one or a few, but it does not require something like a universal franchise with political rights accorded equally to everyone. That construction of democracy remained robust until recently when excluded groups demanded full citizenship and the franchise was extended to them. At the minimum, calls for inclusion initially meant the political rights available to citizens (usually propertied, white men), such as voting and holding office, should be open to those who had been excluded. This is the thrust of women suffragettes in the nineteenth and early twentieth centuries. For them, women deserve the same rights as men and for the same reason that men want rights: everyone is entitled to find his or her own sphere. It is not good enough, they argue, that women be represented by their fathers, husbands, or sons. With an exuberant optimism, they expect that with the vote, the condition of women will change positively.[1]

In the late twentieth century, Anne Phillips sees inclusion requiring more. She finds that the gendered division of labor, as witnessed in the family, at home, at work, and elsewhere in society, "has political consequences." For this reason, she wants to pay attention to the details of social practice as a means of asking more sweeping questions about equality and participation. Details matter to Phillips because she sees them affecting all kinds of outlooks, practices, opportunities, and obstacles. In particular, they shape the way people conceive of politics; whether citizens are actually or only formally free; whether an authentic participatory politics is possible; and whether the concerns of women are taken seriously and occupy an important place on the political agenda. This means that many areas once thought to be outside of politics should be explicitly politicized. For Phillips, all sites of power need to be challenged openly and persistently in order to realize the dual promise of democracy as equality and freedom for all citizens.

Cornel West also speaks to questions of inclusion in his interrogation of welfare state liberal and conservative approaches to race. Here he finds that neither of these traditions

251

adequately addresses the issue of race. Accordingly, he wants us to think differently when we talk about race in a country with democratic aspirations. This means it is necessary to address the flaws of society at large as well as reexamine our commitment to equality. For him, the very way we continue to think about this issue in American society is itself a symptom of the profound cleavages that continue to divide citizens from each other. Contemporary responses to the condition of African-American communities have followed a pattern of partial solutions or the selective delegation of blame. Yet neither response, according to West, manages to challenge those perceptions that situate racial communities outside of the national community. The *de facto* segregation of the races illuminates the extent to which America proceeds as if the fate of people of color can still be seen as distinct from the fate of the white community. At the same time, the recent decline in the political commitment to collective goods has coincided with a collapse of various social networks that once provided a sense of connectedness among marginalized groups that now fall victim to fragmentation, isolation, and despair. In order to counter the destructive impact that these trends have upon all citizens, West calls for a reinvigoration of our common goals and a new generation of creative and engaged leadership. He also wants to move beyond interest group politics and anticipates the human rights arguments advanced by several democratic theorists from the third world.

Iris Marion Young enters this discussion to notice that the universal extension of equal legal and political rights remains one of the great accomplishments of human history. Yet just as this ideal is finding its fullest expression in developed democracies, we encounter a set of movements that emerge to challenge the desirability of the principle of uniform equal treatment. What many groups find in the drive toward universal standards is a set of oppressive representations and practices that serve to protect rather than diminish inequality by disguising the ways in which democratic societies unequally distribute privileges and burdens. For Young, a more comprehensive model of justice must allow for the different treatment of historically oppressed groups organized around an alternative understanding of equality. Here, efforts to confront institutionalized and sometimes unconscious forms of inequality call for a democratic cultural pluralism where the universal principles of equality are preserved but also supplemented by a set of procedural protections for the cultural integrity and material interests of systematically disadvantaged groups. These protections, she argues, should take the form of group representation as the best means of countering some of the unjust features of current political arrangements.

READINGS

ANNE PHILLIPS, SELECTION FROM *ENGENDERING DEMOCRACY* (1991)

[I]t may not much matter if what is at issue is the equalization of men and women in the national legislature or local or state government. If they are only given the chance, there will always be a pool of women who make themselves available for election, some by extraordinary efforts of combining politics and children and work, others by remaining childless, others by having well-paid jobs and being able to purchase domestic help. But if democracy is to mean more than the opportunity to vote in periodic elections and the equal right to stand as candidates, it has to involve a more substantial degree of participation, and more genuine openness, regardless of sex, race or class. We might hesitate before the kind of mean-spirited hypothetical that permits only one choice for change, but equalizing the distribution of responsibilities and time in each household will surely figure as a candidate on the list. If men and women are to be political equals in any more substantial sense than the equal right to vote, then this *is* a key condition.

This is part then of what feminism has to contribute to the debates on democracy: the importance of transforming the familial, domestic, 'private' sphere; of laying the groundwork for a democratic society by democratizing sexual relations in the home. But the arguments so far follow a well-worn track, extending established connections between social and political life. Equality in the household is being presented as a means to an end, as a necessary condition for what we really want, which is democracy in the wider sphere. To this extent, the argument does not capture the full flavour of 'the personal is political.' Taking an analogy from more general debates between socialists and feminists, it is as if the equality of the sexes is being promoted because it has been discovered that it contributes to the development of socialism, but is not valued as an end in itself. Yet the personal is political has usually meant more than that the personal *affects* the political; even in its most sober guises, it is saying that the personal is political too. The second meaning attached to the slogan is thus one that stresses the ubiquity of power. Never mind the learning process, never mind the equalization of time, never mind the cumulative effects of household equality on political participation outside. Democracy is *as* important in the household as anywhere else, for in the household there is unequal power.

Power As All Pervasive

It is frequently noted that each new wave of feminism has to rediscover what previous generations found out, and that, in a pattern that seems to bury all the earlier contributions, each period thinks itself unique. Bearing this in mind, I will nonetheless hazard a comment. When the women's movement re-emerged in the late 1960s, it was particularly insistent on women's unhappiness in the family—through boredom, lack of control and because of violence. While the external world of jobs and pay and media and politics figured significantly in campaigns and on the agenda of demands, the more burning preoccupations were often closer to home. In the consciousness raising groups that were so vital in this period, women began to grapple with their sense of identity and frustration, and, as Sheila Rowbotharn describes in her account of the British movement, moved from a puzzled indictment of men's emotional incapacity and women's emotional dependence to a starker sense of coercion and control (1989, 6–10). Men and women were supposed to be related through love, but sexuality seemed to be distorting our relations with those who were not our lovers and bringing vulnerability and pain with those who were. Heterosexual love began to look like a trap. Stripped of its romantic gloss, the family began to emerge as a site of male power, a power that in its more benign aspects got women working excessively long hours for minimal reward, and in its worst could expose them to physical and sexual abuse. The family was no haven in a heartless world, the lover no guarantee of harmony or bliss.

This harsher view of family and sexual relations carried with it a more pervasive definition of power. Many had thought of problems they had with husbands or lovers in terms of individual psychology—maybe we're not compatible? maybe I want what's impossible? maybe he just doesn't care?—but in the process of exploring individual experiences, they came to identify general patterns of power. Feminists then disagreed profoundly over who was responsible (was it men or capitalism or structures or roles?) but were reasonably united in stressing the subordination of women in the home. In relation to democracy, this implied a good deal more than the idea that equality in the household is a condition for democracy in the state. It was not just that women were prevented from participating in external activities by the pressures and constraints of the home; women's impotence and subordination, their submission and dependence, crucially mattered in themselves. The personal was *as* political as anything else, and as devastatingly destructive of our human development as anything that governments could do.

This broader conception of power has been cited as one of feminism's major innovations, and those theorists who have focused attention on the different spaces within which democracy is required often make their bow towards women for their help in changing the agenda. Samuel Bowles and Herbert Gintis, for example, commend the women's movement for identifying the heterogeneity of power and for reminding us that domination is no respecter of place. Placing it in the broad tradition of 'radical democracy' in which they locate themselves, they link it with a rather ragbag assortment of deviants: 'the seventeenth-century leveller, the nineteenth-century chartists and agrarian populists, and the twentieth-century feminists and advocates of worker councils' (1986, 8). All these, they argue, have conceived of politics as a matter of 'becoming,' as something which cannot be reduced to a bid for resources but which involves transforming the very interests it pursues. The other common denominator is that all have viewed oppression as multi-layered, spanning the family, economy and state. For Bowles and Gintis, there will be many arenas in which democracy is vital. Concentrating on contemporary Western societies, they select out three crucial sites: the liberal democratic state, the capitalist economy, and the patriarchal family. The issue of domination arises wherever there is a 'socially consequential yet democratically unaccountable power' (101); where these two come together, there is a case for democratization.

All this makes it sound a good deal simpler than it is and leaves us with some uneasy questions about the differences between democratizing the family, household or community, democratizing the workplace, and democratizing the state. The democratization of the workplace, for example, can occur through state intervention, through legislation that requires firms to set up decision-making structures that will involve employees or their representatives, that dictates the nature and range of decisions that must be put to the employees, or, more ambitiously, that enforces a transfer of ownership to the workers. The 'democratization of everyday life' is not open to the same kind of process. We can perhaps imagine the kind of decision-making structures that would equalize power within the household, but would we welcome the household inspectorate whose job it might be to enforce them? In the first case, we can regulate for democracy. In the second, we are calling on participants to take democracy into their own hands. It is one thing to say that both spheres are characterized by democratically unaccountable power, but once we turn to what might be the democratic solutions, there are important distinctions of kind.

Among critics of contemporary feminism, the main distinction is to do with scale of significance, and the questions are designed with pathetic intent. How can equalizing the decisions over who changes the nappies be comparable with equal rights to vote? This is a game that anyone can play, and the more fruitful line of enquiry is whether an over-assimilation of the personal and political endangers what is positive about private life. Carole Pateman signalled an early qualification when she noted that 'the interdependence of the personal and the political can be recognized, as can the fact that any relationship can, in certain circumstances, have political effects, but this is not the same as arguing that the criteria and principles that should order our interactions and decision-making as citizens should be exactly the same as those that should underlay our relationships with friends and lovers' (1975, 467). More polemically and critically, Jean Bethke Elshtain has presented 'the personal is political' as an outrageous slogan of radical feminism and one that teems with totalitarian intent. 'Note,' she says, 'that the claim is not that the personal and political are interrelated in important and fascinating ways previously hidden to us by sexist ideology and practice; nor that the personal and the political may be analogous to one another along certain axes of power and privilege, but that the personal *is* political' (1981, 217). This simple equation, she argues, denies what are important distinctions between one kind of activity and another and blurs everything into ramifications of the same masculine power. 'The social world from top to bottom, is one long, unmediated conduit permeated throughout by male oppression of the female, whether the male is defined as a natural aggressor, a demon, a member of the universal male sex-class, or a simple oppressor who throughout history has taken advantage of his superior physical strength' (212). Public and private are collapsed into one, leaving no area of human existence that is deemed to exist outside of politics and no exemptions from political control.

Elshtain argues this in the context of a sustained critique of existing divisions between public and private, and in particular of the way that liberalism recast these as determinedly separate spheres. The result, she suggests, was disastrous. Into the public sphere went all the rationality of prudential calculation; while the private soaked up the sentimental remains. The conceptual links between politics and the familial were severed, and politics became defined as the most crass individualism, something that began and ended 'with mobilization of resources, achieving maximum impacts, calculating prudentially, articulating interest group claims, engaging in reward distribution functions' (Elshtain 1981, 246). The heart went out of politics. The triumph of individualism emptied the public sphere of most of what politics should be about, while the pressure to extend individualist or contractarian principles into the innermost chambers of the private sphere threatens what deeper humanity still remains. This, she believes, is where the dangers of radical feminism come in, for in its simple equations of personal and political, it encourages the very worst tendencies in the modern world.

As many of her feminist critics have noted, Elshtain retains a sanguine view of the family (see, for example, Ehrenreich 1983; Siltanen and Stanworth 1984; Stacey 1986). 'I begin,' she says in *Public Man, Private Woman,* 'with an affirmation: familial ties and modes of child-rearing are essential to establish the minimal foundations of human, social existence' (1981, 326). Collective forms of childcare are said to sacrifice the child to the career of the mother and, while she indicates some sympathy with current notions of shared parenting, she gives no attention to any mechanisms that might bring this about. If feminists go down the 'me too' road of selfish rights and interests (dumping their children in institutionalized care, making a child's life a misery by squabbling with the father over who does most work) then instead of providing us with an alternative vision of society, they will be capitulating to the very forces that limit and coarsen our life.

Jean Bethke Elshtain's argument barely engages with the difficult conditions in which many children grow up: the resentments and depressions of isolated mothers; the enveloping swathes of a maternal love that can find no other object; the absence or indifference of too many fathers; the poverty of families living on only one income. I can think of few feminists who claim to have found the answer, but this hardly justifies giving up on the question. As Judith Stacey notes, 'Elshtain appears uninterested in, even hostile to, the subject of male domination . . . She rarely seems to comprehend what all the feminist fuss is about' (1986, 232). The family is equated with the private, and the private with personal life, and in her main point of contact with classical liberalism (which otherwise is an object of critique), Elshtain seeks to defend this private world from the excesses of politicization.

Her own version of the distinction between public and private rests on a notion of *activities* that are different. It is not that politics exists 'out there' in a recognizable space of its own, but that some things we do are political and other things we do are not. If we drift into thinking that everything in our lives is a political problem, then we lay ourselves open to thinking everything has a political solution. 'Part of the struggle,' she observes, 'involves reflecting on whether our current misery and unhappiness derive entirely from faulty and exploitative social forms that can, and therefore must, be changed or whether a large part of that unhappiness derives from the simple fact of being human, therefore limited, knowing that one is going to die' (Elshtain 1981, 301). This kind of comment can always be a recipe for complacency, and Elshtain's defense of the family can be faulted along such lines. As long as the seemingly intimate relations between men and women (or parents and children) are structured by state regulation, economic conditions and patriarchal power, then these relations are already politicized whether we want it or no. Elshtain's warning therefore carries only a residual weight. Difficult as it is to know where to draw the distinction (is poverty just part of being human? is frustration just evidence that we want too much?), there will be some things in life that must be left up to us, either to change, or simply accept. If we treat the personal as thoroughly identical to the political, we run the twin risks of believing our lives can be made perfect (with all the associated unhappiness when the belief proves ill-founded) and of handing over to others the responsibility for making them so.

A Woman's Right to Choose

Jean Bethke Elshtain is centrally concerned with combating what she sees as feminist attacks on the family. Ironically perhaps, the problems she identifies have arisen most directly in relation to abortion. The contemporary women's movement has tended to see a woman's right to abortion—her right to decide for herself whether or not to continue with a pregnancy—as the quintessentially feminist demand. A woman who cannot choose what is done with her body is no better than a slave; how could anyone else claim to make this decision? Yet almost as soon as it was articulated, 'a woman's right to choose' became a source of anxiety. It was such a defiant assertion of individual rights, such a refusal of social intervention. In most of the issues that have provoked feminist campaigns, the division between public and private was being identified as a crucial element in the subordination of women, something that excused society from its responsibilities for caring for the young and old, that confined women to a (lesser) realm they had not chosen to inhabit and, in such phrases as 'the Englishman's home is his castle,' legitimated domestic violence. Over abortion, feminism seemed to be going the opposite way.

The slogan chanted on many demonstrations—'not the church and not the state, women must decide their fate'—claimed absolute autonomy for women in choosing whether or not to bear a child and derived much of its power from the widely shared belief that having babies is a private affair. In the USA, the crucial case of *Roe v. Wade* was settled by reference to a woman's right of privacy, which in the words of the Supreme Court was 'broad enough to encompass a woman's decision whether or not to terminate her pregnancy' (cited in Petchesky 1986, 290). As Rosalind Petchesky notes, this was not meant to vindicate a woman's right to choose, for the 1973 decision gave the doctor responsibility for making the choice and reserved to the state a right to intervene (to prohibit abortion) at later stages in the pregnancy. That said, the legal decision that did most to extend the availability of abortion to U.S. women was based on a notion of the individual as autonomous in the private sphere. And in 1989, when this availability was being challenged in all quarters and state after state was introducing more restrictive legislation, the notion of abortion being a matter for the women themselves still retained amazing support. A national survey conducted by the *Los Angeles Times* revealed that, while 61 percent of Americans thought abortion morally wrong and a stunning 57 percent considered it murder, nonetheless 74 percent of respondents believed abortion was a decision that must be made by each woman for herself (cited in Dworkin 1989).

Feminists have long been uneasy with the implications. Commenting on the breadth of support for a woman's right to decide for herself whether to have an abortion or not, Susan Himmelweit suggests that 'the popularity of the idea of private choice in reproduction is a reflection and acceptance of the existing division,' in which having babies is a private, and of course female, concern (1980, 67). People respond readily enough because it fits with their existing convictions—and yet these convictions themselves are part of what feminism has attacked. The case for greater social provision for children, for example, has often been argued on the grounds that children are *not* exclusively their mother's concern. With the exception of babies conceived by artificial insemination by donor, each child has both a father and a mother, so why is it only the latter who takes care of the child? Each child will grow up to contribute to the society, so why doesn't society do more to help? The modern counter-argument can all too easily be fuelled by the woman's right to choose whether or not to have babies: 'well, you chose to have them, so stop complaining and get on with the job.' It is hard (though not impossible) to argue both cases simultaneously, hard to call on fathers and/or society to shoulder more responsibility for those children who are born, and yet in the same breath deny the fathers or society any voice in making the decision.

For some socialist feminists, the argument then becomes contingent on the social arrangements for bringing up children. Thus as long as society makes the woman responsible for nurture and care and support, no one other than the woman can decide. But if and when societies do assume responsibility for the welfare of children, she can no longer claim this right. Once her 'private' choice has clearly 'public' effects—when, for example, her decision to have ten children instead of one means a substantial redirection of social resources—then we cannot say it is entirely her affair. It is worth noting (and is an indication of how strongly feminists have felt on the issue of abortion) that even here the examples given are usually of women who want more children not fewer. In this future scenario in which the care of children has become a social concern, the issue raised is not so much whether a woman can be forced to continue with a pregnancy that she does not want, but whether she can freely choose more children than the norm. Even among feminists who regard the right to choose as contingent on social conditions, the fact that it is women's bodies in which pregnancies occur remains a disturbing factor.

The issues of reproductive choice have generated much thoughtful literature (see, for example, Petchesky 1986 and Birke et al. 1990) and a lot of this revolves around the relationship between public and private and the extent to which any decision can be a matter for one individual alone. With further developments in reproductive technology, new dilemmas arise. Should, for example, a woman have the right to abort a foetus that happens to be of the wrong sex? Should a woman have the right to 'rent' out her womb as a surrogate mother? Are these also dimensions of 'a woman's right to choose'? There is no consensus on these questions, and within feminism there has been a strong antiliberal tendency that has argued against certain kinds of choice (see Corea 1985).

Many maintain, however, that even in the best of all possible worlds, certain aspects of reproductive and sexual relations will remain irreducibly personal affairs. 'Can we really imagine,' asks Rosalind Petchesky, 'the social conditions in which we would be ready to renounce control over our bodies and reproductive lives to give over the decision as to whether, when and with whom we will bear children to the "community as a whole"?' (1986, 13). If women are not free to make such choices for themselves, then they are being compelled into pregnancy and childbirth and this 'is incompatible with the existence of women as moral agents and social beings' (388). To link this with the arguments developed by Carole Pateman, a womb is not something that can be rented out like a house, or taken under legal charge by a judge who decides a foetus must live. The body is part of the self, and it is only the extraordinary male conceptions of the individual that could ever have conceived of them as so separate and distinct.

If abortion is the testing ground for dissolving all differences between public and private, then most feminists fail. When it comes down to it, they do want to retain distinctions between some areas or activities that are open to public decision and others that should remain personal concerns. The argument does not usually depend on how democratically public decisions are made, for women will want to retain control over certain aspects of their lives no matter how impressive the procedures have become. At the same time, however, feminists have wanted to challenge the enforced separation between public and private, and though this may sound too much like having one's cake and eating it, it is not, in fact, inconsistent. As Iris Marion Young has argued (1987), there ought to be certain aspects of our lives from which we are entitled to exclude others, about which we can say they are nobody's affair but our own. (We will argue endlessly about what fits into this category, but that is not to say the category itself is absurd.) Equally important, however, is that there should be no aspect of our lives which we are compelled to keep private. There is no inconsistency, for example, in saying that our sexuality should be our private concern but that homophobia should be on the public agenda. In similar vein, there is no inconsistency in saying that abortion is a decision we must make for ourselves, but that the treatment of children should be a public concern.

Most feminist writing implies a distinction of sorts between public and private—and the fact that Kate Millett is so often invoked as the example of what not to do suggests that there are not too many to choose from who have abandoned all distinction! In terms of democracy, this means that the sphere of sexual and family relations cannot be treated in exactly the same way as the sphere of work or the sphere of conventional politics. First, there are some decisions that must be regarded as an individual and not a social affair, and under any conditions that I can envisage, a woman's right to decide for herself whether or not to continue with a pregnancy remains the clearest example of this. When women are denied access to abortion, they are being denied the freedom to make this choice themselves, and are being treated as if their bodies belonged to somebody else. Democracy is not supposed to coexist with slavery, and no society can present itself as fully democratic if it compels women into unwanted pregnancy and childbirth. This seems to me indisputable, but it is worth noting that this version of democracy has a markedly liberal tone.

In the more mundane (if often more pressing) areas of who cleans the house and who cooks the meals, the women's movement has certainly said that democracy should be extended to the private sphere. People rarely make any formal analogy between the equal right to vote in elections and an equal say in household affairs: it is hardly a question of secret ballots on who cleans the bathroom, or formal majorities on what to have for tea. But when women have noted that men presume the authority to take major decisions because they bring in the money on which the household survives, there are strong resonances of what is a classic argument for democracy. Income and wealth should be entirely irrelevant; each individual should have an equal voice. (Women also, of course, argue that incomes should be equalized, and query the complacent formalism of liberal ideas. But the claim on equal standing in household decisions is not made to depend on this.)

Anything that is a decision should be taken by equals. Things that have been taken for granted as if they were ordained by nature should be decided by open discussion and mutual consent. It should not be assumed, for example, that there is a particular division of labour between the sexes: that the woman cleans the house and the man cleans the car; that the woman gives up her job when a baby is born; that the man's occupation is always more important; that the whole family moves when he gets a new job. All these should enter the realm of democratic discussion, to be treated as matters of choice. It is part of the success of the women's movement—and simultaneously of the strength of what the movement must contest—that household inequalities do not depend only on men asserting their authority, but as often as not on men and women sharing an uncritical consensus about how things should be. Even so, interviews with women workers continue to throw up the comment that 'my husband wouldn't let me work while the baby was young' or 'my husband would never allow me to work nights.' Important decisions are still taken by men.

On abortion, women have demanded the right to take a decision by themselves and not be dictated to by what others say or do. But in other aspects, too, there is a limit to how much we can assimilate private and public spheres. 'Household' democracy, in particular, is not really a matter of regulation, imposition, guarantee. There are all kinds of social intervention that can help make relations between the sexes more democratic, and various ways in which public policy or public resources can contribute to a process of change. The provision of refuges and affordable accommodation can give more women a choice about leaving relationships that are beyond redemption; changes in the hours that men and women work can increase the chances for equalizing the distribution of household tasks; changes in the practices of mortgage companies, landlords and insurance offices can give women more of a say. All these can empower women, making it more possible for them to claim their place as equals and encouraging the practices of democracy in the home. None of these, however, can dictate what goes on between lovers or husbands and wives—and with the exception of bodily injury, most people prefer it this way. At the end of the day, what happens will depend on the individuals themselves, on how much they insist on change.

Means and Ends

This is no news to the women's movement, and indeed it is much of what 'the personal is political' has meant to feminists over the last twenty years. Part of the slipperiness of the slogan is that it takes us out of our personal preoccupations and experiences, and simultaneously lets us treat these experiences as the political centre of our life. Thus, on the one hand, it has helped women see that what they thought of as peculiar to themselves (personal, unique and perhaps basically their fault) may be part of a general pattern of sexual relations that is then available to political change. On the other hand, it gives women the confidence to claim the kind of changes they can already make (refusing to cook the dinner or type the leaflet, maybe even throwing him out) as politically important. Politics then becomes something other than procedures or rules or programmes for change. It is what we do in our everyday life.

Politics had become associated with alien or grandiose concerns, either because it was thought to happen in particular places (from which women were absent), or because it dealt with matters of earth-shattering importance (on which women could have nothing to say). Contemporary feminism has challenged this, theoretically in terms of the abstract way men have thought about power, and practically in saying politics has no integrity until it is grounded in everyday life. Drawing attention to the detailed texture of our daily lives, 'the personal is political' has claimed a continuum between those things that were previously considered the most trivial and minor and those to which the term politics could be confidently attached. But instead of referring to a particular place (the household), this version of 'the personal' stresses aspects that will be present in every activity, no matter where or when it takes place. This is perhaps the most characteristic of all the meanings associated with the slogan and the one that will be most familiar to those who have been active in the women's movement over the last decades. What implications does it have for democracy?

When women in the civil rights or socialist movement said the personal was political, part of what they were stressing was the relationship between means and end. There was something pretty suspect about organizations that could see themselves as dedicated to liberation but treated the women involved as if they had no abilities or minds of their own. The ideals were being subverted by the daily practice, and yet most men seemed to think this a silly complaint. The new women's movement was convinced that it did indeed matter and consistently emphasized the ways women related to one another as a crucial part of what the movement was about. You could not claim to be involved in a politics of liberation if you unthinkingly exploited other people's time and energies and continually put people down. The division of labour mattered, so did inequalities in confidence or capacities, and so did any separation into leaders and led. Feminism meant thinking about all these issues, regarding the way you organized as something that was as important and revealing as your goals. [. . . .]

The Public Arena

When Hannah Arendt defines politics in terms of the pursuit of public happiness or the taste for public freedom, she is employing a terminology almost the opposite to that adopted within the contemporary women's movement, though anyone who has experienced the heady delights of political involvement will have some inkling of what she means. The impulse that drives people into an endless round of meetings, demonstrations and discussion groups must be more than the imperative of material need, and leaving aside those cases where politics has become a career, it fits in some way with a taste for 'public freedom.' When people complain that they cannot arouse others from their private affairs—when, for example, an exhaustive leafleting of twenty streets has produced only one new face at the meeting—their despair echoes Arendt's ideals. Few of us may live up to her other definition of politics as the striving for excellence 'regardless not only of social status and administrative office but even of achievement and congratulation' (1963, 280), but again we probably know what she means. Certainly the women's movement was quick to spot the distracting appeals of the 'star system' and to query the good faith of those whose political involvement seemed a route to public acclaim.

Yet in most ways the principles of republican democracy seem antagonistic to women's movement concerns. None of its theorists is an enthusiast for dissolving the boundaries between public and private, or for transforming the way decisions are made in every arena of social life. Those who have devoted their energies to democratizing the 'little world' of factory or office or community are at best patronized for their limited ambitions, and at worst criticized for a dangerous distraction. There seems no obvious bridge between this and feminist perspectives. When women argue that 'democratic ideals and politics have to be put into practice in the kitchen, the nursery and the bedroom' (Pateman 1983, 216) they are pointing in just the opposite direction.

Feminists have criticized the orthodox division between public and private, presenting a powerful and radical challenge to existing notions of democracy. They have broadened our understanding of the preconditions for democratic equality, and brought into the discussion the sexual division of labour at home and at work. They have challenged (though with some important reservations) the notion that what goes on in private is a private concern, and made what seems an unanswerable case for democratizing relations and decisions in the home. They have enlarged our conception of the practices that are relevant, pulling into the orbit of democracy the way we talk to one another, the way we organize, the way we write. They have attached themselves to a vision of democracy as something that matters in every detail and wherever we are. With all these wonderful extensions, do feminists remain stuck in what Sheldon Wolin (1982, 28) considers the politics of their own backyard?

The question is posed most starkly by those who accuse feminists of collapsing into the cosiness of inter-personal dynamics, and who cite as examples the counter-cultural focus on lifestyle politics, or the more recent growth of feminist therapies. In either case, the equation of the personal with the political is said to have legitimated women in retreating from political concerns. In the first instance, women abandoned their efforts at changing the world and chose to live out an exclusive alternative with those of like mind. The rhetoric might sound defiant and, if we take Mary Daly as a possible exemplar, claimed a more risky and less compromised existence than that available to those who continued to engage with the masculine world. But it hardly mattered whether the choice was expressed in the cloying language of wonderful women or the angry denunciation of patriarchy and men. Whichever it was, women had stepped out of the political arena to build their strength in an alternative world. In the case of feminist therapies, women were said to be turning even further in on themselves. Here there was not even the pretence of constructing a different kind of world: just an unhealthy obsession with the problems of self.

These aspects of contemporary feminism have very little to do with democracy, beyond perhaps a shared language of partnership or discussion. But they are also so far from exhausting what the women's movement is about that I do not find this particularly disturbing. The more troublesome issues arise where the women's movement has clearly engaged with democratic concerns. Where there is an explicit focus on democracy, feminism has tended to associate itself with those who argue for a revitalized and reconstituted civil society. Few have noticed, fewer still commented on, the division that is growing up between those who emphasize civil society as the focus for democratic development and those who stress the state or, more broadly, the public sphere (for one exception, see Pierson 1989). For those in the first camp, the main focus will be on the layer of social activity that is intermediate between the personal, or individual, and the state. They will aim to multiply therefore the contexts in which people can choose to assert control over their lives, contexts which include our places of work but also community-based centres and voluntary organizations. As John Keane puts it, in a list that makes direct overtures to feminism: 'the self-governed enterprise, the democratic trade union, the rape crisis centre, the gay and lesbian collective, the housing co-operative, and other public spheres of civil society' (1988a, 145). This seems very close to what feminists have been saying and doing over the last twenty years. It extends the principles of participation out of their previous workplace confines and projects a notion of democracy as something that should permeate every social activity and sphere. But, implicitly or explicitly, it suggests that democracy is a matter of building blocks: the more we have the better the edifice will be. In this sense, it dodges the relationship between particular and general and denies any peculiarity about a public sphere.

Writers like Arendt or Wolin would, by contrast, claim a qualitative leap from the specific to the general and would say that however democratic we are in running our rape crisis centre, we are not yet engaged in politics per se. Politics arises only when we are faced with people who are different and have to work out with them our common and shared concerns. Or, as Benjamin Barber puts it, 'essential contestability is the premise of politics' (1984, 57), and politics only happens when we do not agree. This criterion alone will not dismiss the rape crisis centre from the realm of politics, for disagreement may be furious and any decisions strongly contested. But think of the next stage up. Members from the centre attend a meeting of the elected council which controls local finances, in order to put their case for funding. Here they represent just one among many demands on resources and can only put their case as effectively and clearly as possible, making sure all councillors know what the issues are. Obviously they would hope that some of the councillors would volunteer to further their cause, but if all the elected members went in with their votes fixed (each one nobbled beforehand by some group), the meeting would be a depressing occasion. Discussion would be desultory and irrelevant, and each vote would have been decided in advance. The groups with no automatic allies in the council (this would very likely include the crisis centre) would complain bitterly, for they would have been deprived of their chance to influence the meeting and win new support to their side. And on any definition of democracy, their complaints would surely be justified. We do not want politics reduced to a mere counting of numbers, with all decisions sewn up in advance. Imagine that someone from the centre was also an elected member of the council: most people would hope she could stand back a bit from the centre's interests and not just campaign on a single concern. We would expect her decisions on the council to be influenced by the knowledge and experience she brought from the rape crisis centre, but we would not want her to be a cipher for a single group and unable to connect with other concerns.

As in the preceding discussion of the representation of women, it is important to separate out two aspects. The first is the desirability of ensuring that our representatives include people from previously marginalized groups: there are all too many councils on which no one person understands what a rape crisis centre involves. But the second is that there are levels of representation, and that failing to acknowledge these would collapse all levels of decision-making into one. There is a connection, and some continuity, between the specific and the general, but there is also an important and distinctive shift. When the small collective that produces a feminist newsletter struggles to work in democratic fashion, its members are learning the kind of confidence, competence and respect for the opinions of others that will help them change for the better any other organization to which they subsequently belong. In this sense, every democratized forum in civil society is a kind of building block out of which we get democracy as a whole; and the more there are, the better things will be. But there are also things that the members of the collective will have to *un*learn in a different situation. Small collectives often generate an all-enveloping enthusiasm, in which nothing else seems of comparable importance or worth. This is not a helpful attitude to carry into a wider arena, for it can prematurely close debate or understanding. We cannot, and should not, be expected to 'leave ourselves behind' when we enter the political arena, but we ought nonetheless to be able to look at ourselves in a different kind of light. In this sense, extending democracy is not just about democratizing all our practices in every aspect of our lives. There remains a distinction between the general and the particular, and it is important not to blur this divide.

For a variety of reasons, then, I am arguing that we *do* need a distinction between private and public, and that rather than abandoning this distinction, the emphasis should be on uncoupling it from the division between women and men. First, there are some decisions which will remain individual ones, and no matter how thoroughly democratized public debate and decision-making may become, there are matters we will want to reserve to ourselves. The clearest example of this is a woman's decision about continuing or terminating a pregnancy, but a less gender-specific example might be the choices we make about our sexuality. Second, even within the much larger category of decisions where a number of people are involved and each is then entitled to an equal voice, there is a distinction between spheres within which democracy can be imposed and spheres within which it should be enabled. If we take the simplest definition of democracy as saying that everyone should have a vote and nobody more than one, there will be certain areas where this can and should be enforced by law (it should be illegal to vote twice in elections) and others where it would be nonsense to have formal regulation. Feminism has brought the domestic sphere much more clearly into the orbit of democratic debate, but the argument is that women should be empowered so that they can insist on the equality themselves, and in this sense it still retains a distinction.

Finally, the equation of the personal with the political has drawn attention to the details of how people relate and organize and has thus been linked to the democratization of whatever association (including places of work) we find ourselves in. On this point, however, feminists have sometimes acted as if there were an amorphous continuum in which there are no distinctions beyond those of size. Here, too, we need to differentiate. There is a difference between extending control over decisions to everyone involved in a particular venture or place of work, and increasing participation in what has been traditionally defined as politics. The one does not lead inexorably to the other. Feminism rightly queries the exclusive emphasis on 'politics' as conventionally defined and has stressed the often more immediate issues of taking control where we work and live. This positive insistence on the democratization of everyday life should not become a substitute for a more lively and vital political life.

References

Arendt, Hannah. 1963. *On revolution*. Faber and Faber.
Barber, Benjamin. 1984. *Strong democracy: Participatory politics for a new age*. University of California Press.

Birke, Lynda, Susan Himmelweit, and Gail Vines. 1990. *Tomorrow's child: Reproductive technologies in the '90s.* Virago.

Bowles, Samuel, and Herbert Gintis. 1986. *Democracy and capitalism: Property, community and the contradictions of modern social thought.* London: Routledge and Kegan Paul.

Corea, Gena. 1989. *The mother machine: Reproductive technologies from artificial insemination to artificial wombs.* New York: Harper & Row.

Dworkin, Ronald. 1989. The great abortion case. *New York Review of Books,* 29 June.

Ehrenreich, Barbara. 1983. On feminism, family, and community. *Dissent,* winter.

Elshtain, Jean Bethke. 1981. *Public man, private woman: Women in social and political thought.* Princeton, N.J.: Princeton University Press.

Himmelweit, Susan. 1980. Abortion: Individual choice and social control. *Feminist Review* 5.

Keane, John. 1988. *Democracy and civil society: On the predicaments of European socialism, the prospects for democracy, and the problem of controlling social and political power.* New York: Verso.

Pateman, Carole. 1975. Sublimation and reification: Locke, Wolin and the liberal democratic conception of the political. *Politics and Society* 6.

———. 1983. Feminism and democracy. In *Democratic theory and practice,* edited by Graeme Duncan. Cambridge: Cambridge University Press.

Petchesky, Rosalind. 1985. *Abortion and woman's choice: The state, sexuality and reproductive freedom.* Boston: Northeastern University Press.

Rowbotharn, Sheila. 1989. *The past is before us: Feminism in action since the 1960s.* Boston: Beacon.

Siltanen, Janet, and Michelle Stanworth. 1984. The politics of private woman and public man. In *Women and the public sphere,* edited by J. Siltanen and M. Stanworth. New York: St. Martin's Press.

Stacey, Judith. 1986. Are feminists afraid to leave home? The challenge of conservative pro-family feminism. In *What Is Feminism?* edited by Juliet Mitchell and Ann Oakley. Oxford: Basil Blackwell.

Wolin, Sheldon. 1982. What revolutionary action means today. *Democracy* 2.

Young, Iris Marion. 1987. Impartiality and the civic public. In *Feminism As critique: On the politics of gender,* edited by Seyla Benhabib and Drucilla Cornell. Minneapolis: University of Minnesota Press.

CORNEL WEST, SELECTION FROM *RACE MATTERS* (1993)

What happened in Los Angeles in April of 1992 was neither a race riot nor a class rebellion. Rather, this monumental upheaval was a multiracial, trans-class, and largely male display of justified social rage. For all its ugly, xenophobic resentment, its air of adolescent carnival, and its downright barbaric behavior, it signified the sense of powerlessness in American society. Glib attempts to reduce its meaning to the pathologies of the black underclass, the criminal actions of hoodlums, or the political revolt of the oppressed urban masses miss the mark. Of those arrested, only 36 percent were black, more than a third had full-time jobs, and most claimed to shun political affiliation. What we witnessed in Los Angeles was the consequence of a lethal linkage of economic decline, cultural decay, and political lethargy in American life. Race was the visible catalyst, not the underlying cause.

The meaning of the earthshaking events in Los Angeles is difficult to grasp because most of us remain trapped in the narrow framework of the dominant liberal and conservative views of race in America, which with its worn-out vocabulary leaves us intellectually debilitated, morally disempowered, and personally depressed. The astonishing disappearance of the event from public dialogue is testimony to just how painful and distressing a serious engagement with race is. Our truncated public discussions of race suppress the best of who and what we are as a people because they fail to confront the complexity of the issue in a candid and critical manner. The predictable pitting of liberals against conservatives, Great Society Democrats against self-help Republicans reinforces intellectual parochialism and political paralysis.

The liberal notion that more government programs can solve racial problems is simplistic—precisely because it focuses *solely* on the economic dimension. And the conservative idea that what is needed is a change in the moral behavior of poor black urban dwellers (especially poor black men, who, they say, should stay married, support their children, and stop committing so much crime) highlights immoral actions while ignoring public responsibility for the immoral circumstances that haunt our fellow citizens.

The common denominator of these views of race is that each still sees black people as a "problem people," in the words of Dorothy I. Height, president of the National Council of Negro Women, rather than as fellow American citizens with problems. Her words echo the poignant "unasked question" of W. E. B. Du Bois, who, in *The Souls of Black Folk* (1903), wrote:

> They approach me in a half-hesitant sort of way, eye me curiously or compassionately, and then instead of saying directly, How does it feel to be a problem? they say, I know an excellent colored man in my town. . . . Do not these Southern outrages make your blood boil? At these I smile, or am interested or reduce the boiling to a simmer, as the occasion may require. To the real question, How does it feel to be a problem? I answer seldom a word.

Nearly a century later, we confine discussions about race in America to the "problems" black people pose for whites rather than consider what this way of viewing black people reveals about us as a nation.

This paralyzing framework encourages liberals to relieve their guilty consciences by supporting public funds directed at "the problems"; but at the same time, reluctant to exercise principled criticism of black people, liberals deny them the freedom to err. Similarly, conservatives blame the "problems" on black people themselves—and thereby render black social misery invisible or unworthy of public attention.

Hence, for liberals, black people are to be "included" and "integrated" into "our" society and culture, while for conservatives they are to be "well behaved" and "worthy of acceptance" by "our" way of life. Both fail to see that the presence and predicaments of black people are neither additions to nor defections from American life, but rather *constitutive elements of that life*.

To engage in a serious discussion of race in America, we must begin not with the problems of black people but with the flaws of American society—flaws rooted in historic inequalities and longstanding cultural stereotypes. How we set up the terms for discussing racial issues shapes our perception and response to these issues. As long as black people are viewed as a "them," the burden falls on blacks to do all the "cultural" and "moral" work necessary for healthy race relations. The implication is that only certain Americans can define what it means to be American—and the rest must simply "fit in."

The emergence of strong black-nationalist sentiments among blacks, especially among young people, is a revolt against this sense of having to "fit in." The variety of black-nationalist ideologies, from the moderate views of Supreme Court Justice Clarence Thomas in his youth to those of Louis Farrakhan today, rest upon a fundamental truth: white America has been historically weak-willed in ensuring racial justice and has continued to resist fully accepting the humanity of blacks. As long as double standards and differential treatment abound—as long as the rap performer Ice-T is harshly condemned while former Los Angeles Police Chief Daryl F. Gates's antiblack comments are received in polite silence, as long as Dr. Leonard Jeffiies's anti-Semitic statements are met with vitriolic outrage while presidential candidate Patrick J. Buchanan's anti-Semitism receives a genteel response—black nationalisms will thrive.

Afrocentrism, a contemporary species of black nationalism, is a gallant yet misguided attempt to define an African identity in a white society perceived to be hostile. It is gallant because it puts black doings and sufferings, not white anxieties and fears, at the center of discussion. It is misguided because—out of fear of cultural hybridization and through silence on the issue of class, retrograde views on black women, gay men, and lesbians, and a reluctance to link race to the common good—it reinforces the narrow discussions about race.

To establish a new framework, we need to begin with a frank acknowledgment of the basic humanness and Americanness of each of us. And we must acknowledge that as a people—*E Pluribus Unum*—we are on a slippery slope toward economic strife, social turmoil, and cultural chaos. If we go down, we go down together. The Los Angeles upheaval forced us to see not only that we are not connected in ways we would like to be but also, in a more profound sense, that this failure to connect binds us even more tightly together. The paradox of race in America is that our common destiny is more pronounced and imperiled precisely when our divisions are deeper. The Civil War and its legacy speak loudly here. And our divisions are growing deeper. Today, 86 percent of white suburban Americans live in neighborhoods that are less than 1 percent black, meaning that the prospects for the country depend largely on how its cities fare in the hands of a suburban electorate. There is no escape from our interracial interdependence, yet enforced racial hierarchy dooms us as a nation to collective paranoia and hysteria—the unmaking of any democratic order.

The verdict in the Rodney King case, which sparked the incidents in Los Angeles, was perceived to be wrong by the vast majority of Americans. But whites have often failed to acknowledge the widespread mistreatment of black people, especially black men, by law enforcement agencies, which helped ignite the spark.

The verdict was merely the occasion for deep-seated rage to come to the surface. This rage is fed by the "silent" depression ravaging the country—in which real weekly wages of all American workers since 1973 have declined nearly 20 percent, while at the same time wealth has been upwardly distributed.

The exodus of stable industrial jobs from urban centers to cheaper labor markets here and abroad, housing policies that have created "chocolate cities and vanilla suburbs" (to use the popular musical artist George Clinton's memorable phrase), white fear of black crime, and the urban influx of poor Spanish-speaking and Asian immigrants—all have helped erode the tax base of American cities just as the federal government has cut its supports and programs. The result is unemployment, hunger, homelessness, and sickness for millions.

And a pervasive spiritual impoverishment grows. The collapse of meaning in life—the eclipse of hope and absence of love of self and others, the breakdown of family and neighborhood bonds—leads to the social deracination and cultural denudement of urban dwellers, especially children. We have created rootless, dangling people with little link to the supportive networks—family, friends, school—that sustain some sense of purpose in life. We have witnessed the collapse of the spiritual communities that in the past helped Americans face despair, disease, and death and that transmit through the generations dignity and decency, excellence and elegance.

The result is lives of what we might call "random nows," of fortuitous and fleeting moments preoccupied with "getting over"—with acquiring pleasure, property, and power by any means necessary. (This is not what Malcolm X meant by this famous phrase.) Post-modern culture is more and more a market culture dominated by gangster mentalities and self-destructive wantonness. This culture engulfs all of us—yet its impact on the disadvantaged is devastating, resulting in extreme violence in everyday life. Sexual violence against women and homicidal assaults by young black men on one another are only the most obvious signs of this empty quest for pleasure, property, and power.

Last, this rage is fueled by a political atmosphere in which images, not ideas, dominate, where politicians spend more time raising money than debating issues. The functions of parties have been displaced by public polls, and politicians behave less as thermostats that determine the climate of opinion than as thermometers registering the public mood. American politics has been rocked by an unleashing of greed among opportunistic public officials—who have followed the lead of their counterparts in the private sphere, where, as of 1989, 1 percent of the population owned 37 percent of the wealth and 10 percent of the population owned 86 percent of the wealth—leading to a profound cynicism and pessimism among the citizenry.

And given the way in which the Republican Party since 1968 has appealed to popular xenophobic images—playing the black, female, and homophobic cards to realign the electorate along race, sex, and sexual-orientation lines—it is no surprise that the notion that we are all part of one garment of destiny is discredited. Appeals to special interests rather than to public interests reinforce this polarization. The Los Angeles upheaval was an expression of utter fragmentation by a powerless citizenry that includes not just the poor but all of us.

What is to be done? How do we capture a new spirit and vision to meet the challenges of the post-industrial city, post-modern culture, and post-party politics?

First, we must admit that the most valuable sources for help, hope, and power consist of ourselves and our common history. As in the ages of Lincoln, Roosevelt, and King, we must look to new frameworks and languages to understand our multilayered crisis and overcome our deep malaise.

Second, we must focus our attention on the public square—the common good that undergirds our national and global destinies. The vitality of any public square ultimately depends on how much we *care* about the quality of our lives together. The neglect of our public infrastructure, for example our water and sewage systems, bridges, tunnels, highways, subways, and streets—reflects not only our myopic economic policies, which impede productivity, but also the low priority we place on our common life.

The tragic plight of our children clearly reveals our deep disregard for public well-being. About one out of every five children in this country lives in poverty, including one out of every two black children and two out of every five Hispanic children. Most of our children—neglected by overburdened parents and bombarded by the market values of profit-hungry corporations—are ill-equipped to live lives of spiritual and cultural quality. Faced with these facts, how do we expect ever to constitute a vibrant society?

One essential step is some form of large-scale public intervention to ensure access to basic social goods—housing, food, health care, education, child care, and jobs. We must invigorate the common good with a mixture of government, business, and labor that does not follow any existing blueprint. After a period in which the private sphere has been sacralized and the public square gutted, the temptation is to make a fetish of the public square. We need to resist such dogmatic swings.

Last, the major challenge is to meet the need to generate new leadership. The paucity of courageous leaders—so apparent in the response to the events in Los Angeles—requires that we look beyond the same elites and voices that recycle the older frameworks. We need leaders—neither saints nor sparkling television personalities—who can situate themselves within a larger historical narrative of this country and our world, who can grasp the complex dynamics of our peoplehood and imagine a future grounded in the best of our past, yet who are attuned to the frightening obstacles that now perplex us. Our ideals of freedom, democracy, and equality must be invoked to invigorate all of us, especially the landless, propertyless, and luckless. Only a visionary leadership that can motivate "the better angels of our nature," as Lincoln said, and activate possibilities for a freer, more efficient, and stable America—only that leadership deserves cultivation and support.

This new leadership must be grounded in grass-roots organizing that highlights democratic accountability. Whoever *our* leaders will be as we approach the twenty-first century, their challenge will be to help Americans determine whether a genuine multiracial democracy can be created and sustained in an era of global economy and a moment of xenophobic frenzy.

Let us hope and pray that the vast intelligence, imagination, humor, and courage of Americans will not fail us. Either we learn a new language of empathy and compassion, or the fire this time will consume us all.

Iris Marion Young, Selections from *Justice and the Politics of Difference* (1990)

There was once a time of caste and class, when tradition decreed that each group had its place, and that some are born to rule and others to serve. In this time of darkness, law and social norms defined rights, privileges, and obligations differently for different groups, distinguished by characteristics of sex, race, religion, class, or occupation. Social inequality was justified by church and state on the grounds that people have different natures, and some natures are better than others.

Then one day Enlightenment dawned, heralding a revolutionary conception of humanity and society. All people are equal, the revolutionaries declared, inasmuch as all have a capacity for reason and moral sense. Law and politics should therefore grant to everyone equal political and civil rights. With these bold ideas the battle lines of modern political struggle were drawn.

For over two hundred years since those voices of Reason first rang out, the forces of light have struggled for liberty and political equality against the dark forces of irrational prejudice, arbitrary metaphysics, and the crumbling towers of patriarchal church, state, and family. In the New World we had a head start in this fight, since the American War of Independence was fought on these Enlightenment principles, and our Constitution stood for liberty and equality. So we did not have to throw off the yokes of class and religious privilege, as did our Old World comrades. Yet the United States had its own oligarchic horrors in the form of slavery and the exclusion of women from public life. In protracted and bitter struggles these bastions of privilege based on group difference began to give way, finally to topple in the 1960s.

Today in our society a few vestiges of prejudice and discrimination remain, but we are working on them, and have nearly realized the dream those Enlightenment fathers dared to propound. The state and law should express rights only in universal terms applied equally to all, and differences among persons and groups should be a purely accidental and private matter. We seek a society in which differences of race, sex, religion, and ethnicity no longer make a difference to people's rights and opportunities. People should be treated as individuals, not as members of groups; their life options and rewards should be based solely on their individual achievement. All persons should have the liberty to be and do anything they want, to choose their own lives and not be hampered by traditional expectations and stereotypes. [. . . .]

Enlightenment ideals of liberty and political equality did and do inspire movements against oppression and domination, whose success has created social values and institutions we would not want to lose. A people could do worse than tell this story after big meals and occasionally call upon one another to live up to it.

The very worthiness of the narrative, however, and the achievement of political equality that it recounts, now inspires new heretics. In recent years the ideal of liberation as the elimination of group difference has been challenged by movements of the oppressed. The very success of political movements against differential privilege and for political equality has generated movements of group specificity and cultural pride.

In this . . . [essay] I criticize an ideal of justice that defines liberation as the transcendence of group difference, which I refer to as an ideal of assimilation. This ideal usually promotes equal treatment as a primary principle of justice. Recent social movements of oppressed groups challenge this ideal. Many in these movements argue that a positive self-definition of group difference is in fact more liberatory. [. . . .]

An emancipatory politics that affirms group difference involves a reconception of the meaning of equality. The assimilitionist ideal assumes that equal social status for all persons requires treating everyone according to the same principles, rules, and standards. A politics of difference argues, on the other hand, that equality as the participation and inclusion of all groups sometimes requires different treatment for oppressed or disadvantaged groups.

Competing Paradigms of Liberation

In "On Racism and Sexism," Richard Wasserstrom (1980) develops a classic statement of the ideal of liberation from group-based oppression as involving the elimination of group-based difference itself. A truly nonracist, nonsexist society, he suggests, would be one in which the race or sex of an individual would be the functional equivalent of eye color in our society today. While physiological differences in skin color or genitals would remain, they would have no significance for a person's sense of identity or how others regard him or her. No political rights or obligations would be connected to race or sex, and no important institutional benefits would be associated with either. People would see no reason to consider race or gender in policy or everyday interactions. In such a society, social group differences would have ceased to exist.

Wasserstrom contrasts this ideal of assimilation with an ideal of diversity much like the one I will argue for, which he agrees is compelling. He offers three primary reasons, however, for choosing the assimilationist ideal of liberation over the ideal of diversity. First, the assimilationist ideal exposes the arbitrariness of group-based social distinctions which are thought natural and necessary. By imagining a society in which race and sex have no social significance, one sees more clearly how pervasively these group categories unnecessarily limit possibilities for some in existing society. Second, the assimilationist ideal presents a clear and unambiguous standard of equality and justice. According to such a standard, any group-related differentiation or discrimination is suspect. Whenever laws or rules, the division of labor, or other social practices allocate benefits differently according to group membership, this is a sign of injustice. The principle of justice is simple: treat everyone according to the same principles, rules, and standards. Third, the assimilationist ideal maximizes choice. In a society where differences make no social difference people can develop themselves as individuals, unconstrained by group norms and expectations. [. . . .]

The power of this assimilationist ideal has inspired the struggle of oppressed groups and the supporters against the exclusion and denigration of these groups, and continues to inspire many. Periodically in American history, however, movements of the oppressed have questioned and rejected this "path to belonging" (Karst 1986). Instead they have seen self-organization and the assertion of a positive group cultural identity as a better strategy for achieving power and participation in dominant institutions. Recent decades have witnessed a resurgence of this "politics of difference" not only among racial and ethnic groups, but also among women, gay men and lesbians, old people, and the disabled. [. . . .]

Emancipation through the Politics of Difference

Implicit in emancipatory movements asserting a positive sense of group difference is a different ideal of liberation, which might be called democratic cultural pluralism (cf. Laclau and Mouffe 1985, 166–71; Cunningham 1987, 186–99; Nickel 1988). In this vision the good society does not eliminate or transcend group difference. Rather, there is equality among socially and culturally differentiated groups, who mutually respect one another and affirm one another in their differences. What are the reasons for rejecting the assimilationist ideal and promoting a politics of difference? [. . . .]

[For some], group difference is an invidious fiction produced and perpetuated in order to preserve the privilege of the few. Others, such as Wasserstrom, may agree that social groups do now exist and have real social consequences for the way people identify themselves and one another, but assert that such social group differences are undesirable. The assimilationist ideal involves denying either the reality or the desirability of social groups.

Those promoting a politics of difference doubt that a society without group differences is either possible or desirable. Contrary to the assumption of modernization theory, increased urbanization and the extension of equal formal rights to all groups has not led to a decline in particularist affiliations. If anything, the urban concentration and interactions among groups that modernizing social processes introduce tend to reinforce group solidarity and differentiation (Rothschild 1981; Ross 1980; Fischer 1982). Attachment to specific traditions, practices, language, and other culturally specific forms is a crucial aspect of social existence. People do not usually give up their social group identifications, even when they are oppressed.

Whether eliminating social group difference is possible or desirable in the long run, however, is an academic issue. Today and for the foreseeable future societies are certainly structured by groups, and some are privileged while others are oppressed. New social movements of group specificity do not deny the official story's claim that the ideal of liberation as eliminating difference and treating everyone the same has brought significant improvement in the status of excluded groups. Its main quarrel is with the story's conclusion, namely, that since we have achieved formal equality, only vestiges and holdovers of differential privilege remain, which will die out with the continued persistent assertion of an ideal of social relations that make differences irrelevant to a person's life prospects. The achievement of formal equality does not eliminate social differences, and rhetorical commitment to the sameness of persons makes it impossible even to name how those differences presently structure privilege and oppression.

Though in many respects the law is now blind to group differences, some groups continue to be marked as deviant, as the Other. In everyday interactions, images, and decisions, assumptions about women, Blacks, Hispanics, gay men and lesbians, old people, and other marked groups continue to justify exclusion, avoidance, paternalism, and authoritarian treatment. Continued racist, sexist, homophobic, ageist, and ableist institutions and behavior create particular circumstances for these groups, usually disadvantaging them in their opportunity to develop their capacities. [. . . .]

Today in American society, as in many other societies, there is widespread agreement that no person should be excluded from political and economic activities because of ascribed characteristics. Group differences nevertheless continue to exist, and certain groups continue to be privileged. Under these circumstances, insisting that equality and liberation entail ignoring difference has oppressive consequences in three respects.

First, blindness to difference disadvantages groups whose experience, culture, and socialized capacities differ from those of privileged groups. The strategy of assimilation aims to bring formerly excluded groups into the mainstream. So assimilation always implies coming into the game after it is already begun, after the rules and standards have already been set, and having to prove oneself according to those rules and standards. In the assimilationist strategy, the privileged groups implicitly define the standards according to which all will be measured. Because their privilege involves not recognizing these standards as culturally and experientially specific, the ideal of a common humanity in which all can participate without regard to race, gender, religion, or sexuality poses as neutral and universal. The real differences between oppressed groups and the dominant norm, however, tend to put them at a disadvantage in measuring up to these standards, and for that reason assimilationist policies perpetuate their disadvantage. [. . . .]

Second, the ideal of a universal humanity without social group differences allows privileged groups to ignore their own group specificity. Blindness to difference perpetuates cultural imperialism by allowing norms expressing the point of view and experience of privileged groups to appear neutral and universal. The assimilationist ideal presumes that there is a humanity in general, an unsituated group-neutral human capacity for self-making that left to itself would make individuality flower, thus guaranteeing that each individual will be different. . . . [B]ecause there is no such unsituated group-neutral point of view, the situation and experience of dominant groups tend to define the norms of such a humanity in general. Against such a supposedly neutral humanist ideal, only the oppressed groups come to be marked with particularity; they, and not the privileged groups, are marked, objectified as the Others.

Thus, third, this denigration of groups that deviate from an allegedly neutral standard often produces an internalized devaluation by members of those groups themselves. . . . The aspiration to assimilate helps produce the self-loathing and double consciousness characteristic of oppression. . . . When participation is taken to imply assimilation the oppressed person is caught in an irresolvable dilemma: to participate means to accept and adopt an identity one is not, and to try to participate means to be reminded by oneself and others of the identity one is. [. . . .]

Under these circumstances, a politics that asserts the positivity of group difference is liberating and empowering. In the act of reclaiming the identity the dominant culture has taught them to despise (Cliff 1980), and affirming it as an identity to celebrate, the oppressed remove double consciousness. [. . . .]

Reclaiming the Meaning of Difference

[A]s Martha Minow (1985; 1987; 1990) suggests, group differences should be conceived as relational rather than defined by substantive categories and attributes. A relational under-standing of difference relativizes the previously universal position of privileged groups, which allows only the oppressed to be marked as different. When group difference ap-pears as a function of comparison between groups, whites are just as specific as Blacks or Latinos, men just as specific as women, able-bodied people just as specific as disabled people. Difference thus emerges not as a description of the attributes of a group, but as a function of the relations between groups and the interaction of groups with institutions (cf. Littleton 1987). [. . . .]

In general, then, a relational understanding of group difference rejects exclusion. Dif-ference no longer implies that groups lie outside one another. To say that there are dif-ferences among groups does not imply that there are not overlapping experiences, or that two groups have nothing in common. The assumption that real differences in affinity, culture, or privilege imply oppositional categorization must be challenged. Different groups are always similar in some respects, and always potentially share some attributes, experiences, and goals. [. . . .]

Respecting Difference in Policy

The issue of formally equal versus group-conscious policies arises primarily in the context of workplace relations and access to political power. . . . [P]olicies that are universally formulated and thus blind to differences of race, culture, gender, age, or disability often perpetuate rather than undermine oppression. Universally formulated standards or norms, for example, ac-cording to which all competitors for social positions are evaluated, often presume as the norm capacities, values, and cognitive and behavioral styles typical of dominant groups, thus dis-advantaging others. Racist, sexist, homophobic, ageist, and ableist aversions and stereotypes, moreover, continue to devalue or render invisible some people, often disadvantaging them in economic and political interactions. Policies that take notice of the specific situation of op-pressed groups can offset these disadvantages.

It might be objected that when facially neutral standards or policies disadvantage a group, the standards or policies should simply be restructured so as to be genuinely neutral, rather than replaced by group-conscious policies. For some situations this may be appropriate, but in many the group-related differences allow no neutral formulation. [. . . .]

More important, however, some of the disadvantages that oppressed groups suffer can be remedied in policy only by an affirmative acknowledgment of the group's specificity. The op-pressions of cultural imperialism that stereotype a group and simultaneously render its own experience invisible can be remedied only by explicit attention to and expression of that group's specificity. [. . . .]

The dilemma of difference exposes the risks involved both in attending to and in ignor-ing differences. The danger in affirming difference is that the implementation of group-conscious policies will reinstate stigma and exclusion. In the past, group-conscious policies were used to separate those defined as different and exclude them from access to the rights and privileges enjoyed by dominant groups. A crucial principle of democratic cultural plural-ism, then, is that group-specific rights and policies should stand together with general civic and political rights of participation and inclusion. Group-conscious policies cannot be used to justify exclusion of or discrimination against members of a group in the exercise of general political and civil rights. A democratic cultural pluralism thus requires a dual system of rights: a general system of rights which are the same for all, and a more specific system of group-conscious policies and rights (cf. Wolgast 1980, chap. 2). [. . . .]

The Heterogeneous Public and Group Representation

I have argued that participatory democracy is an element and condition of social justice. Contemporary participatory democratic theory, however, inherits from republicanism a commitment to a unified public that in practice tends to exclude or silence some groups. Where some groups are materially privileged and exercise cultural imperialism, formally democratic processes often elevate the particular experiences and perspectives of the privileged groups, silencing or denigrating those of oppressed groups. [. . . .]

I assert, then, the following principle: a democratic public should provide mechanisms for the effective recognition and representation of the distinct voices and perspectives of those of its constituent groups that are oppressed or disadvantaged. Such group representation implies institutional mechanisms and public resources supporting (1) self-organization of group members so that they achieve collective empowerment and a reflective understanding of their collective experience and interests in the context of the society; (2) group analysis and group generation of policy proposals in institutionalized contexts where decisionmakers are obliged to show that their deliberations have taken group perspectives into consideration; and (3) group veto power regarding specific policies that affect a group directly, such as reproductive rights policy for women, or land use policy for Indian reservations.

Specific representation for oppressed groups in the decisionmaking procedures of a democratic public promotes justice better than a homogeneous public in several ways, both procedural and substantial (cf. Beitz 1988, 168–69). First, it better assures procedural fairness in setting the public agenda and hearing opinions about its items. Social and economic privilege means, among other things, that the groups which have it behave as though they have a right to speak and be heard, that others treat them as though they have that right, and that they have the material, personal, and organizational resources that enable them to speak and be heard. As a result, policy issues are often defined by the assumptions and priorities of the privileged. Specific representation for oppressed groups interrupts this process, because it gives voice to the assumptions and priorities of other groups.

Second, because it assures a voice for the oppressed as well as the privileged, group representation better assures that all needs and interests in the public will be recognized in democratic deliberations. The privileged usually are not inclined to protect or advance the interests of the oppressed, partly because their social position prevents them from understanding those interests, and partly because to some degree their privilege depends on the continued oppression of others. While different groups may share many needs, moreover, their difference usually entails some special needs which the individual groups themselves can best express. If we consider just democratic decisionmaking as a politics of need interpretation, as I have already suggested, then democratic institutions should facilitate the public expression of the needs of those who tend to be socially marginalized or silenced by cultural imperialism. Group representation in the public facilitates such expression. [. . . .]

Group representation, third, encourages the expression of individual and group needs and interests in terms that appeal to justice, that transform an "I want" into an "I am entitled to," in Hannah Pitkin's words. . . . [P]ublicity itself encourages this transformation because a condition of the public is that people call one another to account. Group representation adds to such accountability because it serves as an antidote to self-deceiving self-interest masked as an impartial or general interest. Unless confronted with different perspectives on social relations and events, different values and language, most people tend to assert their perspective as universal. When social privilege allows some group perspectives to dominate a public while others are silent, such universalizing of the particular will be reaffirmed by many others. Thus the test of whether a claim upon the public is just or merely an expression of self-interest is best made when those making it must confront the opinion of others who have explicitly different, though not necessarily conflicting, experiences, priorities, and needs (cf. Sunstein 1988, 1588). As a person of social privilege, I am more likely to go outside myself and have regard for social justice when I must listen to the voice of those my privilege otherwise tends to silence.

Finally, group representation promotes just outcomes because it maximizes the social knowledge expressed in discussion, and thus furthers practical wisdom. Group differences are manifest not only in different needs, interests, and goals, but also in different social locations and experiences. People in different groups often know about somewhat different institutions, events, practices, and social relations, and often have differing perceptions of the same institutions, relations, or events. For this reason members of some groups are sometimes in a better position than members of others to understand and anticipate the probable consequences of implementing particular social policies. A public that makes use of all such social knowledge in its differentiated plurality is most likely to make just and wise decisions.

I should allay several possible misunderstandings of what this principle of group representation means and implies. First, the principle calls for specific representation of social groups, not interest groups or ideological groups. By an interest group I mean any aggregate or association of persons who seek a particular goal, or desire the same policy, or are similarly situated with respect to some social effect—for example, they are all recipients of acid rain caused by Ohio smokestacks. Social groups usually share some interests, but shared interests are not sufficient to constitute a social group. A social group is a collective of people who have affinity with one another because of a set of practices or way of life; they differentiate themselves from or are differentiated by at least one other group according to these cultural forms.

By an ideological group I mean a collective of persons with shared political beliefs. Nazis, socialists, feminists, Christian Democrats, and anti-abortionists are ideological groups. The situation of social groups may foster the formation of ideological groups, and under some circumstances an ideological group may become a social group. Shared political or moral beliefs, even when they are deeply and passionately held, however, do not themselves constitute a social group.

A democratic polity should permit the expression of all interests and opinions, but this does not imply specific representation for any of them. A democratic public may wish to provide representation for certain kinds of interests or political orientations; most parliamentary systems, for example, give proportional representation to political parties according to the number of votes they poll. The principle of group representation that I am arguing for here, however, refers only to social groups.

Second, it is important to remember that the principle calls for specific representation only of oppressed or disadvantaged groups. Privileged groups are already represented, in the sense that their voice, experience, values, and priorities are already heard and acted upon. The faces of oppression . . . provide at least beginning criteria for determining whether a group is oppressed and therefore deserves representation.[2] Once we are clear that the principle of group representation refers only to oppressed social groups, then the fear of an unworkable proliferation of group representation should dissipate.

Third, while I certainly intend this principle to apply to representative bodies in government institutions, its application is by no means restricted to that sphere. . . . [S]ocial justice requires a far wider institutionalization of democracy than currently obtains in American society. Persons should have the right to participate in making the rules and policies of any institution with authority over their actions. The principle of group representation applies to all such democratized publics. [. . . .]

This principle of group representation, finally, does not necessarily imply proportional representation, in the manner of some recent discussions of group representation (see Bell 1987, chap. 3; Beitz, 1988, 163). Insofar as it relies on the principle of "one person one vote," proportional representation retains the assumption that it is primarily individuals who must be represented in decision-making bodies. Certainly they must, and various forms of proportional representation, including proportional representation of groups or parties, may sometimes be an important vehicle for representing individuals equally. With the principle I argue for here, however, I am concerned with the representation of group experience, perspectives, and interests. Proportional representation of group members may sometimes be too little or too much to accomplish that aim. [. . . .]

Some might object that implementing a principle of group representation in governing bodies would exacerbate conflict and divisiveness in public life, rendering decisions even more difficult to reach. Especially if groups have veto power over policies that fundamentally and uniquely affect members of their group, it seems likely, it might be claimed, that decisionmaking would be stalled. This objection presupposes that group differences imply essential conflicts of interest. But this is not so; groups may have differing perspectives on issues, but these are often compatible and enrich everyone's understanding when they are expressed. To the extent that group differences produce or reflect conflict, moreover, group representation would not necessarily increase such conflict and might decrease it. If their differences bring groups into conflict, a just society should bring such differences into the open for discussion. Insofar as structured relations of privilege and oppression are the source of the conflict, moreover, group representation can change those relations by equalizing the ability of groups to speak and be heard. Thus group representation should mitigate, though not eliminate, certain kinds of conflict. If, finally, the alternative to stalled decision-making is a unified public that makes decisions ostensibly embodying the general interest which systematically ignore, suppress, or conflict with the interests of particular groups, then stalled decisionmaking may sometimes be just.

A second objection might be that the implementation of this principle can never get started. For to implement it a public must be constituted to decide which groups, if any, deserve specific representation in decision-making procedures. What principles will guide the composition of such a "constitutional convention"? Who shall decide what groups should receive representation, and by what procedures shall this decision be made? If oppressed groups are not represented at this founding convention, then how will their representation be ensured at all? And if they are represented, then why is implementation of the principle necessary?

These questions pose a paradox of political origins which is not specific to this proposal, and which no philosophical argument can resolve. No program or set of principles can found a politics, because politics does not have a beginning, an original position. It is always a process in which we are already engaged. Normative principles such as those I have proposed . . . [here] can serve as proposals in this ongoing political discussion, and means of envisioning alternative institutional forms, but they cannot found a polity. In actual political situations application of any normative principle will be rough and ready, and always subject to challenge and revision. If democratic publics in American society accept this principle of group representation, as I have suggested a few have, they also are likely to name candidates for groups within them that deserve specific representation. Such an opening might sensitize the public to the need for other groups to be represented. But if it does not, these groups will have to petition with arguments that may or may not be persuasive. I see no practical way out of this problem of origin, but that does not stand as a reason to reject this or any other normative principle.

One might ask how the idea of a heterogeneous public which encourages self-organization of groups and group representation in decision-making differs from . . . interest-group pluralism. . . . Interest-group pluralism, I suggest, operates precisely to forestall the emergence of public discussion and decision-making. Each interest group promotes its own specific interest as thoroughly and forcefully as it can, and need not consider the other interests competing in the political marketplace except strategically, as potential allies or adversaries in its own pursuit. The rules of interest-group pluralism do not require justifying one's interest as right, or compatible with social justice. A heterogeneous public, however, is a *public*, where participants discuss together the issues before them and come to a decision according to principles of justice. Group representation, I have argued, nurtures such publicity by calling for claimants to justify their demands before others who explicitly stand in different social locations.

References

Beitz, Charles. 1988. Equal opportunity in political representation. In *Equal Opportunity*, edited by Norman Bowie. Boulder: Westview.

Bell, Derek. 1987. *And we are not saved: The elusive quest for racial justice.* New York: Basic.

Cliff, Michelle. 1980. *Reclaiming the identity they taught me to despise.* Watertown, Mass.: Persephone.

Cunningham, Frank. 1987. *Democratic theory and socialism.* Cambridge, Mass.: Cambridge University Press.

Fischer, Claude. 1982. *To dwell among friends: Personal networks in town and city.* Chicago: University of Chicago Press.

Karst, Kenneth. 1986. Paths to belonging: The constitution and cultural identity. *North Carolina Law Review* 64 (January): 303–77.

Laclau, Ernesto, and Chantal Mouffe. 1985. *Hegemony and socialist strategy.* London: Verso.

Littleton, Christine. 1987. Reconstructing sexual equality. *California Law Review* 75 (July): 1279–1337.

Minow, Martha. 1985. Learning to live with the dilemma of difference: Bilingual and special education. *Law and Contemporary Problems* 48 (spring): 157–211.

———. 1987. "Justice Engendered." *Harvard Law Review* 101 (November): 11–95.

———. 1990. *Making All the Difference.* Ithaca: Cornell University Press.

Nickel, James. 1988. Equal opportunity in a pluralistic society. In *Equal Opportunity*, edited by Ellen Frankel Paul, Fred D. Miller, Jeffrey Paul, and John Ahrens. Oxford: Blackwell.

Ross, Jeffrey. 1980. Introduction to *The mobilization of collective identity*, edited by Jeffrey Ross and Ann Baker Cottrell. Lanham, Md.: University Press of America.

Rothschild, Joseph. 1981. *Ethnopolitics*. New York: Columbia University Press.

Sunstein, Cass R. 1988. Beyond the republican revival. *Yale Law Journal* 97 (July): 1539–90.

Wasserstrom, Richard. 1980. On racism and sexism. In *Philosophy and Social Issues*. Notre Dame: Notre Dame University Press.

Wolgast, Elizabeth. 1980. *Equality and the rights of women*. Ithaca, N.Y.: Cornell University Press.

NOTES

1. For an earlier statement of women's rights, see Mary Wollstonecraft, *Vindication of the Rights of Women* (Penguin, 1975). First published 1792.

2. Young identifies oppression as a complex phenomena that does not necessarily require an intentionally oppressive actor group. It can also operate through inherited practices, orientations and institutional arrangements that structure a given society. Here she offers five "faces of oppression" to articulate the diverse forms of systematic oppression. They are exploitation, marginalization, powerlessness, cultural imperialism, and violence. For a more detailed treatment of these categories, see *Justice and the Politics of Difference*, chapter 2. *Eds*.

VOICES OUTSIDE THE WEST

The democratic theories we have been examining are Western. For many, these theories are meant to apply universally, not necessarily in every detail but in their broad outlines and procedures. Many outside of the economically developed nations of the West take exception to this universalizing impulse of Western democratic theory. This is not because they want nondemocratic political systems but because they want their democracy to reflect their own conceptions of the good community and fear that Western theories sometimes restrict this possibility or do not speak to their specific circumstances. In this section, we look at the work of several writers who take up the question of democracy from a non-Western perspective.[1] For all of their many differences, they agree that democracy must mean more than a set of institutional procedures.

Mahatma Gandhi, leader of India's nonviolent independence movement, presents a decentralized version of democracy and ties his vision to a civil society that emphasizes the equality and dignity of everyone. His democracy is about self-rule or what he calls *Hind Swaraj*. This means not only that India must be free of foreign domination but that each Indian must be free from domestic domination. In Gandhi's democracy, the equality of everyone requires the elimination of the steep economic, social, and political inequalities. To continue practices that degrade women, ignore the poor, or legitimize untouchability means, for him, that democracy has not yet really arrived. Moreover, he insists that no good regime can rely on violence, even if this reflects the sentiments of the majority. For this reason, Gandhi means to limit the scope of democratic rule. Clearly, a democratic government needs to make rules that enable its citizens to live together and face common opportunities and challenges; but, Gandhi argues, it has no warrant to expect the decisions of a majority to cancel the deep moral commitments of any of its citizens. With this in mind, he offers civil disobedience as a political method when conventional ones fail and not only for those who live under nondemocratic regimes; he also invites it against a democratic government that fails to respect the autonomy of everyone.

Hind Swaraj takes the form of a dialogue between a reader and an editor, who is Gandhi. This work has been seen as Gandhi's single most important writing and lays out his vision for self-rule for India and for Indians. The problem that India faces, he claims, is not just or even primarily colonialism but a state of mind that has infected India, namely the view that modern civilization is superior to traditional Indian civilization. If Indians accept this outlook, Gandhi argues they accept the terms of debate set by the colonial power and work within the context provided by the imperial system. In introducing his own terms of debate, Gandhi holds that independence is about more than national sovereignty—it includes the autonomy of each individual. To achieve these aims, Gandhi calls for nonviolent civil disobedience or passive resistance.[2]

Gandhi has several things in mind when he talks about the power of truth and love. For him, the actual flow of life is not one of conflict—that is the story that he sees history telling; rather he sees it as a repetitious cycle of mutual understanding and cooperation. Moreover, courageous nonviolent resistors take control over their own lives and this does not depend on their physical strength or weapons. As he understands matters, this kind of courage, expressed by even one person or a small group, can change or, to use one of his favorite expressions, convert opponents regardless of how physically powerful or numerous they are. Gandhi also repeatedly warns Indians that if they win independence from the British but are tied to materialistic standards of success, they will squander their freedom. Democracy for him does not mean great advances in the economy but in the moral development of self-governing men and women.

Desmond Tutu, a Nobel laureate who served as chairman of the Truth and Reconciliation Commission in South Africa, calls for forgiveness following the elimination of apartheid in his country. Without coming to terms with profound past injustices, he argues, it will be impossible for his country to face the present and the future democratically. He finds that forgiveness is a great human miracle, enabling very different people with radically different views to protect themselves from injustices perpetrated in the past and to find ways to live together peacefully and in dignity. This is a promise of democracy that cannot be achieved as long as recrimination and hatred continue to guide political decisions.

But Tutu makes it clear that forgiveness does not mean forgetting and that appeals for forgiveness cannot be only verbal. He wants people to remember, if for no other reason than because it enables them to guard against the very things happening in the future that they are forgiving in the present. And he wants actions to move beyond the admission of wrongdoing; for him, it is necessary to concretely remedy past evils by addressing the issues of the deep inequalities that mark South African society. For Tutu, the importance of reconciliation applies not only to South Africa but to the other regions of the earth, which are torn by strife, particularly if they have democratic aspirations.

Aung San Suu Kyi of Burma, who is also a Nobel laureate, insists that every country must find its own way to democracy. But that does not mean some democratic aspirations do not cut across borders and one of the most important is bound up in the idea of human rights. For her, this means that a country that denies such basic rights as free speech and assembly cannot really qualify as a democracy. Suu Kyi goes on to argue that if human rights are violated and if civil society is laced with fear, then popular government cannot flourish.

Another aspiration that transcends boundaries, according to Suu Kyi, is that democracy aims at economic justice and not economic growth. Like Gandhi, she is concerned about the economic conditions of the least well-off members of society and means to make economic development in a democracy to take account of this group, not as an afterthought but as one of its focal points. She wants to eliminate the many forms of economic inequality that stifle individual development and dignity. Indeed, one reason democracy is important to her is that it empowers individuals and their cultures, neither of which should be objects of manipulation and control. Central to this view of empowerment is the idea that different people can live harmoniously and cooperatively in a multiracial, pluralist society. Obviously, her pluralism departs markedly from the interest-group pluralism of Bentley and Dahl and reflects the deep-seated localized identities in her country.

Suu Kyi is not unlike many other democrats outside the West who see their own tradition carrying a strong democratic element. She finds that Buddhism continually emphasizes the connectedness between the governor and the governed and the accountability and responsibilities that the former owe to the latter. Her version of democracy wants to bypass the interest-attentiveness of pluralist and performance democracy and instead aims at a common good, which is something she finds central in traditional Buddhist thought about governance. With these traditional resources in hand, she finds the ordinary people of her country are ready to assume the responsibilities of democratic citizenship.

Another Nobel laureate, Adolfo Pérez Esquivel, is also concerned with the connection between human rights and democracy. In his presentation to a hearing of the European Parliament he considers this question in terms of the role and responsibilities of international financial aid organizations. He fears that the domestic obstacles to democracy are fortified by international organizations and foreign countries that do not make democracy abroad a priority. Donor countries and institutions, Pérez Esquivel argues, have routinely failed to hold governments receiving aid accountable to credible standards of human rights and democratic procedure. He finds that international treaties and agreements are often used to justify current distributions of power and wealth. For Pérez Esquivel, this means that the vast disparities of economic and judicial power that characterize many Latin American countries go unchanged. As a result, the poor are left without the political resources to defend their most immediate interests and to participate democratically in the politics of their respective countries. Under these conditions, Pérez Esquivel argues, international aid has functioned as a de-democratizing force in the region. We also find in Pérez Esquivel an argument that appears in much non-Western theorizing about democracy, namely that economic development cannot be separated from democratic politics and that economic policies must speak to the good of everyone, including the poor.

In a speech delivered to the United Nations in 1991, Jean-Bertrand Aristide, the first freely elected President of Haiti following the fall of a long-standing dictatorship, calls attention to his country's special contribution to the cause of free government. At the same time, he notes how the history of his nation has been one of great hardship and oppression, underscoring the remarkable turn of events that led to Haiti's peaceful transition to democracy.[3] Yet like all momentous historical transitions, the emergence of democracy did not solve all of Haiti's problems in one stroke. Rather, for Aristide, it embodied a promising beginning, but one that will require the concerted efforts of dedicated democrats, both within and outside of his country.

Like other non-Western democrats considered here, Aristide insists that Haitian democracy must be a living commitment to human rights, which for him includes economic rights such as the right to work and to earn adequate sustenance. But it is also a commitment to reestablish the rights of economic sovereignty against international arrangements that he believes have served to deplete the resources of Haiti without fair compensation to its citizens. Against those political models that rely on violence, Aristide reaffirms democracy as a model that relies on ballots rather than bullets in the distribution of power. For him, this commitment to nonviolence embodies a psychological and moral investment in democracy as a prerequisite to humanitarian governance and a respect for human beings as the highest form of wealth.

Readings

Mahatma Gandhi, Selection from "Speech at Muir College Economic Society" (1916)

Before I take you to the field of my experiences and experiments, it is perhaps best to have a mutual understanding about the title of this evening's address: *Does economic progress clash with real progress?* By economic progress, I take it, we mean material advancement without limit and by real progress we mean moral progress, which again is the same thing as progress of the permanent element in us. The subject may therefore be stated thus: "Does not moral progress increase in the same proportion as material progress?" I know that this is a wider proposition than the one before us. But I venture to think that we always mean the larger one even when we lay down the smaller. For we know enough of science to realize that there is no such thing as perfect rest or repose in this visible universe of ours. If therefore material progress does not clash with moral progress, it must necessarily advance the latter. Nor can we be satisfied with the clumsy way in which sometimes those who cannot defend the larger proposition put their case. They seem to be obsessed with the concrete case of thirty million of India stated by the late Sir William Wilson Hunter to be living on one meal a day. They say that before we can think or talk of their moral welfare, we must satisfy their daily wants. With these, they say, material progress spells moral progress. And then is taken a sudden jump: what is true of thirty millions is true of the universe. They forget that hard cases make bad law. I need hardly say to you how ludicrously absurd this deduction would be. No one has ever suggested that grinding pauperism can lead to anything else than moral degradation. Every human being has a right to live and therefore to find the wherewithal to feed himself and where necessary to clothe and house himself. But, for this very simple performance, we need no assistance from economists or their laws.

"Take no thought for the morrow"[4] is an injunction which finds an echo in almost all the religious scriptures of the world. In well-ordered society, the securing of one's livelihood should be and is found to be the easiest thing in the world. Indeed, the test of orderliness in a country is not the number of millionaires it owns, but the absence of starvation among its masses. The only statement that has to be examined is whether it can be laid down as a law of universal application that material advancement means moral progress.

Now let us take a few illustrations. Rome suffered a moral fall when it attained high material affluence. So did Egypt and so perhaps most countries of which we have any historic record. The decedents, kinsmen of the royal and divine Krishna, too, fell when they were rolling in riches. We do not deny to the Rockefellers and the Carnegies possession of an or-dinary measure of morality but we gladly judge them indulgently. I mean that we do not even expect them to satisfy the highest standard of morality. With them material gain has not nec-essarily meant moral gain. In South Africa, where I had the privilege of associating with thou-sands of our countrymen on most intimate terms, I observed almost invariably that the greater the possession of riches, the greater was their moral turpitude. Our rich men, to say the least, did not advance the moral struggle of passive resistance as did the poor. The rich men's sense of self-respect was not so much injured as that of the poorest. If I were not afraid of treading on dangerous ground, I would even come nearer home and show you that possession of riches has been a hindrance to real growth. [. . . .]

[I]nsofar as we have made the modern materialistic craze our goal, insofar are we going downhill in the path of progress. I hold that economic progress in the sense I have put it is antagonistic to real progress. Hence the ancient ideal has been the limitation of activities pro-moting wealth. This does not put an end to all material ambition. We should still have, as we have always had, in our midst people who make the pursuit of wealth their aim in life. But we have always recognized that it is a fall from the ideal. It is a beautiful thing to know that the wealthiest among us have often felt that to have remained voluntarily poor would have been a higher state for them. That you cannot serve God and Mammon is an economic truth of the highest value. We have to make our choice. Western nations today are groaning under the heel of the monster-god of materialism. Their moral growth has become stunted. They measure their progress in £. s. d.[5] American wealth has become the standard. She [sic] is the envy of the other nations. I have heard many of our countrymen say that we will gain Amer-ican wealth but avoid its methods. I venture to suggest that such an attempt if it were made is foredoomed to failure. We cannot be 'wise, temperate and furious'[6] in a moment. I would have our leaders to teach us to be morally supreme in the world. This land of ours was once, we are told, the abode of the gods. It is not possible to conceive gods inhabiting a land which is made hideous by the smoke and the din of mill chimneys and factories and whose road-ways are traversed by rushing engines dragging numerous cars crowded with men mostly who know not what they are after, who are often absent-minded, and whose tempers do not improve by being uncomfortably packed like sardines in boxes and finding themselves in the midst of utter strangers who would oust them if they could and whom they would in their turn oust similarly. I refer to these things because, they are held to be symbolical of material progress. But they add not an atom to our happiness. [. . . .]

Under the British aegis, we have learnt much, but it is my firm belief that there is little to gain from Britain in intrinsic morality, that if we are not careful, we shall introduce all the vices that she has been a prey to, owing to the disease of materialism. We can profit by that connection only if we keep our civilization, and our morals, straight, i.e., if instead of boasting of the glorious past, we express the ancient moral glory in our own lives and let our lives bear witness to our past. Then we shall benefit her and ourselves. If we copy her because she provides us with rulers, both they and we shall suffer degradation. We need not be afraid of ideals or of reducing them to practice even to the uttermost. Ours will only then be a truly spiritual nation when we shall show more truth than gold, greater fearless-ness than pomp of power and wealth, greater charity than love of self. If we will but clean our houses, our palaces and temples of the attributes of wealth and show in them the at-tributes of morality, we can offer battle to any combinations of hostile forces without hav-ing to carry the burden of a heavy militia.

Mahatma Gandhi, Selections from *Hind Swaraj* (1909)

Why Was India Lost?

READER: You have said much about civilization—enough to make me ponder over it. I do not now know what I should adopt and what I should avoid from the nations of Europe, but one question comes to my lips immediately. If civilization is a disease and if it has attacked England, why has she been able to take India, and why is she able to retain it?

EDITOR: Your question is not very difficult to answer, and we shall presently be able to examine the true nature of Swaraj; for I am aware that I have still to answer that question. I will, however, take up your previous question. The English have not taken India; we have given it to them. They are not in India because of their strength, but because we keep them. Let us now see whether these propositions can be sustained. They came to our country originally for purposes of trade. Recall the Company[7] Bahadur[8]. Who made it Bahadur? They had not the slightest intention at the time of establishing a kingdom. Who assisted the Company's officers? Who was tempted at the sight of their silver? Who bought their goods? History testifies that we did all this. In order to become rich all at once we welcomed the Company's officers with open arms. We assisted them. If I am in the habit of drinking *bhang* and a seller thereof sells it to me, am I to blame him or myself? By blaming the seller, shall I be able to avoid the habit? And, if a particular retailer is driven away, will not another take his place? A true servant of India will have to go to the root of the matter. If an excess of food has caused me indigestion, I shall certainly not avoid it by blaming water. He is a true physician who probes the cause of disease, and if you pose as a physician for the disease of India, you will have to find out its true cause.

READER: You are right. Now I think you will not have to argue much with me to drive your conclusions home. I am impatient to know your further views. We are now on a most interesting topic. I shall, therefore, endeavour to follow your thought, and stop you when I am in doubt.

EDITOR: I am afraid that, in spite of your enthusiasm, as we proceed further, we shall have differences of opinion. Nevertheless, I shall argue only when you stop me. We have already seen that the English merchants were able to get a footing in India because we encouraged them. When our Princes fought among themselves, they sought the assistance of Company Bahadur. That corporation was versed alike in commerce and war. It was unhampered by questions of morality. Its object was to increase its commerce and to make money. It accepted our assistance, and increased the number of its warehouses. To protect the latter it employed an army which was utilized by us also. Is it not then useless to blame the English for what we did at that time? The Hindus and the Mahomedans were at daggers drawn. This, too, gave the Company its opportunity and thus we created the circumstances that gave the Company its control over India. Hence it is truer to say that we gave India to the English than that India was lost.

READER: Will you now tell me how they are able to retain India?

EDITOR: The causes that gave them India enable them to retain it. Some Englishmen state that they took and they hold India by the sword. Both these statements are wrong. The sword is entirely useless for holding India. We alone keep them. Napoleon is said to have described the English as a nation of shop-keepers. It is a fitting description. They hold whatever dominions they have for the sake of their commerce. Their army and their navy are intended to protect it. When the Transvaal offered no such attractions, the late Mr. Gladstone[9] discovered that it was not right for the English to hold it. When it became a paying proposition, resistance led to war. Mr. Chamberlain[10] soon discovered that England enjoyed a suzerainty over the Transvaal. It is related that someone asked the late President Kruger[11] whether there was gold in the moon. He replied that it was highly unlikely because, if there were, the English would have annexed it. Many problems can be solved by remembering that money is their God. Then it follows that we keep the English in India for our base self-interest. We like their commerce; they please us by their subtle methods and get what they want from us. To blame them for this is to perpetuate their power. We further strengthen their hold by quarrelling amongst ourselves. If you accept the above statements, it is proved that the English entered India for the purposes of trade. They remain in it for the same purpose and we help them to do so. Their arms and ammunition are perfectly useless. In this connection I remind you that it is the British flag which is waving in Japan and not the Japanese. The English have a treaty with Japan for the sake of their commerce, and you will see that if they can manage it, their commerce will greatly expand in that country. They wish to convert the whole world into a vast market for their goods. That they cannot do so is true, but the blame will not be theirs. They will leave no stone unturned to reach the goal. [. . . .]

How Can India Become Free?

READER: I appreciate your views about civilization. I will have to think over them. I cannot take them in all at once. What, then, holding the views you do, would you suggest for freeing India?

EDITOR: I do not expect my views to be accepted all of a sudden. My duty is to place them before readers like yourself. Time can be trusted to do the rest. We have already examined the conditions for freeing India, but we have done so indirectly; we will now do so directly. It is a world-known maxim that the removal of the cause of a disease results in the removal of the disease itself. Similarly if the cause of India's slavery be removed, India can become free.

READER: If Indian civilization is, as you say, the best of all, how do you account for India's slavery?

EDITOR: This civilization is unquestionably the best, but it is to be observed that all civilizations have been on their trial. That civilization which is permanent outlives it. Because the sons of India were found wanting, its civilization has been placed in jeopardy. But its strength is to be seen in its ability to survive the shock. Moreover, the whole of India is not touched. Those alone who have been affected by Western civilization have become enslaved. We measure the universe by our own miserable foot-rule. When we are slaves, we think that the whole universe is enslaved. Because we are in an abject condition, we think that the whole of India is in that condition. As a matter of fact, it is not so, yet it is as well to impute our slavery to the whole of India. But if we bear in mind the above fact, we can see that if we become free, India is free. And in this thought you have a definition of Swaraj. It is Swaraj when we learn to rule ourselves. It is, therefore, in the palm of our hands. Do not consider this Swaraj to be like a dream. There is no idea of sitting still. The Swaraj that I wish to picture is such that, after we have once realized it, we shall endeavour to the end of our life-time to persuade others to do likewise. But such Swaraj has to be experienced, by each one for himself. One drowning man will never save another. Slaves ourselves, it would be a mere pretension to think of freeing others. Now you will have seen that it is not necessary for us to have as our goal the expulsion of the English. If the English become Indianized, we can accommodate them. If they wish to remain in India along with their civilization, there is no room for them. It lies with us to bring about such a state of things.

READER: It is impossible that Englishmen should ever become Indianized.

EDITOR: To say that is equivalent to saying that the English have no humanity in them. And it is really beside the point whether they become so or not. If we keep our own house in order, only those who are fit to live in it will remain. Others will leave of their own accord. Such things occur within the experience of all of us.

READER: But it has not occurred in history.

EDITOR: To believe that what has not occurred in history will not occur at all is to argue disbelief in the dignity of man. At any rate, it behoves us to try what appeals to our reason. All countries are not similarly conditioned. The condition of India is unique. Its strength is immeasurable. We need not, therefore, refer to the history of other countries. I have drawn attention to the fact that, when other civilizations have succumbed, the Indian has survived many a shock.

READER: I cannot follow this. There seems little doubt that we shall have to expel the English by force of arms. So long as they are in the country we cannot rest. One of our poets says that slaves cannot even dream of happiness. We are day by day becoming weakened owing to the presence of the English. Our greatness is gone; our people look like terrified men. The English are in the country like a blight which we must remove by every means.

EDITOR: In your excitement, you have forgotten all we have been considering. We brought the English, and we keep them. Why do you forget that our adoption of their civilization makes their presence in India at all possible? Your hatred against them ought to be transferred to their civilization. But let us assume that we have to drive away the English by fighting, how is that to be done? [. . . .]

Passive Resistance

READER: Is there any historical evidence as to the success of what you have called soul-force or truth-force? No instance seems to have happened of any nation having risen through soul-force. I still think that the evil-doers will not cease doing evil without physical punishment.

EDITOR: The poet Tulsidas has said: "Of religion, pity, or love, is the root, as egotism of the body. Therefore, we should not abandon pity so long as we are alive." This appears to me to be a scientific truth. I believe in it as much as I believe in two and two being four. The force of love is the same as the force of the soul or truth. We have evidence of its working at every step. The universe would disappear without the existence of that force. But you ask for historical evidence. It is, therefore, necessary to know what history means. The Gujarati equivalent means: "It so happened." If that is the meaning of history, it is possible to give copious evidence. But, if it means the doings of kings and emperors, there can be no evidence of soul-force or passive resistance in such history. You cannot expect silver ore in a tin mine. History, as we know it, is a record of the wars of the world, and so there is a proverb among Englishmen that a nation which has no history, that is, no wars, is a happy nation. How kings played, how they became enemies of one another, how they murdered one another, is found accurately recorded in history, and if this were all that had happened in the world, it would have been ended long ago. If the story of the universe had commenced with wars, not a man would have been found alive today. Those people who have been warred against have disappeared as, for instance, the natives of Australia of whom hardly a man was left alive by the intruders. Mark, please, that these natives did not use soul-force in self-defence, and it does not require much foresight to know that the Australians will share the same fate as their victims. "Those that take the sword shall perish by the sword." With us the proverb is that professional swimmers will find a watery grave.

The fact that there are so many men still alive in the world shows that it is based not on the force of arms but on the force of truth or love. Therefore, the greatest and most unimpeachable evidence of the success of this force is to be found in the fact that, in spite of the wars of the world, it still lives on.

Thousands, indeed tens of thousands, depend for their existence on a very active working of this force. Little quarrels of millions of families in their daily lives disappear before the exercise of this force. Hundreds of nations live in peace. History does not and cannot take note of this fact. History is really a record of every interruption of the even working of the force of love or of the soul. Two brothers quarrel; one of them repents and re-awakens the love that was lying dormant in him; the two again begin to live in peace; nobody takes note of this. But if the two brothers, through the intervention of solicitors or some other reason take up arms or go to law—which is another form of the exhibition of brute force— their doings would be immediately noticed in the Press, they would be the talk of their neighbours and would probably go down to history. And what is true of families and communities is true of nations. There is no reason to believe that there is one law for families and another for nations. History, then, is a record of an interruption of the course of nature. Soul-force, being natural, is not noted in history.

READER: According to what you say, it is plain that instances of this kind of passive resistance are not to be found in history. It is necessary to understand this passive resistance more fully. It will be better, therefore, if you enlarge upon it.

EDITOR: Passive resistance is a method of securing rights by personal suffering; it is the reverse of resistance by arms. When I refuse to do a thing that is repugnant to my conscience, I use soul-force. For instance, the Government of the day has passed a law which is applicable to me, I do not like it. If by using violence I force the Government to repeal the law, I am employing what may be termed body-force. If I do not obey the law and accept the penalty for its breach, I use soul-force. It involves sacrifice of self.

Everybody admits that sacrifice of self is infinitely superior to sacrifice of others. Moreover, if this kind of force is used in a cause that is unjust, only the person using it suffers. He does not make others suffer for his mistakes. Men have before now done many things which were subsequently found to have been wrong. No man can claim that he is absolutely in the right or that a particular thing is wrong because he thinks so, but it is wrong for him so long as that is his deliberate judgment. It is therefore meet that he should not do that which he knows to be wrong, and suffer the consequence whatever it may be. This is the key to the use of soul-force.

READER: You would then disregard laws—this is rank disloyalty. We have always been considered a law-abiding nation. You seem to be going even beyond the extremists. They say that we must obey the laws that have been passed, but that if the laws be bad, we must drive out the law-givers even by force.

EDITOR: Whether I go beyond them or whether I do not is a matter of no consequence to either of us. We simply want to find out what is right and to act accordingly. The real meaning of the statement that we are a law-abiding nation is that we are passive resisters. When we do not like certain laws, we do not break the heads of law-givers but we suffer and do not submit to the laws. That we should obey laws whether good or bad is a new-fangled notion. There was no such thing in former days. The people disregarded those laws they did not like and suffered the penalties for their breach. It is contrary to our manhood if we obey laws repugnant to our conscience. Such teaching is opposed to religion and means slavery. If the Government were to ask us to go about without any clothing, should we do so? If I were a passive resister, I would say to them that I would have nothing to do with their law. But we have so forgotten ourselves and become so compliant that we do not mind any degrading law.

A man who has realized his manhood, who fears only God, will fear no one else. Man-made laws are not necessarily binding on him. Even the Government does not expect any such thing from us. They do not say: "You must do such and such a thing," but they say: "If you do not do it, we will punish you." We are sunk so low that we fancy that it is our duty and our religion to do what the law lays down. If man will only realize that it is unmanly to obey laws that are unjust, no man's tyranny will enslave him. This is the key to self-rule or home rule.

It is a superstition and ungodly thing to believe that an act of a majority binds a minority. Many examples can be given in which acts of majorities will be found to have been wrong and those of minorities to have been right. All reforms owe their origin to the initiation of minorities in opposition to majorities. If among a band of robbers a knowledge of robbing is obligatory, is a pious man to accept the obligation? So long as the superstition that men should obey unjust laws exists, so long will their slavery exist. And a passive resister alone can remove such a superstition.

To use brute-force, to use gunpowder, is contrary to passive resistance, for it means that we want our opponent to do by force that which we desire but he does not. And if such a use of force is justifiable, surely he is entitled to do likewise by us. And so we should never come to an agreement. We may simply fancy, like the blind horse moving in a circle round a mill, that we are making progress. Those who believe that they are not bound to obey laws which are repugnant to their conscience have only the remedy of passive resistance open to them. Any other must lead to disaster.

READER: From what you say I deduce that passive resistance is a splendid weapon of the weak, but that when they are strong they may take up arms.

EDITOR: This is gross ignorance. Passive resistance, that is, soul-force, is matchless. It is superior to the force of arms. How, then, can it be considered only a weapon of the weak? Physical-force men are strangers to the courage that is requisite in a passive resister. Do you believe that a coward can ever disobey a law that he dislikes? Extremists are considered to be advocates of brute force. Why do they, then, talk about obeying laws? I do not blame them. They can say nothing else. When they succeed in driving out the English and they themselves become governors, they will want you and me to obey their laws. And that is a fitting thing for their constitution. But a passive resister will say he will not obey a law that is against his conscience, even though he may be blown to pieces at the mouth of a cannon.

What do you think? Wherein is courage required—in blowing others to pieces from behind a cannon, or with a smiling face to approach a cannon and be blown to pieces? Who is the true warrior—he who keeps death always as a bosom-friend, or he who controls the death of others? Believe me that a man devoid of courage and manhood can never be a passive resister.

This, however, I will admit: that even a man weak in body is capable of offering this resistance. One man can offer it just as well as millions. Both men and women can indulge in it. It does not require the training of an army; it needs no Jiu-Jitsu. Control over the mind is alone necessary, and when that is attained, man is free like the king of the forest and his very glance withers the enemy.

Passive resistance is an all-sided sword, it can be used anyhow; it blesses him who uses it and him against whom it is used. Without drawing a drop of blood it produces far-reaching results. It never rusts and cannot be stolen. Competition between passive resisters does not exhaust. The sword of passive resistance does not require a scabbard. It is strange indeed that you should consider such a weapon to be a weapon merely of the weak.

READER: You have said that passive resistance is a speciality of India. Have cannons never been used in India?

EDITOR: Evidently, in your opinion, India means its few princes. To me it means its teeming millions on whom depends the existence of its princes and our own.

Kings will always use their kingly weapons. To use force is bred in them. They want to command, but those who have to obey commands do not want guns: and these are in a majority throughout the world. They have to learn either body-force or soul-force. Where they learn the former, both the rulers and the ruled become like so many madmen; but where they learn soul-force, the commands of the rulers do not go beyond the point of their swords, for true men disregard unjust commands. Peasants have never been subdued by the sword, and never will be. They do not know the use of the sword, and they are not frightened by the use of it by others. That nation is great which rests its head upon death as its pillow. Those who defy death are free from all fear.[12] For those who are labouring under the delusive charms of brute-force, this picture is not overdrawn. The fact is that, in India, the nation at large has generally used passive resistance in all departments of life. We cease to co-operate with our rulers when they displease us. This is passive resistance.

I remember an instance when, in a small principality, the villagers were offended by some command issued by the prince. The former immediately began vacating the village. The prince became nervous, apologized to his subjects and withdrew his command. Many such instances can be found in India. Real Home Rule is possible only where passive resistance is the guiding force of the people. Any other rule is foreign rule.

DESMOND TUTU, SELECTIONS FROM *NO FUTURE WITHOUT FORGIVENESS* (1999)

In relations between individuals, if you ask another person for forgiveness you may be spurned; the one you have injured may refuse to forgive you. The risk is even greater if you are the injured party, wanting to offer forgiveness. The culprit may be arrogant, obdurate, or blind; not ready or willing to apologize or to ask for forgiveness. He or she thus cannot appropriate the forgiveness that is offered. Such rejection can jeopardize the whole enterprise. Our leaders were ready in South Africa to say they were willing to walk the path of confession, forgiveness, and reconciliation with all the hazards that lay along the way. And it seems their gamble might be paying off, since our land has not been overwhelmed by the catastrophe that had seemed so inevitable.

It is crucial, when a relationship has been damaged or when a potential relationship has been made impossible, that the perpetrator should acknowledge the truth and be ready and willing to apologize. It helps the process of forgiveness and reconciliation immensely. It is never easy. We all know just how difficult it is for most of us to admit that we have been wrong. It is perhaps the most difficult thing in the world—in almost every language the most difficult words are, "I am sorry." Thus it is not at all surprising that those accused of horrendous deeds and the communities they come from, for whom they believed they were committing these atrocities, almost always try to find ways out of even admitting that they were indeed capable of such deeds. They adopt the denial mode, asserting that such-and-such has not happened. When the evidence is incontrovertible they take refuge in feigned ignorance. The Germans claimed they had not known what the Nazis were up to. White South Africans have also tried to find refuge in claims of ignorance. The former apartheid cabinet member Leon Wessels was closer to the mark when he said that they had not wanted to know, for there were those who tried to alert them. For those with eyes to see there were accounts of people dying mysteriously in detention. For those with ears to hear there was much that was disquieting and even chilling. But, like the three monkeys, they chose neither to hear, nor see, nor speak of evil. When some did own up, they passed the blame to others, "We were carrying out orders," refusing to acknowledge that as morally responsible individuals each person has to take responsibility for carrying out unconscionable orders.

We do not usually rush to expose our vulnerability and our sinfulness. But if the process of forgiveness and healing is to succeed, ultimately acknowledgment by the culprit is indispensable—not completely so but nearly so. Acknowledgment of the truth and of having wronged someone is important in getting to the root of the breach. If a husband and wife have quarreled without the wrongdoer acknowledging his or her fault by confessing, so exposing the cause of the rift; if a husband in this situation comes home with a bunch of flowers and the couple pretend all is in order, then they will be in for a rude shock. They have not dealt with their immediate past adequately. They have glossed over their differences, for they have failed to stare truth in the face for fear of a possible bruising confrontation. They will have done what the prophet calls healing the hurt lightly by crying, "Peace, peace where there is no peace."[13] They will have only papered over the cracks and not worked out why they fell out in the first place. All that will happen is that, despite the beautiful flowers, the hurt will fester. One day there will be an awful eruption and they will realize that they had tried to obtain reconciliation on the cheap. True reconciliation is not cheap. It cost God the death of His only begotten Son.

Forgiving and being reconciled are not about pretending that things are other than they are. It is not patting one another on the back and turning a blind eye to the wrong. True reconciliation exposes the awfulness, the abuse, the pain, the degradation, the truth. It could even sometimes make things worse. It is a risky undertaking but in the end it is worthwhile, because in the end dealing with the real situation helps to bring real healing. Spurious reconciliation can bring only spurious healing.

If the wrongdoer has come to the point of realizing his wrong, then one hopes there will be remorse, or at least some contrition or sorrow. This should lead him to confess the wrong he has done and ask for forgiveness. It obviously requires a fair measure of humility, especially when the victim is someone in a group that one's community had despised, as was often the case in South Africa when the perpetrators were government agents.

The victim, we hope, would be moved to respond to an apology by forgiving the culprit. As I have already tried to show, we were constantly amazed in the commission at the extraordinary magnanimity that so many of the victims exhibited. Of course there were those who said they would not forgive. That demonstrated for me the important point that forgiveness could not be taken for granted; it was neither cheap nor easy. As it happens, these were the exceptions. Far more frequently what we encountered was deeply moving and humbling.

In forgiving, people are not being asked to forget. On the contrary, it is important to remember, so that we should not let such atrocities happen again. Forgiveness does not mean condoning what has been done. It means taking what happened seriously and not minimizing it; drawing out the sting in the memory that threatens to poison our entire existence. It involves trying to understand the perpetrators and so have empathy, to try to stand in their shoes and appreciate the sort of pressures and influences that might have conditioned them.

Forgiveness is not being sentimental. The study of forgiveness has become a growth industry. Whereas previously it was something often dismissed pejoratively as spiritual and religious, now because of developments such as the Truth and Reconciliation Commission in South Africa it is gaining attention as an academic discipline studied by psychologists, philosophers, physicians, and theologians. In the United States there is an International Forgiveness Institute attached to the University of Wisconsin, and the John Templeton Foundation, with others, has started a multimillion-dollar Campaign for Forgiveness Research. Forgiving has even been found to be good for your health.

Forgiving means abandoning your right to pay back the perpetrator in his own coin, but it is a loss that liberates the victim. In the commission we heard people speak of a sense of relief after forgiving. A recent issue of the journal *Spirituality and Health* had on its front cover a picture of three U.S. ex-servicemen standing in front of the Vietnam Memorial in Washington, D.C. One asks, "Have you forgiven those who held you prisoner of war?" "I will never forgive them," replies the other. His mate says: "Then it seems they still have you in prison, don't they?[14]

Does the victim depend on the culprit's contrition and confession as the precondition for being able to forgive? There is no question that, of course, such a confession is a very great help to the one who wants to forgive, but it is not absolutely indispensable. Jesus did not wait until those who were nailing him to the cross had asked for forgiveness. He was ready, as they drove in the nails, to pray to his Father to forgive them and he even provided an excuse for what they were doing. If the victim could forgive only when the culprit confessed, then the victim would be locked into the culprit's whim, locked into victimhood, whatever her own attitude or intention. That would be palpably unjust.

I have used the following analogy to try to explain the need for a perpetrator to confess. Imagine you are sitting in a dank, stuffy, dark room. This is because the curtains are drawn and the windows have been shut. Outside the light is shining and a fresh breeze is blowing. If you want the light to stream into that room and the fresh air to flow in, you will have to open the window and draw the curtains apart; then that light which has always been available will come in and air will enter the room to freshen it up. So it is with forgiveness. The victim may be ready to forgive and make the gift of her forgiveness available, but it is up to the wrongdoer to appropriate the gift—to open the window and draw the curtains aside. He does this by acknowledging the wrong he has done, so letting the light and fresh air of forgiveness enter his being.

In the act of forgiveness we are declaring our faith in the future of a relationship and in the capacity of the wrongdoer to make a new beginning on a course that will be different from the one that caused us the wrong. We are saying here is a chance to make a new beginning. It is an act of faith that the wrongdoer can change. According to Jesus,[15] we should be ready to do this not just once, not just seven times, but seventy times seven, without limit—provided, it seems Jesus says, your brother or sister who has wronged you is ready to come and confess the wrong they have committed yet again.

That is difficult, but because we are not infallible, because we will hurt especially the ones we love by some wrong, we will always need a process of forgiveness and reconciliation to deal with those unfortunate yet all too human breaches in relationships. They are an inescapable characteristic of the human condition.

Once the wrongdoer has confessed and the victim has forgiven, it does not mean that is the end of the process. Most frequently, the wrong has affected the victim in tangible, material ways. Apartheid provided the whites with enormous benefits and privileges, leaving its victims deprived and exploited. If someone steals my pen and then asks me to forgive him, unless he returns my pen the sincerity of his contrition and confession will be considered to be nil. Confession, forgiveness, and reparation, wherever feasible, form part of a continuum.

In South Africa the whole process of reconciliation has been placed in very considerable jeopardy by the enormous disparities between the rich, mainly the whites, and the poor, mainly the blacks. The huge gap between the haves and the have-nots, which was largely created and maintained by racism and apartheid, poses the greatest threat to reconciliation and stability in our country. The rich provided the class from which the perpetrators and the beneficiaries of apartheid came and the poor produced the bulk of the victims. That is why I have exhorted whites to support transformation taking place in the lot of blacks.

For unless houses replace the hovels and shacks in which most blacks live, unless blacks gain access to clean water, electricity, affordable health care, decent education, good jobs, and a safe environment—things which the vast majority of whites have taken for granted for so long—we can just as well kiss reconciliation goodbye.

Reconciliation is liable to be a long-drawn-out process with ups and downs, not something accomplished overnight and certainly not by a commission, however effective. The Truth and Reconciliation Commission has only been able to make a contribution. Reconciliation is going to have to be the concern of every South African. It has to be a national project to which all earnestly strive to make their particular contribution by learning the language and culture of others; by being willing to make amends; by refusing to deal in stereotypes by making racial or other jokes that ridicule a particular group; by contributing to a culture of respect for human rights, and seeking to enhance tolerance—with zero tolerance for intolerance; by working for a more inclusive society where most, if not all, can feel they belong—that they are insiders and not aliens and strangers on the outside, relegated to the edges of society.

To work for reconciliation is to want to realize God's dream for humanity—when we will know that we are indeed members of one family, bound together in a delicate network of interdependence.

Simon Wiesenthal in the anthology, *The Sunflower: On the Possibilities and Limits of Forgiveness,* tells the story of how he was unable to forgive a Nazi soldier who asked to be forgiven. The soldier had been part of a group that rounded up a number of Jews, locked them up in a building, and proceeded to set it alight, burning those inside to death. The soldier was now on his deathbed. His troubled conscience sought the relief that might come through unburdening himself, confessing his complicity and getting absolution from a Jew. Simon listened to his terrible story in silence. When the soldier had ended his narration, Simon left without uttering a word, certainly not one of forgiveness. He asks at the end of his account, "What would you have done?"

The Sunflower is a collection of the responses of various people to Simon Wiesenthal's question. An updated version[16] contains a contribution from me. The dilemma Wiesenthal faced was very real. His own view, which seems to be that of many Jews, is that the living have no right to forgive on behalf of those who were killed, those who suffered in the past and are no longer alive to make the decision for themselves. One can understand their reluctance, since if they were to forgive it might appear they were trivializing the awful experience of the victims; it also might seem the height of presumption to speak on behalf of people who suffered so grievously, especially perhaps if one had not oneself suffered to the same extent. I understand the nature of their dilemma and would not want to seem to minimize it, but I hold a slightly different view.

At the end of 1990 the various South African churches gathered in Rustenburg to the west of Pretoria in one of the most fully ecumenical and representative church meetings to have taken place in our country. This meeting was called the Rustenburg Conference. Present were those churches that had been very vocal in opposing apartheid through their membership in the South African Council of Churches, as well as the major white Dutch Reformed Church (Nederduitse Gereformeerde Kerk, or DRC), which had supported apartheid by providing its theological rationale (but which had already retreated significantly from that posture). Then there were the many so-called charismatic or pentecostal churches that had tried to be apolitical, though they must have been aware that their imagined neutrality in reality supported the unjust status quo. There were representatives, too, from overseas partner churches and from the so-called African independent churches, which had taken varying political stances.

Quite early in the proceedings a leading DRC theologian, Professor Willie Jonker, made an eloquent plea for forgiveness to his black fellow Christians on behalf of Afrikaners, specifically those in the Dutch Reformed Church. It was not clear whether he had a mandate to be a spokesperson for his church, but as its official delegation subsequently endorsed his statement we can say he was representing that denomination. One could well have asked whether he could claim to speak for past generations of its members, though it would be an oddly atomistic view of the nature of a community not to accept that there is a very real continuity between the past and the present and that the former members would share in the guilt and the shame as in the absolution and the glory of the present. A church is a living organization; otherwise history is of no significance and we should concentrate only on those who are our contemporaries. But clearly this is not how human beings normally operate. We boast about the past achievements of those who are no longer with us and point to them with pride even when they are in the dim and distant past. Their influence is as real as when the achievements were first attained, if not more so. It is the same with failures and disgraces: they too are part of who we are, whether we like it or not. When we speak, we speak as those who are aware of the cloud of witnesses surrounding us. No one would doubt that ultimately a confession such as that made by Dr. Jonker, if it was not repudiated by those on whose behalf it was purportedly being made, would be accepted as speaking for the living and the dead, for those present and those no longer with us.

I consulted with Frank Chikane, who was at the time general secretary of the South African Council of Churches, and we agreed that such an impassioned plea, such a heartfelt confession, could not be treated as just another example of rhetoric. Theologically, we knew that the gospel of our Lord and Savior constrained us to be ready to forgive when someone asked for forgiveness. This was also happening at an important time in the history of our land. Nelson Mandela had been released earlier that year and there was a genuine striving for a negotiated settlement to help the delicate transition from repression to democracy. If the churches, with their immense potential as agents of reconciliation, could not reconcile with each other it could very well send the wrong message to the politicians and to the people of God. If the churches, despite their distressing baggage, could find one another in a public act of forgiveness and reconciliation, that would be a massive shot in the arm for a peaceful transition. And so I got up to say that we accepted the deeply moving and sincere plea for forgiveness.

This could, of course, have been interpreted as a monstrous act of presumption on my part. Who had given me the right to claim to speak on behalf of the millions of contemporary victims of apartheid and, even more seriously, for those many millions who were no longer alive? The DRC had introduced apartheid into church structures, establishing separate churches for members classified under apartheid as black, Indian, and "Coloured." Some of the black delegates at the conference, particularly those from these segregated churches— first called the "daughter" and later the "sister" churches of the DRC—were quite incensed with me because they felt the white church was being allowed to get away with murder, literally and figuratively. They questioned the seriousness of the confession since they were upset that the DRC was dragging its feet on the question of uniting with the black churches. They were also distressed because the white denomination was balking at the prospect of accepting the "Belhar Confession," which the other churches in the DRC family had endorsed. This confession, among other things, condemned apartheid as a heresy. However, while I was challenged to justify my position, which I did try to do, happily I was not repudiated, and what happened at Rustenburg perhaps did advance the cause of a peaceful transition. [. . . .]

If we are going to move on and build a new kind of world community there must be a way in which we can deal with a sordid past. The most effective way would be for the perpetrators or their descendants to acknowledge the awfulness of what happened and the descendants of the victims to respond by granting forgiveness, providing something can be done, even symbolically, to compensate for the anguish experienced, whose consequences are still being lived through today. It may be, for instance, that race relations in the United States will not improve significantly until Native Americans and African Americans get the opportunity to tell their stories and reveal the pain that sits in the pit of their stomachs as a baneful legacy of dispossession and slavery. We saw in the Truth and Reconciliation Commission how the act of telling one's story has a cathartic, healing effect.

If the present generation could not legitimately speak on behalf of those who are no more, then we could not offer forgiveness for the sins of South Africa's racist past, which predates the advent of apartheid in 1948. The process of healing our land would be subverted because there would always be the risk that some awful atrocity of the past would come to light that would undermine what had been accomplished thus far; or that people would say: "It is all right so far as it goes in dealing with the contemporary situation, but it is all utterly ineffectual because it has failed to deal with the burden of the past."

True forgiveness deals with the past, all of the past, to make the future possible. We cannot go on nursing grudges even vicariously for those who cannot speak for themselves any longer. We have to accept that what we do we do for generations past, present, and yet to come. That is what makes a community a community or a people a people—for better or for worse.

I have wished desperately that those involved in seeking solutions for what have seemed intractable problems in places such as Northern Ireland and the Middle East would not despise the value of seemingly small symbolic acts that have a potency and significance beyond what is apparent. I have been distressed to learn that some of those most intimately connected to the peace process in Northern Ireland have not been seen shaking hands in public, that some have gone to odd lengths not to be photographed together with those on the other side, their current adversaries. It was wonderful that, at the funeral of King Hussein of Jordan, President Ezer Weizman of Israel had the courage to shake hands with the leader of a radical Palestinian group. It was a gesture that helped to humanize his adversary where before much had conspired to demonize him. A small handshake can make the unthinkable, the improbable—peace, friendship, harmony, and tolerance—not quite so remote.

I also hope that those who are at this moment enemies around the world might consider using more temperate language when describing those with whom they disagree. Today's "terrorist" could very well be tomorrow's president. That has happened in South Africa. Most of those who were vilified as terrorists are today our cabinet ministers and others sitting in the government benches of our National Assembly. If those we disagree with today are possibly going to be our colleagues tomorrow, we might begin by trying to describe them in language that won't be an embarrassment when that time of change does come.

It is crucial too that we keep remembering that negotiations, peace talks, forgiveness, and reconciliation happen most frequently not between friends, not between those who like one another. They happen precisely because people are at loggerheads and detest one another as only enemies can. But enemies are potential allies, friends, colleagues, and collaborators. This is not just utopian idealism. The first democratically elected government of South Africa was a government of National Unity made up of members of political parties that were engaged in a life-and-death struggle. The man who headed it had been incarcerated for twenty-seven years as a dangerous terrorist. If it could happen there, surely it can happen in other places. Perhaps God chose such an unlikely place deliberately to show the world that it can be done anywhere.

If the protagonists in the world's conflicts began to make symbolic gestures for peace, changed the way they described their enemies, and began talking to them, their actions might change too. For instance, what is it doing for future relations in the Middle East to go on constructing Jewish settlements in what is accepted to be Palestinian territory when this causes so much bitterness and resentment among the Palestinians, who feel belittled and abused? What legacy does it leave for the children of those who are destined to be neighbors? I have asked similar questions when Arab nations have seemed so completely unrealistic in thinking they could destroy Israel. What a wonderful gift to the world, especially as we enter a new millennium, if true peace would come in the land of those who say *salama*, or *shalom*, in the land of the Prince of Peace.

Peace *is* possible, especially if today's adversaries were to imagine themselves becoming friends and begin acting in ways that would promote such a friendship developing in reality. It would be wonderful if, as they negotiated, they tried to find ways of accommodating each other's needs. A readiness to make concessions is a sign of strength, not weakness. And it can be worthwhile sometimes to lose a battle in order in the end to win the war. Those who are engaged in negotiations for peace and prosperity are striving after such a splendid, such a priceless goal that it should be easier to find ways for all to be winners than to fight; for negotiators to make it a point that no one loses face, that no one emerges empty handed, with nothing to place before his or her constituency. How one wishes that negotiators would avoid having bottom lines and too many preconditions. In negotiations we are, as in the process of forgiveness, seeking to give all the chance to begin again. The rigid will have a tough time. The flexible, those who are ready to make principled compromises, end up being the victors.

I have said ours was a flawed commission. Despite that, I do want to assert as eloquently and as passionately as I can that it was, in an imperfect world, the best possible instrument so far devised to deal with the kind of situation that confronted us after democracy was established in our motherland. With all its imperfections, what we have tried to do in South Africa has attracted the attention of the world. This tired, disillusioned, cynical world, hurting so frequently and so grievously, has marveled at a process that holds out considerable hope in the midst of much that negates hope. People in the different places that I have visited and where I have spoken about the Truth and Reconciliation process see in this flawed attempt a beacon of hope, a possible paradigm for dealing with situations where violence, conflict, turmoil, and sectional strife have seemed endemic, conflicts that mostly take place not between warring nations but within the same nation. At the end of their conflicts, the warring groups in Northern Ireland, the Balkans, the Middle East, Sri Lanka, Burma, Afghanistan, Angola, the Sudan, the two Congos, and elsewhere are going to have to sit down together to determine just how they will be able to live together amicably, how they might have a shared future devoid of strife, given the bloody past that they have recently lived through. They see more than just a glimmer of hope in what we have attempted in South Africa.

AUNG SAN SUU KYI, "IN QUEST OF DEMOCRACY" (1991)

Opponents of the movement for democracy in Burma have sought to undermine it by on the one hand casting aspersions on the competence of the people to judge what was best for the nation and on the other condemning the basic tenets of democracy as un-Burmese. There is nothing new in Third World governments seeking to justify and perpetuate authoritarian rule by denouncing liberal democratic principles as alien. By implication they claim for themselves the official and sole right to decide what does or does not conform to indigenous cultural norms. Such conventional propaganda aimed at consolidating the powers of the establishment has been studied, analyzed and disproved by political scientists, jurists and sociologists. But in Burma, distanced by several decades of isolationism from political and intellectual developments in the outside world, the people have had to draw on their own resources to explode the twin myths of their unfitness for political responsibility and the unsuitability of democracy for their society. As soon as the movement for democracy spread out across Burma there was a surge of intense interest in the meaning of the word 'democracy,' in its history and its practical implications. More than a quarter-century of narrow authoritarianism under which they had been fed a pabulum of shallow, negative dogma had not blunted the perceptiveness or political alertness of the Burmese. On the contrary, perhaps not all that surprisingly, their appetite for discussion and debate, for uncensored information and objective analysis, seemed to have been sharpened. Not only was there an eagerness to study and to absorb standard theories on modern politics and political institutions, there was also widespread and intelligent speculation on the nature of democracy as a social system of which they had had little experience but which appealed to their common-sense notions of what was due to a civilized society. There was a spontaneous interpretative response to such basic ideas as representative government, human rights and the rule of law. The privileges and freedoms which would be guaranteed by democratic institutions were contemplated with understandable enthusiasm. But the duties of those who would bear responsibility for the maintenance of a stable democracy also provoked much thoughtful consideration. It is natural that a people who have suffered much from the consequences of bad government should be preoccupied with theories of good government.

Members of the Buddhist *sangha* in their customary role as mentors have led the way in articulating popular expectations by drawing on classical learning to illuminate timeless values. But the conscious effort to make traditional knowledge relevant to contemporary needs was not confined to any particular circle—it went right through Burmese society from urban intellectuals and small shopkeepers to doughty village grandmothers.

Why has Burma with its abundant natural and human resources failed to live up to its early promise as one of the most energetic and fastest-developing nations in South-east Asia? International scholars have provided detailed answers supported by careful analyses of historical, cultural, political and economic factors. The Burmese people, who have had no access to sophisticated academic material, got to the heart of the matter by turning to the words of the Buddha on the four causes of decline and decay: failure to recover that which had been lost, omission to repair that which had been damaged, disregard of the need for reasonable economy, and the elevation to leadership of men without morality or learning. Translated into contemporary terms, when democratic rights had been lost to military dictatorship sufficient efforts had not been made to regain them, moral and political values had been allowed to deteriorate without concerted attempts to save the situation, the economy had been badly managed, and the country had been ruled by men without integrity or wisdom. A thorough study by the cleverest scholar using the best and latest methods of research could hardly have identified more correctly or succinctly the chief causes of Burma's decline since 1962.

Under totalitarian socialism, official policies with little relevance to actual needs had placed Burma in an economic and administrative limbo where government bribery and evasion of regulations were the indispensable lubricant to keep the wheels of everyday life turning. But through the years of moral decay and material decline there has survived a vision of a society in which the people and the leadership could unite in principled efforts to achieve prosperity and security. In 1988 the movement for democracy gave rise to the hope that the vision might become reality. At its most basic and immediate level, liberal democracy would mean in institutional terms a representative government appointed for a constitutionally limited term through free and fair elections. By exercising responsibly their right to choose their own leaders the Burmese hope to make an effective start at reversing the process of decline. They have countered the propagandist doctrine that democracy is unsuited to their cultural norms by examining traditional theories of government.

The Buddhist view of world history tells that when society fell from its original state of purity into moral and social chaos a king was elected to restore peace and justice. The ruler was known by three titles: *Mahasammata*, 'because he is named ruler by the unanimous consent of the people'; *Khattiya*, 'because he has dominion over agricultural land'; and *Raja*, 'because he wins the people, to affection through observance of the *dhamma* (virtue, justice, the law).' The agreement by which their first monarch undertakes to rule righteously in return for a portion of the rice crop represents the Buddhist version of government by social contract. The *Mahasammata* follows the general pattern of Indic kingship in South-east Asia. This has been criticized as antithetical to the idea of the modern state because it promotes a personalized form of monarchy lacking the continuity inherent in the western abstraction of the king as possessed of both a body politic and a body natural. However, because the *Mahasammata* was chosen by popular consent and required to govern in accordance with just laws, the concept of government elective and *sub lege* is not alien to traditional Burmese thought.

The Buddhist view of kingship does not invest the ruler with the divine right to govern the realm as he pleases. He is expected to observe the Ten Duties of Kings, the Seven Safeguards against Decline, the Four Assistances to the People, and to be guided by numerous other codes of conduct such as the Twelve Practices of Rulers, the Six Attributes of Leaders, the Eight Virtues of Kings and the Four Ways to Overcome Peril. There is logic to a tradition which includes the king among the five enemies or perils and which subscribes to many sets of moral instructions for the edification of those in positions of authority. The people of Burma have had much experience of despotic rule and possess a great awareness of the unhappy gap that can exist between the theory and practice of government.

The Ten Duties of Kings are widely known and generally accepted as a yardstick which could be applied just as well to modern government as to the first monarch of the world. The duties are: liberality, morality, self-sacrifice, integrity, kindness, austerity, non-anger, non-violence, forbearance and non-opposition (to the will of the people).

The first duty of liberality (*dana*) which demands that a ruler should contribute generously towards the welfare of the people makes the tacit assumption that a government should have the competence to provide adequately for its citizens. In the context of modern politics, one of the prime duties of a responsible administration would be to ensure the economic security of the state.

Morality (*sila*) in traditional Buddhist terms is based on the observance of the five precepts, which entails refraining from destruction of life, theft, adultery, falsehood and indulgence in intoxicants. The ruler must bear a high moral character to win the respect and trust of the people, to ensure their happiness and prosperity and to provide a proper example. When the king does not observe the *dhamma,* state functionaries become corrupt, and when state functionaries are corrupt the people are caused much suffering. It is further believed that an unrighteous king brings down calamity on the land. The root of a nation's misfortunes has to be sought in the moral failings of the government.

The third duty, *paricagga, is* sometimes translated as generosity and sometimes as self-sacrifice. The former would constitute a duplication of the first duty, *dana, so* self-sacrifice as the ultimate generosity which gives up all for the sake of the people would appear the more satisfactory interpretation. The concept of selfless public service is sometimes illustrated by the story of the hermit Sumedha who took the vow of Buddhahood. In so doing he who could have realized the supreme liberation of *nirvana* in a single lifetime committed himself to countless incarnations that he might help other beings free themselves from suffering. Equally popular is the story of the lord of the monkeys who sacrificed his life to save his subjects, including one who had always wished him harm and who was the eventual cause of his death. The good ruler sublimates his needs as an individual to the service of the nation.

Integrity (*ajjava*) implies incorruptibility in the discharge of public duties as well as honesty and sincerity in personal relations. There is a Burmese saying: 'With rulers, truth, with (ordinary) men, vows.' While a private individual may be bound only by the formal vows that he makes, those who govern should be wholly bound by the truth in thought, word and deed. Truth is the very essence of the teachings of the Buddha, who referred to himself as the *Tathagata* or 'one who has come to the truth.' The Buddhist king must therefore live and rule by truth, which is the perfect uniformity between nomenclature and nature. To deceive or to mislead the people in any way would be an occupational failing as well as a moral offence. 'As an arrow, intrinsically straight, without warp or distortion, when one word is spoken, it does not err into two.'

Kindness (*maddava*) in a ruler is in a sense the courage to feel concern for the people. It is undeniably easier to ignore the hardships of those who are too weak to demand their rights than to respond sensitively to their needs. To care is to accept responsibility, to dare to act in accordance with the dictum that the ruler is the strength of the helpless. In *Wizaya*, a well-known nineteenth-century drama based on the *Mahavamsa* story of Prince Vijaya, a king sends away into exile his own son, whose wild ways had caused the people much distress: 'In the matter of love, to make no distinction between citizen and son, to give equally of loving kindness, that is the righteousness of kings.'

The duty of austerity (*tapa*) enjoins the king to adopt simple habits, to develop self-control and to practice spiritual discipline. The self-indulgent ruler who enjoys an extravagant lifestyle and ignores the spiritual need for austerity was no more acceptable at the time of the *Mahasammata* then he would be in Burma today.

The seventh, eighth and ninth duties—non-anger (*akkodha*), non-violence (*avihamsa*) and forbearance (*khanti*)—could be said to be related. Because the displeasure of the powerful could have unhappy and far-reaching consequences, kings must not allow personal feelings of enmity and ill will to erupt into destructive anger and violence. It is incumbent on a ruler to develop the true forbearance which moves him to deal wisely and generously with the shortcomings and provocations of even those whom he could crush with impunity. Violence is totally contrary to the teachings of Buddhism. The good ruler vanquishes ill will with loving kindness, wickedness with virtue, parsimony with liberality, and falsehood with truth. The Emperor Ashoka who ruled his realm in accordance with the principles of non-violence and compassion is always held up as an ideal Buddhist king. A government should not attempt to enjoin submission through harshness and immoral force but should aim at *dhamma-vijaya*, a conquest by righteousness.

The tenth duty of kings, non-opposition to the will of the people (*avirodha*), tends to be singled out as a Buddhist endorsement of democracy, supported by well-known stories from the *Jakatas*. Pawridasa, a monarch who acquired an unfortunate taste for human flesh, was forced to leave his kingdom because he would not heed the people's demand that he should abandon his cannibalistic habits. A very different kind of ruler was the Buddha's penultimate incarnation on earth, the pious King Vessantara. But he too was sent into exile when in the course of his strivings for the perfection of liberality he gave away the white elephant of the state without the consent of the people. The royal duty of non-opposition is a reminder that the legitimacy of government is founded on the consent of the people, who may withdraw their mandate at any time if they lose confidence in the ability of the ruler to serve their best interests.

By invoking the Ten Duties of Kings the Burmese are not so much indulging in wishful thinking as drawing on time-honored values to reinforce the validity of the political reforms they consider necessary. It is a strong argument for democracy that governments regulated by principles of accountability, respect for public opinion and the supremacy of just laws are more likely than an all-powerful ruler or ruling class, uninhibited by the need to honor the will of the people, to observe the traditional duties of Buddhist kingship. Traditional values serve both to justify and to decipher popular expectations of democratic government.

The people of Burma view democracy not merely as a form of government but as an integrated social and ideological system based on respect for the individual. When asked why they feel so strong a need for democracy, the least political will answer: 'We just want to be able to go about our own business freely and peacefully, not doing anybody any harm, just earning a decent living without anxiety and fear.' In other words they want the basic human rights which would guarantee a tranquil, dignified existence free from want and fear. 'Democracy songs' articulated such longings: 'I am not among the rice-eating robots . . . Everyone but everyone should be entitled to human rights.' 'We are not savage beasts of the jungle, we are all men with reason, it's high time to stop the rule of armed intimidation: if every movement of dissent were settled by the gun, Burma would only be emptied of people.'

It was predictable that as soon as the issue of human rights became an integral part of the movement for democracy the official media should start ridiculing and condemning the whole concept of human rights, dubbing it a western artifact alien to traditional values. It was also ironic—Buddhism, the foundation of traditional Burmese culture, places the greatest value on man, who alone of all beings can achieve the supreme state of Buddha-hood. Each man has in him the potential to realize the truth through his own will and endeavor to help others to realize it. Human life therefore is infinitely precious. 'Easier is it for a needle dropped from the abode of Brahma to meet a needle stuck in the earth than to be born as a human being.'

But despotic governments do not recognize the precious human component of the state, seeing its citizens only as a faceless, mindless—and helpless—mass to be manipulated at will. It is as though people were incidental to a nation rather than its very life-blood. Patriotism, which should be the vital love and care of a people for their land, is debased into a smoke-screen of hysteria to hide the injustices of authoritarian rulers who define the interests of the state in terms of their own limited interests. The official creed is required to be accepted with an unquestioning faith more in keeping with orthodox tenets of the biblical religions which have held sway in the West than with the more liberal Buddhist attitude:

> It is proper to doubt, to be uncertain . . . Do not go upon what has been acquired by repeated hearing. Nor upon tradition, nor upon rumors . . . When you know for yourself that certain things are unwholesome and wrong abandon them . . . When you know for yourself that certain things are wholesome and good, accept them.

It is a puzzlement to the Burmese how concepts which recognize the inherent dignity and the equal and inalienable rights of human beings, which accept that all men are endowed with reason and conscience and which recommend a universal spirit of brotherhood, can be inimical to indigenous values. It is also difficult for them to understand how any of the rights contained in the thirty articles of the Universal Declaration of Human Rights can be seen as anything but wholesome and good. That the declaration was not drawn up in Burma by the Burmese seems an inadequate reason, to say the least, for rejecting it, especially as Burma was one of the nations which voted for its adoption in December 1948. If ideas and beliefs are to be denied validity outside the geographical and cultural bounds of their origin, Buddhism would be confined to north India, Christianity to a narrow tract in the Middle East and Islam to Arabia.

The proposition that the Burmese are not fit to enjoy as many rights and privileges as the citizens of democratic countries is insulting. It also makes questionable the logic of a Burmese government considering itself fit to enjoy more rights and privileges than the governments of those same countries. The inconsistency can be explained—but not justified—only by assuming so wide a gulf between the government and the people that they have to be judged by different norms. Such an assumption in turn casts doubt on the doctrine of government as a comprehensive spirit and medium of national values.

Weak logic, inconsistencies and alienation from the people are common features of authoritarianism. The relentless attempts of totalitarian regimes to prevent free thought and new ideas and the persistent assertion of their own rightness bring on them an intellectual stasis which they project on to the nation at large. Intimidation and propaganda work in a duet of oppression, while the people, lapped in fear and distrust, learn to dissemble and to keep silent. And all the time the desire grows for a system which will lift them from the position of 'rice-eating robots' to the status of human beings who can think and speak freely and hold their heads high in the security of their rights.

From the beginning Burma's struggle for democracy has been fraught with danger. A movement which seeks the just and equitable distribution of powers and prerogatives that have long been held by a small élite determined to preserve its privileges at all costs is likely to be prolonged and difficult. Hope and optimism are irrepressible but there is a deep underlying premonition that the opposition to change is likely to be vicious. Often the anxious question is asked: will such an oppressive regime *really* give us democracy? And the answer has to be: democracy, like liberty, justice and other social and political rights, is not 'given,' it is earned through courage, resolution and sacrifice.

Revolutions generally reflect the irresistible impulse for necessary changes which have been held back by official policies or retarded by social apathy. The institutions and practices of democracy provide ways and means by which such changes could be effected without recourse to violence. But change is anathema to authoritarianism, which will tolerate no deviation from rigid policies. Democracy acknowledges the right to differ as well as the duty to settle differences peacefully. Authoritarian governments see criticism of their actions and doctrines as a challenge to combat. Opposition is equated with 'confrontation,' which is interpreted as violent conflict. Regimented minds cannot grasp the concept of confrontation as an open exchange of major differences with a view to settlement through genuine dialogue. The insecurity of power based on coercion translates into a need to crush all dissent. Within the framework of liberal democracy, protest and dissent can exist in healthy counterpart with orthodoxy and conservatism, contained by a general recognition of the need to balance respect for individual rights with respect for law and order.

The words 'law and order' have so frequently been misused as an excuse for oppression that the very phrase has become suspect in countries which have known authoritarian rule. Some years ago a prominent Burmese author wrote an article on the notion of law and order as expressed by the official term *nyein-wut-pi-pyar.* One by one he analyzed the words, which literally mean 'silent-crouched-crushed-flattened,' and concluded that the whole made for an undesirable state of affairs, one which militated against the emergence of an articulate, energetic, progressive citizenry. There is no intrinsic virtue to law and order unless 'law' is equated with justice and 'order' with the discipline of a people satisfied that justice has been done. Law as an instrument of state oppression is a familiar feature of totalitarianism. Without a popularly elected legislature and an independent judiciary to ensure due process, the authorities can enforce as 'law' arbitrary decrees that are in fact flagrant negations of all acceptable norms of justice. There can be no security for citizens in a state where new 'laws' can be made and old ones changed to suit the convenience of the powers that be. The iniquity of such practices is traditionally recognized by the precept that existing laws should not be set aside at will. The Buddhist concept of law is based on *dhamma,* righteousness or virtue, not on the power to impose harsh and inflexible rules on a defenseless people. The true measure of the justice of a system is the amount of protection it guarantees to the weakest.

Where there is no justice there can be no secure peace. The Universal Declaration of Human Rights recognizes that 'if man is not to be compelled to have recourse, as a last resort, to rebellion against tyranny and oppression,' human rights should be protected by the rule of law. That just laws which uphold human rights are the necessary foundation of peace and security would be denied only by closed minds which interpret peace as the silence of all opposition and security as the assurance of their own power. The Burmese associate peace and security with coolness and shade:

> The shade of a tree is cool indeed
> The shade of parents is cooler
> The shade of teachers is cooler still
> The shade of the ruler is yet more cool
> But coolest of all is the shade of the Buddha's teachings.

Thus to provide the people with the protective coolness of peace and security, rulers must observe the teachings of the Buddha. Central to these teachings are the concepts of truth, righteousness and loving kindness. It is government based on these very qualities that the people of Burma are seeking in their struggle for democracy.

In a revolutionary movement there is always the danger that political exigencies might obscure, or even nullify, essential spiritual aims. A firm insistence on the inviolability and primacy of such aims is not mere idealism but a necessary safeguard against an Animal Farm syndrome where the new order after its first flush of enthusiastic reforms takes on the murky colors of the very system it has replaced. The people of Burma want not just a change of government but a change in political values. The unhappy legacies of authoritarianism can be removed only if the concept of absolute power as the basis of government is replaced by the concept of confidence as the mainspring of political authority: the confidence of the people in their right and ability to decide the destiny of their nation, mutual confidence between the people and their leaders and, most important of all, confidence in the principles of justice, liberty and human rights. Of the four Buddhist virtues conducive to the happiness of laymen, *saddha*, confidence in moral, spiritual and intellectual values, is the first. To instill such confidence, not by an appeal to the passions but through intellectual conviction, into a society which has long been wracked by distrust and uncertainty is the essence of the Burmese revolution for democracy. It is a revolution which moves for changes endorsed by universal norms of ethics.

In their quest for democracy the people of Burma explore not only the political theories and practices of the world outside their country but also the spiritual and intellectual values that have given shape to their own environment.

There is an instinctive understanding that the cultural, social and political development of a nation is a dynamic process which has to be given purpose and direction by drawing on tradition as well as by experiment, innovation and a willingness to evaluate both old and new ideas objectively. This is not to claim that all those who desire democracy in Burma are guided by an awareness of the need to balance a dispassionate, sensitive assessment of the past with an intelligent appreciation of the present. But threading through the movement is a rich vein of the liberal, integrated spirit which meets intellectual challenges with wisdom and courage. There is also a capacity for the sustained mental strife and physical endurance necessary to withstand the forces of negativism, bigotry and hate. Most encouraging of all, the main impetus for struggle is not an appetite for power, revenge and destruction but a genuine respect for freedom, peace and justice.

The quest for democracy in Burma is the struggle of a people to live whole, meaningful lives as free and equal members of the world community. It is part of the unceasing human endeavor to prove that the spirit of man can transcend the flaws of his own nature.

ADOLFO PÉREZ ESQUIVEL, "CONDITIONALITY, HUMAN RIGHTS, AND DEMOCRACY" (1996)

I come from a continent of great wealth and great poverty—a region where the misery and exclusion of millions of women and men, boys and girls, is growing daily, at a rate that is only surpassed by the sustained growth of the concentration of income and of the power of consumption in the hands of very few. Our political history has been, and continues to be, strongly marked by intervention, authoritarianism, repression and state terror: the enforced disappearance of persons, torture, murder, persecution and arrest, in a situation where the very cultural identity of our peoples faces great challenges and threats.

The Latin American reality is one which suffers permanent conditionality, both internally and from outside. It should be recognized, as was the case at the recent World Conference on Social Development, that structural adjustment programs, the external debt, and the policies imposed by the International Monetary Fund and the World Bank constitute *de facto* conditionalities which gravely affect the enforcement of our people's human rights and democracy.

The asymmetry which characterizes inter-State relations also constitutes a serious condition on any agreement between "donor" and "benefactor" countries. This conditionality itself suggests a balance of power and is commonly applied in accordance with the interests that dominate that balance. To speak explicitly about this conditionality makes it more visible and perhaps more available to scrutiny and control. However, a swift glance over our recent history suggests the breadth of the challenge: the blockade of Cuba, the interventions in Panama, Grenada and the Dominican Republic, the absence or weakness of the measures taken against the dictatorships and the national security policies are all clear manifestations of the forms, and the results, of "bulk" conditionality policies.

On the other hand, human rights, which are conceived of as tools in the struggle to place limits on power, suggest in themselves a conditionality on the exercise of State power—one which implies mutual obligations taken on by the State Party with regard to the respective covenants and treaties, and by the members of the international community as a whole, along with the recognition of individuals and peoples as subjects of international law.

From this perspective, and in the context of the realities and experiences to which I have just referred, we wish to address the issue of conditionality in relation to the principles of democracy and human rights.

If we begin by recognizing the pre-existence of strong conditions that are placed on the relationships and agreements in question, the challenge then lies in making it possible for conditionality to be established in conformity with the purpose and meaning of human rights, which serves to place global limits on the exercise of power. In this sense, the legitimacy of any clause or system of conditionality should be based on clear criteria that are applied in a consistent rather than a selective manner, through the use of consensual and democratic participatory mechanisms.

The Conceptualization of Violations to Democratic and Human Rights Related Principles

I believe that it is very important to determine the extent of human rights violations and violations to the system of democracy.

One hundred years ago we could have said, from a Latin American perspective, that a system is democratic to the extent that it can be identified with the rule of law. In other words, the extent to which it includes the following characteristics:

- The rule of law, as an expression of the general will manifested through its representatives
- The separation of powers
- A legally constituted administration
- Basic rights and freedoms

As we enter the twenty-first century, these standards of the rule of law are insufficient for determining the existence of a "process of democracy building." It is important to recognize that every democratic system can be improved upon, and that such improvement permits the possibility of advancement. To reject this possibility is to take a step backwards.

In Latin America, the democratic processes, especially the separation of powers, possess a marked tendency toward the concentration of power in one of the branches of government, usually the Executive Branch. This concentration is functional and is necessary for the application of economic policies that are blatantly inequitable and unjust.

Electoral systems do not, in and of themselves, guarantee community participation. The high rate of voter absenteeism is but one manifestation of this reality. Nor does the community participate in the decisions that affect it. While a wave of democratic processes appeared once the dictatorial systems had exhausted themselves, these processes are not synonymous with democracy.

One of the basic guarantees of a system based on the rule of law is found in the independence of the Judicial Branch. Judges are supposed to uncover cases and concrete occurrences of violations to basic guarantees and freedoms and to seek the restoration of justice and equality under the law. However, in examining the Latin American judicial systems, it can be seen that, as a rule, these systems function under the terms of the pressures of the political and economic powers that oppress our societies, rather than in defense of the dispossessed.

The clients of the criminal justice system are essentially "poor"; that is, poverty is systematically associated with crime. The clients of the civil courts are from sectors where a greater amount of wealth is concentrated. Counterposed to the persecution of poor and marginalized citizens is the impunity granted to white collar crime (which is essentially economic crime) and to the promoters of policies that marginalize and impoverish certain sectors of the population. In Latin America, we watch the growing corruption of our governments while the justice system reacts inadequately, and in those cases where judges decide to apply justice, they are sanctioned by the political powers through removal from duty, or they are transferred or promoted to a different court.

While impunity has been extended to those responsible for the flagrant violation of civil and political rights committed under dictatorships through the terrorist exercise of State powers, an equally serious crime also remains in impunity. I am referring to systematic death caused by the privation of elemental human rights: health, work, food, housing. The hunger of our people is not a product of nature but a consequence of the acts of government and of the exclusive application of the laws of the market economy in "human" relations.

How can we determine the presence of democratic principles in systems of government, and whether or not they are truly functioning? This can only be done by analyzing the extent to which human rights are enforced.

States tend to offer normative answers—laws that are positive to the extent to which they recognize rights. However, national laws, together with the international covenants and treaties, cannot stand up to a comparison with the reality of the infinite number of daily violations which arise from the privation of the right of all people and all peoples to meet their basic needs.

There are laws that benefit our people and laws that harm our people. If the Judicial Branch is not independent, there is a risk that the harmful laws will be applied.

The systematic application of economic, social and cultural policies that benefit 20 percent of the population while excluding the other 80 percent presupposes the inadequacy of the rule of law. This is why our democracies are absolutely conditioned. The logical consequence of this combination is the systematic violation of human rights.

Human Rights As a Criterion of Conditionality

In order to propose the application of human rights as a criterion of conditionality, it is absolutely essential to begin by recognizing the reality I have just described along with the characteristics of violation. There is a marked tendency, however, to limit the conceptualization of human rights, and hence the situations under which they are violated, to that of civil and political rights. This tendency must be reversed.

In order for rights to be "human" they must be considered in the context of all aspects of the life of the individual and of peoples. The Vienna Declaration of 1993 reaffirmed the indivisibility, interdependence and interrelated nature of human rights and committed the international community to uniformly address civil, cultural, economic, political and social rights, along with so-called "third generation" or "solidarity" rights: the right to development, to a healthy environment, to peace, to participation, and the right of all peoples to self-determination. Acceptance of this affirmation becomes a challenge to all of us to seek mechanisms and criteria that respond to this interdependence and indivisibility.

Similarly, the viability and the legitimacy of any policy of conditionality must be based on a logic of reciprocity that reflects the obligations of both the "benefactor" and the "donor" nations. This same criterion applies to the legal force of current international human rights law. Since human rights constitute obligations, and not only on the part of the transgressor State, they must also be interpreted in a way that includes the global context that gives rise to the situation of violation.

We are referring here very concretely to extra-State and extra-territorial elements which, at times, have a determining effect on the actions and policies of a given State. In the Latin American context, where we are far from the centers of political and economic power, we assign special importance to the need to identify and confront with equal force both the internal and the external causes of human rights violations. If this situation is to be transformed, the actions of third countries, of transnational corporations and markets, and of the multilateral organizations—some of which we have already mentioned—must be subject to the same criteria of analysis and control as the State-sponsored behaviors of the countries generally subjected to conditionality.

It is necessary to instill this criterion of co-responsibility, while keeping in mind the clear precepts that already exist in international human rights law. The Universal Declaration of Human Rights enshrines the right of all people "to establish a social and international order in which the proclaimed rights and freedoms . . . may be fully enforced." The International Covenant on Economic, Social and Cultural Rights also commits each State Party to "take steps, both individually and through international assistance and cooperation . . . with a view to achieving progressively . . . the full enforcement of the rights recognized in the present Covenant. . . ."[17]

Similarly, the World Conference on Human Rights in Vienna reaffirmed the right to development and the commitment of the States to cooperate among themselves to achieve development; however, the Conference also ratified the following statement:

> ongoing progress toward the realization of the right to development requires efficient national policies as well as equal economic relations and a favorable international economic environment.

Making Conditionality Measures Operable

The transparent and non-selective application of the agreed-upon criteria constitutes another essential element to the development of a policy of conditionality that effectively contributes to the enforcement of human rights and democratic principles.

First of all, in order for the established mechanisms to be operable, they must ensure the application of the criteria in the steps taken to establish any agreement, be it an agreement on development aid or at a commercial or military level. In other words, the mutual obligations of the contracting States for the promotion of human rights and democracy should influence the very conception of the agreement, thereby allowing the impact and the priority of the proposed initiative to be evaluated from the perspective of the rights of the dispossessed. This also implies a creative and consistent search for forms of participation that involve the dispossessed right from the onset. This is an objective which was strongly highlighted at the 1995 World Summit on Social Development.

Similarly, the operability on conditionality implies strengthening the existing international mechanisms and institutions that monitor the enforcement of human rights, and creating whatever new mechanisms are necessary in light of the fact that, on an operational level, the existing mechanisms and institutions appear to be insufficient and inefficient.

The conventions on Civil and Political Rights and on Economic, Social and Cultural Rights, as well as other conventions of the international human rights system, the covenants of the International Labour Organization (ILO), and similar agreements, merely constitute a legal foundation, requiring the examination of the reports produced by the State Party. However, the nature of the measures taken by these competent instruments, which are in the form of recommendations, is inadequate for enforcing the human rights described in the treaties.

How do we reverse these insufficiencies?

When the States report on the laws that guarantee human rights, it is common for them to deliberately avoid describing the real situation, that is, how these rights are put into practice and to what extent they include the dispossessed. One instrument of positive and effective action are the periodic reports in which, regardless of the national legislation and the international laws adopted by the State, the States must present information on particular sectors: the situation of children, adolescents, workers, retired people, women, in which all rights must be addressed as a whole rather than individually. In spite of the fact that these types of reports tend to be elaborated only by human rights organizations, it is the duty of the States not to conceal information from their co-signatories.

Procedures for presenting periodic reports require that the States grant participation to the organizations that work in the defense of human rights. This incorporation of civil society in the monitoring of the application of democratic principles would be innovative since, in practice, our participation is restricted.

The recommendations that arise from the evaluation should include a time limit during which the State must reverse the violation. During this period, the State must be offered all necessary cooperation, along with adequate monitoring, so that the cause, and not just the effect, of the violation is reversed.

In addition to promoting these ideas for strengthening the system, the European Parliament should ensure the effectiveness of these international procedures by assigning them an adequate budget and adopting new instruments for legal action, including a facultative protocol to the International Covenant on Economic, Social and Cultural Rights.

Not only should these international mechanisms and their results be included in the specific agreements between the European Union and third-party States, but the Union should also take measures to ensure the necessary distribution of information and transparency of the evaluations undertaken, as well as adequate and democratic participation of the various groups involved, both governments and civil society. Similarly, at the time agreements are negotiated, the supervision and decision-making relative to the application of measures of conditionality, whether positive or negative, should be based on the needs of all the parties involved.

Finally, in cases where sanctions ("negative measures") are to be applied, care must be taken to ensure that such measures be imposed gradually and in ways that do not harm the population, thereby making the situation worse. Clear criteria must be used to determine which violations require which types of sanctions. The practice of imposing sanctions only in cases of flagrant abuse (such as forced disappearances or the disruption of democracy through a *coup d'etat*) is inadequate, since the same result is produced by other types of abuses—the destruction of a human being through hunger, for example. A high percentage of current rights violations are based on the privation of basic needs, which tends to be cyclical, permanent and ongoing, and confirms a "system of violations" while using the State as a tool.

To avoid harming the population through the application of sanctions, such measures should be aimed at limiting the power of the State to make war. For example, arms embargos do not harm the population, and may have a positive effect. Here, too, the criteria of reciprocity and co-responsibility implies the need for measures to be shared by the "recipient" State, by the "benefactor" and by the international community.

With regard to commercial conditionality, it is doubly necessary to make progress in laws and control mechanisms in order to keep from making piecemeal decisions and to confront those powers that are becoming increasingly uncontrollable. These include the transnational companies, the financial market, the International Monetary Fund (IMF), and the World Bank.

It is a challenge for the European Union and Parliament to determine which types of commercial relations benefit economic groups and, therefore, do not benefit the people, and which function inversely, benefitting the most needy. Once the nature of the relationship has been discerned, the first model should be suspended and the latter sustained and effectively monitored to assure compliance.

Conclusion

The experience of Latin America makes it difficult to place one's hopes in policies of conditionality that cannot be differentiated in criteria and application from the interests and conditionalities that currently affect us so strongly. However, from the perspective of the logic of human rights, which seeks to activate democratic participation by individual men and women as well as by peoples, in the process of placing limits on the exercise of power and of constructing just alternatives, we remain firm in our hope and our willingness to contribute to the proposed debate and to the generation of adequate instruments.

References

United Nations. International Covenant on Civil and Political Rights. General Assembly. 1967. Twenty-first Session. Official Records. Supplement 16. Resolution 2200 (XXI), A/6316 (reprinted in 6 I.L.M. 368, 1967; entered into force 23 March 1976).

United Nations. International Covenant on Economic, Social and Cultural Rights. General Assembly. 1967. Twenty-first Session. Official Records. Supplement 16. Resolution 2200 (XXI), A/6316 (reprinted in 6 I.L.M. 360, 1967; entered into force 3 January 1976).

United Nations. Vienna Declaration and Programme of Action, World Conference on Human Rights. 1993. Doc. A/CONF.157/24/(1993).

JEAN-BERTRAND ARISTIDE, SELECTION FROM "TEN COMMANDMENTS OF DEMOCRACY IN HAITI" (1991)

At the moment when the international community is absorbed in the shifting of the geopolitical axes of the planet, let us turn to our dear Haiti, that rebellious and faithful daughter,

Rebellious toward every imperialist dictate,
Faithful to every democratic precept.

Let us also speak primarily of ten glowing beacons christened "the ten commandments of democracy," arising out of our democratic praxis. Indeed, our message is limited to the democratic arena where they stand in a straight line. [. . . .]

The First Commandment of Democracy: Liberty or Death

As you know, Haiti was one of the first beacons of liberty in the western hemisphere. In 1791 we presented to the world the first slave revolution, through which hundreds of thousands of blacks freed themselves from the yoke of oppression. The leaders of that victorious revolution helped to finance the liberating crusades of Simon Bolivar in South America. It was in Haiti that slavery was abolished for the first time: a giant step toward the liberation of humanity. The roots of the Declaration of Human Rights arose from the Haitian revolution. The Haiti of Boukmann, of Dessalines, of Toussaint-Louverture is and remains the first black republic in the world.

Haiti shone in the eyes of all as a star of liberty. Throughout our history, often glorious, sometimes troubled, we have always remembered with pride the unprecedented exploits of our ancestors. The cries of "Liberty or death, liberty or death," far from being stifled by a sterile past, have resounded steadily in the heart of a people who have become, forever, a free nation.

Throughout our long march toward 1991, in spite of our contribution to the free world, Haiti has never been able to open all the doors of the international community. The colonials of those days and their allies have been afraid of freedom: our leaders and the traditional oligarchy have feared it as well. From white colonials to black colonials, we have had to break the yoke of the black dictators and their international allies.

Happily, in 1986, to the astonishment of the whole world, the Haitian people overthrew a dictatorial regime that had lasted thirty years. That was the beginning of the end of a dictatorship whose marks are ineffaceable. The more those marks stare us in the face, the louder we cry out: "Liberty or death, liberty or death!"

The Second Commandment of Democracy: Democracy or Death

After having banished the oppressive and corrupt regime of the Duvaliers on February 7, 1986, at the end of that long and courageous struggle, the people of Charlemagne Péralte had only one choice: to install, once and for all, a democratic regime in Haiti. In that light, "liberty or death" is no different from "democracy or death." Hence we have conducted an unremitting struggle for the conquest of our rights against minority groups who have monopolized power since 1986. The struggle is unremitting and legitimate because that power has not worked to change the nature of a government that, for a long time, has created the objective conditions for maintaining the status quo and for sustaining the operation of the machinery of exploitation and oppression.

Finally, on December 16, 1990, thanks to the heroic courage of the Haitian people, thanks to their contribution, we for the first time carried out free, honest, and democratic elections! Honor to the Haitian masses! Glory to our ancestors, who put a stop to colonialism throughout the nineteenth century! Bravo to the international community! Bravo and applause to the United Nations!

Indeed, this was a great beginning in history. For once, through a brilliant tactical movement, a nation had carried out a revolution through the ballot box. The election of the president of the republic by more than 70 percent on the first ballot symbolized simultaneously

The victory of the people
The power of the people
The demands of the people.

These free, honest and democratic elections are, in sum, the outcome of a strategy proper to us, that is to say, the historic rise of *Lavalas*. In union there is strength: is that not our slogan? With the fork of division, we said, no one can drink the soup of elections. In the same way, no one can drink the soup of democracy with the fork of division. [. . . .]

The Third Commandment of Democracy: Fidelity to Human Rights

If human beings have duties, they certainly have rights: rights to respect and to be respected. It is, in the last analysis, to guarantee those rights that a just government is established.

The Universal Declaration of Human Rights is and remains sacred. It lays on us the heavy responsibility of faithfully obeying the constitutional mandate to "guarantee our inalienable and indefeasible rights to life, liberty and the pursuit of happiness," according to our Act of Independence of 1804 and the Universal Declaration of Human Rights of 1948.

We respect the Constitution on behalf of "a Haitian nation that is socially just, economically free and politically independent."

We respect the Constitution for the sake of establishing an ideological pluralism and political succession, to strengthen national unity, to eliminate distinctions between city and country, to insure the harmonious separation and distribution of the powers of the executive, the judiciary and the parliament, that is, to install a governmental regime based on fundamental freedoms and respect for human rights, and to assure the cooperation and participation of the whole population in the great decisions involving the life of the nation through an effective decentralization.

The Fourth Commandment of Democracy: The Right to Eat and to Work

It goes without saying that the right to eat is naturally included in the list of the rights belonging to every person. The reality of people who are starving because they are exploited is an immediate accusation against the oppressor as well as the authorities who are responsible for seeing that the inalienable and indefeasible rights of life are respected.

In Haiti, the victims have difficulty eating because they themselves are being eaten by the international axes of exploitation.

With respect to the arms race, "all countries taken together devote more than $500 billion dollars per year, i.e., one billion four hundred million dollars per day. With only fifteen days of this expenditure, it would be possible to eliminate hunger throughout the planet for several years."

The drama of the starving has nothing to do with a lack of food, but rather with a lack of social justice. Work, work, and more work: that is what they need to earn their bread by the sweat of their brows. Some people have shown that if, instead of a single B1 bomber, one were to build houses, for the same amount of money one could employ seventy thousand people.

How can we justify the fact that 71 percent of Haitian farmers cultivate plots of less than 1.2 square hectares?

How can we justify the fact that, in our country, 3 percent of the richest landowners possess more than two-thirds of the arable land?

Certainly, we have to get past the traditional indifference of the dominant political and economic sectors in order to demand respect for the right to eat and to work. [. . . .]

Work for everyone in and for a civilization based on work—in that way we can strike at the roots of hunger. The hunger of one person is the hunger of humanity itself.

In order to get beyond the limitations of language, let us explore a few trails of reality going back to February 7, 1991. In fact, since that date, the government of *Lavalas* has begun to bring order into our administration. The resources of the government have increased sharply. . . .

But an increase in food production has proved to be indispensable. To achieve that, we are undertaking the agrarian reform envisaged by the Constitution, Article 248, and placing at the disposal of the peasants the necessary framework within which they can produce.

The participation of the private sector is essential for the creation of highly labor-intensive industries. While in the past illicit practices have enabled certain sectors to despoil the country at the expense of the majority of the population, our *Lavalas* government, on the contrary, is on the alert to see that the rights of all are respected. These include the right to invest according to the constitutional norms, and the right to work for human and economic growth.

To you, our dear friends and foreign investors, Haiti desires, now and in the future, to extend the warmest and most cordial welcome.

The Fifth Commandment of Democracy:
The Right to Demand What Rightfully Belongs to Us

"What belongs to us is ours. Ours is not yours."

The contribution of the Haitian people to the democratic struggle that has been set in motion throughout the last five years all over the world is remarkable and exceptional.

At the intersection of the democratic streams of Eastern Europe, Asia, the Middle East, South Africa, Central and South America, there erupted among us, in Haiti, a democratic avalanche christened *Lavalas*. No democratic nation can exist by itself, without weaving geopolitical, diplomatic, economic and international connections.

Today we are recording our right to demand what is rightfully ours in the context of that network of relationships where we have first acknowledged the fruits of a rich but impoverished past. Today we also acknowledge the fruits of a present that is exploited but the bearer of hope, and this thanks to the possibility of reconciling a colonized past with a democratic present.

Heraclitus of Ephesus rightly said: "People who are awake have only one world, but those who are asleep each have a world of their own."

As Haitian women and men who are awake, we have one world: the world of justice. Justice for everyone: for Haitians, women and men, too often the victims of social injustice at the international level! If we scan the horizons of this world of justice we wonder how long the impoverished will have to cry out with Democritus: "We seek the good and do not find it; we find evil without seeking it."

Convinced that . . . the Spirit moves the mass, our politics remain alert and attentive to the masses whose voices demand, in respect and dignity, that which is owed to them. It arises out of the treatment inflicted on a great number of our Haitian sisters and brothers who are living in foreign lands.

The Sixth Commandment of Democracy: Legitimate Defense of the Diaspora

Driven out until 1991 by the blind brutality of the repressive machine or by the structures of exploitation erected in an anti-democratic system, our Haitian sisters and brothers have not always had the good fortune to find a promised land. Illegal because the brutes have not had the forethought to give their victims certificates of torture properly signed; illegal because they have had to travel as boat people or without being provided with legal documents, they have nevertheless made great contributions to the economic prosperity of their patrons, preferring to do all the hardest work rather than to take charity. [. . . .]

In the hope that the international bodies concerned will help us to ensure that the fundamental rights of the person are respected, now and hereafter, and that they will act in solemn fashion, we proclaim with pride and dignity that:

> *Never again*
> *Never again*
> *will our Haitian sisters and brothers*
> *be sold*
> *to convert their blood into bitter sugar.*

The Seventh Commandment of Democracy: No to Violence, Yes to Lavalas

A political revolution without armed force in 1991: is it possible? Yes. Incredible, but true. The pedagogy of *Lavalas*, the tactical and strategic convergence of democratic forces, brandished the weapon of unity against that of violence. A stunning victory! An historic surprise!

Schooled by the poor, the pedagogy of active nonviolence and unity triumphed over institutionalized violence. After 1804, the date of our first independence, 1991 opened the era of our second independence.

Does there exist a democratic nation that is capable of remaining indifferent to that victory of nonviolence precisely in the place where the structures of economic violence still hold sway? Is it right to test the patience of the victims of economic violence? If there is no such thing as a politics unconnected with force, neither is there such a thing as an economy unconnected with interests.

The capital of nonviolence that the Haitians have already invested represents considerable economic interests, thanks to the restoration of peace. A simple social-psychological approach speaks volumes. In fact, the less the social self is under attack by the antiquated oligarchy, the more psychological, political and economic health it enjoys.

The pedagogy of nonviolence may support a collective raising of consciousness with regard to our country of nonviolence—a nonviolent country where, nevertheless, 85 percent of the population, crushed under the weight of economic violence, is still illiterate: illiterates who are not animals. Teaching these victims to read, today, is a challenge to the true friends of the Haitian people: I am not speaking of friends, but of true friends. You who are our true friends, do not be observers. Be actors, inasmuch as you are citizens of the world.

Together, let us participate in a campaign for literacy. Can we count on your cooperation? We hope so. All cooperation at this level testifies to a willingness to struggle against economic violence through active nonviolence. [. . . .]

The Eighth Commandment of Democracy: Fidelity to the Human Being, the Highest Form of Wealth

To speak of the human being as the highest form of wealth may imply that we are forgetting gold, oil, or greenbacks. Far from it. There is wealth, and then there is wealth. According to certain experts, if America's hydroelectric potential were fully exploited, it would be able to furnish more energy than all the oil that is consumed by the whole world.

All this wealth should be at the service of human beings, the pivot on which the whole politics of *Lavalas* turns. We, too, are ready to prove our fidelity to humanity, embracing everything that promotes its full development. [. . . .]

We are also working at the intersection of our south-south relations, between our neighbors in South America and ourselves. South-south relations are not the only important ones for Haiti. In fact, we share a political heritage with the United States, whose independence reminds us of the Haitian pioneers who, precisely for the sake of that independence, were beaten and killed. Like France, with which we also share a political heritage together with the United States, the other countries of North America, Europe, the Middle East, Africa, and other parts of the globe are situated together with us within the network of interdependence that binds all the nations of the globe.

We offer patriotic greetings to the Haitian women and men living in Cuba, without forgetting Cuba and the Cuban people to whom we express our wishes for peace and growth in democracy.

We want to address these same wishes for peace and growth in democracy to the Middle East and South Africa.

The Ninth Commandment of Democracy: Fidelity to Our Culture

Lavalas interlaces the cultural bonds at the very heart of the political universe. Resistance to cultural alienation guarantees the psychological health of the democratic tissue. In fact, every kind of cultural suicide results in deviance in the social body and inevitably threatens the democratic cells.

To live, and to live fully, also means nourishing oneself at the sources of one's culture; it means plunging the roots of one's being into those sources.

Those cultural sources incorporate the whole life of a people. We are speaking of a density of nature that has to be studied and explored. By that nature we mean a fabric of multi-dimensional relationships. Defining the human being not as an end but as a bridge, Friedrich Nietzsche situated humanity, whether that was his intention or not, at the intersection of acculturation and inculturation. It is a question of the transmission of cultural seeds capable of vivifying or wounding a being in its very essence.

The seeds of pathological guilt transmitted by contact between the cultures that are called dominant and dominated can only injure any democratic encounter.

The politics of *Lavalas* endeavors to validate our cultural identity. No truly deep change can be accomplished democratically without an articulation of the indigenous values that are closely linked with any genuine socio-cultural fabric.

That fidelity to the culture of humanity invites us to share the concerns of the Kurdish people, the Palestinian people, the Jewish people, the peoples of Iraq—all of them firmly attached to the roots of their own being. [. . . .]

The Tenth Commandment of Democracy: Everyone around the Same Table

> *Yes, everyone around the democratic table*
> *Not a minority on the table*
> *Not a majority under the table*
> *But everyone around the same table.*

That, I think, is the historic meeting place as we approach 1992; on the eve of the celebration of five hundred years of evangelization for more than one country, but primarily and before all, of resistance on the part of us Haitians, women and men. For throughout those five hundred years we have resisted in order to follow and protect our freedom and our dignity. That is why, on the eve of the celebration of these five hundred years, which we call the five centuries of resistance—quantitative and qualitative—we can speak of this gathering around the table. It is truly and genuinely a challenge to be accepted on the threshold of the third millennium.

Sisters and brothers of Jamaica, Barbados, Trinidad, Cuba, the Dominican Republic, Guadeloupe, Martinique: our past struggle against colonialism has led us inevitably toward the establishment of deeper ties in the course of our long march toward the democratic table.

A new social contract at the Caribbean, Latin American and international level is clearly necessary for us to join together one day, all of us, around the democratic table.

We others in Haiti, since December 16, 1990, the date of our elections under the supervision of the United Nations, are on the march toward that meeting place.

To get there—and so that we may all get there—it is time that indebtedness cease to be the condition that governs the net transfer of the resources of our impoverished countries to the rich nations—I do not talk about "developed countries," but rather "countries that are called developed"—a transfer that has increased to the level of $115 billion. For the single year 1989, that transfer reached almost $60 billion—financial resources that the southern countries need absolutely for their own growth.

NOTES

1. For a review of recent non-Western theorizing on democracy, see Fred Dallmayr, *Beyond Orientalism: Essays on Cross-Cultural Encounter* (Albany: SUNY Press, 1996).

2. He later dropped this term in favor of *satyagraha* or "truth force."

3. Aristide's *Lavalas* Party is a coalition of democratic organizations that came to power in Haiti with the establishment of democracy.

4. *St. Matthew*, VI, 34.

5. That is, in money. *Eds.*

6. "Who can be wise, amazed, temperate and furious, / Loyal and neutral, in a moment? / No man."—*Macbeth*, II, iii.

7. East India Company.

8. Literally, 'brave,' here 'powerful,' 'sovereign.'

9. William Ewart Gladstone (1809–1898), Prime Minister of Great Britain, 1868–74, 1880–85, 1886, and 1892–94.

10. Joseph Chamberlain (1836–1914), Secretary of State for the Colonies, 1895.

11. Stephanus Johannes Paulus Kruger (1825–1904), Boer leader and State President of the South African Republic; *vide* "Memorial to Chamberlain," 16-5-1899.

12. The original adds: "True, I am exaggerating somewhat."

13. Jeremiah 6:14 and 8:11.

14. Vol. 2, no. 1 (New York, Trinity Church: Spirituality & Health Publishing).

15. Matthew 18:22.

16. Harry James Cargas and Bonny V. Fetterman, eds. (New York: Schocken Books, 1998).

17. Part II, Article 2, International Covenant on Economic, Social and Cultural Rights.

BIBLIOGRAPHY

PART ONE: LIBERALISM AND REPUBLICANISM

The Evolving Liberal Tradition

Berlin, Isaiah. *Four Essays on Liberty*. Oxford: Oxford University Press, 1969.

Damico, Alfonso. "The Democratic Consequences of Liberalism." In *Liberals on Liberalism*, edited by Alfonso Damico. Totowa, N.J.: Rowman & Littlefield, 1986.

Dworkin, Ronald. "Liberalism." In *Public and Private Morality*, edited by Stuart Hampshire. Cambridge: Cambridge University Press, 1978.

———. *Taking Rights Seriously*. Cambridge, Mass.: Harvard University Press, 1978.

Flathman, Richard. *Willful Liberalism*. Ithaca, N.Y.: Cornell University Press, 1992.

Gewirth, Alan. *The Community of Rights*. Chicago: University of Chicago Press, 1996.

Glaston, William. *Liberal Purposes: Goods, Virtues and Diversity in the Liberal State*. New York: Cambridge University Press, 1992.

Glendon, Mary. *Rights Talk: The Impoverishment of Political Discourse*. New York: Free Press, 1991.

Gray, John. *Liberalisms*. London: Routledge, 1989.

Green, Thomas Hill. *Lectures on the Principles of Political Obligation*. Cambridge: Cambridge University Press, 1986.

Gutting, Gary. *Pragmatic Liberalism and the Critique of Modernity*. Cambridge: Cambridge University Press, 1999.

Hardin, Russell. *Liberalism, Constitutionalism and Democracy*. New York: Oxford University Press, 1999.

Hobhouse, Leonard. *Liberalism and Other Writings*. Cambridge: Cambridge University Press, 1994.

Kloppenberg, James T. *The Virtues of Liberalism*. New York: Oxford University Press, 1998.

Kymlicka, Will. "Liberalism and Communitarianism." *Canadian Journal of Philosophy* 18 (1988): 181–203.

———. *Liberalism, Community, and Culture*. Oxford: Oxford University Press, 1989.

Locke, John. *An Essay Concerning Human Understanding*, edited by Peter Midditch. Oxford: Oxford University Press, 1979.

———. *Two Treatises of Government*, edited by Peter Laslett. Oxford: Oxford University Press, 1988.

Macpherson, C. B. *The Political Theory of Possessive Individualism*. Oxford: Oxford University Press, 1962.

Mansbridge, Jane. "Self-Interest in Political Life." *Political Theory* 18 (February 1990): 132–53.

Mill, J. S. *Considerations on Representative Government*. In *Collected Works*, vol. 19. Toronto: University of Toronto Press, 1977.

———. "De Tocqueville." In *Collected Works*. Toronto: University of Toronto Press, 1977.

———. *On Liberty*. In *Collected Works*, vol. 18. Toronto: University of Toronto Press, 1977.

———. *Utilitarianism*. In *Collected Works*, vol. 10. Toronto: University of Toronto Press, 1969.

Moon, J. Donald. *Constructing Community: Moral Pluralism and Tragic Conflicts*. Princeton, N.J.: Princeton University Press, 1993.

Rawls, John. "Justice As Fairness: Political Not Metaphysical." *Philosophy and Public Affairs* 14 (1985): 223–57.

———. *Political Liberalism.* New York: Columbia University Press, 1993.

———. "The Priority of Right and Ideas of the Good." *Philosophy and Public Affairs* 17 (1988): 251–76.

———. *A Theory of Justice.* Cambridge, Mass.: Harvard University Press, 1971.

Raz, Joseph. *The Morality of Freedom.* Oxford: Clarendon, 1986.

Smith, Adam. *An Inquiry into the Nature and Causes of the Wealth of Nations.* Oxford: Oxford University Press, 1976.

———. *Lectures on Jurisprudence.* Oxford: Oxford University Press, 1978.

———. *The Theory of Moral Sentiments.* Edited by D. Raphael and A. L. Macfie. Oxford: Oxford University Press, 1976.

Shapiro, Ian. *Democratic Justice.* New Haven, Conn.: Yale University Press, 1999.

Spragens, Thomas A. *Civic Liberalism: Reflections on Our Democratic Ideals.* Lanham, Md.: Rowman & Littlefield, 1999.

Terchek, Ronald J. "The Fruits of Success and the Crisis of Liberalism." In *Liberals on Liberalism,* edited by Alfonso J. Damico. Totowa, N.J.: Rowman & Littlefield, 1986.

Tocqueville, Alexis de. *Democracy in America.* Translated by Henry Reeve. New York: Vintage, 1957.

The Civic Republican Tradition and Communitarians

Aristotle. *The Politics.* Chicago: University of Chicago Press, 1984.

———. *Nicomachean Ethics.* Indianapolis: Hackett Publishing, 1985.

Barber. Benjamin. *Strong Democracy: Participatory Politics for a New Age.* Berkeley: University of California Press, 1984.

Bellah, Robert N. *Habits of the Heart: Individualism and Commitment in American Life.* Berkeley: University of California Press, 1985.

Bloom, Allan. *The Closing of the American Mind.* New York: Simon and Schuster, 1987.

Cicero, Marcus Tullius. *On the Commonwealth.* Indianapolis: Bobbs-Merrill, 1976.

Etzioni, Amitai. *New Communitarian Thinking.* Charlottesville: University Press of Virginia, 1995.

———. *The New Golden Rule: Community and Morality in a Democratic Society.* New York: Basic Books, 1996.

Fowler, Robert Booth. *The Dance with Community.* Lawrence: University of Kansas Press, 1991.

Glendon, Mary Ann. *Rights Talk.* New York: Free Press, 1992.

Green, Philip. *Retrieving Democracy: In Search of Civic Equality.* Totowa, N.J.: Rowman & Littlefield, 1985.

Machiavelli, N. *The Art of War.* Indianapolis: Library of Liberal Arts Press, 1965.

———. *Discourses.* New York: Random House, 1940.

———. *History of Florence.* London: Dent, 1975.

———. *The Prince.* New York: Random House, 1940.

MacIntyre, Alasdair. *After Virtue.* Notre Dame: University of Notre Dame Press, 1981.

———. *Whose Justice? Which Rationality?* Notre Dame: University of Notre Dame Press, 1988.

Pettit, Phillip. *Republicanism.* Oxford: Oxford University Press, 1997.

Phillips, Derek. *Looking Backward: A Critical Appraisal of Communitarian Thought.* Princeton, N.J.: Princeton University Press, 1993.

Pocock, J. G. A. *The Machiavellian Moment.* Princeton, N.J.: Princeton University Press, 1975.

Rousseau, J. J. *A Discourse on Political Economy.* London: Dent, 1983.

———. *A Discourse on the Origin of Inequality.* London: Dent, 1983.

———. *The Government of Poland.* Indianapolis: Library of Liberal Arts, 1972.

———. *The Social Contract.* London: Dent, 1983.

Salkever, Stephen G. *Finding the Mean: Theory and Practice in Aristotelian Political Philosophy.* Princeton, N.J.: Princeton University Press, 1990.

Sandel, Michael. *Democracy's Discontent*. Cambridge, Mass.: Harvard University Press, 1996.
———. *Liberalism and the Limits of Justice*. New York: Cambridge University Press, 1982.
———. "The Procedural Republic and the Unencumbered Self." *Political Theory* 12 (1984): 81–96.
Shuman, Michael. *Going Local: Creating Self-Reliant Communities in a Global Age*. New York: Routledge, 2000.
Skinner, Quentin. *The Foundations of Modern Political Thought,* vol. 1. Cambridge: Cambridge University Press, 1978.
———. *Liberty before Liberalism*. Cambridge: Cambridge University Press, 1998.
Seligman, Adam. *The Idea of Civil Society*. Princeton, N.J.: Princeton University Press, 1992.
Sullivan, William M. *Reconstructing Public Philosophy*. Berkeley: University of California Press, 1982.
Taylor, Charles. *Sources of the Self*. Cambridge, Mass.: Harvard University Press, 1989.
Terchek, Ronald. *Republican Paradoxes and Liberal Anxieties*. Lanham, Md.: Rowman & Littlefield, 1997.
Terchek, Ronald, and David K. Moore. "Recovering the Political Aristotle." *American Political Science Review* 94 (December, 2000).
Walzer, Michael. "The Communitarian Critique of Liberalism." *Political Theory* 18 (1990): 6–23.
———. *Spheres of Justice: A Defense of Pluralism and Equality*. New York: Basic Books, 1983.
Wood, Gordon. *Creation of the American Republic*. New York: Norton, 1969.
Yack, Bernard. *The Problems of a Political Animal: Community, Justice, and Conflict in Aristotelian Political Thought*. Berkeley: University of California Press, 1993.

PART TWO: CONTEMPORARY THEORIES OF DEMOCRACY

Protective Democracy

Friedman, Milton. *Capitalism and Freedom*. Chicago: University of Chicago Press, 1962.
Hayek, Friedrich A. *The Political Order of a Free People*. Chicago: University of Chicago Press, 1979.
———. *Road to Serfdom*. Chicago: University of Chicago Press, 1944.
———. *Rules and Order*. Chicago: University of Chicago Press, 1973.
———. *Studies in Philosophy, Politics, and Economics*. London: Routledge, 1967.
Madison, James, Alexander Hamilton, and John Jay. *The Federalist Papers*. Edited by Isaac Kramnick. Middlesex: Penguin, 1987.
Mandeville, Bernard. *Fable of the Bees*. Oxford: Oxford University Press, 1924.
Mises, Ludwig von. *Theory and History*. New Haven, Conn.: Yale University Press, 1957.
Nozick, Robert. *Anarchy, State, and Utopia*. New York: Basic Books, 1974.
Oakeshott, Michael. *Rationalism and Politics*. London: Methuen, 1962.
Paine, Thomas. *Common Sense*. New York: Penguin Books, 1986.
Riker, William. *Liberalism against Populism: A Confrontation between the Theory of Democracy and the Theory of Social Choice*. San Francisco: W. H. Freeman, 1982.
Spencer, Herbert. *The Man versus the State*. Caldwell, Idaho: Caxton Printers, 1965.
Sumner, William Graham. *What Social Classes Owe to Each Other*. Caldwell, Idaho: Caxton, 1963.
Whitman, Walt. *Democratic Vistas and Other Papers*. London: W. Scott Publishing, 1970.

Pluralist Democracy

Bachrach, Peter, and Morton Baratz. "Two Faces of Power." *American Political Science Review* LVI (December, 1962).
Bellamy, Richard. *Liberalism and Pluralism: Towards a Politics of Compromise*. London: Routledge, 1999.
Bentley, Arthur. *The Process of Government*. Evanston, Ill.: Principia Press, 1908.

Berry, Jeffrey. *The Interest Group Society.* New York: Longman, 1997.

Dahl, Robert. *After the Revolution.* New Haven, Conn.: Yale University Press, 1970.

——. *Democracy and Its Critics.* New Haven, Conn.: Yale University Press, 1989.

——. *Dilemmas of Pluralist Democracy.* New Haven, Conn.: Yale University Press, 1982.

——. *On Democracy.* New Haven, Conn.: Yale University Press, 1998.

——. *Who Governs?* New Haven, Conn.: Yale University Press, 1961.

Downs, Anthony. "An Economic Theory of Democracy." *Journal of Political Economy* 64 (1957): 135–52.

Edleman, Murray. *The Symbolic Uses of Power.* Urbana: University of Illinois Press, 1967.

Follett, Mary Parker. *The New State: Group Organization the Solution to Poplar Government.* University Park: Pennsylvania State University Press, 1998.

Grillo, A. *Pluralism and the Politics of Difference.* Oxford: Clarendon Press, 1998.

Hirst, Paul. *From Statism to Pluralism.* London: UCL Press, 1997.

Kariel, Henry. *The Decline of American Pluralism.* Stanford, Calif.: Stanford University Press, 1961.

Lowi, Theorode. *The End of Liberalism.* New York: Norton, 1979.

Manley, John. "Neo-Pluralism: A Class Analysis of Pluralism I and Pluralism II." *American Political Science Review* 77 (1983): 368–83.

McClure, Kristie. "On the Subject of Rights: Pluralism, Plurality, and Political Identity." In *Dimensions of Radical Democracy: Pluralism, Citizenship, Community,* edited by Chantal Mouffe (New York: Verso, 1992).

McConnell, Grant. *Private Power and American Democracy.* New York: Knopf, 1966.

Truman, David. *The Governmental Process.* New York: Knopf, 1951.

Walker, Jack. "A Critique of the Elitist Theory of Democracy." *American Political Science Review* 60 (June 1966): 285–95.

Walzer, Michael. *Spheres of Justice: A Defense of Pluralism and Equality.* New York: Basic Books, 1983.

Performance Democracy

Bell, Daniel. *The Cultural Contradictions of Capitalism.* New York: Basic Books, 1976.

Berelson, B., P. Lazarfeld, and W. McPhee. *Voting.* Chicago: University of Chicago Press, 1954.

Buchanan, James, and Gordon Tullock, *The Calculus of Consent.* Ann Arbor: University of Michigan Press, 1962.

Campbell, Angus, et al. *The American Voter.* New York: Wiley, 1960.

Heertje, Arnold, ed. *Schumpeter's Vision: Capitalism, Socialism, and Democracy after 40 Years.* New York: Prager, 1981.

Holmes, Stephen. "The Secret History of Self-Interest." In *Beyond Self-Interest,* edited by Jane Mansbridge. Chicago: University of Chicago Press, 267–86.

Key, V. O. *The Responsible Electorate.* Cambridge, Mass.: Harvard University Press, 1966.

Lindblom C. E. *Politics and Markets.* New York: Basic Books, 1977.

Marcuse, Herbert. *One Dimensional Man.* Boston: Beacon, 1964.

Marquand, David. *The New Reckoning: Capitalism, States, and Citizens.* London: Polity Press, 1997.

Offe, Claus. *Contradictions of the Welfare State.* Cambridge, Mass.: MIT Press, 1984.

Olson, Mancur. *The Rise and Decline of Nations: Economic Growth, Stagflation, and Social Rigidities.* New Haven, Conn.: Yale University Press, 1983.

Przeworski, Adam. *Capitalism and Social Democracy,* Cambridge, Mass.: Cambridge University Press, 1991.

Schumpeter, Joseph A. *Capitalism, Socialism, and Democracy.* New York: Harper, 1942.

Shattschneider, E. F. *The Semi-Sovereign People.* New York: Reinhart and Winston, 1960.

Wood, John C., ed. *Joseph Schumpeter: Critical Assessments.* 4 vols. London: Routledge, 1991.

Participatory Democracy

Bachrach, Peter, and Aryeh Botwinick. *Power and Empowerment: A Radical Theory of Participatory Democracy.* Philadelphia: Temple University Press, 1992.

Barber, Benjamin. *A Passion for Democracy.* Princeton, N.J.: Princeton University Press, 1998.

———. *Strong Democracy.* Berkeley: University of California Press, 1984.

Berger, Peter, and Richard Neuhaus. *To Empower People: The Role of Mediating Structures in Public Policy.* Washington, D.C.: The American Enterprise Institute, 1977.

Burnheim, John. *Is Democracy Possible? The Alternative to Electoral Politics.* Berkeley: University of California Press, 1985.

Cohen, Joshua, and Joel Rogers. "Secondary Associations and Democratic Governance." *Politics and Society* 20 (1992): 393–472.

Dewey, John. *The Public and Its Problems.* Athens, Ohio: Swallow Press, 1954.

Fischer, Frank. "Citizen Participation and the Democratization of Policy Expertise." *Policy Studies* 26 (1993): 165–87.

Hirschman, Albert. *Exit, Voice, and Loyalty.* Cambridge, Mass.: Harvard University Press, 1970.

Inglehart, Ronald. *Modernization and Postmodernization: Cultural, Economic, and Political Change in 43 Societies.* Princeton, N.J.: Princeton University Press, 1997.

Johnston, Hank, and Bert Klandermans, eds. *Local Movements and Culture.* Minneapolis: University of Minnesota Press, 1995.

Kelly, Petra. *Fighting for Hope.* Translated by Howarth Marianne. Boston: South End Press, 1984.

Macpherson, C. B. *Democracy Theory: Essays in Retrieval.* Oxford: Oxford University Press, 1973.

Mattson, Kevin. *Creating a Democratic Republic.* University Park: Pennsylvania State University Press, 1998.

Offe, Claus. "New Social Movements: Challenging the Boundaries of Institutional Politics." *Social Research* 52, 4 (1985): 817–68.

Orlie, Melissa. *Living Ethically, Acting Politically.* Ithaca, N.Y.: Cornell University Press, 1997.

Pateman, Carole. *Participation and Democratic Theory.* Cambridge: Cambridge University Press, 1970.

Pennock, J. Roland, and John Chapman, eds. *Nomos*, vol. 16, *Participation in Politics.* New York: Lieber-Atherton, 1975.

Putnam, Robert. "Bowling Alone: America's Declining Social Capital." *Journal of Democracy* 6 (1995): 65–78.

———. "Tuning In, Turning Out: The Strange Disappearance of Social Capital in America." *PS: Political Science and Politics* 28 (December, 1955): 664–83.

Rosenblum, Nancy. *Membership and Morals: The Personal Uses of Pluralism in America.* Princeton, N.J.: Princeton University Press, 1998.

Ryan, Alan. *John Dewey and the High Tide of American Liberalism.* New York: W. W. Norton, 1995.

Thompson, Dennis. *The Democratic Citizen: Social Science and Democratic Theory in the Twentieth Century.* London: Cambridge University Press, 1970.

Thoreau, Henry David. "Civil Disobedience." In *Walden and Other Writings.* New York: Modern Library, 1981.

Verba, Sidney, and Norman Nie. *Participation in America: Political Democracy and Social Equality.* New York: Harper & Row, 1972.

Walzer, Michael. "A Day in the Life of a Socialist Citizen." In *Radical Principles.* New York: Basic Books, 1989.

Warren, Mark. *Democracy and Association.* Princeton, N.J.: Princeton University Press, 2000.

PART THREE: CRITIQUES OF CONTEMPORARY DEMOCRATIC THEORY AND PRACTICE

The Realist and Neorealist Critiques

Arendt, Hannah. *The Human Condition.* New York: Doubleday, 1958.

———. *On Revolution.* New York: Penguin Books, 1977.

Bobbio, Norberto. *Democracy and Dictatorship.* Minneapolis: University of Minnesota Press, 1989.

———. *The Future of Democracy: A Defence of the Rules of the Game.* London: Polity Press, 1987.

———. *Liberalism and Democracy.* London: Verso, 1990.

Isaac, Jeffrey. *Democracy in Dark Times.* Ithaca, N.Y.: Cornell University Press, 1998.

———. "Realism and Reality." *Journal of the Theory of Social Behavior* 20 (1990): 1–31.

Lippmann, Walter. *Essays in Public Philosophy.* Boston: Little, Brown, [1955].

Michles, Robert. *Political Parties.* New York: Dover, 1959.

Morgenthau, Hans J. *Politics Among Nations.* 2nd ed. New York: Knopf, 1954.

———. *Scientific Man vs. Power Politics.* Chicago: University of Chicago Press, 1946.

Murray, Alastair. *Reconstructing Realism.* Edinburgh: Keele University Press, 1997.

Niebuhr, Reinhold. *The Children of Light and the Children of Darkness: A Critique of Democracy and Its Traditional Defenders.* New York: Scribners, 1944.

———. *The Irony of American History.* New York: Scribners, 1962.

———. *Moral Man and Immoral Society.* New York: Scribners, 1932.

Pareto, Vilfredo. *The Mind and Society.* New York: Dover Publications, 1935.

Rosenthal, Joel. *Righteous Realists.* Baton Rouge: Louisiana State University Press, 1991.

Schattschneider, E. F. *The Semi-Sovereign People: A Realist View of Democracy in America.* New York: Reinhart and Winston, 1960.

Shklar, Judith. *The Faces of Injustice.* New Haven, Conn.: Yale University Press, 1990.

Thucydides. *The Peloponnesian Wars.* New York: Penguin, 1954.

Villa, Dana. *Politics, Philosophy, Terror: Essays on the Thought of Hannah Arendt.* Princeton, N.J.: Princeton University Press, 1999.

Weber, Max. *Economy and Society.* Edited by Guenther Roth and Claus Wittich. 2 vols. Berkeley: University of California Press, 1978.

———. "Politics as a Vocation." In *From Max Weber,* edited by Hans Gerth and C. W. Mills. New York: Galaxy, 1958.

Zolo, Danilo. *Democracy and Complexity.* University Park: Pennsylvania State University Press, 1992.

———. "Democratic Citizenship in a Post-Communist Era." In *Prospects for Democracy,* edited by David Held. Cambridge: Polity Press, 1993.

Postmodernist Critiques

Best, Steven, and Douglas Kellner. *Postmodern Theory: Critical Interrogations.* New York: Guilford Press, 1991.

Botwinick, Aryeh. *Postmodernism and Democratic Theory.* Philadelphia: Temple University Press, 1993.

Connolly, William E. *Identity/Difference: Democratic Negotiations of Political Paradox.* Ithaca, N.Y.: Cornell University Press, 1991.

———. *The Ethos of Pluralization.* Minneapolis: University of Minnesota Press, 1993.

———. *Politics and Ambiguity.* Madison: University of Wisconsin Press, 1987.

———. *Why I Am Not a Secularist.* Minneapolis: University of Minnesota Press, 1999.

Foucault, Michel. *Discipline and Punish.* New York: Vintage Books, 1977.

———. *Politics, Philosophy, Culture: Interviews and Other Writings, 1977–1984.* Translated by Lawrence Kritzman. New York: Routledge, 1988.

———. *Power/Knowledge.* New York: Pantheon Books, 1972.

Jameson, Fredric. *Postmodernism: Or, the Cultural Logic of Late Capitalism.* Durham: Duke University Press, 1992.

Jarvis, Darryl S. L. "Postmodernism: A Critical Typology." *Politics & Society* 26 (March 1998).

Laclau, Ernesto. *New Reflections on the Revolution of Our Time.* New York: Verso, 1990.

Lyotard, Jean-Francois. *The Postmodern Condition: A Report on Knowledge.* Minneapolis: University of Minnesota Press, 1988.

Mouffe, Chantal. *The Democratic Prospect.* London: Verso, 2000.

———, ed. *Dimensions of Radical Democracy: Pluralism, Citizenship, and Community.* London: Routledge, 1992.

———. "Radical Democracy: Modern or Postmodern?" In *Universal Abandon,* edited by Andrew Ross. Minneapolis: University of Minnesota Press, 1988.

———. *The Return of the Political.* London: Verso, 1993.

Nietzsche, Friedrich. *Thus Spoke Zarathustra.* In *The Portable Nietzsche,* edited by Walter Kaufmann. New York: Viking, 1954.

Rorty, Richard. *Contingency, Irony, and Solidarity.* Cambridge: Cambridge University Press, 1989.

Rosenau, Pauline Marie. *Post-Modernism and the Social Sciences: Insights, Inroads, and Intrusions.* Princeton, N.J.: Princeton University Press, 1992.

Smith, Anna Marie. *Laclau and Mouffe: The Radical Democratic Imaginary.* London: Routledge, 1998.

White, Stephen. *Political Theory and Postmodernism.* Cambridge: Cambridge University Press, 1991.

Discourse and Democracy

Akerman, Bruce. *Social Justice and the Liberal State.* New Haven, Conn.: Yale University Press, 1980.

Benhabib, Seyla, ed. *Democracy and Difference: Contesting the Boundaries of the Political.* Princeton, N.J.: Princeton University Press, 1966.

———. "Toward a Deliberative Model of Democratic Legitimacy." In *Democracy and Difference: Contesting the Boundaries of the Political,* edited by Seyla Benhabib. Princeton, N.J.: Princeton University Press, 1996.

Bickford, Susan. *The Dissonance of Democracy: Learning, Conflict, and Citizenship.* Ithaca, N.Y.: Cornell University Press, 1996.

Blaug, Ricardo. *Democracy, Real and Ideal: Discourse Ethics and Radical Politics.* Albany, N.Y.: State University of New York Press, 1999.

Chambers, Simone. *Reasonable Democracy: Jürgen Habermas and the Politics of Discourse.* Ithaca, N.Y.: Cornell University Press, 1996.

Cohen, Jean, and Andrew Arate. *Civil Society and Political Theory.* Cambridge, Mass.: MIT Press, 1992.

Dallmayr, Fred. *Polis and Praxis.* Cambridge, Mass.: MIT Press, 1984.

Dryzek, John. *Democracy in Capitalist Times.* New York: Oxford University Press, 1996.

Elster, Jon, ed. *Deliberative Democracy.* Cambridge: Cambridge University Press, 1998.

———. "The Market and the Forum." In *Foundations in Social Choice,* edited by J. Elster and A. Hylland. Cambridge: University of Cambridge Press, 1986.

Fishkin, James. *Democracy and Deliberation.* New Haven, Conn.: Yale University Press, 1991.

Forester, John. *The Deliberative Practioner.* Cambridge, Mass.: MIT Press, 1999.

Frohock, Fred M. *Public Reason: Mediated Authority in the Liberal State.* Ithaca, N.Y.: Cornell University Press, 1999.

Gutmann, Amy, and Dennis Thompson. *Democracy and Disagreement.* Cambridge, Mass.: Harvard University Press, 1996

Habermas, Jürgen. *On the Pragmatics of Communication.* Cambridge: MIT Press, 1998.

———. *Structural Transformation of the Public Sphere: An Inquiry into a Category of Bourgeois Society.* Cambridge, Mass.: MIT Press, 1989.

———. *The Theory of Communicative Actions.* 2 vols. Translated by Thomas McCarthy. Boston: Beacon Press, 1984–87.

————. "Three Normative Models of Democracy." *Constellations* 1 (April 1994): 1–10.

Honneth, Axel, and Hans Joas. *Communicative Action*. Cambridge, Mass.: MIT Press, 1991.

Macedo, Stephen. *Deliberative Politics*. New York: Oxford University Press, 1999.

Mansbridge, Jane. *Beyond Adversary Democracy*. Chicago: University of Chicago Press, 1983.

Mattson, Kevin. *Creating a Democratic Republic*. University Park: Pennsylvania State University Press, 1998.

McCarthy, Thomas. *The Critical Theory of Jürgen Habermas*. Cambridge, Mass.: MIT Press, 1978.

Rosenfeld, Michael, and Andrew Arato. *Habermas on Law and Democracy: Critical Exchanges*. Berkeley: University of California Press, 1998.

Spragens, Thomas. *Reason and Democracy*. Durham: Duke University Press, 1990.

Wolin, Sheldon. "The Liberal/Democratic Divide." *Political Theory* 24 (1996): 97–142.

Pushing for Inclusion

Anthony, Susan B. *An Account of the Proceedings on the Trial of Susan B. Anthony, on the Charge of Illegal Voting, at the Presidential Election in Nov., 1872*. New York: Arno Press, 1974.

Bartlett, Katherine, and Rosanne Kennedy, eds. *Feminist Legal Theory*. Boulder, Colo.: Westview Press, 1991.

Benhabib, Seyla. *Democracy and Difference: Contesting the Boundaries of the Political*. Princeton, N.J.: Princeton University Press, 1996.

Brown, Wendy. *States of Injury: Power and Freedom in Late Modernity*. Princeton, N.J.: Princeton University Press, 1995.

Carmichael, Stokely, and Charles Hamilton. *Black Power: The Politics of Liberation in America*. New York, Random House, 1967.

Du Bois, W. E. B. *Color and Democracy: Colonies and Peace*. New York: Harcourt, Brace, 1945; reprint Millwood, N.Y.: Kraus-Thomson Organization, [1975].

————. *The Souls of Black Folk*. Boston: Bedford Books, [1997].

Delgado, Richard, ed. *Critical Race Theory*. Philadelphia: Temple University Press, 1995.

Elshtain, Jean Behke. *Public Man, Private Woman: Women in Social and Political Thought*. Princeton, N.J.: Princeton University Press, 1981.

Franklin, John Hope. *The Color Line: Legacy for the Twenty-first Century*. Columbia: University of Missouri Press, 1993.

Freeman, Jo. *The Politics of Women's Liberation*. New York: McKay, 1975.

Gould, Carol. *Rethinking Democracy*. Cambridge: Cambridge University Press, 1988.

Guinier, Lani. *The Tyranny of the Majority*. New York: Free Press, 1994.

Hirshmann, Nancy. *Rethinking Obligation*. Ithaca, N.Y.: Cornell University Press, 1992.

Hochschild, Jennifer. *Facing Up to the American Dream: Race, Class and the Soul of the Nation*. Princeton, N.J.: Princeton University Press, 1995.

Jackson, Jesse. *Legal Lynching: Racism, Injustice, and the Death Penalty*. New York: Marlowe, 1996.

————. *Straight from the Heart*. Edited by Roger D. Hatch and Frank E. Watkins. Philadelphia: Fortress Press, 1987.

King, Martin Luther, Jr. *Where Do We Go from Here?* New York: Bantam, 1967.

————. *Why We Can't Wait*. New York: HarperCollins, 1963.

Kymlicka, Will. *Multicultural Citizenship*. Oxford: Clarendon Press, 1995.

MacKinnon, Catherine. *Feminism Unmodified*. Cambridge, Mass.: Harvard University Press, 1987.

————. *Towards a Feminist Theory of the State*. Cambridge, Mass.: Harvard University Press, 1989.

Malcom X. *Autobiography*. New York: Random House, 1964.

Marx, Anthony. *Making Race and Nation: A Comparison of the United States, South Africa, and Brazil*. Cambridge: Cambridge University Press, 1998.

Mills, Charles. *The Racial Contract*. Ithaca, N.Y.: Cornell University Press, 1997.

Okin, Susan. *Justice, Gender, and the Family.* New York: Basic Books, 1989.

Parekh, Bhikhu. *Rethinking Multiculturalism: Cultural Diversity and Political Theory.* Cambridge, Mass.: Havard University Press, 2000.

Pateman, Carole. *Sexual Contract.* Stanford, Calif.: Stanford University Press, 1988.

Phillips, Anne. *Engendering Democracy.* Cambridge: Polity Press, 1991.

———. "Must Feminists Give Up on Liberal Democracy?" In *Prospects for Democracy,* edited by David Held. Cambridge: Polity Press, 1993.

———. *The Politics of Presence.* Oxford: Oxford University Press, 1995.

Stanton, Elizabeth Cady. *Eighty Years and More: Reminiscences, 1815–1897.* New York: Schocken Books, 1971.

Taylor, Charles *Multiculturalism and "The Politics of Recognition."* Princeton, N.J.: Princeton University Press, 1992.

West, Cornel. *Keeping Faith: Philosophy and Race in America.* New York: Routledge, 1994.

———. *Race Matters.* Boston: Beacon Press, 1993.

Winant, Howard. *Racial Conditions: Politics, Theory, Comparisons.* Minneapolis: University of Minnesota Press, 1994.

Wollstonecraft, Mary. *Vindication of the Rights of Women.* Penguin, 1975. First published 1792.

Young, Iris Marion. *Justice and the Politics of Difference.* Princeton, N.J.: Princeton University Press, 1990.

Voices Outside the West

Appiah, Kwame Anthony. "Identity, Authenticity, Survival." In *Multiculturalism,* edited by Amy Gutmann. Princeton, N.J.: Princeton University Press, 1994.

———. *In My Father's House: Africa in the Philosophy of Culture.* New York: Oxford University Press, 1992.

Aristide, Jean Bertrand. *Dignity.* Charlottesville: University Press of Virginia. 1996.

———. *Eyes of the Heart: Seeking a Path for the Poor in the Age of Globalization.* Monroe, Maine: Common Courage Press, 2000.

Aung San Suu Kyi. *Freedom from Fear and Other Writings.* New York: Penguin, 1995.

Chatterjee, Partha. *Nationalist Thought and the Colonial World: A Derivative Discourse.* New Delhi: Oxford University Press, 1986.

Dallmayr, Fred. *Alternative Visions: Paths in the Global Village.* Lanham, Md.: Rowman & Littlefield, 1998.

———. *Beyond Orientalism: Essays on Cross-Cultural Encounter.* Albany, N.Y.: SUNY Press, 1996

Esquivel, Adolfo Pérez. *Christ in a Poncho: Testimonials of the Nonviolent Struggles in Latin America.* Edited by Charles Antoine. Maryknoll, N.Y.: Orbis Books, [1983].

Frei Montalva, Eduardo. *Latin America, The Hopeful Option.* Maryknoll, N.Y.: Orbis Books, 1978.

Gandhi, Mahatma. *Constructive Programme.* Ahmedabad, India: Navajivan Publishing, 1941.

———. *Democracy, Real and Deceptive.* Ahmedabad, India: Navajivan Publishing, 1961.

———. *Hind Swaraj.* Edited by Anthony Parel. Cambridge: Cambridge University Press, 1997.

Khatami, Mohammad. *Hope and Challenge.* Binghamton, N.Y.: Institute for Global Cultural Studies, Binghamton University, 1997.

———. *Islam, Liberty, and Development.* Binghamton, N.Y.: Institute for Global Cultural Studies, Binghamton University, 1998.

Kothari, Rajni. *Footsteps into the Future.* New York: Free Press, 1974.

Mandela, Nelson, *Long Walk to Freedom.* Boston: Little, Brown, 1994.

———. *Symbol of Resistance and Hope for a Free South Africa: Selected Speeches Since His Release.* Edited by E. S. Reddy. New Delhi: Sterling, 1990.

Menchu Rigoberta. *Crossing Borders.* London: Verso, 1998.

Nandy, Ashis. *Traditions, Tyranny and Utopia.* New Delhi: Oxford University Press, 1987.

Nkrumah, Kwame. *Africa Must Unite*. London: Panaf, 1963.

Nyerere, Julius. *Freedom and Development: Uhuru na Maendeleo. A Selection from Writings and Speeches, 1968–1973*. London: Oxford University Press, 1974.

Pantham, Thomas. *Political Theories and Social Reconstruction*. New Delhi: Sage, 1995.

Parekh, Bhikhu. *Colonialism, Tradition, and Reform*. 2nd ed. New Delhi: Sage, 1999.

———. *Gandhi's Political Philosophy*. Notre Dame: Notre Dame University Press, 1989.

Parel, Anthony, ed. *Gandhi, Freedom, and Self-Rule*. Lanham, Md.: Rowman & Littlefield, 2000.

Said, Edward. *Orientalism*. New York: Vintage Books, 1979.

Terchek, Ronald. *Gandhi: Struggling for Autonomy*. Lanham, Md.: Rowman & Littlefield, 1998.

Wiredu, Kwasi. *Cultural Universals and Particulars: An African Perspective*. Bloomington: Indiana University Press, 1996.

INDEX

ABOUT THE EDITORS

Ronald J. Terchek is professor of government and politics at the University of Maryland, College Park, and the author of *Republican Paradoxes and Liberal Anxieties: Retrieving Neglected Fragments of Political Theory* and *Gandhi: Struggling for Autonomy*.

Thomas C. Conte has taught in the department of government and foreign affairs at the University of Virginia and is currently an assistant professor at Gettysburg College.